Pray for Dor

JOHN CARROLL

OF

BALTIMORE

1735-1815

By the same author

ELIZABETH BAYLEY SETON

Courtesy, Georgetown University, Washington, D. C.

Archbishop John Carroll—the Gilbert Stuart Portrait

JOHN CARROLL

of Baltimore

FOUNDER
OF THE AMERICAN CATHOLIC HIERARCHY

by

ANNABELLE M. MELVILLE

**NEW
YORK**

CHARLES SCRIBNER'S SONS

Library of Congress Catalogue Card No. 55-7195

Nihil Obstat
JOHN M. A. FEARNS, S.T.D.
Censor Librorum

Imprimatur
✠ FRANCIS CARDINAL SPELLMAN
Archbishop of New York

The *Nihil Obstat* and *Imprimatur* are official declarations that a book or pamphlet is free of doctrinal or moral error. No implication is contained therein that those who have granted the *Nihil Obstat* and *Imprimatur* agree with the contents, opinions or statements expressed.

TO

MY GODCHILDREN

ELLEN, MICHAEL, NORMAN,

PETER, and STEPHEN

PREFACE

TO THE biographer of a man whose career proved nearly all-engrossing for half a decade, the task of prefatory justification is not only anticlimactic but onerous. It places the writer in the scarcely tolerable position of apologizing for an old friend, of defending the longevity of the friendship. Nevertheless, some glance askance is inevitably accorded any new title and, since a new life of John Carroll can be reasonably justified, the writer must give her reasons.

In the first place, at the time this work was undertaken the only other reasonably complete biography of John Carroll was out of print, and had been for some time. Even if Peter Guilday's *Life and Times of John Carroll* had been easily accessible, it still left something to be desired. Completed as it was before 1922, Guilday's work proposed some interpretations which later research had proved untenable. Again, owing to the voluminous nature of the biography, errors in small factual details had crept into the text and the documentation. The chief disadvantage, from the point of view of the average reader, was that the man was lost in the times. Certainly no one who has used the Guilday volumes, as this writer has done both extensively and with appreciation, would wish to deny the invaluable contribution the *Life and Times of John Carroll* made, if it were only for the generous publication of complete texts of documents from European archives not available to writers of that day. Any future biographer of John Carroll must continue to owe a debt of magnitude to the Guilday *Carroll*. Yet the work has its imperfections, and Guilday himself was considering a revision of his own work, as his personal papers revealed after his death.

This present volume does not presume to supply either a definitive biography or a revision of the larger study of Guilday, which is fortunately available to the student of church history once more. Rather, this work is offered as testimony to the author's conviction that John Carroll merits more than one biographer. A great man in his day, which was a day of great men, Carroll as surely as Washington, Jefferson, Madison, and those other giants of the Republic, can not be exhausted by a single study. This limited volume is dual in its aims: those of revealing the man in all his subtlety, probity, and warmth of character, and of estimating his peculiar contribution to the later success of that institution whose hierarchy he founded, the Catholic Church in the United States. Many monographs offer better studies of individual institutions and movements which were contemporaneous with the life of the first Archbishop of Baltimore. But within its limited purposes, this biography may claim to be carefully documented, truthfully reported, and interpreted with caution and respect for the sanctity of personality. If a man's whole truth can be recaptured a century and a half after he lived, that is the obligation of the biographer. If this writer has worked with fidelity then John Carroll was a man any American, of whatever persuasion, is entitled to call his compatriot with pride and affection. His career should no longer remain the special province of the church historian alone.

No book of this kind is the product of one mind, and it would be impossible to gauge the exact influence of all who contributed to the writing of this study. The writer is immeasurably indebted to everyone who had a part in shaping the final work, and takes this way of expressing her gratitude for the scholarship and generosity which were so consistently available during the past five years.

Again, no book of this kind is possible without the generosity of the archivists and librarians who unstintingly assist in finding the materials which are the blood-stream of biography. The writer is especially indebted to the Reverend Henry J. Browne, of the Department of Archives and Manuscripts of the Catholic University of America, not only for making available the vast resources of the Carroll Papers which were collected by him as the secretary for the Committee on the John Carroll Papers, but also for the direction he gave to the documentation of this biography. The writer is also most grateful to the Reverend Paul Love of the Archives of the Archdiocese of Baltimore, the Reverend Hugh Philips of the Archives of Mount Saint Mary's College, Emmitsburg, Maryland, Sister-Archivist of Saint Joseph Central House, Emmitsburg, Maryland, and Sister-Archivist of Mount Saint Vincent on the Hudson. Equally generous in their assistance were the staffs of the Mullen Library of the Catholic University of America, the Enoch Pratt

Library of Baltimore, the Maryland Historical Society, the Library of Congress, and the State Library of Albany, New York. The writer is indebted to the Reverend John Rudd of Llanelly, Wales, for materials on the restoration of Lulworth Chapel and to Dr. Clement C. Maxwell, President of the State Teachers College, Bridgewater, Massachusetts, and Dr. Ralph S. Bates, Associate Professor of History, for critical copy reading.

Bridgewater, Massachusetts
1955

CONTENTS

JOHN CARROLL

OF

BALTIMORE

1735-1815

CHAPTER
I

THE BOY FROM UPPER
MARLBOROUGH

A JANUARY child comes close upon the heels of Christmas and heralds wintry weather. John Carroll was one of these, entering this world as he did on January 8, 1735, in the middle of the octave of the Epiphany. A later generation of American mothers might look with loving scrutiny at the face of each newborn son and wonder if he might become one day the President of his country. But Eleanor Darnall Carroll, if she wondered at all as she tenderly examined the wrinkled, red, little face of her fourth child, might have asked herself the older question: "Is this the one? Is this the son to be the priest?" She could not know, of course, that although no man would ever love his country more, John Carroll was destined to serve it best as the first Catholic bishop of the infant Republic, and as the first Archbishop of Baltimore.

The son who was born to Eleanor and Daniel Carroll at Upper Marlborough more than four decades before the signing of the Declaration of Independence came from distinguished forebears and was kin to some of the country's most illustrious founders. Through his father he was part of the family of Keane Carroll of Ireland, who seems to have been the eldest brother of the Charles Carroll who migrated to America to serve as Attorney-General to the colony of Maryland. At any rate, the descendants of Charles the Attorney certainly thought so, for the third Charles who earned his fame as a signer of the Declaration of Independence repeated the belief to the Countess of Auzouer, referring to his grandfather Charles as the second son of Daniel Carroll of Litterlouna in King's County, and adding, "Keane, we believe, the first son." [1]

The two lines of Maryland Carrolls developed contemporaneously in the colony. The third generation of Keane's line followed much the same pattern as the third generation of Charles the

Attorney. Both Daniel III and Charles III were sent abroad to study at St. Omer in French Flanders; and while Charles Carroll of Carrollton returned to Maryland to sign the Declaration of Independence, Daniel of Rock Creek became famous in his turn as a signer of the United States Constitution in 1787.

Through his mother, the infant John Carroll was related to the Darnalls, the family whose American branch had been founded by the brother-in-law of Lord Baltimore, Colonel Henry Darnall. Eleanor Darnall Carroll's grandfather had come to Maryland in 1672, and had quickly risen in wealth and reputation. At the time of his death his holdings had embraced 40,000 acres of land, including the lovely manors: "My Lord's Kindness," "Portland," "Joseph's Park," "Girl's Portion," "Promise," and "Resurrection."

Eleanor's father had inherited many of these properties at his father's death, and he had acquired by his marriage to Anne Digges "Warburton Manor." Although he either sold or mortgaged much of his property in later years, her father provided Eleanor with a happy childhood. Eleanor Darnall grew up in serenity and security, and her earliest recollections were of the large red brick English manor house with its many wings, its seventy-two corridors and numberless rooms. At an early age she was sent by her father to a select school in France where, developing her excellent and discriminating mind, she acquired those refinements of behavior so essential to the lady of the manor. When Daniel Carroll brought her to Upper Marlborough to grace his smaller mansion, it was generally agreed that he had acquired a treasure far beyond the value that mere riches could confer.

Eleanor Darnall married wisely when she joined her fortunes in 1727 to those of the young merchant of Prince George's County. Daniel Carroll had come to Maryland some time before 1725, and had settled on the Patuxent River. His earliest purchase of land was the "Four Hills and Partnerswick" which he secured from the London factor, John Hyde, on October 19, 1725. During the following year he added 500 more acres in Howard County to his holdings; and on May 13, 1727, he acquired by his marriage the tracts, "Darnall's Chance" and "Addition." As his marriage prospered, so did his fortunes. At the time of his death Daniel Carroll left six children, and to one son alone lands worth between £4,000 and £5,000.[2]

While his wealth was invested chiefly in land, livestock, and slaves, Daniel Carroll's profits were reaped largely from his importing activities and his general store in Upper Marlborough, and were closely interwoven with the fabric of the single-staple tobacco economy which dominated the Maryland colony. As Benedict Leonard Calvert, the Governor of Maryland, remarked to the Proprietor, his brother, in 1729, "Tobacco, as our staple, is our all; and indeed leaves no room for anything else." The tobacco planter, however, could exercise a certain choice as to the way in which he exported his crop. Larger producers whose manors stretched down to the river or bay might consign their leaf directly to London, but many another shipment of tobacco left the colony by way of the middlemen: through the factors of the European companies, or through the independent merchants in Maryland. Scottish firms like James Brown and Company, and Jamieson, Johnstone and Company had their own factors and stores in Bladensburg and Upper Marlborough. But much of the London trade was handled by provincial planters such as Charles Carroll, or by the independent merchants like Daniel.

Although the role of the independent Maryland merchants is still not fully understood, it is certain that their activities brought some novelty and variety into the trade of the colony in the eighteenth century. They were the commercial adventurers, the innovators; and it was often due to their efforts that new markets were discovered, or that new manufactures were introduced into the colony. Through sheer doggedness and not a little ingenuity they soon outstripped their European rivals, even while using the factors for their own ends. Both factors and independent merchants offered an astonishing variety of wares to entice their customers. There were textiles such as plushes, velvets, linens, fine India cottons and chintzes, and coarse Irish canvas. There were household goods including blankets, rugs, and window draperies. Hardware, stationers' supplies, and mariners' wares were displayed on shelves or were transferred for tobacco, paper bills, or sterling, or, as was more often the case, charged against the expected payment of tobacco later. Daniel Carroll's inventories showed such a wide variety of goods, and there is little doubt that his store was an important *entrepôt* for the flourishing trade along the Patuxent River.

John Carroll's boyhood was spent amid this mercantile environment in a most momentous period in Maryland's development. Historians now attribute much importance to these years of political and economic crisis between 1725 and 1740. In many respects, of course, Maryland remained typically English during that first half of the eighteenth century. In its architecture the colony was strongly reminiscent of the English country houses, and the Maryland manor with its three masses, its great central structure of two or three stories and high facing chimneys, the two flanking lesser wings for domestic servants and office space, was deliberately suggestive of its English model. Interiors were elaborately decorated in fine wood and plaster work; and exteriors, as in England, were charming in their simplicity, relying upon symmetry and balance achieved in lovely dull, salmon-colored brick to produce a final beauty which age could only enhance. In the intellectual realm the Maryland gentleman, like his English cousin, was molded by a classical education, was often preoccupied by literary journalism, and preserved a dogged devotion to the parliamentary ideal. And although a diminishing number of Marylanders now imbibed this culture from its original font, since comparatively few of John Carroll's contemporaries were of English birth, English education, English conceits in writing, and English political philosophy continued to tinge the thought processes of the heirs of the landed gentry.[3]

On the other hand, much of the colonial society was the direct product of peculiarly American influences. The tobacco-staple economy, the slave labor system, the avid speculation in the abundant land with the accompanying surge westward—these were American and tended to make the colonist a man apart and, on occasion, quite incomprehensible to his English relatives across the Atlantic. True, the Maryland economic system naturally benefited most those families who achieved the largest estates and, as in England, the power of the government was in the hands of the landed aristocracy. High office in Maryland went to the owners of twenty or more thousand acres, to the Darnalls, the Dulanys, the Bennetts, and the Carrolls. But this combination of land and power produced in those who controlled it a more than ordinary interest in law. The Maryland country squire was something of a petty lord in his own locality, and some degree of legal knowledge was presumed essential.

Charles Carroll II expressed the general belief when he wrote to his son, the third Charles, who was studying law at the Inner Temple in London, "It is a shame for a gentleman to be ignorant of the laws of his country and to be dependent on every dirty pettifogger. On the other hand," he continued, "how commendable it is for a gentleman of independent fortune not only not to stand in need of mercenary advisers, but to be able to advise his friends, relations, and neighbors of all sorts." And when the younger Charles displayed a reluctance to continue his legal studies, his father wrote him more compellingly:

> Would it not be of infinite advantage to England if every man who serves in Parliament were a sound lawyer and well acquainted with the Constitution? Will not the knowledge of the Law enable you to transact your affairs with ease and security? Will it not enable you to state your own Cases, to instruct those you employ, and if you find them ignorant, knavish, or conceited, direct you to employ others? [4]

This preoccupation with the law would, in the second half of the eighteenth century, make many a Maryland gentleman take the lead in shaping the civil liberties of the new Republic. And, indeed, localism was only natural in a colony where the economic and social life was so decentralized. While the colonies to the north developed their large commercial cities: Boston, New York, and Philadelphia, where the wealth and power of extensive areas converged and where prestige grew with power, the tobacco-staple system with its many scattered depots and merchants left Maryland without a single great commercial town. True, Annapolis was very gay when the governor was in residence. Then cannon were fired with wild enthusiasm, bonfires glowed against the evening sky, and the populace outside gulped down the contents of hogsheads opened for the occasion, while within the mansion the notables of Maryland offered politer toasts to His Excellency's health. One French visitor to the city, Abbé Claude C. Robin, wrote of Annapolis:

> The furniture of the houses here is of the costliest description. They have light and elegant carriages which are drawn by fine horses. The coachmen are slaves and are richly dressed. There appears to be more wealth and luxury in Annapolis than in any other city I have visited in this country, and the extravagance of the women surpasses that of our Provinces. A French hairdresser is a man of great importance. A lady here pays hers a thousand crowns a year. [5]

But Annapolis was important only because it was the seat of government. Any small tobacco port had as much connection with the world beyond, and culture reached the scattered population through as many arteries as there were wharves to receive ships.

John Carroll's father had chosen an excellent location in the midst of this Anglo-American environment. Marlborough had been the county seat of Prince George's County since 1727 and had taken its name from the much-toasted hero of Blenheim, John Churchill, the Duke of Marlborough. Upper Marlborough lay just above it on the Patuxent River, and when Philip Fithian visited there in 1774 he was impressed with the fine houses he found. An earlier traveller from France described Upper Marlborough as the "very center of pleasures in Maryland," and surely it must have seemed so to young Jacky Carroll as he played about his spacious home or watched wide-eyed as ships edged carefully toward the wharf where the Negroes waited to unload the cargoes. After his brother Henry was drowned, and Dan went off to Flanders to school, Jacky was the only boy left in a household of girls. It is small wonder that the bonds between the serious young lad and his aristocratic, charming, and pious mother were strengthened. Much of the ease, the dignity, and refinement which marked John Carroll in later life he owed to the close relationship he enjoyed with his mother. Certainly throughout her life Eleanor Carroll was the constant object of her son's affection and devotion.

While the rising fortunes of Daniel Carroll the merchant freed the family from financial cares, the problem of educating the children, particularly the sons, remained a perplexing one. During that period of Maryland's colonial history which saw the Anglican Church established there, the lot of Roman Catholics was not an enviable one. As if trying to blot out the memory of Catholic predominance during the seventeenth century, the Maryland Assembly in the eighteenth passed the most rigorous anti-Catholic laws in America; not only did it proscribe Catholic voters and officeholders, it also forbade the erection of churches or the employment of Catholic teachers as well. A law of 1704 made it a crime for "Popish priests" to baptize children in the faith or to offer Mass. The Catholics who were disenfranchised in 1718 for their supposed sympathies toward the Jacobite cause were further penalized in later years by double taxation.[6] Catholic sensitivities were sorely tried during the French and Indian Wars when ministers of the Church of England like James Sterling of Annapolis denounced the "Rome-imp'd Priests" who "refin'd simple Savages into human Tygers and to enlarge their Creed have totally corrupted whatever they knew of Morals before." And, although the Carrolls were by implication exonerated, the eloquent orator went on to urge that "Ye Sons of the Reformation, confirmed by the Death of so many bright martyrs, guard your holy Religion from Papal Persecution, Idolatry, Irish Massacres, Gun-Powder Treasons and worse than Smithfield Fires!" [7]

Most keenly felt was the discrimination which aimed at the very roots of the faith, that is, the education of the children. Since the English penal code prevailed in the colonies, Maryland as well as English Catholics suffered under the law of 1700 which stipulated that parents who tried to send their children abroad to be educated in the Roman religion should forfeit £100. Parents who dared to send their sons to the English Catholic colleges on the continent might even face a charge of treason. Charles Carroll of Annapolis wrote to his son in England in 1760 that he should show "a proper resentment" to Mr. Calvert when he visited the Proprietor, having already complained, "I leave you to judge whether Maryland be a tolerable residence for a Roman Catholic. Were I younger I would certainly quit it." [8]

These anti-Catholic strictures did not always produce the desired results, however. As in England after the "Glorious" Revolution of 1688 which exiled the Catholic Stuarts and confirmed the Anglican domination, legislation was one thing, enforcement another. Tacit tolerance was inevitable where wealth encouraged some winking at the law. As a matter of fact, Protestant citizens often had occasion to denounce the persistent power of leading Catholics. Dr. Charles Carroll of the Protestant branch of the family wrote in an aggrieved tone to his son in 1753:

You desire to know how Mr. Carroll [the Catholic Charles of Annapolis] has proceeded. He has filed a Bill in Court here against me and if such a Chancellor as we have had should determine his Claim, no doubt it would not be in my favour as he was my declared enemy. I shall battle it with him as long as I can until I have reason to hope for Equal Justice. His money and influence are Two Things that are two powerful for me. . . . The whole Popish Interest have Levelled their Artillery against me and are strongly associated with the government. A new Governor is daily expected. I hope he will prove a more unprejudiced one than our former. It stands you upon [end] to make yourself Capable of rubbing through what you may Expect here, to wit, all the injury a Popish Faction can do you.[9]

Again, the resistance of the Catholics nullified much of the legislation regarding education and in August, 1753, the parochial Anglican clergy met at Annapolis to consider addressing the Proprietor on the subject of the dangerous encroachments of Popery in Maryland. So great was their indignation that by October these gentlemen had produced seventeen queries which filled three sides of a paper folder and listed their complaints against "Popery and Jacobitism." Among the grievances cited were: that Popish school masters were teaching publicly and even had Protestant children under their care, and that Papists were not only sending their own children to St. Omer but also tried to persuade Protestants to send theirs there as well. The latter accusation led to some public recriminations in the Maryland *Gazette* when Mr. Wootton, the High Sheriff of Prince George's County, was reported to have told a friend that a Papist named Basil Warren had tried to persuade him to send his son to St. Omer, "mentioning the Great Care taken of Youth, and the Cheapness of the Commons and Education there as Inducements." Wootton later denied this in an affidavit published in the *Gazette,* but non-Catholics remained convinced that soliciting for St. Omer was common practice; and the *Gazette* continued to report, as it did on October 17, 1754, that "great numbers of their Catholic youth were sent this year to foreign Popish seminaries." [10]

The truth was, of course, that Maryland Catholic parents were determined to preserve the faith in their children and had struggled to secure schools of some sort since the very founding of the colony. Father Andrew White, S.J., who came with the first expedition in 1634, was fresh from the English colleges at Valladolid and Seville, and he tried to forward the establishment of a Jesuit college in the Maryland colony. Although this project never materialized, private teachers continued to work among the Catholic children. Brother Ralph Crouch, S.J., conducted a private school at Newton for twenty years until the persecutions stemming from the Orange Rebellion of 1688 forced its abandonment. As usual, the English fear at home of a Catholic dynasty or of Irish rebels was reflected in the colonies across the seas. It was only in secret that the outlaws of the Irish "sheltering hedge and mountain fern" could teach in Maryland Catholic manor houses or conduct small schools supported by the parents of the locality.[11]

The eighteenth century saw sporadic attempts to organize schools for secondary education as well, and the school at Bohemia Manor near the Pennsylvania border was one of these. It was at Bohemia that young Jacky Carroll received his first taste of formal schooling; and for a century thereafter his school chair used at the manor was preserved as a testimony thereof. Both the school building and the chair have long since been lost to posterity, but the short-lived experiment in secondary education is remembered because its most famous pupil later founded Georgetown University and served as a link between the two institutions. When Jacky Carroll came to Bohemia Manor at the age of twelve he found the brick school house standing a few feet south of the manse or rectory of the Jesuits. Bohemia, one of the earliest permanent Catholic settlements in Maryland, was situated on the immense tract of land granted to Augustine Herman. Time and custom had attached the title of the tract of land to the Catholic church there and to the Jesuit residence; by the time Jacky arrived, "Bohemia Manor" meant the school where he would be prepared for St. Omer across the sea.

The Bohemia academy was scarcely established when Daniel and Eleanor Carroll enrolled their son John. It had opened during the pastorate of Father Thomas Poulton at the manor chapel dedicated to Saint Francis Xavier.[12] The Daniel Carrolls were not the only parents eager to try out this latest venture in Catholic education. Charles Carroll of Annapolis sent his only son there and Carroll cousins studied and played with the Neale brothers, Benedict and Edward, as well as with James Heath and Robert Brent. Indeed, the academy at one time housed twenty boarders and offered instruction to forty pupils, and for two years it was the institution which laid the foundations of John Carroll's education. There he could take courses in reading and writing, simple figures, and begin his Latin. The boys who limited their studies to the elementary courses paid thirty pounds, but those who studied Latin and more advanced work paid forty. Until July 8, 1748, young Carroll pursued his studies at Bohemia, interrupted only by vacations spent at home.

In this year, however, his brother Daniel returned from Europe and it was decided to send John abroad in his place. Dan at eighteen was a sensible, energetic young man, well-prepared after six years of continental study to enter his father's mercantile establishment and to take over some of the increasing burdens of that enterprise. It was now Jacky's turn to go to St. Omer. That same year Charles Carroll of Annapolis decided to send his son Charles

to Flanders, and the two boys crossed the ocean together along
with another Bohemia classmate, Robert Brent. John was only in
his fourteenth year, and his cousin Charles was more than two years
younger. Their departure from Annapolis was bound to be an
occasion for mingled emotions.

Passage across the Atlantic Ocean in the mid-eighteenth century
was both expensive and dangerous. Catholic parents were not only
compelled to face the necessity of forwarding large remittances
abroad, for Marylanders in Europe were already famous for their
extravagances, but there was the immediate and terrible possibility
of heartbreaking delays or actual wreck of the vessels which carried
their sons away. Even after news of safe arrivals filtered back
through the devious routes of trans-Atlantic correspondence, the
separation was still acute. Young Charlie was his father's only son,
and Daniel and Eleanor Carroll had already lost one boy by
drowning. It required a very present belief that the soul was more
important than the body to persuade these Catholic parents that
duty required this shattering of the family circle.

Departures were always pregnant with change. Although neither
boy knew it on that day at the wind-swept wharf, each young
Carroll bidding his family adieu was gazing on the face of one
parent he would never see again. For John Carroll's father died
on February 27, 1751, and young Charles lost his mother ten years
later while both young men were still across the sea. The young
voyagers might chafe uneasily at delays and long restlessly for sails
to unfurl. But the older members of the family savored the reprieve,
storing up the look of adolescent freshness of face, or awkwardness
of mien, against the day when this lad would return a man, or
not at all.

CHAPTER
II

THE MAKING OF A PRIEST

THE school to which the Carroll boys were sent in 1748 was
conducted by English Jesuits in French Flanders. Although
Charles Carroll of Carrollton later admitted its limitations, com-
menting that for a mercantile career it was "ill-judged" to keep
a boy too long at St. Omer since its "education is only fit for
priests," [1] the college in the eighteenth century was still the most
popular preparatory institution in the minds of American Catholic
parents.

Carrolls had been going to St. Omer since the family removed
to Maryland. Charles Carroll I, the Attorney-General, had sent
his three sons, Henry, Charles, and Daniel to Flanders. Although
Henry died at sea while returning to Annapolis in 1719, both
Charles II of Annapolis and Daniel of Duddington carried the
mark of St. Omer to America, and it was to be expected that the
third Charles would be sent across the sea in his turn. "You can lay
a foundation," his father admonished him, "for other studies which
may hereafter be profitable to yourself and useful to your friends." [2]
Jacky Carroll, too, was repeating a family pattern; for his brother
Dan had spent six years at St. Omer before entering his father's
business.

St. Omer was an old school, going back to September 18, 1592,
when it had been founded by the English Jesuit, Father Robert
Parsons. In spite of the penal legislation which wiped out Catholic
education in England after the Protestant Revolt, English parents
persevered in their intention of sending their sons to Catholic
schools; if they could not exist on the island, these schools must
migrate to the continent. They remained essentially English in
character, of course, and the French townspeople were at first
considerably annoyed at the frequent ringing of the bells with
which St. Omer celebrated every English event. The French fear

of spies, too, led to an early stipulation that the rectors of the school should not be English. But as the centuries passed, St. Omer came to be an accepted part of the town; and by 1730, when the tower on old St. Denise collapsed, the burghers gave 500 livres on the condition that the college bell could be heard all over town. Certainly the college was English in its Spartan regime and was quite competent in turning out Jesuit novices or English gentlemen's sons, whether they came from across the Channel or from across the Atlantic Ocean. Here "all the arts and sciences" were to be had for the annual sum of twenty-four pounds. It was not to be wondered at that the fame of the Flemish school spread to distant lands.

The daily life at St. Omer was at first very strange to the young American cousins who had grown up in the leisurely luxury of a Maryland manor. The dormitory in which the younger students slept was a long, neat room furnished on each side with little beds over which square bits of board proclaimed the names of the prospective incumbents. As they grew older many students chose the "Commons" or chambers where fifteen or sixteen students could live together rather inexpensively. Since Charles Carroll was an only son and his father seemed to consider expense inevitable, Anthony Carroll, an Irish cousin of the family, suggested that Charles take a room with only one or two others and supply his own "fire, furniture, candles, maintenance of his tutor, servants' wages and several other expenses." Less prosperous students, however, were attracted to St. Omer by the economy of the "Commons." The lads from Maryland seemed to adapt themselves rather easily to the rigors of this life, for Charles wrote to his "Papa" in 1750, "Cousin Watty Hoxton and Jacky Carroll give their service to you. They are very well and mightily beloved in the house." [3]

The diet at St. Omer was most meagre in those days. A winter's breakfast consisted of one dish of boiled milk for every six boys, with "bread at discretion." The rhetoricians were entitled to a dish much larger than the rest and were the envy of the less intellectual. The last days at St. Omer were particularly parsimonious due to the regime of Brother Joe Blyde, but the hungry young men could always anticipate the feast days when mince pie endeared St. Thomas of Canterbury to their hearts, or St. Stephen's black pudding came around. Many a tone-deaf young cleric revered St. Cecilia if only for the roast turkey enjoyed in her honor. Christmas and Easter, properly enough, were especially graced with an extra bottle of wine for every four. Certainly the scanty fare did not hamper the progress of the Americans, for Charles Carroll wrote home, "I believe Cousin Jack Carroll will make a good scholar for he is often the first. Most of our Marylanders do very well and they are said to be as good as any, if not the best boys in the house." [4]

In Flanders John Carroll went through little figures, which troubled him much less than they did his younger cousin, and he advanced without effort to rudiments or great figures. He soon left middle grammar behind and applied himself to upper grammar, or syntax. Rhetoric and the humanities were the crowning achievements of this curriculum in the liberal arts, and places or rank were determined by the "compositions" which sometimes ran as many as nine a year. It was this early training in careful expression that made John Carroll the precisely polished writer and speaker of his later career. It is interesting to note on the first drafts of his correspondence in adult life how he crossed out and rearranged the words and phrases until he had achieved the exact meaning he intended.

All in all it was not an unhappy life for the young men so far from home. They bore the same protective coloring: the white canvas doublet, knee breeches, and worsted stockings at St. Omer, and afterwards at Liège, their grey coats, yellow leather breeches, and black stockings. They took their monthly holidays at Blandyke, an hour's walk from town; in the interim they played at ninepins, trap bat and ball, or handball. The college stage or "domestic theatre" was a great diversion at St. Omer, and boys learned there the "genteel way of behaving, and carriage, to Brake them of the Bashfulness so natural to ye English." Plays of the genre of the Latin *Leonidas* or the French *Humiades* were presented and gave an extra fillip to their classical education. In Lent they took particular pleasure from the traditional sport of "Sawing the Witch" at Laetare, a custom borrowed from the Spanish and one which indicated the half-way mark in Lent by sawing the figure of an old woman in two. It was a boisterous, rowdy affair and many a man remembered it in later years with twitching lips or outright laughter. [5]

After four years of rising at five and retiring at nine, Charles Carroll was anxious to go on to new fields of learning and a more colorful life. In his seventeenth year his father permitted him to go to Rheims, accompanied by his cousin Anthony. Charles never forgot the good habits learned at St. Omer, and late in life still cherished, he said, "these good practices I learned under the Jesuits at the College at St. Omer's." [6] But in 1754 he was eager to be gone.

John Carroll's was a different case. His father, Daniel Carroll of Upper Marlborough, had died quite unexpectedly on February 27, 1751. The Maryland *Gazette* on Wednesday, March 6, deplored the passing of such a "Gentleman of Great worth and esteem." But there was no question of an interruption of John's studies in 1751. His brother Dan had probated their father's will on May 22, 1751, and it was clear from its terms that it had been the older Daniel's wish to have both of his sons educated and provided for. "Joseph's Park" was bequeathed

> unto my loving sons Daniel Carroll and John Carroll . . . to be Equally divided between them as they shall severally arrive to the age of twenty-one years till which time my will and desire is and I hereby Direct . . . my Dear Wife Eleanor Carroll to receive and Take the Rents Issues and Profits thereof for the better maintenance and Education of said Dear Sons Daniel and John.[7]

Dan's education was long since completed and at twenty-one he was ready and willing to assume the responsibilities as male head of the family. A year later he married Eleanor W. Carroll, a distant cousin of the Duddington branch of the family who was sometimes called Elizabeth, and Dan became the founder of a family in his own right. There was no reason why the young student at St. Omer should be deprived of his education as well as of his parent. Since both his mother and brother wished to see Daniel Carroll's will executed, John would stay on in Flanders.

While Cousin Charles was straining at the leash and impatient for his father's consent to depart from the confining walls of the Jesuit college, John was content to stay. By the time he was eighteen, this Maryland Carroll knew that in the uncluttered, stimulating environment of the clerical, academic world he had found his spiritual home. With high hopes already directed toward the day when he, too, might teach and preach, the earnest young man "went up the hill" in 1753 to Watten, the Jesuit novitiate just seven miles away.[8]

The house John Carroll entered that September day was an old abbey which had been given by a former bishop for its special purpose. Here under the novice-master, Father Henry Corbie, Carroll began his two years of meditation, manual labor, and prayer. He went eagerly through the ten days of orientation and instruction in the Jesuit rule. After a brief spiritual retreat, having proved himself acceptable and worthy, the novice was permitted to don the clerical habit. Even the rich elegance of his bishop's robes in after years would never bring John Carroll the exquisite pleasure he experienced when he put on his simple black cassock for the first time. He prayed that he might be forgiven the fleeting vanity which plagued him as he strode through the chilly halls with the skirts of his new habit whipping against his thin legs in constant reminder of his new estate. Wearing the uniform of the soldier of Jesus Christ, he entered the next phase of his training, and by 1755 he had successfully passed the requirements for a Jesuit scholastic.

The next ten years of John Carroll's life are not clearly limned. His earlier biographers do not agree as to the exact chronology, and the sources for this period are scanty and scattered. All agree that Carroll went from Watten to Liège where Jesuit scholastics continued with their studies of philosophy and theology; there is disagreement, however, as to whether he then taught at Liège or went back to St. Omer to teach for a time. If Carroll went to St. Omer at all after the Watten novitiate it is highly questionable that he stayed there any length of time. His cousin Anthony Carroll wrote to Charles Carroll of Annapolis on February 8, 1759, "Jack is still at Liège and continues to do well; he is esteemed and beloved." [9] When Charles Carroll III relayed the news of the flight of St. Omer to Bruges in a letter to his father on November 11, 1762, he made no mention of his cousin Jack's being involved. He said simply:

> The English Jesuites have been obliged in consequence of the dissolution of their order in France to quit St. Omer's. Their college is now in the Possession of the Secular Priests of Douay. The students and Jesuites have removed to Bruges by an invitation of that city from the Empress Queen who promises them her protection.[10]

It seems probable that if his relative and former classmate had been part of the hegira Charles would have mentioned it.

As a matter of fact, when Charles visited Bruges the following year his letter home indicated that John was not there at that time. Charles wrote:

> From Dunkirk I proceeded to Bruges where I found my old Preceptors removed from St. Omer's. They are at present settled in the vieux government, an old and roomy building but never intended for a College, and therefore notwithstanding all their contrivances, their situation is inconvenient. They are waiting to see what turn affairs are likely to take. Should the King of France live much longer they may give up all thought of returning to that Kingdom.

In this same letter Charles mentioned meeting "my cousin Jacky" in Antwerp, and the two Marylanders chatted about another compatriot and relative, Henry Darnall, who was living at Ghent.[11] John had probably come over from Liège to meet his cousin Charles, for the latter had a few months earlier mentioned to his father, "I have wrote to my Cousin at Liège for an account of Mr. Darnall's conduct and manner of living at Ghent." [12]

All the evidence available now seems to suggest that John Carroll did not take any part in the hasty removal of his old school, St. Omer, to Bruges in 1762. When his brother Dan wrote a letter to their relatives in Ireland in December of that year, after explaining how the family and its fortunes had prospered since their father's death, he added, "My brother John was sent abroad for his education on my return, and is now a Jesuit at Liège, teaching philosophy and eminent in his profession." [13] And at Liège John undoubtedly remained for some time, for he wrote to Dan from that place two years later saying, "I know not if your next will find me at Liège as I am uncertain what destination I may have after having finished my course in Philosophy, which will be now in two months." [14] In the end, it is of little consequence whether Carroll actually accompanied the flight to Bruges or not. His life was unquestionably affected by the occurrences which that migration portended. During the very years that he was so singlemindedly devoting his thought and energies toward a career as a Jesuit priest, clouds were gathering whose deluge would sweep away the Society of Jesus itself.

As early as 1759 rumors had reached Maryland that the Jesuits were being attacked in Portugal. Charles Carroll of Annapolis demanded of his son, "What has been the real occasion of the shocking executions at Lisbon?" He could scarcely believe what he read in the Annapolis papers, and was very displeased at what he called this "lugging of the Jesuits" into every plot. "I know the envy their superior merit draws on them," he told his son. "They are not only too virtuous, but too wise to engage in assassinations, however illy treated." [15]

Odd as it may seem, the older Carroll in America had received news of the unsavory actions of Portugal's Marquis de Pombal before his son now in London had. After a political raid on Tavora Mansion on December 12, 1758, Sebastian Joseph Carvalho, or Pombal, had implicated the Jesuits in an alleged regicidal plot. On February 16, 1759, all Jesuit houses in Portugal were surrounded by soldiers, and before long Jesuit martyrdoms began. Maryland owed a great debt to the Jesuits and, since the present family chaplain of the Carrolls was a member of that order, Carroll of Annapolis continued to press his son for news, asking, on February 13, 1761, for a copy of a Jesuit memorial which rumor claimed defended their position. Young Charles answered, "I know of no memorial published by the Jesuits. The troubles in Portugal so far as they relate to Jesuits are as much a secret here as with you. Some Italian letters have been published, written as is said, by the Pope's nephew in vindication of that order." Charles explained that he had sent a copy of the Italian pamphlets to his old preceptor at St. Omer for his opinion, but he had been told they shed no light on the Portuguese attitude. "The Italian apologies do not lay open the mysteries of Lisbon," Charles concluded, "but sets the character of the sufferers in a favourable light, and vindicates them from the imputation of trade, ambition, and rebellion." [16]

The young man in London was apparently unaware that the accusations of trade, ambition, and rebellion had already been the levers used by nationalistic ministers to pry kings away from their former loyalties to religious orders. Ever since the Marquis de Pombal had come into power in Portugal in 1750, the Jesuits had been accused of standing in the way of national progress. Covetous eyes had been cast at their colony in Paraguay, and subsequent investigators had declared the Society of Jesus guilty of "scandalous commerce." In France the story was scarcely different. True, a combination of intellectual rivals was a contributing factor. Jansenists, Gallicans, Sorbonnists, *Philosophes,* and Encyclopedists all attacked the Jesuits. But the elements of colonial greed and political pressure were equally present. The hatred for the Jesuits

of the wily Madame de Pompadour, the mistress of King Louis
XV, and the Duc de Choiseul, the king's minister, in the end
counter-balanced the friendship which the royal family had formerly felt for the Society of Jesus. On October 22, 1761, Charles
Carroll sent from London "a Pamphlet with an account of the
late Parliamentary proceedings against the Jesuits in France" for
his father's perusal.[17] The older man answered in bewilderment:

> I am the more astonished that the King of France has
> abandoned the Jesuits, as I cannot see in the *arrêts* of Par-
> liament, and other papers published by them and others
> against them, anything but gross, barefaced Calumny un-
> supported by facts of reason. Inscrutable are the ways of
> God.

He concluded sententiously, *"Quos vult perdere, primo de-
mentat."* [18]

For a time father and son did not see eye to eye on the controversy being waged on the continent of Europe. To the younger
man the evidence presented in the French legal proceedings seemed
to "discover the extensive, too extensive, privileges conferred by
the former Popes on that order." He was of the newer generation
who, impressed by the nascent nationalism of the eighteenth century, were beginning to speculate whether statecraft's rapid development might not have rendered incompatible the former great powers
of the religious societies. He told his father:

> If these bulls, constitutions, and letters are faithfully quoted
> I can but coincide with the Parliament in judging them
> dangerous to the State. . . . No one has a greater regard for
> the Jesuits than myself. I revere the virtue, I esteem the
> learning, I respect the apostolic labours of individuals; but
> am forced to acknowledge their institute and plan of
> government liable to great abuses.[19]

His father in America was more concerned with the stricter
justice and canonical aspects of the case. It seemed to him that
the French *parlements* had exceeded their jurisdiction in censuring
the constitutions of the Jesuits, which he felt could "only fall
properly under the cognizance of an ecclesiastical tribunal." He
commented rather astutely:

> The Popes' extravagant privileges to the Society amount to

no more than an Expression of their sense of their great merit; they were not so ignorant as not to know the power of the Successors would be equal to their own. The implicit Obedience professed by the Jesuits cannot be meant . . . to extend beyond things innocent, indifferent and just. Have they murdered, burnt or destroyed in virtue of their Obedience? I say it as my Sentiment, their Eminent Merit and Virtue had provoked this persecution.

Then he admonished his only son, "I have, I thank God, been bred among them, and if you do what they have taught you and nothing contrary to it, you will be happy here and hereafter!" [20]

It was not long before the younger Carroll, perhaps swayed by his father's opinions, perhaps impressed by the events which followed, began to alter his views. The attack launched in Paris spread rapidly to the provinces. Thirty books and other pieces containing the constitution and doctrines of the Jesuits were publicly burned at Rouen pursuant to the order of the *Parlement* of Normandy on February 12, 1762, which enjoined the Jesuits to evacuate their houses before the first of July. Charles began to note how slight were the majorities which were effecting the ruin of the society in France. In Rouen the vote had been twenty to fifteen, at Rennes thirty-one to twenty-eight; Toulouse and Aix had majorities of only two votes each, while at Perpignan the vote was five to four. Of the six decisions taken, Charles found that "a majority of eighteen votes only . . . has subverted an order confirmed by several Popes, approved by the Council of Trent, and patronized by all the present Bishops of France—one only excepted, Fitzjames Bishop of Soissons." [21] The American law student became more sympathetic to the persecuted society as he perceived the slight preponderance of support for suppression.

To his father these events only proved the extent to which monarchy in France had decayed. He commented rather bitterly:

It seems to me the king of France is not sincerely the friend of the Jesuits. Considering how small the Majority in the several Parliaments was against them, could not he, if in earnest, have commanded a great majority in their favour? It is natural to suppose Pompadour not to be their friend, and the surprising influence she has, I doubt not, has been exerted against them. In short, it is no wonder a King of France, who gives up his Authority by suffering the Executive part of the Government to be exercised by such Parliaments,

should connive at their unjust and unprecedented proceedings against the Jesuits. Louis XIV or any king of Spirit
would have chastized their villainy and insolence.[22]

But while his kinsmen debated the relative powers of kings and
the justice of legal majorities, John Carroll found the attacks on
the Society of Jesus a more personal matter. The Paris ultimatum
of August 6, 1762, meant the end of St. Omer in Flanders. On
August 9 the exodus began. The younger lads went first, the others
followed. They travelled on foot, by canal boats, or in wagons.
Without luggage of any kind and carrying nothing to excite suspicion, they left the college in detachments, as if on walking
parties. But these walking parties never returned. Some of the
hikers reached Bruges on August 11, and the last party was safe
in the mice-infested old House of Seven Towers by August 17.
For eleven years the college carried on bravely in the midst of a
dreary Flemish countryside, under the suspicious stares of the
unfriendly inhabitants of the town. It was here at Bruges that
John Carroll would do his last teaching in a Jesuit institution.

It is probably due to this period of confusion in Jesuit affairs
that the exact date of John Carroll's ordination can not be finally
ascertained. There seems to be more reason to accept the date 1769
than any other, but this date is not the last word possible. There
is no way of knowing, either, precisely when John renounced his
rights to his father's legacy in favor of his brothers and sisters.
Some biographers suggest the date 1762, others prefer 1771. It
seems fairly certain that he was still living on money forwarded
from Maryland in 1764, however, for he wrote to Dan in May
of that year complaining of delays. He told his brother that it
had been a year since he had received any communication from
Upper Marlborough. If he had not heard from his uncle, John said,
"I should be at a loss to know whether my friends there were
dead or alive." He concluded his letter with the complaint, "I
am at a loss, for want of letters from you to know whom to apply
to for money this year."[23]

While John lived in uncertainty at Liège, Daniel was preparing
to come to Europe himself. Eleanor Carroll, his wife, had finally
succumbed after a long illness on April 12, 1763. In his grief Dan
found himself wishing for a change of scene. He began to think
of a trip abroad. Conditions were more favorable since the French
had agreed to the humiliating Peace of Paris in February, and

the long war with England was ended at last. Dan found himself longing for a talk with his brother and he began to make plans for a European voyage. On October 13, 1763, he put his first notice of his intentions in the Maryland *Gazette,* and announced to the general public.

> The Subscriber intending to Europe in the Spring has to Let his Dwelling-House and Out Houses, with his Meadows, near the Landing; To save Trouble none need apply but of genteel Family.[24]

These notices continued to appear until November 24, 1763, when it is presumed a sufficiently "genteel" party applied. The news went the rounds of the family and the Darnall girls wrote to their father in Liège that Cousin Daniel was coming to Europe to pay John a visit. When John got the news from his uncle who was then boarding at the convent of English nuns, he wrote happily to Dan, "My uncle is advised by his daughters that you design to come to Europe this year and to see us in Flanders. If this prove true I shall derive abundant compensation from the pleasure of your conversation." John might not be at Liège by the time Dan got to Europe, of course, but the latter could always locate him through Wright the English banker in Henriette Street, Covent Garden. He concluded excitedly, "Write as soon as possible and believe me to be, Dear Brother, your most affectionate Brother, John Carroll." [25]

Dan did come to Europe in 1764, and the brothers had a fine reunion on the continent. If the older man was disappointed not to be able to visit his school at St. Omer, it was at least very reassuring to find John in such good health and so highly esteemed among his fellows. That summer of 1764, too, seemed to be ushering in a period of better times for his brother's order, the Society of Jesus. The death of Pompadour in the spring seemed a harbinger of a new era in France. While she lived it had been known that Louis XV had kept a Jesuit confessor near in case of serious illness, but that the king would have been told to rid himself of his mistress if he had approached the confessor. While her "reign" lasted, from 1746 to 1764, she had never relaxed her hatred for the Jesuits, but with her death on April 15, 1764, Jesuit spirits lifted briefly. John told his brother:

The death of the famous Marchioness de Pompadour will,

it is generally believed by our French brethren, occasion some great change in their circumstances. So far is certain, that they are delivered by this event from their greatest enemy, I mean the most powerful one, and who by her interest and influence over the king of France could more easily than anyone else prevail upon him to view tamely the proceedings against the Jesuits. . . .[26]

The Jesuits were basing their new hopes upon the declared attachment of all the royal family to the society's interests. It was now anticipated that the resumed intimacy between the king and his wife and children, combined with the zealous intercession of the bishops, the nobility, and the town magistrates, would bring about a change of policy on the part of the French government. John Carroll, in his innermost heart, was not so sure that these sanguine hopes would be fulfilled; but, engrossed as he was with the joys of a spiritual life, he went on about his work undismayed. It was his conviction that to the man persuaded of the existence of God, even though publicly accused of crimes as the Jesuits had been, there was always the comfort of this reflection: "That an all powerful and infinitely just Being cannot consistently with these attributes refuse him in another life that justice which passion and iniquity have denied him in this." Persecution in this life, it seemed to the fervent young Jesuit, was only one more proof of man's immortality.

There was nothing of the French mystic about John Carroll. His cheerfulness and zeal were the result of a straight, unwavering scrutiny of things as they were. "To pretend, as some ancient and modern unbelievers have done," he maintained, "that virtue and a good conscience is its own reward argues very little knowledge of the human heart; for many a hardy villain, from a natural alacrity and cheerfulness of mind, and possessed of worldly enjoyments, seldom finds, at least for any long time, his remorse to prey much upon him or disturb his pleasures." On the contrary, he believed, many a good man because of an unhappy disposition or sickly constitution might rarely feel a tangible happiness from his own virtue. Common sense indicated that it was futile to look anywhere but upward. It was this practical kind of pursuit of perfection which in later years made Carroll the ideal man to cope with the persistent imperfections in the human equation of the first Catholic bishopric in the United States. The priest and bishop never surrendered an iota of the Church's valid authority in these relationships, but the man and philosopher was never scandalized nor discouraged by the frequent proofs of human frailty. These years in Europe were to develop this habit, "this train of Philosophising," as he called it, as the "best relief amidst so many affecting and melancholy scenes." [27]

The events of the near future seemed designed to test this fortitude. After the famous "hat riot" in Madrid in 1766 the Jesuits had come under attack by Charles III, and the following year they were suppressed in Spain. John's cousin Charles, who was now home in Maryland, spoke in a tone strongly reminiscent of his father's earlier one when he commented:

> General accusations against a body of men, of great crimes and misdemeanors, without particular proof, are to me strong confirmation of the falsity of those accusations. It is my private opinion that the Roman Catholic princes are desirous of rooting out the regular clergy in their dominions, not only with a view of seizing their estates and enriching with their plunder a few court favorites, but to ease their people of a dead weight and themselves of a political encumbrance. [28]

Now that Charles was in the new world environment of his native Maryland he was more aware of the evils inherent in Old Regime Europe. The privileged classes, it seemed to him, were growing too expensive and too cumbersome. The suppression of the Jesuits was to be a temporary alleviation of the costly anachronism of a corrupt court.

Then in February, 1769, Pope Clement XIII died. There was a rumor that Lorenzo Cardinal Ganganelli would suppress the Jesuits if he were elected by the conclave of cardinals. Father Carroll told his brother:

> In human appearance nothing could have happened more unfortunate to us. . . . How matters will go in the conclave, and after the election of the new Pope, Heaven knows. Humanly speaking we have everything to dread from the combination formed against us. Yet when I reflect on the atrocious falsehoods, injustices, cruelties, and mean artifices employed against us, I greatly confide that God's providence will not permit our dissolution to be effected by such wicked means.

It was a bitter portion to accept at the very beginning of his priesthood, this possibility that the Society of Jesus might be universally destroyed. But his training had given him patterns of thought which quickly asserted themselves, and he concluded his letter to Dan with the words:

> I know His kingdom is not of this world, and that they who seek to do His divine will and promote His glory are not to expect a visible interposition in their favour on every occasion, or to receive in this life an apparent testimony of innocence and divine approbation.[29]

Nevertheless, the newly ordained priest hoped that this might be the exception. And for three years disaster seemed to stay its hand.

CHAPTER III

AN EIGHTEENTH-CENTURY TOURIST

IN ENGLAND in the eighteenth century it was considered highly desirable for the sons of the landed gentry to have a wide acquaintance with conditions in other realms. Many an education was chiefly the product of an extended tour taken under the direction of a capable tutor. Father Carroll had taught only a few months at Bruges, following his profession in 1771, when Charles, Lord Stourton, an English Catholic nobleman, prevailed upon Carroll's superiors to allow the American priest to accompany his son on a tour of the continent. Charles-Philippe, who was to become the sixteenth Lord Stourton, was eighteen that summer, and it was with no little satisfaction that his father saw him start off in the company of the thirty-six-year-old priest whose reputation for prudence and learning was already a by-word at Bruges.

After the American Revolution had separated the English colonies from their parent, a host of European travellers were to descend on the United States to roam its length and penetrate its interior. Chateaubriand's *Voyage en Amérique* would comment vividly upon the hazards of travel. Hector St. John de Crèvecoeur would explain his views of American agriculture in two languages in *Letters* dedicated to a variety of patrons. Brissot de Warville would comment on urban life; de Tocqueville would expound his concepts of *American Democracy*. European tourists after 1776 were fascinated by the spectacle of a new nation being born in a virgin wilderness. But John Carroll's tour in the years 1771-1772 was a different sort. He was witnessing the last days of a declining society. His journal recorded an American's reactions to the symptoms of decay he found on an ancient continent. He wrote of the Old Regime.

Jean Jacques Rousseau had commented nine years earlier, "Man is born free and is everywhere in chains;" and the phrase was

25

snatched up by radicals everywhere as the last word on the Old Regime. From an economic or social point of view his appraisal was valid, certainly. The antiquated machinery of feudalism clanked and groaned as it ground out the heavy chains which shackled trade or bound the peasant to his misery. France which produced the loudest critics was in reality more enlightened than eastern or central Europe. The intolerable conditions which the Encyclopedists decried, and the Physiocrats meant to remedy, were less oppressive than those in Germany or Italy. Frenchmen could chafe under the evils of tax-farming and the absence of a royal budget, but in Naples a thousand different kinds of feudal dues still were levied, while one trip along the Rhine from Strasbourg to Holland exacted as many as thirty tolls. The higher clergy and the nobility comprised the first and second estates in France and controlled the political and social life; but in Germany the divisions of society were even more complex. Imperial cities like Nuremburg, Augsburg, and Ulm were in the grasp of a few families; the nobility controlled the army recruited from the peasantry; and industry, like religion, became an affair of state. East of the Elbe serfdom still prevailed.

Most of Father Carroll's knowledge of Europe up to this time had been confined to the Channel villages in Flanders. Engaged as he had been in study or teaching in English colleges, his opportunities had been comparatively limited. The tour of central Europe, upon which he embarked in 1771, lasted nearly two years and was destined to broaden his horizons. Typical of the eighteenth-century traveller, Carroll kept a journal of much of the tour. A nineteenth-century reader of the journal found it "remarkable for its just and wise reflections," and thought its style "replete with the classical taste and erudition of the writer;" while a twentieth-century critic found it to be commonplace and "on the whole disappointing." But anyone interested in discovering the man that John Carroll was, will still find in the journal many clues to his character and personality. The historian of the Old Regime will find it an engaging commentary on central Europe as seen through an American's eyes.[1]

Carroll and his young charge began their travels by way of Alsace, that fertile province which had been in the possession of France since the Treaty of Münster in 1648. The tutor was quite intrigued with the sharp contrast in legal procedure which he noted in the province. For one thing, the Roman law still prevailed even when contrary to the ordinances of the kings of France, "if you except some few which were enacted since the cession of Alsace." For another, the advocates-general exerted very little influence in the Court of Colmar, *le Conseil Souverain d'Alsace*. Carroll wrote in his journal:

> This may appear extraordinary to an Englishman, since with us it is a certain mark of great eminence in the law to be raised to the rank of king's council. But this surprise will vanish when it is considered that the charges of judicature in France are considered saleable, and that they are transmitted as an inheritance from father to son.

He found, too, that Strasbourg still retained many of her former privileges as an imperial town, and was the only town under the French crown where the intervention of the royal judges was not necessary to condemn a criminal to death.

A true son of the Maryland manor, Father Carroll was impressed with the amazing fertility of the soil, and the odd customs of land tenure which prevailed in that province. As a student and teacher he was appalled at the abuses in the University of Strasbourg, where young men of sufficient fortune could spend but a few months to secure a degree of licentiate and immediately qualify as a counsellor at the court of Colmar. "The venality introduced by Louis XII, Francis I, and the succeeding kings of France occasioned this great abuse, which calls aloud for redress," he noted in his journal. Always interested in the manners and customs of a people, he was unfavorably impressed by what he termed the "want of courtesy and affability" that he found among the Alsatian people. As a Catholic priest he was interested to learn of the rapid increase among the Lutherans in Alsace, and he recorded that they were "bred up in a strong aversion to Catholicity." The thing that pleased him most was, of course, the cathedral of Strasbourg with its choir which had been built by Charlemagne and its spire which soared even higher than the dome of St. Peter's in Rome. He gazed up in silent pleasure at the "admirable gilding of the stucco work of the ceilings." He was impressed, too, by the bishop's palace which he found very grand but which apparently did not satisfy the present incumbent, for an even grander one was in the process of being built nine leagues away at Taverne.

From Alsace Father Carroll and his pupil went into Lorraine where the older man was struck by the terribly human implications

of ruthless transfers of territories. Everywhere he met reminders of
the heartbreak the people of Lorraine had suffered at the transfer
of their homeland to the French by the peace of 1737, when
Francis, the Duke of Lorraine, gave his paternal duchy to France
in return for the Grand Duchy of Tuscany in Italy. Carroll was
sobered by the speculation whether "any compensation could be
made to men of liberal understandings for transferring them without their consent or concurrence, like so many slaves, from dominion
to dominion." It was in Lorraine, on the other hand, that the
travellers came into contact with some of the tangible benefits
which resulted from "benevolent" or "enlightened" despotism.
Later historians might devote their comments to the reigns of a
Frederick of Prussia or a Catherine of Russia; John Carroll was
edified by the benevolent zeal of Stanislaus of Poland. The peace
of 1737 had stipulated that Lorraine should be ceded to Stanislaus
during his life, and should thereafter devolve to France. It was
Stanislaus who softened the passage from their own prince to
France. In an age when too few princes were concerned with the
welfare of their subjects, Carroll found in the Polish king an
admirable example, and he wrote:

> He beautified Nancy, their capital, making it one of the
> finest towns in Europe. He instituted noble foundations
> for the relief of his subjects, without any detriment to their
> industry. He encouraged all the fine arts; he propagated by
> his example and authority a true spirit of religion, which
> he knew to be the best foundation of political as well as
> future happiness. He maintained at the same time a splendid
> court; and what is most remarkable, performed so many great
> things with a revenue which would hardly suffice for the
> hunting parties of many sovereign princes. As far as he was
> above meanness, (and no prince ever carried into his ex-
> penses nobler or more extensive views of the public good,)
> with so strict an economy did he administer his little revenues
> he ought in every age to be held out to princes, as the *Man
> of Ross* is by our great poet to private fortune, for an example
> of what great things may be done by small sums, by a prudent
> and active zeal.

Whether the Polish prince was truly the paragon that the
American priest imagined, Carroll's eulogy gives a fairly accurate
summary of his own theories of the functions of good government.
It was in some ways an amazingly prophetic sketch of what the

Americans were to devise in the way of a blueprint for political and public welfare before the century was out. More than that, it was a prediction of the values which would shape the policies Carroll himself would promulgate when he became a "prince of the Church." He believed in economy which would achieve great things through moderate expenditures. Perhaps, it was the influence of his family background, perhaps the result of his religious life as a Jesuit, but as a bishop John Carroll remained as thrifty and foresighted as he was in theory in 1771. As a bishop, too, he would encourage cultural agencies, serving himself for nearly twenty years as the president of the Baltimore Library Company. Himself a "propagator by example and authority" of the true spirit of religion, he never lost sight of his earlier belief that the industry and zeal of the individual must be preserved. Carroll was never carried away by the weight of his own authority. More than one recalcitrant priest could marvel at the patience and charity of this great prelate.

After leaving Lorraine, the tourists crossed the Rhine into the Holy Roman Empire. Here the priest marked the ease with which they made their entry; and he recorded that France would have an easy access to Germany any time she wished, little suspecting that another century would reverse the direction of invasions through this area. Once across the Rhine the older man's health began to suffer, and he was taken ill with fever and ague which continued to plague him as they progressed from Rastadt to Carlsruhe, from Carlsruhe to Brucksal. In spite of his weakness, however, Carroll remained inquisitive and he continued to keep his journal. Although the capital of Catholic Baden-Baden was the town of that name, the count of the district lived at the strongly fortified town of Rastadt. The priest and his pupil visited the palace and gardens which were laid out in the traditional taste of the country, and they sampled the *vin du marepusat* which was thought to be so far superior to the wines of Alsace. Pushing north to the Protestant section of the province called Baden-Dourlach, they came to the residence of the Prince of Dourlach in Carlsruhe fourteen miles away. His illness prevented Father Carroll from doing much exploring of the city but he gathered as much information as he could through conversations, and he wrote in his journal of the ruler:

> I heard in particular that he provided every parish with an able schoolmaster, who taught the children reading, writing, arithmetic and surveying, without being any charge to the

parents. All the children are obliged to frequent the school; and, while employing their hands in forming the alphabet, they are taught to read and write on such subjects as may ever occur to them.

It was the American's first glimpse of a general, compulsory system of elementary education in Europe, and he was pleased to observe that even for the girls there were schools for instruction proper to their sex.

The route of their tour continued northward through the university town of Heidelberg, on to Mannheim which was now the seat of the Elector Palatine. The previous elector, piqued at what he considered the ingratitude of the citizens of Heidelberg, had removed his court to Mannheim, and as a result that strongly fortified city at the confluence of the Neckar and the Rhine had recently undergone some refurbishing. The streets were all re-laid so as to lead directly to the palace, a magnificent affair of red sandstone. Carroll in later years was to spend many an hour in another city so designed to honor the seat of government, the city of Washington, whose planning was undertaken while his own brother Dan was a commissioner on the board of surveyors.

At Mannheim Carroll met some famous Jesuit scholars, Fathers Desbillons and Mayer. François Joseph Terrasse Desbillons was a French Jesuit who excelled in Latin poetry and composed the *Fabulae Aesopicae* on such salutary subjects as "The Art of Being Well" or "The Art of Preserving Health." He was reputed to be the man most versed in knowledge of both the Latin classics and the Latin language, and his fables were formed on the style of Phaedrus. It seemed to the visiting priest a pity that the fables carried with them such "an air of pedantry," but he joined with the learned Germans in their eager anticipation of the Jesuit's forthcoming work which was to be entitled the *History of the Latin Language*. Carroll was more fascinated by the studies of Andreas Mayer which were entirely devoted to astronomy, and had merited for their author the recently accepted invitation of Catherine the Great, Empress of Russia, that Mayer come to St. Petersburg to observe the latest "transit of Venus."

After some forays out from Mannheim to Cologne, Worms, and Trèves, Father Carroll directed his charge's steps toward Augsburg in Swabia. Here they were depressed by the strange contrast between the magnificence of the ducal court and the poverty of the masses. The tutor wrote in his journal, "There is indeed to be observed in every country a great difference between the gentry and lower class of people; but in none does this difference strike one so much as in many parts of Germany. It is natural to imagine that it arises there chiefly from the nature of the feudal government." He found it ample cause for reflection. Although he had not been in America for nearly a quarter of a century, Carroll was not unfamiliar with the advanced political philosophy of his compatriots, and it gave him pause to find that these German subjects, for the most part, "never conceive an idea of the original equality or of the common rights of mankind." For all his continental education and experience John Carroll was viewing central Europe through American eyes, and the miserable beggars who infested the roads into Bavaria filled his heart with enormous pity for "the distress of so many fellow creatures."

Munich followed, then the Tyrol. Once more Carroll was struck by the geopolitical aspects of these European border districts. He observed:

> Austria, to whom the country of Tyrol belongs, makes it a capital point of politics to preserve this passage into Italy in its own hands. Indeed, the country appears to be of little importance to the court of Vienna besides its serving to connect together its German and Italian states.

As the travellers approached the city of Trent they were impressed by the picturesque appearance of the historic old settlement. It was very imposing with its old Gothic castle, its embattled walls, its church spires rising against the cerulean sky, and it seemed the very prototype of medieval urban design. Inside the feudal walls, however, the houses were very Italian and the numerous canals gave the city an exotic tone all its own. It was in Trent that the priest and his companion first noticed the Italian language being spoken. Trent naturally meant more to Father Carroll than to his pupil. This city on the left bank of the Adige had been the seat of the last and most famous ecumenical council of the Church during the years 1545-1563. When he visited the Church of Saint Mary Major, Carroll could only think that this was the very place, and "the remembrance of that august assembly, which met in it so often, and procured so great services to Christianity" made him view it as one of the most awe-inspiring sanctuaries in the world.

He went down on his knees in deep humility to utter his prayer of thanksgiving "to the Author of all good."

The most interesting part of Italy for Father Carroll was the papal domain, the States of the Church which severed the north from the south. They entered by way of "Bolonia" as Carroll spelled it, and were charmed by the hillside villas which overlooked the prosperous plain where vineyards and fields of grain bore testimony to the good living of the inhabitants.[2] The priest was only too familiar with the denunciations of English writers such as Addison, who liked to deplore the wretched condition of the Pope's domain, the thinness of the population, and the miserable condition of agriculture. Now Carroll found that, with the exception of the countryside around Rome, the Pontiff's subjects appeared "infinitely more happy and at their ease than in many parts of Italy, to say nothing of several provinces in France and Germany." The American priest commented rather astutely:

> It appears to me that the great error of travellers in discoursing of the Pope's states arises from a comparative view of their former and present condition. When they behold the remains of ancient magnificence, and reflect on the immense population of former times, their imagination takes fire, and they give way to popular declamations against priestly government, a monastical life, and the tyranny of Rome. These topics favor their prejudices; their trite and common-place reflections are esteemed profound philosophy; and they give themselves no farther trouble to find out more general causes of the present decay. . . . I might mention many other causes of the present decay than the indolence of government, not that I deny this latter to have no part in producing the downfall.

And then Carroll added a comment which marked him as the admirer of discipline that he was. "Abuses there are in every government," he admitted; but, he continued, "they are greatest where the government is mildest." As first bishop of the United States after 1790, he would be quite consistent in his deep admiration and support of the administration of George Washington. He would by the same logic prove less sympathetic to the Jeffersonian theory that the best government is that which governs least. It was, perhaps, Carroll's greatest contribution to the struggling Church on the frontier, this insistence upon a full and firm authority.

At last Father Carroll and Charles Stourton arrived in Rome. What impressions the Eternal City might have made upon him in another era, Carroll could not imagine. But in October, 1772, the city which treasured the remains of Saint Ignatius, the founder of the Society of Jesus, was now rife with antagonism to all Jesuits. Instead of finding unadulterated joy in this first entrance into the center of Christendom the travellers were chilled by the sentiments they found there. The American priest felt constrained to seek safety in an *incognito,* and advised his friends at Liège and Bruges to address his mail to "Mons. Carroll, Seigneur Anglois," or to enclose it with letters for the English College in Rome. He was forced to seek out Father John Thorpe in a most furtive manner, and resigned himself to avoiding the Jesuit houses in the city. It was all very obnoxious to a man of Carroll's forthrightness, and his wrath at being compelled to act like a sneak-thief colored his views of the city. There was little incentive for remaining in Rome that autumn, and the two travellers went south to Naples for a few months in the sun.[3]

By the time young Stourton and his tutor returned to Rome after their Neapolitan jaunt, things were going even worse for the Society of Jesus.[4] The Family Compact by which France and Spain secretly pledged themselves to aid and abet each other's nefarious designs in 1761 was bearing fruit of bitter flesh. Floridablanca, formerly Don José Monino, had been appointed by Charles III of Spain in 1772 to press the Spanish designs at Rome. Floridablanca was not a man to be diverted from his intentions, and it was he who led the committee which drafted the doom of the Jesuits. Since the election of Cardinal Ganganelli to the Papacy after the death of Clement XIII ominous rumors suggested that the new Pope was committed to a policy of suppression of the Jesuits. Father Carroll had told his brother Dan at the time of Clement's death, "Nothing could have happened more unfortunate to us, especially in the critical moment when an answer was to have been given to the memorials of three united courts of the family compact, France, Spain, and Naples, requiring the immediate dissolution of the society."[5] Now in January, 1773, it looked as if the pressure being brought to bear upon Pope Clement XIV would produce a victory for the Bourbon faction. Carroll wrote to Liège, "Our catastrophe is near at hand, if we must trust to the present appearances, and the talk of Rome. . . . I am assured that some of our best friends in the Sacred College, tho' not admitted to state secrets yet now look upon the determination of our fate as entirely certain." He enclosed a particularly obnoxious attack on the Society of Jesus written in the form of a Mass, and he commented indignantly, "That so horrid a profanation of the Church prayers and the most august sacrifice should pass unnoticed gives a strange idea of the toleration allowed here to everything done or said against us." [6]

One month later Father Carroll was able to relay to Liège the exact details of the extent to which Spanish political ambitions had triumphed. In a letter of February 3, 1773, he said:

> The articles of agreement are said to be, 1, depriving the Jesuits of their general, 2, subjecting them to the ordinaries as a congregation of priests, 3, forbidding them to admit any supplies into their body, 4, Avignon to be restored, the town of Aquila with its dependencies to be ceded to the pope in lieu of Benevento, 6, Castro and Ronciglione to be recognized formally as belonging to the Holy See.

He had heard that this arrangement between the Pope and Spain would be made public by Easter. Moreover, it was said that the Jesuits at Rome were to be sent out of the city at least twenty miles, "that they may not keep up a spirit of fanaticism and blind zeal amongst the cardinals and prelates." [7] If the tone of this letter was rather bitter, Carroll saw nothing during the rest of his winter in Rome to temper his judgments. The political manoeuvres of the cardinals, the personal prejudices, the open attacks of the press on the growing devotion to the Sacred Heart, a devotion the Jesuits fostered,—none was obscured from his observing eyes. "What a revolution of ideas," he reflected soberly, "do all these proceedings produce in a mind accustomed to regard this city as the seat of religion, and the bulwark against the encroachments of irreligion and impiety." [8]

It was withal a salutary experience. John Carroll was not an idealistic dreamer with eyes piously closed to the imperfections of human nature. Nevertheless, this glimpse of the Church as a temporal as well as a spiritual body forced him to readjust his concepts of Rome and her relations to the rest of the Catholic world. He was neither scandalized nor disillusioned. But in the years to come he would remember this complex, and often cumbersome, machinery as he had seen it in operation. Unreasoning awe would never be his portion.

Toward the end of March the two travellers set out for home.

They passed in a leisurely fashion through Florence, Genoa, Turin, Lyons, Paris, and thus at last to Liège and Bruges. After "consigning Mr. Stourton into his father's hands" in the early summer of 1773, Carroll accepted a post as prefect of the sodality at Bruges. But he was uneasy at heart. He was filled with a growing compulsion to go to his family in Maryland. It was not that he lacked good friends at Bruges. Charles Plowden was there, as was William Aston. Thomas Weld of Lulworth Castle was studying there; and men of all ages were devoted to the American priest at Bruges as they had been before at Liège and St. Omer. Years later as Aston's life was nearing its close, he recalled his friendship for Carroll through the years at St. Omer, Watten, Liège, and Bruges, and he told his friend who was now a bishop, "Of all the men I ever knew, you are without any comparison the one whom I most sincerely loved, whom on trial I found most valuable, and with whom I would now choose to finish my career." [9] But in 1773 closer ties were pulling Father Carroll toward America, while events in Rome were severing the ones that bound him to Europe.

On July 21, 1773, the Holy See spoke the words which produced the dissolution of the Jesuits. Kept a secret there until August 16, the shocking news did not reach Bruges until September 5. The blow had finally fallen. With an expression of emotion quite foreign to his letters, Father Carroll wrote to Dan on September 11:

> The enemies of the Society, and above all the unrelenting perseverance of the Spanish and Portuguese Ministries, with the passiveness of the court of Vienna, have at length obtained their ends; and our so long persecuted, and I must add holy, Society is no more. God's holy will be done. . . . I am not, and perhaps never shall be, recovered from the shock of this dreadful intelligence. The greatest blessing which in my estimation I could receive from God would be immediate death; but if he deny me this, may his holy and adorable designs on me be wholly fulfilled.[10]

Although it is easy to suspect Carroll's sentiments of some coloring of nationalistic prejudice or the natural partisanship of a member of the order, his views were in fact neither unique nor exaggerated. The disaster which visited the Society of Jesus in 1773 was widely acknowledged by men of all creeds and opinion to be a blow sustained by the intellectual and spiritual life of the western world. Voltaire, that harsh critic of the Church, did not hesitate to describe the Jesuits as "writers of rare merit, men of learning, orators, and geniuses," while his friend and patron, Frederick II of Prussia, knew of no better teachers for his Catholic subjects than the Jesuit order and told Voltaire he still hoped "to preserve some of its precious stock so as to be able to supply those who might desire to cultivate so rare a plant." Speaking later in the French Chamber of Deputies, Joseph Jerome Lalande, the eminent astronomer, recalled the Jesuits as the most astonishing reunion of science and virtue ever seen. "Pombal and Choiseul," he said direfully, "have destroyed the finest work of man." [11]

As for Father Carroll, momentarily his grief brooked no disguise. It was an almost unbearable deprivation, this snatching away of the pattern of life to which he had been so forcibly attracted almost from the beginning of his education in Flanders. The Jesuit rule of life had so exactly suited his yearnings, had so precisely delineated the pathway to perfection, that for one brief moment he thought death would be preferable to a life without the society. But in almost the same breath his deep piety canceled out the repugnance. In spite of his anguish over the destruction of his fondest hopes his fortitude was equal to the crisis. If Daniel Carroll perceived his brother's sorrow, he never doubted the complete sincerity of those words, "May His holy and adorable designs on me be wholly fulfilled." Only John Carroll knew the terrific effort it took to sustain that hard-won resignation.

Scarcely more than a month later, on the night of October 14, 1773, the college at Bruges was invaded by Austrian officials, and Fathers Angier, Plowden, and Carroll were temporarily arrested. Through the intervention of Lord Arundell of Wardour Castle no physical harm came to the ex-Jesuits; but Bruges, like St. Omer before it, was doomed. Plowden and some of the others went to Liège and joined the secularized Jesuit college there; but John Carroll chose to go with the great majority across the Channel to England.

Lord Arundell, whose intervention in his official capacity as a Count of the Holy Roman Empire had tried to prevent the destruction of the college, now came forward to offer the exiles a refuge in his English castle. Scrimping old Brother Joe Blyde lived out his days there. But in spite of Arundell's plea that he stay on as the family chaplain, Father Carroll could not be persuaded. After trying fruitlessly to get some reparation from the Austrian and French governments for the loss of the Jesuit properties at St. Omer and

Bruges, Carroll abandoned his post as secretary for the remonstrating migrants and made plans to set sail for America in the spring.

"In returning to Maryland," he told his brother with calm resignation, "I shall have the comfort of not only being with you, but of being farther out of reach of scandal and defamation, and removed from the scenes of distress of many of my dearest friends, whom God knows, I shall not be able to relieve." [12] It was a harsh termination to a career begun with such fervor. John Carroll was nearing forty when his Jesuit vocation was so abruptly denied him. In the eighteenth century life was not so prone to "begin at forty," and a lesser man would have been despondent and defeated. But Father Carroll's spirits could not be kept down. There was always a bright side, and he was going home at last.

CHAPTER IV

A FRUITLESS MISSION

FATHER John Carroll and his cousin, the Reverend Anthony Carroll, arrived in America in the late spring of 1774. Anthony was the nephew of James Carroll of All Hallows Parish in Ann Arundel County, and had come to America hoping to settle some difficulties over the family estate, part of which had come to him by his uncle's will of February 12, 1728. In a letter to James Earle of Easton on June 15, 1809, John Carroll recalled that visit with the words:

> The Rev. Mr. Anthony Carroll who passed a few months in Maryland and Pennsylvania in the years 1774-1775, was the nephew and heir of a Mr. James Carroll, who held considerable estates in Maryland. Mr. Dominic Carroll, as I have heard, was likewise a nephew, but not a brother of Anthony, who knew that Dominic's heirs were numerous and he was unable to ascertain them and divide the small sum to which they were entitled.[1]

With the failure of his efforts to locate the missing heirs, Anthony Carroll returned to Europe. But John Carroll was home to stay.

Father Carroll was welcomed by his sisters and their families at Richland on the Potomac River. It was the lovely season of white dogwood and the shocking-pink of Judas trees in Virginia, and it must have been a happy reunion for the brother who had been gone some twenty-seven years from his native land. Richland was the family seat of William Brent, Eleanor's husband, and was not far from the home of Robert Brent who had married Anne Carroll. "Bobby Brent's Landing" was becoming a well-known stop on the river in 1774, but John Carroll found that there was little to remind him of his youth except the affection shining from his sisters' faces, and the reminiscences of Robert who had been with him at Bohemia and St. Omer. Therefore, after a two-day visit in Virginia he hastened to Rock Creek to the side of his mother for whose sake alone, he confessed to Charles Plowden, he had "sacrificed the best place in England." [2]

The Maryland to which the travellers had returned was caught up in the mercantile web with which England was determined to ensnare colonial profits; like the other colonies on the mainland she was threshing about in wild efforts to escape. Although some theorists on the American side of the Atlantic held that an imperial parliament could solve the present difficulties, the majority on both sides still preserved the illusion of colonial dependency which had been the accepted mercantile pattern of English-American relations. Colonies were expected to furnish cheap raw materials in tobacco, iron, and furs, to offer markets for finished English products, and to fill the ranks of the army or man the topsails of His Majesty's fleet if need be. English mercantilists, like the Spanish and French before them, did not question the right of the mother country to legislate for the colonies, and, ever since the master-pattern had been devised by Oliver Cromwell in the Navigation Act of 1651, England had gone ahead, by fits and starts, syphoning off surplus colonial profits. Adam Smith's *Wealth of Nations* with its critical glance at mercantile regulation was still two years away when Father Carroll set foot on Maryland soil.

Maryland in 1774 was a thriving commercial colony whose ports on the Potomac River and Chesapeake Bay sent across the Atlantic annually 28,000 hogsheads of tobacco, and whose own sloops and schooners numbering nearly thirty carried corn, wheat, and bread to the West Indies and the northern colonies. In answer to the queries recently expressed by the Lords of Trade, and those of Lord Dartmouth's letter of July 5, 1773, the Marylanders assured England that their colony engaged in no trades or manufactures "hurtful to Great Britain," but there were many iron mines furnishing the eight furnaces for pig iron and the ten forges for making iron bars. The vessels which returned from England carried "all sorts of fine and coarse Woollens and Linnens, great quantities of wrought Leather, wrought Iron and almost all kinds of British manufactures and East India goods." Even George Town was beginning to hint of her future as a thriving port and the day when she would become the center of operations for James Barry, that staunch friend of Maryland's first Catholic bishop.[3]

But it was the temper of the times which most intrigued the late arrival. In the decade which had elapsed since Daniel Dulany had published Maryland's denunciation of the Stamp Act and all internal taxation, and the Maryland *Gazette* had deplored the "Dreadful, Dismal, Dolorous, and Dollarless times" in gloomy alliteration, little remained of the optimism with which the citizens of Queen Anne's County had dug their hole to "bury Discord" and to erect a pillar dedicated to Harmony. The twenty-two toasts drunk on that happy occasion to "Pitt and Concord" were now forgotten, and Charles Carroll of Carrollton wrote to his father from Philadelphia that the toasts recently drunk at the "Treat" given to the First Continental Congress included such stirring phrases as: "May no man enjoy Freedom who has not the spirit to defend it," and "May every American hand down to posterity pure and untainted the Liberty he had derived from his Ancestor!" [4]

Maryland had learned during the colonial resistance to the hated Stamp Act that boycotting could be a powerful weapon, and, when the English Townshend Duties of 1767 became known, she revived her non-importation tactics of 1765. Annapolis sent back to London the *Good Intent* with her $50,000 cargo of India goods untouched. Although the later repeal of most of the Townshend Duties cajoled the other commercial colonies Maryland remained adamant; when Rhode Island reneged on her non-importation pledge to Maryland, her ships, the *Industry* and *Speedwell*, were refused in Maryland ports. The journalistic argument over taxation the year before John Carroll's return, a debate in which his cousin Charles had used the pen-name "First Citizen" to retort to "Antillon" who was in reality Daniel Dulany, only served to point up the radicalism of Cousin Charles' attack and the unpopularity of any defense of British taxation even when voiced by a Dulany. Marylanders made no secret of their opposition to British imperial legislation by 1774, and if further proof were needed to convince Father Carroll of their belligerence it came in the October following his return with the burning of the *Peggy Stewart*.

The brigantine, *Peggy Stewart*, was owned by Anthony Stewart and his father-in-law, James Dick. On October 15, 1774, it arrived at Annapolis carrying merchandise including 2,000 pounds of tea consigned to Thomas C. Williams and Company. The tea had been wrapped in blankets by the senior member of the firm who was conveniently in London when the *Peggy Stewart* sailed. When Stewart applied to the Annapolis customs, he asked to enter all of the cargo except the tea, but the officials said he must enter all or nothing. Reluctantly Stewart entered the entire cargo and fearfully awaited the consequences.

He did not have long to wait. The local committee of resistance met at once and voted that the tea must be burned. Public wrath against Stewart mounted rapidly and, while the committee waited for the Anne Arundel citizens to voice their opinion, Stewart tried futilely to defend himself by issuing handbills which claimed that the shipmaster, Richard Jackson, was unaware of the tea's presence on board until the vessel had passed Gravesend. The meeting in Anne Arundel County on October 19, framed an apology to be signed by Stewart and the Williams partners, but by this time the more radical mob which had long suspected Stewart of Tory sentiments were in no mood for such a mild solution. They threatened the unfortunate fellow with violence and burned a gallows outside the window where Mrs. Stewart was confined by childbirth. Her protests and her father's pleading forced Stewart to cater to the mob. The *Peggy Stewart* was doomed.

The whole affair showed to what extent the mob would ignore the counselings of the more moderate men of the colony. Robert Caldelaugh's affidavit to England testified that both "Mr. Matthias Hammond and Mr. Charles Carroll, Barrister, did propose as an atonement for the crime that the Tea should be carried under the Gallows and there burned." But the radical ringleaders had insisted that both brigantine and tea must go. There was even some reason to believe that the Maryland *Gazette* had been intimidated by threats to wreck its press if any vindications of Stewart were published. Edmund Burke commented in Parliament, "These people of the Southern colonies are much more strongly and with an higher and more stubborn spirit attached to liberty than those to the northward." [5] Parliament generally, however, chose to ignore the Annapolis tea party, and Father Carroll's own part in the Revolution was to be provoked in another quarter. It was the Quebec Act of 1774 which indirectly caused his appearance on the troubled political scene.

Viewed in retrospect, the notorious Quebec Act has been deemed an epochal event in religious and political statecraft by both American and British historians. Time has softened the harsh judgments of the revolutionary era, and present opinion rates the builders of the act, Sir Guy Carleton and Lord North, wiser than even they knew. The act became, within a few decades of its passage, the master-plan for British government in "the second empire" which flourished after the American colonies were lost, an empire based on large territories inhabited by non-Europeans. The Quebec Act became the precedent and model of crown-colony government in non-British dependencies in the nineteenth century. It evolved during the decade following the acquisition of French Canada by the British in 1763.

As early as 1766, when James Murray the first governor general was recalled, the broad lines of British policy had begun to emerge. When Sir Guy Carleton landed in Quebec in September of that year, he continued to build upon the foundations Murray had laid. Carleton saw that Canada would remain predominantly French not only in language and culture but in civil law as well. One of his first acts was to undertake a compilation of French-Canadian law and, shortly after its completion in 1769, he requested to be allowed to return to London in order to present the Canadian cause in person. The picture he drew for Parliament was that of more than 50,000 Canadians almost wholly French and Roman Catholic, whose claims must be superior to those of the 600 British immigrants. For three years the soldier-statesman labored at home to secure for his American dominion religious freedom, the retention of local customs in regard to civil law and property rights, and the introduction of British criminal law in the other areas of control.

There is no question that the Boston Tea Party in December of 1773 and Parliament's subsequent decision to take penal measures made Carleton's policies in regard to Canada more attractive in London; but evidence seems to point to the conclusion that the bill for Quebec was substantially complete before 1774, and that fear of war with France and Spain was as much a factor in the passage of the Quebec Act as any fleeting desire to punish Massachusetts.[6] Nevertheless, the act raised a storm of outraged protest in the Protestant colonies south of the new Quebec boundary line. In Massachusetts on September 6, 1774, the famous Suffolk County Resolutions asserted that "the late act of Parliament for establishing the Roman Catholic Religion and the French laws in. . . Canada is dangerous in an extreme degree to the Protestant religion and to the civil rights and liberties of all Americans." American patriots entrenched at Bunker Hill appealed to the British soldiers not to participate in this attempt England was making to compel submission to "Popery and Slavery." Daniel Barber, who became a Catholic himself in 1818, admitted, "We were all ready to swear that King George, by granting the Quebec Bill, had thereby become a traitor, had broken his coronation oath, was secretly a papist." [7]

The Continental Congress gave official expression to these colonial sentiments in October when the delegates framed two petitions to the mother country. On Friday, October 21, 1774, they addressed the people of Great Britain, expressing astonishment that a British Parliament should ever consent to establish "a religion that has deluged your island in Blood, and disbursed impiety, bigotry, persecution, murder and rebellion through every part of the world." The second petition, addressed to King George III, the following Wednesday used less colorful language but included the Quebec Act among the intolerable measures protested by the Congress. [8]

And yet at the very time these reproaches were being leveled against trans-Atlantic policy, this same Congress at Philadelphia was trimming its sails to the possibility of Canadian collaboration in North America. On the same day that George III was maligned for subjecting great numbers of English freemen to absolute government and Roman Catholicism in Canada, the Continental Congress sent an address to the Canadians couched in conciliatory phrases. "We are too well acquainted," they assured their northern neighbors, "with the liberality of sentiment distinguishing your nation, to imagine that difference of religion will prejudice you against a hearty amity with us." The truth was that the neophyte statesmen at Philadelphia were trying to steer the perilous course between the Charybdis of American bigotry and the Scylla of Canada's geopolitical importance. Congress felt compelled to voice the colonial anger at the Quebec Act; but the delegates dared not ignore the hard, cold facts of military strategy. The whole lesson of the colonial terrain in the wars of the eighteenth century had been the vital importance of the St. Lawrence-Lake Champlain-Lake George theatre. Ticonderoga and the "northwest passage" were still words to conjure with. So it was that while Congress tried through diplomatic channels to win Canada over to the American cause, military expeditions were undertaken to remove the northern threat by force. John Carroll's journey to Canada took place between Benedict Arnold's abortive siege of Quebec in January, 1776, and his defeat by the Canadian general, Sir Guy Carleton, at Valcour Island in October of the same year. Sir William Howe was not the only one carrying an olive branch in one hand while the other brandished a sword.

However ridiculous such a Janus-faced policy may appear in retrospect, the Philadelphia Congress was acting upon advice. Early in February, 1776, their French agents, Preudhomme la Jeunesse and Jean Dantremond, had arrived from Canada with recommendations that some persons from Congress should go to Canada "to explain *viva voce* to the People there the Nature of our Dispute with England." On February 15, therefore, it was resolved that a committee of three be appointed to proceed to Canada, "there to pursue such instructions as shall be given them by Congress." [9] When John Hancock notified Charles Lee in New York a few days later that the Canadian deputies would probably be ready in a short time, Lee replied:

> I should think that if some Jesuit or Religieuse of any other Order (but he must be a man of liberal sentiments, enlarged mind and a manifest friend to Civil Liberty) could be found out and sent to Canada, he would be worth battallions to us. This thought struck me some time ago, and I am pleased to find from the conversation of Mr. Price and his fellow travellers that the thought was far from a wild one. Mr. Carroll has a relative who exactly answers the description. [10]

The Congress had already been struck with the same idea. On February 15 they had further resolved that Charles Carroll of Carrollton be requested to prevail on Father John Carroll to accompany the committee to Canada. And John Adams wrote to his friend, James Warner, three days later, "Dr. Franklin and Mr. Chase of Maryland and Mr. Charles Carroll of Carrollton are chosen a committee to go to Canada." Then he added, "But we have done more. We have empowered the Committee to take with them another gentleman of Maryland, Mr. John Carroll, a Roman Catholic Priest, and a Jesuit, and a gentleman of learning and Abilities." Adams believed Father Carroll's functions would be "to administer Baptism to the Canadian children and bestow Absolution upon such as have been refused it by the Toryfied Priests in Canada." [11]

Obviously John Carroll was not aware of Adams' notion that disgruntled Canadian Catholics could be lured to the patriot cause by his priestly offices, for his own thoughts while weighing the invitation were concerned with quite different compunctions. In

referring to the distinguished and unexpected honor the Congress
had done him in asking him to accompany the committee to Canada
Carroll said, "I should betray the confidence put in me by the
Honourable Congress, and perhaps disappoint their expectations,
were I not to open my mind to them with the utmost sincerity, and
plainly tell them how little service they can hope to derive from
my assistance." He believed that the Congress expected him to
engage in diplomatic conversations, and he was loath to accept such
a responsibility. "In the first place," he explained, "the nature and
functions of that profession in which I have engaged from a very
early period of life, render me, as I humbly conceive, a very unfit
person to be employed in a negotiation of so new a kind to me."
Carroll believed that the priest's place was at the altar, in the confessional, or in some other post where he might serve his flock. "I
have observed," he said, "that when ministers of religion leave the
duties of their profession to take a busy part in political matters,
they generally fall into contempt, and sometimes even bring dis-
credit to the cause in whose service they are engaged." His priestly
vocation pressed upon him and he said, "I cannot help feeling my
character." [12]

Quite apart from his doubts in regard to his own personal
qualifications for such a mission, Father Carroll was dubious as to
the real value of such an undertaking. He had taken a keen interest
in the rising storm of opposition to British imperial policy since
his return to America, and from the information which he had been
able to collect concerning the inhabitants of Canada he was convinced that they were in no wise eager either to molest the American colonies or to aid the British in repelling the American inva-
sion. Sir Guy Carleton had in the mid-summer of the previous
year, 1775, only a few thousand regular troops at his disposal and
could hardly expect more than 300 volunteers from the Englishmen
living in Montreal and Quebec. The main populace, if the few
seigneurs and bourgeois merchants were discounted, were French
farmers or trappers who could be relied upon for very little assistance by either side. The American failures to take Canada thus far
had been more the work of incautious planning, lack of proper
boats, food shortages, and smallpox.

On the other hand, Carroll saw little hope of persuading the
Canadians that they possessed the same motives for taking up arms
against England as those which justified the American malcontents.
Their grievances against their new mother country had been sub-

stantially considered by the Quebec Act, and their governor was the very man who had steered its perilous passage through the British Parliament. The Maryland *Gazette* on October 27, 1774, had carried the text of the Canadian clergy's address to Sir Guy Carleton, thanking him for his part in its passage. "History will rank your name among the bravest of warriors, and the wisest of politicians," they asserted, "but gratitude is already imprinted in the heart of every Canadian." The clergy assured the Canadian governor that he would always find them good and faithful subjects of their most gracious sovereign, the king of England. "We desire through you," they proclaimed, "to offer . . . our assurances of the most profound respect, our attachment and inviolable fidelity (confirmed by an oath) to assure him that he has no subjects more faithful or dutiful than the Canadians." [13]

As a matter of fact, the clergy of French Canada were outspoken in their exhortations to their parishioners that they resist American propaganda. The pastoral letters of the Bishop of Quebec, Joseph Olivier Briand, were fiery in the language of warning. These pastorals of 1775-1776 reminded the French Canadians that no people had been so severe in their persecutions of Catholicism as the Bostonians had been. Nowhere were the clergy more harshly criticized than in Massachusetts. Nowhere were such invectives and blasphemies uttered against veneration of the saints as in the colonies south of the Quebec boundary line. Bishop Briand warned his people against the pretended affections of the Americans and reminded them that they need never take up arms for a freedom which they already possessed. In such a climate of opinion even the sturdiest of overtures was fated to wither. Carroll was, therefore, under no illusions when he accepted the offer from Congress. Nevertheless, he did go. The present distress of his country, he told the Congress, impelled him to disregard his own opinions. Any effort his country required must be made, and personal safety in these times must not be thought of. Armed with nothing more powerful than a letter of introduction from Father Ferdinand Farmer of Philadelphia, John Carroll prepared for the long and arduous journey northward.

Meanwhile the Congress, as Richard Smith recorded in his diary on February 23, ordered that £600 in gold be collected "by the Treasurers for the Expences of our Ambassadors to Canada," and John Adams presented a set of instructions for them. These instructions produced a month of delaying debate. Adams with the collaboration of George Wythe and Roger Sherman had been appointed the committee on instructions on February 17, but sooner or later everyone interested in the Canadian venture took a hand in shaping them. When John Hancock advised Philip Schuyler that the commissioners would call on him on their way to Canada he expressed the opinion, "I expect they will be invested with full powers not only to settle the affairs of that province, but to adjust those matters that have given you uneasiness." It was natural that the exact extent of the commission's powers would be hotly debated, and on March 12 Commissioner Chase's suggested amendments caused the discussion to be carried over to the next day. It was not until March 19 that the last corrections were finally made, and the instructions could be handed over to the commissioners the following day. Richard Smith noted with some satisfaction in his diary on March 24 that the "Canada Commissioners are to set out tomorrow." And Robert Morris wrote with relish born of anticipation to Horatio Gates on April 6:

> I suppose you know that Doctor Franklin, Chase, and the two Mr. Carrolls are gone to Canada, and I hope a sufficient force will be there to put Quebec under their direction for I jump in opinion with you, that Country must be ours at all Events. Should it fall into the hands of the Enemy they will soon raise a Nest of Hornets on our backs that will sting us to the Quick.[14]

As it turned out, on the very day that Morris penned his letter the Canadian commissioners reached Albany and joined General Schuyler there. Father Carroll and the others came by way of Brunswick, New Jersey, from Philadelphia to New York, and the priest had been amused at the odd sights they saw in the New Jersey town. He wrote to his mother at Rock Creek of the Prussian general so swaddled in furs that he could scarcely walk. "Like other Prussian officers," he told her, "he appears to me as a man who knows little of polite life, and yet has picked up so much of it in his passage through France as to make a most awkward appearance." [15] Carroll had been abroad too long himself to be deceived by the false pretensions of newly arrived Europeans, and he was too much of an American to enjoy studied artificiality.

When they reached New York in April it was no longer the gay polite place it was formerly esteemed. Except for the disorganized troops huddled in odd groups about the city, New York was almost deserted. Washington was moving his headquarters to that city and, while the soldiers worked feverishly to erect fortifications, the civilians rushed with equal fervor to remove themselves and their effects from the town. Benjamin Franklin was able to persuade his friend, Mrs. Barron, to remain, but that estimable lady was an exception to the general exodus.[16] After two disagreeable days in New York, the four commissioners boarded a sloop at five o'clock on April 2 to sail up the Hudson to Albany.

John Carroll had made many another trip by river boat in his travels on the continent, but this was the first time that he had been part of an expedition of such military implication. Their first anchorage on the Hudson was a scant thirteen miles from New York, and as the commissioners prepared for their pallets that night they could hear the ominous cannonading which they speculated might be an attack by the British on Bedloe's Island. As they continued up the river the southern gentlemen were given ample opportunity to examine the Hudson Valley more closely. A split mainsail as they rounded St. Anthony's Nose caused them to anchor at Thunder Hill Bay, and the more curious had a chance to acquaint themselves with the wild and romantic shore. Again, on April 5, the sloop anchored off West Point and Mr. Chase and cousin Charles rowed ashore to inspect Fort Constitution which looked so vulnerable that they sent "an express" to Philadelphia urging Congress to strengthen the fort.[17]

The arrival in Albany was a pleasant break in the journey. Father Carroll reported to his mother that the Schuylers entertained them during their stay "with great politeness and very genteely," while cousin Charles' journal received enthusiastic entries describing "lively, agreeable, blackeyed" Betsy and Peggy Schuyler. It was Betsy who later became Mrs. Alexander Hamilton; but in 1776 she graced the family mansion which rose in charming dignity about a mile from town. Joined by the Schuylers and General John Thomas, the commissioners then set off in wagons for Saratoga which was the Schuyler country seat thirty-two miles away. The Carroll cousins found the trip overland very trying. It took all day and was complicated by bad weather and even worse ferry service. Charles was fascinated at Cohoes by the waterfalls which he estimated to be seventy-four feet high and probably a thousand feet wide. His cousin huddled in the jouncing carriage and resigned himself to the fact that any reading of his breviary would have to be done after they arrived. Everyone was dismayed to find Saratoga under six inches of April snow, and it was only the genial courtesy of the general and the gay laughter of his ladies which atoned for the grimness of the surroundings. Saratoga was their farewell to gentle living until the commissioners reached Montreal.

The rest of the journey northward was over the worst roads Father Carroll had ever seen, or else on the Hudson River which now required four hours of laborious rowing to progress a bare seven miles. At ruined Fort Edward the commissioners stayed over night. Again, they were accommodated at Mr. Wing's tavern at Queensbury. At Fort George the priest was relieved to see General Schuyler rejoin their party, and all were glad to get on the boat at Lake George for the trip to Ticonderoga. At "Ti" the shivering commissioners drank hot tea while their thirty-foot craft was hauled across the portage to Lake Champlain, but the warmth of the beverage was all too quickly dispelled as they passed from one abandoned fort to another. To Father Carroll Fort George looked as bad as Fort Edward had, and only "small remains" of Fort William Henry marked its location. Crown Point, like "Ti," was in ruins as well. As the boat traversed the hundred and more miles to St. John, some of the passengers went ashore at night to sleep, protecting themselves against the cold with fires at their feet and under a covering of boughs. But John Carroll had no inclination to lead the life of a scout and he remained on board the transport under the good awning and "plenty of bed clothes." He preferred a raw wind and the slapping of water against the wooden belly of the vessel to the localized heat of crackling boughs or the sounds of prowling animals too close for comfort.[18]

At last, on April 29, 1776, the four representatives of the American Congress arrived safely at Montreal where General Benedict Arnold and "a great body of officers, gentry, etc.," met them with a welcoming cannonade from the citadel in compliment to their official dignity. Carroll looked with curiosity at this man whose daring was part and parcel of the Canadian campaigns, this "Horse Jockey," as Carleton had sneeringly called him. From his hospital bed that winter he had issued the orders that maintained Quebec under the fantastic siege by which a few hundred starving, freezing men had kept twice their number shut up in the fortress town. Now, limping from the wound in his leg newly re-opened by his fall from a horse in April, and stiff with his resentment at the lack of co-operation of Wooster and Thomas, he was at Mont-

real to greet the Philadelphia commissioners.[19] John Carroll wrote
to his mother from Montreal on May 1:

> Being conducted to the general's house, we were served
> with a glass of wine, while people were crowding in to pay
> their compliments, which ceremony being over, we were
> shown into another apartment and unexpectedly met in a
> large assembly of ladies, most of them French. After drinking
> tea, and sitting some time, we went to an elegant supper
> which proved very agreeable, and would have been more so
> if we had not been so much fatigued with our journey.

But if the welcome of the laity at Montreal was warm, the
reception Father Carroll received at the hands of the clergy was
markedly cool. Bishop Briand had ordered that no courtesy be
shown the American priest when he arrived, and if it had not been
for an ex-Jesuit with some American sympathies Carroll might
not have even found a convenient place to offer Mass. Ferdinand
Farmer in Philadelphia had given Carroll a letter for Father Pierre
Floquet, the last superior of the Jesuit mission in Canada. Floquet
was already in disfavor with Briand for his "Bostonnais heart" and
dared not offer the American priest a residence. Carroll was
invited to dine with Floquet exactly once; no further amenities
were proffered. Father Carroll lodged, as did the other commissioners, with Mr. Thomas Walker in "the best built and perhaps
best furnished" house in town.[20]

The long-debated instructions of the Continental Congress had
admonished the commissioners:

> You are further to declare that we hold sacred the rights of
> conscience and may promise to the whole people solemnly
> in our name, the free undisturbed exercise of their religion;
> and to the clergy, the full, perfect and peaceable possession
> and enjoyment of their estates.

But it was quite another thing to find willing listeners to these
protestations of good faith. To Father Carroll's statements of the
Congress' intentions there were such flat contradictions as the presence in Montreal of Father John McKenna, a priest who had very
recently been compelled to flee from the bigotry south of the
Canadian border. Carroll was asked why, if Congress was so tolerant,
they had protested so strongly to London against the Roman Cath-

olic religion. Canadians had not so soon forgotten the rigors and cruelty with which missionaries to the Indians had been treated, nor the tragic history of the Acadians which had left an indelible stain.

Father Carroll could not have denied, even if he had wished, that past performances did not augur well for the future. He was only able to assure the Catholics who cared to listen that the policies of the colonies to the south might guarantee more charity to war-time allies than had been their portions as enemies in the past. The exigencies of war were known to make substantial changes in national aims, and no one could doubt the sincerity of the Congress' attempt to enlist the support of Canada against England. Such support was worth a high bid, and the gentlemen at Philadelphia had sent four of their most honorable citizens as an indication of their sincerity. But none of these considerations could sway the Canadians, Carroll found. And in his heart he could confess to no surprise. He had prophesied the results before ever accepting his commission.

The regular commissioners were meeting with little more success. Even those in Montreal who were disposed to favor the American cause were wary in the face of the constantly decreasing Continental credit and the lack of hard money. The commissioners wrote to Congress:

> It is impossible to give you a just idea of the lowness of the Continental credit here. . . . Therefore, till the arrival of money, it seems improper to propose the federal union of this province with the others, as the few friends we have here will scarce venture to exert themselves in promoting it till they see our credit recovered, and a sufficient army arrived to secure the possession of the country.[21]

Indeed, the lack of money, which led frequently to the conscription by the American military of carriages and other conveniences, had so irritated the Canadians that they were in no mood to listen even if the Americans had proposed collaboration.

As for the American army, the commissioners found it on the verge of starvation, dispirited, and rotten with smallpox. After two weeks of fruitless conversations, the commission learned with dismay that General John Thomas, who had accompanied them on part of their trip, had been surprised by British warships which were able to land a force of 1,000 men and six cannon. When news reached them that the Americans had suffered 250 casualties the commis-

sioners wrote despairingly to Congress on May 10, "We are afraid
it will not be in our power to render our country any further
services in this colony." [22]

Benjamin Franklin was the first to leave. The old sage had been
suffering from boils and swelling of his legs, and on May 11 he
suddenly decided to go home. Knowing he was useless in Montreal,
Father Carroll hastened after the sick old man and caught up with
him before he got past St. John's. He spent two days trying to find
a carriage to carry them southward. No one was willing to admit
ownership of a conveyance in times like these if it could be avoided.
The other two commissioners "after embarrassing Thomas by their
interference, though their authority was partially military and
their intention good," started home toward the end of May. Poor
General Thomas fell sick with smallpox which was no respecter
of rank, and he died before the commissioners ever reached home.

Meanwhile, Father Carroll and his invalid companion continued
their slow journey down through the treacherous terrain, past the
lakes, the abandoned forts, the rugged mountain trails. Before they
left St. John's, they had been dismayed to receive a call from their
former hostess, Mrs. Thomas Walker, who requested that they give
her room in their carriage as far as Saratoga, where her husband
would join her. There was very little the American gentlemen
could say, but the demands of the Walkers destroyed what little
comfort the old man and the priest might have taken in the
journey. The warm memories of the wining and dining of the past
fortnight faded in the harsh light of the hardships of the road, and
Dr. Franklin wrote querulously of the Walkers, "They both took
such liberties in taunting at our conduct in Canada that it came
almost to a quarrel. We continued our care of her, however, and
landed her safe in Albany with her three wagon-loads of baggage,
brought hither without putting her to any expense." [23] The parting
was civil though cool.

At Albany Father Carroll and his peevish companion found the
hospitality of the Schuylers once more a real boon. Franklin, with
an imperious impatience, wanted to borrow a sulky and drive himself back to Philadelphia; but Mrs. Schuyler had had her orders
from the general, and she coaxingly persuaded their crotchety friend
to be driven by their man, Lewis, in a shaise. Frequent changes
of horses made the journey as swift as possible, and Franklin wrote
the Schuylers from New York on May 27 that he and Father Carroll
had arrived the previous evening. To the other commissioners he

confessed, "I find I grow daily more feeble, and I think I could hardly have got along so far but for Mr. Carroll's friendly assistance and tender care of me." [24] In less than a week they were once more in Philadelphia with the news of their fruitless mission, and John Carroll wrote to cousin Charles' father on June 2, 1776:

> I arrived at this place the day before yesterday in company with Dr. Franklin. Cousin Charles and Mr. Chase left Montreal with me on 12th May that they might not be in any danger from a frigate running up the River and getting between them and the Eastern Shore of S. Laurence. As Dr. Franklin determined to return to Philadelphia on account of his health, I resolved to accompany him, seeing that it was out of my power to be of any service after the Commissioners had thought it advisable for them to leave Montreal. Your son and Mr. Chase proposed staying at St. John's or in that neighbourhood till they should know whether our army would keep post at De Chambeau. The former desired me to give you notice of his being safe and well. . . . Nothing new from Canada, nor indeed any advices at all since we left.[25]

In Philadelphia Carroll ran into a fellow priest, and they decided to travel together as far as Bohemia Manor. After two days spent at the serene Maryland scene of his early school days, Father Carroll set off for Rock Creek on June 7 to give a more detailed and personal account of his travels to his waiting mother.[26] By the time Charles Carroll arrived back in Philadelphia on June 10, 1776, the rested priest had already resumed his quiet ministry in St. John's Chapel.

The Canadian fiasco was finished.

CHAPTER V

DR. FRANKLIN REPAYS A FAVOR

THE years which followed the abortive Canadian mission were fraught with change for everyone, and especially so for John Carroll who was now living at Rock Creek with his mother and his two youngest sisters, Mary and Elizabeth. The suppression of the Jesuits, followed by the American bill of political divorcement from England, left the priest without juridical ties or any means of support stemming from his religious vocation. After the Declaration of Independence was signed in 1776, Carroll did not feel inclined to submit to the dictates of Father John Lewis, the vicar-general appointed by the Vicar Apostolic of London, and Lewis in return felt freed of any responsibility for the ex-Jesuit's support. "Because I live with my mother," Carroll explained to his friend Plowden, "and told Mr. Lewis I did not choose to be moved from place to place, now that we had no longer the vow of obedience to entitle us to the merit of it, he does not choose to bear any part of my expense. I do not mention this by way of complaint as I am perfectly easy at present." [1]

Elizabeth Darnall Carroll was quite able, and indeed very proud, to provide for her son. The Carroll plantation at Rock Creek was ably manned by a large number of slaves and brought in an income ample enough for them all to live in ease. The manor house was one of the largest and best-furnished in Montgomery County, and had its chapel where her son could offer his Masses when he was not attending to the spiritual needs of the surrounding countryside. Jacky had always been her favorite, if a mother can allow herself this indulgence, and Father Carroll on his part felt his mother should have some protection in these times of civil rebellion. His Canadian journey had dispelled any lingering illusions he might have had that the colonies would be allowed to go in peace or win a quick and decisive recognition of their claims to independence. Although his mother was destined to live for many years to come, she had already achieved her allotted "three score years and ten," and the priest would have felt uneasy if he had been too far distant in times like these.

There was no question of shirking the duties of his vocation. The family chapel was soon full to overflowing with Sunday worshippers, and it became necessary to build a new chapel, St. John's, on land belonging to Daniel Carroll. When Father Carroll's brother died, a codicil to his will showed that he had bequeathed the two acres on which the church was built to John Carroll and his successors. St. John's Church at Forest Glen, Maryland, thus earned the distinction of being the only part of the Carroll lands to return to the son who had renounced his claims so many years before. He told his English friends, "I have care of a very large congregation. I have often to ride twenty-five or thirty miles to the sick; besides which I go once a month between fifty and sixty miles to another congregation in Virginia." [2] The old wounds received in Europe were beginning to heal.

Although Carroll's Canadian trip had failed to convince Catholics there that the new government at Philadelphia was sincere in its avowals of toleration, events within the rebelling English colonies were more effective in convincing Catholics to the south that religious liberty was in the making. Three years after his return from Montreal, Carroll was able to write to Charles Plowden, his former colleague at Liège:

> You inquire how congress intend to treat the Catholics in this country. To this I must answer you that congress have no authority or jurisdiction relative to the internal government or concerns of the particular states of the Union. These are all settled by the . . . states themselves. I am glad, however, to inform you that the fullest and largest system of toleration is adopted in almost all the American states; public protection and encouragement are extended alike to all denominations, and Roman Catholics are members of congress, assemblies, and hold civil and military posts as well as others.

Then he added pointedly, "I am heartily glad to see the same policy beginning to be adopted in England and Ireland; and I cannot help thinking you are indebted to America for this piece of service." [3]

He was referring to the First Relief Bill, otherwise known as Sir George Savile's Act, which in 1778 relieved English Catholics of some of the worst consequences of former penal legislation and embodied the Irish Oath Act of 1774 by which subjects could swear allegiance to King George III without prejudicing the Pope's spiritual authority.[4]

His glowing report on American toleration ignored the partial or total discrimination still existing in states like New Jersey, New York, North Carolina, and Georgia. But Carroll's letter showed plainly the pride he felt in comparing his own country with others he had known. The Maryland constitution adopted in 1776 had conferred the franchise on all free persons who could meet the requirements of age, residence, and property; while the Declaration of Rights of that same year had stated, "As it is the duty of every man to worship God in such manner as he thinks most acceptable to him, all persons professing the Christian religion are equally entitled to protection in their religious liberty." Relying on the good faith of these two state charters, Carroll invoked them when he wrote to his cousin Charles now in the Maryland State Legislature in 1783:

> I have been informed that some time after the establishment of our present state constitution, a law was continued relating to the administration of orphans' estates, in which, among other provisions, was a clause preventing Roman Catholics from being guardians to Protestant children. . . . As this clause is inconsistent with that perfect equality of rights which by our Constitution is secured to all religions, I make no doubt but you will be able to obtain a general repeal of this and all other laws and clauses of laws enacting any partial regard to one denomination to the prejudice of others.[5]

More pressing than the question of religious toleration in the new nation, however, was the puzzle of his own relation to the Universal Church. The matter of ecclesiastical jurisdiction over the Catholics living in the English colonies had ever been a delicate one, but the American Revolution opened up further speculations and theories. Combined with the problems created by the recent suppression of the Society of Jesus, this question of jurisdiction now infinitely complicated the situation of Catholic priests living in the former English colonies.

From the time the first Charles Carroll had come to Maryland in 1688, it was presumed in England that the Vicar Apostolic of the London District had jurisdiction over all Catholics living in the English colonies in the New World. But since the brief creating the four vicariates in 1688, London among them, did not specifically mention the English colonies, the theory was frequently denied in practice. The Maryland mission was from the very beginning largely a Jesuit one, and American priests tended quite naturally to look to the English provincials of their society as their superiors. As time went on, however, the London vicars apostolic did not hesitate to express their belief in their own powers. In 1722, for example, Bishop Bonaventure Giffard exercised the first recorded jurisdiction of London over holy day regulations for Maryland. The following year Giffard again claimed juridic control over the colony when he defined Maryland as "part of and belonging to the London District."

It is not quite so clear what Rome believed the status of the overseas colonies to be. In 1753 one report from the Antilles to the Congregation of Propaganda Fide in Rome stated:

> Whence the said priests received their faculties the present writer can give no information. He believes, however, that they get them from the Vicars-Apostolic of London; and he thinks he heard before that the Sacred Congregation had assigned this charge to the said Vicar of London. . . . As to the English on the mainland, the greatest number of Catholics are in Maryland, where English Jesuit Fathers have a numerous mission. . . . It is supposed that the missionaries of this province are under the care of a prefect appointed by the Provincial of the Jesuits in England.[6]

Once Rome became interested in the question of American jurisdiction, the claims of London were carefully examined. The Congregation of Propaganda found no authority in the brief of 1688 for London's claims, but Propaganda was willing to validate the action taken by London up to that time. For the future, the London bishop's faculties were formally extended for a period of six years and were again renewed so that the Vicar Apostolic of London was vested with authority over the English colonies until the period of the Revolution.

The suppression of the Society of Jesus by Rome in 1773, followed three years later by the American Declaration of Independence, left the clergy in Maryland in a peculiar position. The former event abolished whatever authority the English provincial of the society had exerted over the American Jesuits, while the latter abrogated for all practical purposes the supervision of an English vicar apostolic on the mainland of North America. The only remaining authority present during the war years, therefore, was that of Father John Lewis, the last Jesuit superior in the colonies who had been made vicar-general by London prior to the war. The ex-Jesuit was a good man, but he was getting on in years and could not, single-handed, combat the listlessness of the clergy during the grim years which witnessed Valley Forge and Yorktown. Carroll wrote in concern to Plowden in 1782:

> The clergymen here continue to live in the old form. . . .
> But I regret that indolence prevents any form of adminis-
> tration being adopted, which might tend to secure to pos-
> terity a succession of Catholic clergymen and secure to these
> a comfortable subsistence. I said that the former system of
> administration (that is, everything being in the power of a
> Superior) continued. But all those checks upon him, so wisely
> provided by former constitutions, are at an end. It is happy
> that the present Superior is a person free from every selfish
> view and ambition. But his successor may not be. And what
> is likewise to be feared, the succeeding generation, which
> will not be trained in the same discipline and habits as the
> present, will in all probability be infected much more
> strongly with interested and private views.[7]

Father Carroll was not one of those who were deluded by any false hopes that the Jesuits would be restored in the near future. Common sense required, he felt, that the former members of the society devise some substitute which would provide for the discipline and support of priests in America. He commented with some irritation to Plowden that the clergy themselves seemed unable to take action. "Ignorance, indolence, delusion (you remember certain prophecies of re-establishment) and above all the irresolution of Mr. Lewis," Carroll complained, "put a stop to every proceeding in this matter."[8] It is the habit of some men to recognize evils, to vent their dissatisfaction among friends, and then to go on their way content. But Carroll was a man who strongly believed that present abuses demanded action. Even though the outcome of the war was still undecided in 1782, he could not remain idle. Unde-

terred by the inertia of his colleagues, he proceeded to formulate
a plan of organization which would solve the American problem.
If no one else could be roused sufficiently to apply his energies to
the task at hand, then he, John Carroll, would act.

The plan which Carroll evolved for the reorganization of the
American ex-Jesuits shows clearly the Carroll family instinct for
the preservation of property, as well as their natural business
acumen. The plan was chiefly concerned with the protection of what
had been Jesuit properties, and the administration of them. Carroll had not forgotten the avaricious encroachments of European
governments upon Jesuit properties, and he had heard rumors
through Plowden that there were those in Rome who looked with
envy even across the Atlantic. He discounted Plowden's fears and
told him:

> Your information of the intention of Propaganda gives me
> no concern farther than to hear that men, whose institution
> was for the service of Religion, should lend their thoughts
> so much more to the grasping of power and the commanding
> of wealth. For they may be assured that they will never get
> possession of a sixpence of our property here. And if any of
> our friends could be weak enough to deliver any real estate
> into their hands or attempt to subject it to their authority,
> our civil government would be called upon to wrest it out
> of their dominion.

There was no question of his loyalty to the Holy See's spiritual
authority involved at all in his mind. But if individual attempts
were made to grasp temporal goods in the new world where no just
claims existed, then Carroll viewed the matter in a local light. His
Americanism came out in deliberate, proud words. "A foreign
temporal jurisdiction will never be tolerated here. . . . They may
send their agents when they please; they will certainly return empty-
handed." [9]

His plan devised in 1782 had as its primary aims the insurance
of the ex-Jesuits' estates against seizure and the guarantee that their
use would be solely for ministering to the faithful and the maintaining of the clergy. With these ends in view, he suggested a meeting of representatives of all the clergy to determine what could be
done. Once the distinction was made clear between spiritual and
temporal powers, their chief concern must be to set up a system
which by checks and balances would protect the clergy's interests
equally from unworthy administrators and bishops. Carroll was

rewarded by seeing his initiative bear early fruit. Father John Lewis sent out a call summoning the regional representatives of the clergy to a general chapter or meeting to discuss these very considerations. On June 27, 1783, six deputies of the clergy met at Whitemarsh, the former Jesuit residence which was situated on the road from Annapolis to George Town. Father Carroll reported to Charles Plowden hopefully, "We are endeavoring to establish some regulations tending to perpetuate a succession of labourers in this vineyard, to preserve their morals, to prevent idleness, and to secure an equitable and frugal administration of temporals." [10]

The times were truly a challenge to men of zeal. The peace just concluded with the British had removed the obnoxious constraints of the Proclamation Line of twenty years earlier, and innumerable Roman Catholics were pouring into the new regions across the Allegheny Mountains where they set up an impatient clamor for priests to attend them. The degree of toleration now existing throughout the immense country insured to apostolic workers freedom from persecution. The time was ripe for some provision for the needs listed in Carroll's letter, and when the clergy's deputies met again on November 6, 1783, their discussions centered around those very questions of maintaining ecclesiastical morality and discipline, and the preservation of church properties for the support of the clergy. Carroll, who with Bernard Diderick represented the Middle District, brought forward his "Plan of Organization" for discussion. From the debates which ensued there emerged three separate documents: a Form of Government, Rules for the Particular Government of Members belonging to the Body of the Clergy, and the Regulations respecting the Management of Plantations.

By the time the final meeting of the First Chapter was held on October 11, 1784, most of John Carroll's hopes were realized. The priests were to be known in the future as the Select Body of Clergy. Their deputies would be officially called Representatives to the Chapter, and the Corporation or Board of Trustees would have charge of administering the properties of the former Jesuits. A petition was framed and forwarded to Rome asking that Father Lewis be confirmed anew as their ecclesiastical superior, and that he be granted the right to bless holy oils, chalices, and altar stones, and be empowered to administer the Sacrament of Confirmation.

Pride in the independence so recently confirmed by the Treaty of Paris colored the phrasing, and the petition asserted:

With all respect to your Holiness, we represent that we, placed under the recent supreme dominion of the United States, can no longer have recourse, as formerly, for necessary spiritual jurisdiction to the Bishops and Vicars-Apostolic residing in different and foreign States (for this has very frequently been intimated to us in very positive terms by the rulers of this Republic) nor recognize any one of them as our ecclesiastical Superior without open offense to this supreme civil magistracy and political government.[11]

The petition re-echoed the words of Carroll to Plowden in September, 1783, when the American priest had said so bluntly, "A foreign temporal jurisdiction will never be tolerated here."

Since Carroll was on the committees which drew up both this and a later petition to Rome it is probable that the phrases reflected something of his own attitude. He saw clearly that the American insistence on religious toleration was to prove a great boon to the Church in the United States. When he forwarded the second petition to Rome, he explained to his Roman intermediary that toleration

is a blessing and advantage which it is our duty to preserve and improve with the utmost prudence, by demeaning ourselves on all occasions as subjects zealously attached to our government and avoiding to give any jealousies on account of any dependence on foreign jurisdiction more than that which is essential to our religion, an acknowledgment of the Pope's spiritual supremacy over the whole Christian world.[12]

From the very outset, the new Republic should be assured of the loyalty of its Catholic clergy. Never, as priest, superior of the mission, bishop, or archbishop, did John Carroll ever deviate from this conviction that while in affairs spiritual he was always a true son of Rome, in concerns temporal and political he was first and last an American.

While the clergy at Carroll's urging were formulating the rules by which they would live and taking measures to protect their properties, the Holy See was by no means oblivious to the march of political events across the sea. Even before England had signed the treaty which confirmed the independence of her former colonies, Rome was pondering over the changes this new state of affairs would render necessary in ecclesiastical control. Having no official through whom to approach the matter directly in the United States, and conscious of the new relations between England and the Americans, Rome decided to use the offices of the French who were known to be the friendly allies of the new nation. As early as January 15, 1783, the Congregation of Propaganda Fide had sent a note to the Apostolic Nuncio at Paris containing these significant phrases:

> The approaching declaration of independence of all those provinces will destroy the bonds of their political and civil subordination to the British government; it will thereby destroy all bonds in religious matters and, therefore, the Vicar-Apostolic of London will be deprived of the influence and direction he has exercised until now in the religious affairs of those provinces.

The nuncio, Archbishop Giuseppe Doria Pamphili, was advised to consult with the court of France to find out if the king might be willing to use his influence with the American peace commissioners to insure the insertion in the peace treaty of some provision "concerning the free exercise and the maintenance of the Catholic religion." [13]

At this time Rome was already considering the desirability of choosing a vicar apostolic for the new nation "from among the subjects of the new Republic," and establishing one of the principal cities as his residence. The Holy See was under the impression, and not mistakenly, that the American Congress might not approve the entrance of a Catholic bishop from abroad. They were quite aware in Rome of the earlier antagonism in the English colonies to any extension of the powers of the Bishop of Quebec into their territories. The priests themselves had resented the suggestion that Bishop Briand go south of his own jurisdiction even for the laudable purpose of confirming those who would otherwise be deprived of that sacrament. As a matter of fact, during the colonial period of their history the Americans had opposed all bishops of whatever denomination; even in the colonies where the Anglican Church had been established, there had never been any unanimity on the subject of an Anglican episcopate.[14] Thus, for many reasons, Rome was inclined to prefer for the time being an official without episcopal power. Having no desire to offend the American Congress, they determined to proceed cautiously and through the channels with which they were familiar at Paris. The nuncio at Paris was instructed to propose the matter to the representatives of the Americans who were then in the French capital for the negotiation of peace, and to indicate that a native American would be sought for the post. If no suitable priest could be found, then Congress was to be asked to allow a foreigner to assume the office. In any case, Congress should have the privilege of deciding whether Rome's choice was acceptable or not.[15]

On February 10 the nuncio replied to Leonardo Cardinal Antonelli, the Prefect of Propaganda, that the French foreign minister, Count de Vergennes, saw no difficulty involved in setting up a vicariate apostolic in the new Republic. Doria Pamphili added that he was now hoping for a conference with Mr. Franklin to discuss the matter with the American commissioner. The Cardinal was pleased with this cheerful report from Paris and awaited further developments.

Six months elapsed before Rome got any more definite news relating to the interview with Benjamin Franklin, but, in the meantime, the Paris nuncio had not neglected the matter. On July 28, 1783, he sent to Franklin a request that he forward to his Congress the enclosed memorandum. The Roman proposal read:

Before the Revolution just consummated in North America, the Catholics and missionaries of the province depended in spiritual affairs upon the Vicar-Apostolic residing at London. This arrangement no longer prevails, but as it is essential that the Catholic subjects of the United States have an ecclesiastical official to govern them in religious concerns, the Congregation of Propaganda Fide existing at Rome for the establishment and preservation of the missions has decided to propose to the Congress that there be appointed in some city of the United States one of their Catholic citizens with powers of a vicar-apostolic and with the character of a bishop, or simply in the capacity of a prefect-apostolic. The establishment of a bishop-vicar-apostolic seems the most suitable in as much as Catholics in the United States could receive Confirmation and Holy Orders in their own country, without being obliged to go to a country under foreign domination. And should it happen at times that no one among the subjects of the United States were found qualified to be intrusted with spiritual government, it would be expedient for Congress to consent to choose from among the subjects of a foreign nation, the most friendly to the United States.

This memorandum to Franklin was in the nature of a tactful and courteous "feeler" setting forth, as it did, two pairs of alternatives. The first related to the extent of the powers of the new vicar, whether they should be those of a bishop, or more limited. The second touched upon the nationality of this spiritual director, whether he should be an American or a man belonging to a friendly European nation. Rome obviously hoped to obtain some pronouncement from the Congress itself. After reading the nuncio's note and reflecting upon it, Franklin replied that in his opinion it would be "absolutely useless to send it to Congress, which according to its power and constitution cannot, and should not in any case, intervene in the ecclesiastical affairs of any sect or any religion established in America." The urbane old fellow added that he was sure that should Rome find it necessary to choose a French ecclesiastic to regulate the spiritual affairs of American Catholics, the Congress would probably tacitly approve. It was all very polite and in accord with the diplomatic exchanges that Franklin enjoyed.

The earlier historians have enjoyed enshrouding this phase of the Franco-American conversations with an atmosphere of deepest intrigue, some going so far as to accuse the venerable Franklin of being "willing, probably anxious, to recompense France by allowing the French government to have control over the Church in the United States." Such extremes of opinion are no longer tenable. In the first place, the intrigue theory rested on the premise that the American peace commissioners had violated the Franco-American Alliance of 1778, had deserted France, in drawing up the preliminary Anglo-American treaty in November of 1782. Franklin, they felt, had a guilty conscience and was obliged to appease Charles Vergennes by selling out his Catholic compatriots to the French government. This was not the case. The only violation practised by the peace commissioners was a violation of the instructions of their own Congress. Now that all the evidence is in, it is no longer possible to criticize Jay, Franklin, Adams, and Laurens for taking this step. The achievement of the Americans in wresting from the skilled diplomats of Europe such a victory was no small triumph.[16]

As for Franklin and Vergennes, the latter had nothing but respect for the former's shrewdness. When Franklin informed the French minister of the terms of the preliminary articles of the treaty, Vergennes' only surprise was at the excellence of the terms the Americans had exacted. He agreed to the additional loan of 6,000,000 livres which Franklin then requested. True, Vergennes belatedly reproved Franklin some days afterward for the brashness of his colleagues' negotiations, and the suave old man agreed that they might have been guilty of some impropriety in the affair. But Franklin slyly observed that the English would be interested to learn of any rift in Franco-American amity, and Vergennes knew enough to drop the matter without further ado. If anything, Vergennes was secretly relieved at the turn the American treaty negotiations had taken.

In the second place, the intrigue theory suggests that the initiative in the matter of an American vicar apostolic was taken by France. Again, this is simply not the case. Rome had been watching the conflict between the colonies and England, chiefly anxious that religious bigotry should not jeopardize the position of Catholics in the liberated areas. She seized the first opportunity which presented itself to offer her services to secure the interests of the Catholic Church in the new nation. Even a casual glance at the original instructions sent to Paris on January 15, 1783, shows that the initiative was taken by the Holy See and that France was simply counted upon to lend its good offices. In acting for the Holy See the French were punctilious and disinterested. Vergennes said quite plainly on one occasion, "We are essentially interested that there should not be in America a French church, since it would be one motive the more to excite the subjects of His Majesty to emigrate."

The theory of French ambition probably originated with a letter Charles Plowden wrote to Carroll on September 2, 1784, in which he declared:

> The note delivered to the nuncio proves their wish to exclude every Jesuit from trust or honor, and equally betrays the policy of the French ministry . . . who by bringing forth a Frenchman, or perhaps an Irish Frenchman, would use religion as an instrument to increase their own influence in America.[17]

But Plowden was decidedly anti-French in politics at this time. He had earlier accused Carroll's country of being under "the trammels of the French" to which Carroll had replied emphatically, "We have never worn her chains, but have treated with her as equals, have experienced from her the greatest magnanimity and moderation, and have repaid it with an honorable fidelity." [18] Carroll agreed that the negotiation cast a reflexion upon the former Jesuits, for he said:

Nothing can place in a stronger light the aversion to the
remains of the Society than the observation made by you
of a negotiation being carried on, relative to the affairs of
religion, with Dr. Franklin, without even deigning to apply
to the Catholic clergy in this country.

But he did not share Plowden's suspicions of French connivance
with Franklin. "When I first heard the nuncio was treating with my
old friend, Dr. Franklin," he told Plowden, "I had thoughts of writing to him, and should certainly have done it had I not been afraid
of placing myself in a conspicuous point of view. . . ." [19] It was
not distrust of Franklin, but fear of seeming to seek office for himself, which kept Carroll from expressing his conviction that the
American clergy ought to have been consulted.

If Carroll was reluctant to approach Franklin in behalf of his
colleagues' interests, others were not. Plowden prevailed upon one
of his friends to write to Dr. Franklin to "expose to him the degree
of respect and consideration due to the missionaries now in
America," and to suggest that no proposals might be admitted
without the participation and consent of Carroll. Thorpe also had
Nicholas Sewall and John Mattingly, two former Jesuits then in
Europe, write to Franklin as well.[20] Father Thorpe commented
dryly, "When the nuncio, M. Doria, at Paris, applied to Mr.
Franklin, the old gentleman remembered you; he had his memory
refreshed before." [21] But none of this supports a theory of French
intrigue.

Finally, if Franklin expressed at the beginning of the conversations an opinion on the advisability of a French vicar apostolic, it
must be remembered that he was acting on his own initiative in a
matter not strictly his province. But, granting this, his attitude is
still comprehensible. His original remark about the acceptability
of a French vicar came in reply to the nuncio's letter containing
the suggested alternative of no suitable American being found. He
was undoubtedly thinking of the necessity for a choice between
European powers. His anxiety shows clearly in the letter he penned
to Vergennes on December 15, 1783:

I understand that the Bishop or spiritual person who
superintends or governs the Roman Catholic clergy in the
United States of America resides in London, and is supposed
to be under obligations to that Court and subject to be in-

fluenced by its ministers. This gives me some uneasiness, and I cannot but wish that one should be appointed to that office who is of this nation and who may reside here among our friends.

A French vicar-general seemed infinitely preferable to Franklin than that England should retain any control over the new nation.

Rome in December, 1783, had not had time to receive the petitions from the American clergy regarding their own preferences, and Franklin could hardly be expected to know that London's jurisdiction was already considered to be at an end. But if Benjamin Franklin failed to understand the developments in the relations between the American clergy and their former supervisors in London, neither did Rome grasp the implications of the new Republic's attitude toward affairs spiritual. Although Franklin had said plainly that Congress had neither the wish nor the power to intervene in the religious affairs of any group, Rome, accustomed as she was to dealing in these matters through the channels of diplomacy, remained reluctant to proceed without some direct negotiations with the government. Accordingly, the French minister at Philadelphia was instructed to approach the Congress. On January 31, 1784, Anne César de la Luzerne replied that Congress had declared itself incompetent to act in ecclesiastical affairs and he elaborated,

> It is a matter that concerns Catholics alone; and the delegates who have spoken to me on the subject have assured me that a Catholic bishop would be very well received in the state of Pennsylvania and much more so in Maryland, where there are many Catholics, providing the prelate avoided to assume any temporal jurisdiction or authority.

He went on to say that the Congress in general would be pleased at the residence of a prelate, who by conferring the sacrament of holy orders on the priests in the United States, would relieve them of the necessity of receiving it in London or Quebec. The letter concluded with the reiteration, "The state legislatures and Congress refrain from entangling themselves with religious matters." It was plain from Luzerne's letter that in the new nation religion was to be free from governmental intervention and that the Congress in return would expect non-intervention of a temporal kind from any foreign power.

Carroll explained his understanding of the event to Plowden on April 10, 1784, saying:

> Dr. Franklin has sent into congress a copy of a note delivered him by the nuncio at Paris, which I shall enclose in this. . . . The answer, I am well informed, is that congress have no answer to give, the matter proposed not being in their department, but resting with the different states. But, this you may be assured of, that the Catholic clergy and laity here know the only connection they ought to have with Rome is to acknowledge the pope as the spiritual head of the church.[22]

The Congress, in turn, made its attitude officially known on May 11, 1784, when it resolved:

> That Dr. Franklin be desired to notify the Apostolic Nuncio at Versailles that Congress will always be pleased to testify their respect to his sovereign and state; but that the subject of his application to Dr. Franklin being purely spiritual, is without the jurisdiction and powers of Congress, who have no authority to permit or refuse it.

Thus the Holy See came to realize that the American government had only these two desires in the matter: the first, to refrain from meddling in ecclesiastical affairs itself; and, second, to see as little connection between the American Catholics and foreign temporalities as possible. The plan of Doria Pamphili, the nuncio to France, or of Vergennes, the French foreign minister, became secondary to the expressed wishes of both clergy and Congress combined. By the spring of 1784 Cardinal Antonelli was prepared to settle upon a suitable prelate within the Republic itself. Writing to Luzerne on May 12 the cardinal said he would like to have "exact knowledge of the conduct and capacities of the ecclesiastics and missionaries . . . which one of them would be the most worthy, and the most acceptable to the assembly of those provinces, to be created Bishop *in partibus* and invested with the character of vicar-apostolic."

Once the decision was made for an American, there was little question as to the most eligible candidate. Doria Pamphili told Luzerne, "The ex-Jesuit, Mr. Carroll of Maryland, has been spoken of to me with eulogy, this Carroll being the same who was educated at St. Omer and who in 1776 was sent by the Congress to Canada with Mr. Franklin and the other Commissioners." Franklin, of course, had only the warmest memories of the Maryland priest and his kindness on that trip back from Montreal. Once Carroll's name entered the discussions, he exerted all his influence to press his good friend's appointment. He could certainly testify to Carroll's tact and good sense, not to mention his breeding and courtesy. When he, Franklin, had found the Walkers well-nigh unbearable, the serene priest had put up with all the irritations of the journey and ministered to the old gentleman as well. There is little doubt that Franklin's influence was considerable. Father John Thorpe wrote from Rome to a friend in Paris "expressly desiring him to thank and congratulate Dr. Franklin" for Carroll's having been named. To Carroll himself Thorpe commented that Archbishop Stefano Borgia, the Secretary of Propaganda, had highly recommended Carroll's letters to Rome. "Your letters," he said, "had convinced both Cardinal Antonelli and himself that you are eminently qualified for the dignity to which Dr. Franklin has commended you." [23]

Other factors, of course, entered into the selection of John Carroll. Rome preferred a younger man than Father John Lewis, who was then sixty-four and had served his time. From Carroll's documents forwarded to Rome the Holy See had gained a high respect for his abilities and modesty. Cardinal Antonelli told the nuncio at Paris that he was convinced that Carroll had never solicited Franklin's recommendation. "Consequently," the cardinal admitted, "it has helped to give him preference over Lewis." In fact, everything about John Carroll conspired to make him the logical choice. His family connections were renowned in the United States; he was vigorous and at forty-nine still in the prime of life; he had had the best education Europe had to offer; and above all, his character was above reproach. Thus, on June 9, 1784, Carroll was made officially the "head of the missions in the provinces of the new Republic of the United States of North America."

The notification from Rome informed him:

As then, Rev. Sir, you have given conspicuous proofs of piety and zeal, and it is known that your appointment will please and gratify many members of that republic, and especially Mr. Franklin, the eminent individual who represents the same republic at the Court of the Most Christian King, the Sacred Congregation with the approbation of his Holiness, has appointed you Superior of the Mission . . .

and has communicated to you the faculties which are necessary to the discharge of that office.[24]

When François Barbé-Marbois, the French *chargé d'affaires* at New
York, forwarded the formal notices to Father Carroll he said to the
new *Missionaire Apostolique,* "I congratulate myself on being one
of the first to assure you that the choice will give general satisfaction." [25] And although he was not actually the first to notify the
American priest, other letters from Rome and France having arrived
during the summer, the *chargé's* prediction was well-taken. No
appointment ever gave more general satisfaction than this one
which marked the beginning of John Carroll's general influence on
the Church of the United States.

CHAPTER
VI

THE CRUCIAL YEARS

A PEOPLE emerge from years of war in a condition of social shock. The pathology of this martial disease is complex and bewilders the amateur physicians who must minister to the patient. Any post-war period is one of exaggerations and excesses, and the Critical Period following the American Revolution was no exception. It was in the midst of these chaotic conditions that John Carroll began his career as superior of the American mission, and many of the problems he faced are understood best when viewed against the background of those troublous times.

The proud exuberance generated by the peace treaty quite naturally resulted at first in some pardonable illusions of grandeur, and more than one American envisaged his homeland as:

> an asylum for the injured and oppressed in all parts of the globe; the delight of God and good men; the joy and pride of the whole earth; soaring on the wings of literature, wealth, population, religion, virtue, and everything that is excellent and happy to a greater height of perfection and glory than the world has ever yet seen.

Even less heady spirits would agree heartily with European observers like William Strickland, who wrote to Father Carroll that "the example of America has been an important lesson to Europe and will have consequences which the most sagacious politicians can not foresee." [1]

But the Revolution left in its wake a confusion of ideas which proved very nearly disastrous when placed in juxtaposition with the problems whose immediacy could not be evaded. Revolt against one aspect of authority inevitably calls into question all authority. The revolutionary propaganda of Thomas Paine had roused men to strike off their chains, and there were many now who looked askance at any fetter. The prolonged colonial struggle against tyranny in its various persons, king, proprietary, or governor, had left its mark. John Jay sagely commented, "It takes time to make sovereigns of subjects." Freedom was a heady wine, and the most intemperate found ample room toward which to direct their erratic footsteps. The vast new lands opened up beyond the Appalachians might serve, as some historians have suggested, as a safety-valve for the relief of radical pressures along the tidewater areas. But the generosity of nature and governmental policy could just as easily aggravate false notions of personal liberty and property rights. The simple fact was that each man interpreted national emancipation in the limited terms of his own private ambitions. The habit of resistance acquired during the Revolution persisted on into the post-war era, only now it had become an individual affair. Taxpayers resisted taxes, debtors resisted creditors, parishioners resisted pastors, priests resisted superiors, militia resisted the very governments that had recruited them; and, at a higher level, states resisted the nation. It would take strong leadership, indeed, to bring order to this chaos.

The post-war period began calmly enough in Maryland. Mrs. Walter Dulany wrote to her son on April 23, 1783:

> Tomorrow we celebrate Peace. I hear there is to be a grand dinner on Squire Carroll's Point, a whole ox to be roasted and I can't tell how many sheep and calves, besides a world of other things. Liquor in proportion. The whole to conclude with illuminations and squibs, etc.[2]

By November the Congress of the United States was ready to acquiesce to Governor William Paca's suggestion that they wind up their war business in Annapolis, and on November 4, 1783, the gentlemen adjourned at Princeton to reconvene in the Maryland capital. When General Washington arrived on December 19, the city was ready to fete the nation's hero on behalf of both state and national legislatures with the customary dinners, balls, and illuminations. Two days later Washington entered the hall to resign his military commission to the Congress. The Maryland *Gazette* reported that "few tragedies ever drew so many tears from so many beautiful eyes."

Congress remained at Annapolis until June 3, 1784, when it adjourned to meet at Trenton the following October. In August the celebrated Marquis de Lafayette favored Annapolis, on his way to Mount Vernon, at the very time that Father John Carroll was reading Father Thorpe's letter from Rome announcing his appointment. By the time Congress was ready to reconvene in Trenton, the official Roman papers had reached François Barbé-Marbois in New York, and that French official forwarded them to Maryland on October 27 with the words, "I am about to start for Trenton, and I wish very much that Maryland would be represented there in the Congress by someone of your relatives." [3]

But the politically-minded Carrolls were not in the federal Congress in 1784. Daniel had been considered ineligible after the last session he had attended in November, 1783, since Maryland law at the time stipulated that delegates to the United States Congress were not eligible for more than three in any term of six years. The new ecclesiastical superior's brother, with his cousin Charles, was busy in the Maryland State Senate over which Charles presided. After Daniel agreed to attend the federal convention in Philadelphia in the spring of 1787, he had two positions to fill, and he divided his time between the state capital and the constitutional convention. Charles preferred not to neglect his state's affairs, and he sent any ideas he had on national government to Philadelphia by Daniel's hand. [4]

While Daniel and Charles Carroll were helping to shape the political destinies of state and nation, Father John Carroll was applying his energies and ingenuity to the equally complex problems of church organization during the Critical Period. One of his most immediate tasks was that of surveying the extent of his territories and responsibilities. The new superior decided to use both correspondence and visitation to accomplish his task. In the letter which contained his appointment he had been requested by Rome to forward as soon as possible a correct report, stating carefully the number of Catholics in each state, their condition, their piety, and the abuses which existed. Rome wanted to know, too, how many missionary priests labored "in the vineyard of the Lord" and what were their qualifications, zeal, and mode of support. Not wishing to delay his initial report to Cardinal Antonelli, Father Carroll began at once to write to his fellow priests, asking them to report on their surrounding districts. He had enough response to his appeals to enable him to make a fairly comprehensive report to Rome on March 1, and his "Relation of the State of Religion in the United States" served the dual purpose of informing himself and Propaganda of the approximate state of Catholic affairs in 1784-1785.

Carroll followed Rome's suggestion in organizing his report and reported his findings under three headings: the size of the Catholic population, the condition and piety of the laity, and the state of the clergy. Maryland, of course, led the list in round numbers of Catholics, having nearly 16,000. Pennsylvania came second with 7,000; New York was in third place with 1,500, and Virginia ranked fourth with not more than 200. "As to the Catholics who are in the territory bordering on the river called the Mississippi," he added, "and all that region which following that river extends to the Atlantic Ocean . . . this tract of country contains . . . many Catholics, formerly Canadians who speak French." He feared that they were destitute of priests, he reported. In the past the jurisdiction of the Bishop of Quebec had extended to part of that region, but Carroll was uncertain whether the Canadian prelate would wish the authority over the area now that its people were subjects of the United States.

The report on population showed three things rather clearly to Carroll and to the Congregation of Propaganda Fide. First, the extent of his domain was vast, extending as it did from the Atlantic to the Mississippi, from British Canada on the north to Spanish Florida on the south. Again, the report revealed the uncertainty which was destined to continue for some time regarding the exact size and precise location of the Catholic population. In the third place, the existing confusion over episcopal jurisdiction in the border areas predicted as much tribulation for ecclesiastical authority as the physical boundaries would cause the civil government of the new Republic.

Carroll's description of the "condition, piety and defects" of the laity revealed other factors which were to become identified with the American Church in the years to come. He noted a sharp difference between the piety of native-born Catholics and that of newcomers from Europe. "While there are few of our native Catholics who do not approach the sacraments of Penance and the Holy Eucharist at least once a year, especially at Easter time," he said, "you can scarcely find any among the newcomers who discharge this duty of religion, and there is reason to fear that the example will be very pernicious, especially in the commercial towns." Future generations in Europe would watch with curiosity and comment with envy upon the growing prosperity of the Church in the United States. But although they were less outspoken in their observations of this other phenomenon, it was the greater piety in practice that was to become the real wonder to the Old World. The causes for the greater regularity in the American Catholic's religious life were not unrelated to another factor noted by Carroll in his report: the fact that the faithful in the new world were faced with "unavoidable intercourse with non-Catholics." In 1785 John Carroll saw in this intercourse the cause for many abuses which had crept into Catholic life. But later observers were not averse to attributing some measure of the American Catholic's zeal and fidelity to this very fact that he was surrounded by a Protestant society which, while tolerating his presence, denied his tenets.

The last section of the report described the clergy, their qualifications, character, and means of support. There were, it seemed, nineteen priests in Maryland, and five in Pennsylvania. Of these, two were more than their allotted "three score years and ten," and three others were nearly that old. Many of the remaining priests were in bad health, but all the clergy led lives "full of labour, as each one attends congregations far apart, and has to be riding constantly and with great fatigue." The clergy were supported either by properties which they held as individuals, or else from the charity of other Catholics. The account, by its very omissions, showed the reluctance of the American superior to rouse Rome's curiosity in regard to the temporal concerns of the ex-Jesuits.[5]

After dispatching this preliminary report to Rome Carroll turned next to an actual visitation of his mission, and during the spring and fall of 1785 he went in person to the centers of his Catholic population to confer with his priests face to face. It is probable that Carroll's first survey was made of the sparse Virginia missions, for Thomas Talbot in London received a letter from him dated April 20, 1785, at Richland, Virginia, where the priest was staying with his sister, Eleanor Carroll Brent. The Virginia congregations which lay scattered along the Potomac River above and below "Bobby Brent's Landing," were poorly organized and depended on the occasional visits they received from the Maryland priests a few times each year. Because of his family connections at Richland and Acquia, John Carroll was particularly interested in the conditions he found in Virginia, and after his return to Rock Creek he wrote to Father Plowden, "The prospect before us is immense, but the want of cultivators to enter the field and improve it is a dreadful and discouraging circumstance." Applications were coming in from every part of the United States, north, south, and west, for clergymen. But Carroll could not ask priests to abandon congregations already formed to go in quest of new ones. He wrote to everyone he could conceive of as a likely prospect and he told Plowden, "I hope you will urge the return hither of Charles and Francis Neale, Leonard Brooke, and Thomson, if his health will allow. . . . Encourage all you can meet with, Europeans or Americans, to come to us." [6]

The Maryland visitation was even more engrossing, owing to the large numbers of Catholics which it involved. Radiating from the early centers of the faith at Whitemarsh, St. Inigoes, Port Tobacco, Newtown, Deer Creek, Bohemia, and Frederick, these Maryland Catholics twice out-numbered the rest of the mission together. Their nineteen priests divided their time among the congregations, "stations," and private manorial chapels. Father Carroll administered the long hoped-for sacrament of confirmation as he went from place to place, and it is probable that he laid the cornerstone of the new church at St. Inigoes on July 13. By the time the oppressive heat of August arrived, he was exhausted and returned to his mother's house for a brief respite before starting northward to complete his survey.

It was becoming apparent to him that Rock Creek was not centrally enough located for the correspondence and journeys his office demanded. "However painful it will be to my dear Mother and myself," he told Charles Plowden, "I apprehend it will be necessary for me to remove to Baltimore as a more centrical situation." [7] Letters were usually carried by vessel or by travelers overland, and Rock Creek was not as consistently crossed by suitable "occasions," as letter-carriers were called. Baltimore was growing rapidly and ships from river ports inland, from coastal cities north and south, and from Europe across the sea vied for place at the busy wharves. By the time the United States received her first bishop, Baltimore was ready to become her first see city.

On September 22 Carroll resumed his travels and went to Philadelphia. During the first week in October he administered confirmation there and inspected the city's two churches, St. Joseph's and St. Mary's. At the home of the prominent Catholic layman, Thomas FitzSimons, the visitor was entertained cordially by the signer of the Constitution. From Fathers Ferdinand Farmer, Robert Molyneux, and the Dominican William O'Brien he learned much concerning the progress of religion in this thriving port. Carroll was interested to see that his clergy were augmented by the chaplains to the French and Spanish officials residing in Philadelphia. Ferdinand Farmer had acted as the vicar-general under the last Jesuit superior, John Lewis, and when Carroll became superior he was glad to rely upon Farmer for the same service. Earlier that year, in April, Farmer had visited New York City in his capacity as Carroll's vicar-general and he now prepared his superior for the difficulties he would find there. Farmer painted a very gloomy picture, and it was with some trepidation and much fervent prayer that John Carroll approached the city on Manhattan Island.

Although New York State had over a thousand Catholics in 1785, the number was not the result of any encouragement given by the government, but stemmed rather from the city's position as a port of ingress for Catholics from Europe. Until 1806 the state required an oath of allegiance which was so worded as to disqualify Catholics from office, while socially the Catholic population were regarded as the "off-scourings" of the city. Nevertheless, the Spanish and French consulates furnished Catholic gentlemen of a transient influence while the Irish immigrants who swarmed off the ships at White Hall Slip or Murray's Wharf settled down and became a permanent part of the city's populace. After the British evacuation of the city in November, 1783, Father Farmer had assembled the Catholics of New York for a Mass of thanksgiving. Other Masses were probably offered from time to time in the houses of Don Thomas Stoughton or Don Diego de Gardoqui, the Spanish diplomats, or at the consulate of France where Hector St. John de Crèvecoeur was in residence.[8]

The first priest offering to serve the general Catholic population, however, was an Irish Capuchin who had arrived in New York in October, 1784. Father Charles Maurice Whelan had been sent by his superiors as a chaplain in the French navy during the Revolution. For a time he had ministered to the sick and wounded French prisoners on the island of Jamaica. By his own account he "administered to three thousand five hundred and sixty-two Frenchmen, eight hundred Spaniards, and thirty-five Americans, without any gratification." At the close of the war, Whelan came to New York where he was befriended by the Portuguese Catholic, José Ruiz Silva, and "that strenuous good friend to religion," the French consul St. John de Crèvecoeur.[9]

Father Farmer had reported the advent of the Irish priest to Carroll adding, "The congregation had received him for a time and allows him consequently, a sustenance." Farmer examined the newcomer's credentials which seemed to be in good order and recommended that Carroll give Whelan faculties for the present.[10] Meanwhile, because neither Carroll nor his vicar-general were certain of the former's precise powers in regard to this matter of granting faculties to new priests, Farmer suggested to the Capuchin Whelan that it might be wise for him to apply through the nuncio at Paris for Propaganda's consent to his ministrations in New York. Father Whelan followed the older man's advice and applied to Rome through the nuncio at Paris, Archbishop Doria Pamphili, on January 28, 1785. The vicar-general was principally concerned with expediency and had no intention of reflecting on Carroll's authority. He wrote to his superior of Whelan's action and explained that his own letter had been forwarded to Europe as well.

Up to this point there seems to have been little to criticize and slight cause for misunderstanding. Each priest involved was obviously motivated by a desire to serve the Catholics of New York to the best advantage. But in his zeal the Irish Capuchin soon acted imprudently. Without waiting for a confirmation of his faculties from either the American superior or the Roman Congregation, he proceeded to hear confessions, to officiate at weddings, to say nothing of offering two Masses every Sunday and holy day. Father Farmer, after visiting New York in April, had remonstrated with Whelan with some success. He reported to Carroll, "Mr. Whelan's conduct I attribute to an ignorance of canon law, through which he persuaded himself that what he could do in Ireland he could also do here." Whelan impressed Farmer as being submissive and ceased his practice of saying two Masses after receiving Farmer's reproof.[11]

But Maurice Whelan was tactless and injudicious in other ways; even after his faculties were confirmed (by Carroll on April 16, 1785, and by Cardinal Antonelli on June 4, 1785), he continued to arouse comment and unfavorable criticism in New York. He was a noticeably poor preacher and, what was more unfortunate, unable to prevent cliques and contentions within his congregation. Too conscious of his debt of gratitude toward his Portuguese benefactor, Whelan tended to ignore the needs of his own Irish countrymen. Before John Carroll ever reached New York one segment of the Catholic congregation was opposed to accepting Father Whelan as their permanent priest.

In spite of the existing friction, however, progress toward a church building was being made. On June 10 the trustees of the

Roman Catholics were incorporated, and soon thereafter they bought the site for a church on Barclay Street. Carroll arrived in time for the laying of the cornerstone, and on November 5, 1785, was thus begun the foundation of the church which was to become famous in the city's history. But poor Whelan's connection with the infant church was a bad omen. The New York congregation would see stormy days, and John Carroll's troubles with their clergy were only beginning.

If Maurice Whelan had been the only priest available to the area, trouble might have been avoided. True, his talents were few, and Carroll admitted to Charles Plowden that Whelan was not "so learned or so good a preacher as I could wish, which mortifies his congregation, and at New York and most other places in America, the different sectaries have scarce any other test of a clergyman than his talents for preaching." [12] The non-Catholic service centered around the sermon, and ministers were valued in proportion to their eloquence in the pulpit. The Catholic minority were not immune to all this talk of oratory and wished for a man of their own to rival the verbal pyrotechnics of the less orthodox. Although Carroll found the Capuchin a zealous, pious, and humble man for the most part, it was unfortunate that a more talented member of Whelan's order arrived on the scene to point up his deficiencies.

Father Andrew Nugent appeared in New York some time prior to Carroll's visitation and began assisting his brother in religion. Nugent was a gifted preacher, and by the time Father Carroll reached the scene seeds of discord had already been planted. Carroll was not only asked to grant Nugent faculties, but the trustees suggested as well that they would welcome Nugent in place of their present shepherd, Father Whelan. Carroll was favorably impressed with the "very good testimonials of his zeal and virtue" which the second Capuchin produced, but he explained to both priest and trustees that his powers did not allow him to give Father Nugent full authority at the moment. At a meeting with the trustees he presented them with some articles of agreement which pledged them to recognize Whelan's ministry, and after securing the consent of the trustees Carroll left a copy of the agreement with Father Whelan. When he left New York Carroll was hopeful that trouble had been averted. Scarcely had he arrived at Rock Creek in December, however, when ominous rumors reached him from New York. On the morning of December 18, he learned, the Nugent faction had appropriated the Sunday collection at Mass,

and schism had flared out openly. Father Farmer reported the conflict to his superior on December 20, deploring the self-interested-
ness of the Capuchins and remarking somewhat cynically that they
seemed to have come to America only to benefit themselves. The
trustees were now decidedly in favor of Nugent, and by Christmas
they went so far as to refuse to pay any salary to his less beloved
confrère. Each priest wrote to Carroll denouncing the other's
effrontery and lauding his own prudence and virtue in the affair.
The trustees, likewise, penned lengthy expositions to the superior
in Baltimore, justifying their position and threatening to use legal
means if necessary to rid themselves of the unfortunate Whelan.

That January John Carroll marked the passing of his fifty-first
birthday. Still vigorous and keenly alert, he was at the same time
mature and dispassionate in his judgment. He possessed that combination of tact and firmness which the occasion demanded, and
he was determined to phrase his letters to New York as skillfully
as he could. A forthright approach to the problem at hand was his
forte, and it served the artful purpose of disarming his adversary
by the device of assuming the other man to be of Carroll's views.
It was his habit to presume in controversy that the opponent was
a man of intelligence and integrity. If the man were a priest, he
further presumed upon his charity and purity of intention. Thus,
to the two Capuchins on January 17 and 18, Carroll wrote urging
each man to make peace with his brother, appealing to the finest
instincts of each as a Christian and a gentleman. To the trustees
Carroll wrote at greater length. The almost flawless tact of this
third letter written on January 25, 1786, attests his fitness for the
task which Carroll frankly admitted was "not an easy nor very
agreeable" one.

He began with a beguiling gentleness. "One circumstance gives
me comfort," he said. "You profess to have no other views than
for the service and credit of religion. And as I make it my endeavor
to be influenced solely by the same motive, I trust that proposing
to ourselves the same end we shall likewise agree in the means of
attaining it." He took the trustees into his confidence and told them
of receiving letters from both Father Whelan and Father Nugent.
He then listed the charges that had been made against the trustees
and their faction: their seizure of the Sunday collection, their re-
fusal to abide by the agreement reached at their meeting with him
in New York, and their contention that the congregation had the
right to choose their parish priests. Carroll made no further com-

ment on the Sunday collection matter, but he said bluntly that any denial of the articles of agreement reflected on his own veracity, a reflection which he found rather shocking. "I considered the matters then agreed on," he asserted, "as right in point of justice, as the renewal of confidence and the foundation of future union." For the trustees now to deny these principles was a contradiction of a solemn pledge which he himself had witnessed.

The most serious matter, he warned them, was their false concept regarding the selection of priests and their jurisdictions. If ever such principles as those attributed to the trustees should prevail "the unity and Catholicity" of the Church would be at an end. Father Carroll was quite aware that the New York Catholics were not immune to the Protestant influences about them. The trustees were bound to be attracted by the practices of the congregational Presbyterians of the neighboring New England states. But they should consider the intrinsic evil in that congregational system. "A zealous clergyman," he pointed out, "performing his duties courageously and without respect of persons would be always liable to be the victim of his earnest endeavours to stop the progress of vice and evil example." A priest more compliant with the passions of the more influential members of the congregation would be called to replace him. "I will refer to your own judgment what the consequence may be," Carroll said, "if the ecclesiastical superior has no control in these instances."

Then the superior went to the heart of the difficulty. The fact of the matter was that both Father Whelan and the trustees were under a misapprehension in their notion of a priest's position in New York City. They seemed to believe that the officiating clergyman was a parish priest, "whereas there is yet no such office in the United States." No American hierarchy had yet been constituted, Carroll reminded them; no parishes were formed. "The clergy coming to the assistance of the faithful are but voluntary labourers in the vineyard of Christ, not vested with ordinary jurisdiction annexed to their office, but receiving it as a delegated, and extra-hierarchical commission." The error was in this clamor on both sides for rights when in reality no such rights yet existed.

As for the particular point at issue, their desire for Nugent instead of Whelan, he must reiterate what he had said in person when present in New York. He had a good opinion of Nugent's abilities, but his present powers did not enable Carroll fully to authorize Nugent. Furthermore, there was no valid reason for revoking Father Whelan's faculties or removing him from New York. "Can I deprive him of these faculties," Carroll asked reasonably, "when neither his morals, his orthodoxy, or his assiduity have been impeached?" As a matter of fact, the superior had no reason to believe that substituting Nugent for Whelan would please a majority of the congregation or heal the rift.

The letter's entire approach was an appeal to reason. The only note of cold authority which crept into its pages related to the trustees' threat of legal action. John Carroll was not a man to be threatened. He commented politely, "I cannot tell what assistance the laws might give you, but allow me to say that you can take no step so fatal . . . or more prejudicial to the Catholic cause. I must therefore entreat you to decline a design so pernicious to all your prospects." Then he added pointedly, "I explicitly declare that no clergyman, be he who he may, shall receive any spiritual powers from me who shall advise or countenance so unnecessary a course." [13]

Unfortunately, before this sound word of caution could temper the passions of the Nugent faction, poor Whelan had been driven to the limits of his endurance. When the turbulent trustees threatened to close the church rather than allow him to officiate, Father Whelan left New York and fled to his brother's farm beyond Albany, up the Hudson. This left Carroll in an unenviable position. Someone must minister to the Catholics in the city. For the time he could rely on a French priest, Father Pierre Huet de la Valinière, to whom Farmer, the vicar-general, had granted temporary powers.[14] But this was no final solution since de la Valinière was only a transient, and sooner or later Nugent would be the only priest left in New York City. It seemed like too easy a victory for Whelan's rival and the rebellious trustees. Nevertheless Carroll notified Rome on March 13, 1786, of his decision. "I finally decided that the mind of the Church was to provide for the care of souls and that my authority was valueless if I could not act in such a danger." He had read the theologians, and had pondered the matter carefully. He did not see any alternative. "Hence I gave faculties to Father Nugent," he explained, "for preaching the Word of God, administering the sacraments of baptism and matrimony, and the rest, whenever it was necessary." [15] He could only hope that Propaganda would approve of his action.

Carroll's decision was characteristic of his whole concept of his office. A lesser man might have eased the edge of his irritation against the trouble-making Nugent by refusing to let him serve a congregation which he had so stirred up. But John Carroll did not allow himself the luxury of private satisfaction. The need for priests was too great in the United States, and the wise superior was willing to endure the frailty of his clergy if their talents could serve the faithful. A less courageous man might have refused to make any decision in Nugent's case pending advice from Rome. But, as he told the Congregation of Propaganda Fide, his office was worthless if he could not act in an emergency to promote the good of souls.

His action was soon vindicated. Two weeks later he received from Rome a letter which clarified his authority and relieved his mind on the score of conferring faculties on the clergy within his jurisdiction. In the future, priests could be empowered to serve congregations without the delays which had formerly tempted them to disregard the superior's authority. Carroll did not feel quite so impotent now. Father Andrew Nugent could serve the New York congregation, and it was to be hoped that he would prove more docile in the future. Carroll privately thought that the more talented Capuchin might in the end prove more suited to the task than his unfortunate predecessor, Whelan, had been. It was too early to predict, of course, but it appeared that the spectre of trusteeism might be banished from New York. The superior of the missions began his second visitation in May with a much lighter heart.

CHAPTER VII

AN AMERICAN "PACIFICUS"

THE last quarter of the eighteenth century witnessed some controversies of quite another sort, and if the antagonists were no less vehement than the New York trustees had proved, modes of expression were at least more literary. While the earlier age of Dryden had ushered in the art of English letter-writing, the age of Swift had produced the political pamphlet with its use of ridicule and the power of its prose. Beginning in 1758 the *Public Advertiser* had featured correspondence bearing such names as "Anti-Sejanus" and "Cato Redivivus," and in 1768 "Junius," the most celebrated of all political correspondents, made his first appearance in its pages.[1] Across the Atlantic pens were no less busy, and the political writing of the Revolutionary period sometimes attained a dignity which stamped the literature of American national beginnings as "superior to the similar literature of any other people anywhere." [2] The period from 1760 to 1775, with its controversies over the Writs of Assistance, the Townshend Duties, and the Coercive Acts had given birth to a veritable deluge of pamphlets from the hands of James Otis, John Adams, Josiah Quincy, John Dickinson, and James Wilson. The war years, 1775-1783, produced the venerated masterpieces of Jefferson, and the persuasive propaganda of Thomas Paine's *Common Sense* and the *Crisis;* while the Critical Period provoked a voluminous journalistic correspondence signed by names like "Cassius," "Fabius," "Agrippa," "Cato," and "Brutus," and the essays by the most famous of all *nom de plumes,* "The Federalist."

Maryland had taken her part, of course, in this age of controversy. The Stamp Act had elicited from Daniel Dulany in 1765 a pamphlet called *Considerations on the Propriety of Imposing Taxes in the British Colonies for the Purpose of Raising a Revenue by Act of Parliament.* It was republished in London, Carroll of Carrollton had recommended it to his friends in England, and William Pitt reiterated its arguments in Parliament when he espoused the repeal of the obnoxious levy. It was, perhaps, the most important single influence which led Maryland to send delegates to the Stamp Act Congress to which Massachusetts had invited the other colonies.[3] The following year Dulany had published a pamphlet on *The Right to the Tonnage, the Duty of Twelve Pence per Hogshead on all Exported Tobacco, and the Fines and Forfeitures in the Province of Maryland.* Then in 1773 Dulany and Carroll of Carrollton entered upon their famous debate in the Maryland *Gazette,* with Dulany adopting the name "Antillon" and Carroll signing himself "First Citizen." [4] Although the main point at issue was the patriot cause, the letters, in true eighteenth-century style, used legal language and Latin quotations to insinuate a wide range of personal innuendo. Dulany taunted Carroll for his Catholicism, and Carroll, with equal irrelevance, sneered at Dulany for having been an indentured servant. Undoubtedly many readers of the *Gazette* were chiefly intrigued by the daring of a disfranchised Catholic's venturing to argue a point of justice with a powerful government official, but in the end it was Carroll's political argument which won the day. Questions of public taxation took precedence over matters of private worship; and William Paca and Matthias Hammond voiced the general opinion when they signed an open letter congratulating Carroll for his denunciation of fees by prerogative as an "act of tyranny, which in a land of freedom cannot, must not, be endured." [5]

Although Maryland pens were laid aside in favor of more formidable weapons during the actual conflict, after independence was won they were grasped with renewed fervor and the closing months of the Critical Period found another Carroll appearing in print. This time it was John Carroll who elected to play his part in the war of pamphlets or battle of the broadsides, and the name of "Pacificus" came in turn to rank with its allusive predecessors. True, John Carroll had spent the formative years of his life far from Maryland's shores; yet in many ways he epitomized the best of the Anglo-American culture which permeated the colony and state in the eighteenth century. In his classical education, his literary facility, and his devotion to the parliamentary ideal, he was distinctly an American of the Maryland genre. He had arrived home in Maryland too late to take sides, even if he had so desired, in the controversies so volubly expounded by his kinsman of

Carrollton before the Revolution. During the months of battle he remained quietly preoccupied with his clerical duties. But when peace came, and with it the problems of defining more carefully the new birth of freedom, John Carroll could not remain aloof.

No man was ever a more ardent believer in religious liberty or a more jealous defender of that principle than John Carroll, and his attention was soon drawn to the dangers inherent in the increasing number of attacks on Catholics which appeared in the newspapers and magazines after the Revolution. During 1786-1787, a Philadelphia magazine, the *Columbian,* had given space to several letters objecting to religious liberty for Catholics. In the summer of 1787 Carroll, feeling compelled to reply to these attacks, addressed a letter to the editor who published it in the December supplement.[6] The tone of the letter was calm and reasonable; the arguments were precise and based on constitutionalism and justice. Thanks to a genuine spirit of Christianity, he said, the federal government had banished intolerance from its system, and many states, likewise, had placed all citizens on an equal footing. But other states like New Jersey had in their new constitutions reserved to Protestants alone the prerogatives of government and legislation. It was against these remnants of intolerance that Carroll protested. "Freedom and independence acquired by the united efforts, and cemented with the mingled blood of Protestants and Catholic fellow-citizens, should be equally enjoyed by all," he firmly maintained.

The superior of the mission felt very strongly on the subject of the Catholic soldier in the Continental Army who had fought as valiantly for freedom as his comrades in arms, and had then been compelled to summon an equal fortitude to face the degrading marks of distrust, the galling yoke of inferiority, forced upon him by his own fellow-citizens, once peace was won. Catholics had fought with a disinterested patriotism, trusting to the wise and generous sentiments which pervaded every corner of the American continent. Should they now be rewarded by being put under slavish subjection to the prejudices imbibed under a narrow British system? Carroll thought not. As he wrote later to Mathew Carey on January 30, 1789:

> After having contributed in proportion to their numbers, equally at least with every other denomination, to the establishment of independence, and run every risk in common with them, it is not only contradictory to the avowed prin-

ciples of equality in religious rights but a flagrant act of injustice to deprive them of those advantages to the acquirement of which they so much contributed.[7]

The powerful pen of protest was next called into play by the insinuations of an article which he read in the *United States Gazette* in May of 1789. When this article appeared in a paper printed under the very eyes of the new federal government meeting in New York City, Carroll could not remain silent. Although the main purpose of the *Gazette* attacks seemed to be to stir up opposition to Catholic office-holding, its author embroidered his theme with arguments that the United States had been founded to preserve Protestantism, that Protestantism was the mother of the arts and sciences, that Great Britain owed her present pre-eminence to her religion, and that in America it had been the Protestant clergy who "boldly and zealously stepped forth, and bravely stood our distinguished sentinels to bring about the late glorious revolution." It was more than Carroll could stomach, and using the pen name of "Pacificus" he wrote a spirited denunciation to the editor of the *Gazette* on June 10, 1789.

At the outset he disposed of the issue of political privilege by reiterating that the blood of Catholics, in proportion to their numbers, had flowed as freely as that of any of their fellow-citizens in the war for independence. With independence won, all Americans had associated in a great national union under the firm conviction that they were to retain every natural right not expressly surrendered. Catholics had concurred, with probably greater unanimity than any other group, in promoting that government "from whose influence America anticipates all the blessings of justice, peace, plenty, good order and civil and religious liberty." Under what pretext could Catholics be deprived of the common rights of nature, or of the stipulated rights of the political society to which they belonged? "What character shall we then give," Carroll demanded, "to a system of policy calculated for the express purpose of divesting of rights legally acquired those citizens who are not only unoffending, but whose conduct has been highly meritorious?" These words, coming from a man whose brother had helped fashion the United States Constitution, and whose cousin had been one of the signers of the Declaration of Independence, rang with an irrefutable logic.

But John Carroll was even more concerned by the insidious claim that the United States was an exclusively Protestant nation, that her culture was a product of purely Protestant arts and sciences, that the defence of American liberty could be only effected by Protestant politics, and the most dangerous of all doctrines: that democracy can only flourish where Protestantism prevails. Proceeding with extreme care for historical impartiality, the superior considered each of the arguments of the *Gazette* thesis. In the first place, he pointed out, history did not bear out the assertion that our forefathers all came to America for the sake of Protestantism. "Did the Roman Catholics . . . leave their native soil for the sake of preserving the Protestant Church? Was this the motive of the peaceable Quakers in the settlement of Pennsylvania?" Even granting that Protestantism laid the foundations of this new and great empire, was it not true that English Protestantism had done its best to crush this empire in its birth, and was still laboring to prevent its growth? "Can we so soon forget," asked Carroll, "that the bitterest enemies of our national prosperity profess the same religion which prevails generally in the United States?" He did not voice the obvious corollary that it was a Catholic power, France, which had made possible the victory at Yorktown, and had signed treaties of amity and commerce which had continued French friendship during the post-war period.

It was ridiculous to say, Carroll asserted, that the Protestant religion is the solitary bulwark of our Constitution. The establishment of the United States was not the work of this or that religion. It had arisen rather from the "generous exertion of all her citizens to redress their wrongs, to assert their rights, and lay its foundations on the soundest principles of justice and equal liberty." No one sect or branch of Christianity has the merit of being the most favorable to freedom. The neglect or contempt of no one body of clergy would cause morality or liberty to expire. "The voice of America will not contradict me," Carroll maintained. The clergy of all religions behaved in the Revolution as any other clergy would have done in similar circumstances.

But men were not always able to comprehend the luminous principles on which the rights of conscience and liberty of religion depend. Religious freedom is not the substitution of a new religion for an old. Nor is it supporting the religion of the majority while tolerating the minority's right to worship. America could not confine her distinguishing favors to the followers of Calvin while keeping a jealous eye on all the others. Carroll was not defending one profession, his own flock, but all religions when he urgently stated his plea. The United States, he firmly believed, must place the preservation of her liberties and her government "on the attachment of mankind to their political happiness, to the security of their persons and their property which is *independent of any religious doctrines and not restrained by any*." [8] America's leading Catholic was clearly on record as a proponent of a separation of Church and State. It remained for his brother, Daniel, to help shape the actual amendment to the Constitution which in 1791 prohibited Congress from making any law respecting an establishment of religion.[9]

Oddly enough, the most serious threats to Carroll's peace of mind came from public writing of quite another sort. Literary debates between men of different beliefs were to be expected and were, in spite of their fervor, usually carried on in good spirit leaving little aftermath of bitterness and recrimination. But during the Critical Period John Carroll found he had to deal with propaganda of another ilk, attacks launched upon the faith, or upon his own person, by men who were not only Catholics but priests as well. Three successive pamphlets, appearing between the years 1784-1789, brought true sorrow and indignation to Carroll's heart and in the end caused him to lay aside his controversial pen, which with one exception he would never grasp again.

In the spring of 1784 while the Reverend Charles Henry Wharton of Maryland was in Philadelphia he took occasion to publish a pamphlet that was destined to shock and sadden all his fellow Catholic clergymen, and to precipitate a controversy which would reverberate throughout the western Catholic world. Charles Wharton was a Maryland priest some dozen years younger than John Carroll to whom he was distantly related.[10] Like Carroll, Wharton had been educated at St. Omer, Liège, and Bruges, had entered the Society of Jesus, and at its dissolution in 1773 had been forced to choose between remaining in Europe or returning to Maryland. Wharton had preferred to remain in England, and after four years there he had been made permanent chaplain to the Catholics of Worcester.

During the American Revolution Father Wharton's sympathies had been quite naturally with the patriots, and he sent to Maryland a *Poetical Epistle to George Washington* which was published in Annapolis in 1778. The poem had an immediate vogue and eventually reached London where it was reprinted in 1780. When peace came in 1783 and the thirteen colonies were severed from their mother England, Wharton decided to return to Maryland. Some rumors preceded him from England, however, suggesting that although his patriotism was above reproach, his religious principles might not be. Carroll was slow to accept the implications of gossip and after a meeting with his relative he told Charles Plowden:

> I find him indeed possessed of considerable knowledge, and endowed with all those talents which render society agreeable. If upon further acquaintance I discover any of those blemishes which some of his companions in England thought they did, it would give me great concern, and I should speak freely to him about them. He has surely too much knowledge, and is too well-grounded in sound philosophy and sacred literature to adopt the incoherent and impious principles of modern infidelity.[11]

But the rumors continued. From London came reports that Wharton had abandoned his faith before he left England, and one friend in America said he had reason to believe as early as 1782 that Wharton was lost to Catholicism. With the publication of the pamphlet in Philadelphia, he confirmed the worst suspicions of his colleagues, and announced that his Catholicism was at an end. *The Letter to the Roman Catholics of the City of Worcester* left no doubt.

Coming as it did at the very beginning of John Carroll's prefectship, the defection of his fellow-priest and relative was a severe blow. The Wharton pamphlet, moreover, was particularly insidious in its method. Its false aura of historical authenticity and its tone of courteous regret were certain to seduce the less informed readers and to vindicate the already prevalent misconceptions of the non-Catholics. Charles Wharton professed to be offering his apology and explanation for leaving the brothers in religion whom he loved and respected. Borrowing the method of Jefferson in the Declaration of Independence, the ex-priest paraphrased the preamble of that liberty document with the words:

> At a period of life when discernment should be ripe, when passions should be calm, and principles settled, if a man relinquishes the opinions of his youth . . . if he abandons connections which he has cherished from his infancy . . . a decent respect to his own character, to the connections which he quits and those which he embraces, seems to call aloud for the motives of so important a change.[12]

Although none of his intimates could be deluded by Wharton's claim to calmness of passions, and some even suspected that license of the flesh lay back of the priest's defection, this *Letter* appeared to many outside the Church as another declaration of freedom, one more proof that American air renders a man free. Wharton argued that his step symbolized an enlargement of ideas, a throwing off of the shackles of Catholicism. He attacked the doctrines of transubstantiation, the infallibility of the teaching Church, and the necessity of the Church to salvation, as well as the practice of clerical celibacy. He developed his argument with scholarly references to authors not readily accessible in the United States, and he concluded with the traditional Protestant apologetic,

> My religion is that of the Bible: whatever that sacred book proposes as an object of my faith, as a rule of my conduct, was inspired by the unerring Spirit of God, and for that reason I admit it with all the faculties of my soul. . . . I solely rely upon the authority of God's word.

After the publication of this defense of his action, Wharton was welcomed into the Protestant Episcopal Church as a minister. That fall he sat in their first general convocation, and in 1785 he was made rector of the Episcopal Church at New Castle, Delaware. The remainder of his life was spent as an exemplary Protestant minister.

From the very outset it was apparent that such a reasonable appeal would carry tremendous weight unless the actual arguments of the ex-priest could be shown to be erroneous. It became John Carroll's task to write the refutation to the Wharton *Letter,* and he knew he must proceed with utmost caution. A friend in Philadelphia, Father Molyneux, wrote encouragingly in August, "I have a snug chamber to rest you in, and a library well fitted up in the choir of the old chapel . . . where you might spend many agreeable hours in study and application, free from noise." [13] But Philadelphia had few of the books which Wharton had used, and Carroll found that Annapolis was better equipped to furnish his needs. So it was at the Maryland capital that he spent the hot summer weeks laboriously drafting his reply. The general chapter of the clergy voted to pay the printing expenses, and by autumn Carroll's refutation was complete and ready for Frederick Green, the Annapolis printer.[14]

The second pamphlet bore the title *An Address to the Roman*

Catholics of the United States of America, and it politely but decisively refuted Wharton's entire attack. The superior began by explaining that had the letter of Wharton reached only those for whom it was professedly intended, the citizens of Worcester in England, he should never have replied to it. But since it had been given a wide circulation in the United States, a regard for truth and the tranquillity of his flock's conscience impelled him to reply. "Ministers of religion should always remember," he felt, "that it is their duty to enlighten the understanding as well as to improve the morals of mankind," and he quoted Saint Matthew's admonition: "You are the light of the world."

Carroll went swiftly on to dispel the illusion of scholarly accuracy which the Wharton work pretended to display. He showed how again and again the ex-priest had misquoted his sources, had garbled texts from Bellarmine, had falsely cited the church councils, and had even gone so far as to attribute to Saint John Chrysostom a fraudulent sixth-century text on Matthew. Examining Wharton's treatment of the theory of "no salvation outside the Church," Carroll demonstrated that nowhere did the fathers of the Church or its present theologians insist on the rigid interpretation which Wharton had deliberately chosen to adopt. There was little room for doubt when Carroll finished that Wharton's misconceptions had no basis in orthodox Catholic theology.

The *Address* concluded on a more personal note, and the older man wrote sorrowfully of his disappointment in this friend with whom he had hoped to have consummated his course "of our common ministry in the service of virtue and religion." He spoke of his particular surprise that a friend of toleration would so "misinform and sow in minds so misinformed the seeds of religious animosity." Carroll had no fear that false doctrine would long prevail; the testament was clear: the Gates of Hell would not prevail against the Church. The present danger in Wharton's attack was this undermining of what was America's greatest blessing, religious liberty. Carroll would ever defend this freedom, "which if we have the wisdom and temper to preserve," he admonished, would enable the United States "to exhibit a proof to the world that general and equal toleration . . . is the most effectual method to bring all denominations of Christians to a unity of faith." As for Wharton's own conscience, Father Carroll concluded, his motives were best known to Wharton and to God. "But I must entreat with an earnestness suggested by the most perfect good will and zealous regard for his welfare," the superior pleaded, "Consider the sanctity of the solemn and deliberate engagement which, at an age of perfect maturity, he contracted with Almighty God."

The impact of the Wharton apostasy was not confined to American circles. News flew back to England and Thomas Talbot, who had long been the temporal agent or procurator of the English ex-Jesuits, wrote to Carroll of his sorrow at having his suspicions of Wharton so sadly confirmed. "Pride and self-conceit have been his ruin," Father Talbot commented. "He has abilities to have made a superior man. The paper he has sent to Worcester will do no harm. His character was lost there long before he left." [15]

Wharton's name soon came to be coupled in England with that of an apostate Benedictine, John Hawkins, and a vacillating ex-Jesuit, Austin Jennison; and, as other apologists took up their pens, the Wharton-Carroll debate expanded on both sides of the Atlantic. In Maryland Carroll himself was encouraged by Talbot's words from London, "I wish to see a good answer, and I think you are equal to the task." [16] Indeed, when Wharton wrote his second treatise in reply to Carroll his arguments seemed to have lost their first cogency and Talbot commented acidly "I am sorry Wharton should have been so weak as to attempt a reply to your answer, but am not surprised at it. His pride will not truckle as long as his vanity is flattered by his pen." [17] In England a Franciscan friar, William Pilling, framed a less skillful reply to Wharton which was printed under the title: *Caveat to the Catholics of Worcester against the Insinuating Letter of Dr. Wharton,* and Father Joseph Berington, who had originally planned answering Wharton himself, directed a pamphlet against John Hawkins, the English apostate. Berington had a facile pen and was already admired by Carroll for his style. The English apologist returned the compliment and used Carroll's *Address* in framing his own *Reflections Addressed to the Rev. John Hawkins.*[18] Quills scratched busily and lengthy phrases were polished and revised. Less literary by-standers wrote private letters denouncing Wharton for his pride and hypocrisy, Jennison for lusts of the flesh and libertinism, and the "conceited puppy" Hawkins as a convert to the "Deity Woman."

Meanwhile Carroll's own pamphlet reached London and was reprinted in an expurgated edition. Carroll's friends there were dismayed to see his *Address* thus "mutilated" not only in regard to the note he had appended, but in the matter of his Latin quotations as well. Father John Thorpe in Rome complained that he was unable to secure Carroll's answer to Wharton in its original form. "I hope," he told Carroll, "that Mr. Talbot will send me a genuine copy of it, because some illiberal alterations are said to have been made in an Irish-London edition of it which I do not care to see." [19] The deleted London version was read avidly enough, however, by others in Rome who were less discriminating, and Abbate Luigi Cuccagni, the Italian rector of the Irish College there, enlisted the aid of some of his students to print a commentary on the Carroll work. The rector's remarks, which were not especially flattering to the American priest, were printed in the *Giornale Ecclesiastico di Roma,* and John Thorpe forwarded them to his friend for his amusement. Charles Plowden in London consoled Carroll with the opinion that Cuccagni was known to be a "red hot champion in litigious theology" who "maddens at the name of Jesuit." [20] It was not until the fall of 1786 that Rome received a true copy of the original *Address.* When Father Thorpe received the well-worn pamphlet from Liège, where Carroll's former colleagues had perused it with pride and pleasure, he said approvingly, "The moderation or rather singular modesty of your pen gives a grace to the goodness of the cause which it defends. You truly treat Mr. Wharton like a father and friend, and I hope that your charitable concern for him will in time be comforted." [21] But the erring priest never repaid Carroll for his fatherly interest. Instead, he continued in the Episcopalian ministry, marrying twice before his death. Yet Wharton never ceased to be of concern to his former associates who felt his defection keenly. "Would to God," Theodore Badin wrote from the Kentucky frontier to Bishop Carroll in 1799, "that the apostate Wharton would open his heart to repentance and his eyes to faith!" [22] But although it preyed upon Carroll's mind to the day of his death, Wharton was lost to the Church.[23]

The next challenge to Father Carroll's instinct for fair play came in a vicious attack on his brothers in religion, the American ex-Jesuits, from the pen of Father Patrick Smyth, an Irish wandering priest whom the superior of the mission had given permission to serve at Frederick, Maryland, in the fall of 1787.[24] Smyth was to prove himself a quarrelsome, contentious person wherever he went, and he was scarcely arrived in Maryland before his complaints became voluble. After a few months at Frederick, he notified Baltimore that he intended to return to Ireland. "The load is become so heavy that I cannot possibly bear it. I will run away. . . . I cannot help it. I must go back to Ireland." It was clear that the hardships of the American mission were not to Smyth's taste, and the rest of his letter indicated that he was also suffering from imaginary slights and rebuffs received at the hands of the Maryland gentry.[25] Carroll sagely advised the sensitive priest not to take offense where he was sure none was intended, but the haughty Irish visitor sailed in high dudgeon in the early part of May, 1788.

During the month he spent in Baltimore, waiting for a ship, Father Smyth was entertained by Carroll, and the latter began to suspect that the priest's grievances went beyond imaginary insults from Catholic laymen. It came back to the superior that Smyth was publicly spreading the charge that he was compelled to leave the United States because of the harsh treatment he had received at the hands of the ex-Jesuit clergy. When reports of this reckless language reached Carroll's ears, he could scarcely believe his guest would so abuse his hospitality while still under his roof, and he determined to question Smyth. That oily fellow smoothly professed to be "shocked that such reports should spread" and assured his host that he could not have been treated with more openness and generosity.[26] Yet so great was his duplicity that the very moment Smyth boarded ship for Dublin he wrote a letter to an acquaintance in Baltimore openly accusing the ex-Jesuits of being hostile to Irish priests, of preventing them from coming to relieve the suffering brethren, and of welcoming only former Jesuits to the American vineyard.[27]

But the worst was still to come. No sooner had Patrick Smyth reached Dublin than the full force of his rancor was made public with the publication of his vilification entitled: *The Present State of the Catholic Missions Conducted by the ex-Jesuits in North America.* There was in reality as little novelty as truth in Smyth's work, repeating as it did the familiar calumnies against the Jesuits: that liberty of the press was endangered by the power of their party, that clergymen occupied superb seats while their poor Catholic subjects hovered around them, starving in the presence of plenty, that shepherds slumbered in the luxuriant climes of Maryland's Eastern Shore while the faithful were neglected in other states.[28] To anyone familiar with the hardships of the Catholic clergy in the United States the fantastic picture drawn by Smyth would have been an occasion for only laughter or disgust. But Smyth was reaching an audience not familiar with American conditions, and he was appealing to the old animus of the Irish against the English when he claimed that only Irish Catholics in the United States remained true to the religion of their fathers while among the English Catholics of Annapolis and Baltimore Catholicism had deteriorated into various other forms of worship. When he could not give credit to the Irish, as in the case of Pennsylvania, he was careful not to bestow it upon the English, and claimed that it was the Germans who were responsible for the success of Catholicism there.

The pamphlet quickly found its way into English hands and Father William Strickland wrote to Carroll from London that it looked as if poor Smyth wanted the United States to be only "an open port for the reception of all Irish ecclesiastics who may wish to try their fortunes in the new world." He added lightly that he had no doubt that Carroll could have all the priests he wanted if he were willing to receive "all whom the irregularity of their behaviour has made more obnoxious to their own country." Then, in a more serious vein, Strickland observed that he thought silent contempt the only answer Smyth's attack deserved.[29]

But when Father Carroll received a copy of the outrageous pamphlet from a Philadelphia publisher in January of 1789 his wrath could not restrain itself. It was one thing to practise prudence and temperate language when refuting non-Catholics or apostates, but Carroll was justly incensed at the base ingratitude of this priest who traduced his own brothers and sought to damage the very cause he was bound in conscience to protect. He reached for his pen and wrote paragraph after scathing paragraph denouncing Smyth and charging him with "bitterness of spirit," "malignant passions," "calumny," and slander. His pen scratched angrily across the wide pages of paper as his righteous indignation vented its force.

But the reply to Smyth never reached print. Archbishop John Thomas Troy, O.P., of Dublin, who was only too familiar with the character of the troublesome fellow, told Carroll that he felt the Irish priest was unworthy of his notice and advised the American superior in February to ignore the petulant pamphlet. Troy further assured Carroll that the Irish hierarchy would do their part to prevent its circulation. By this time Carroll's first anger had subsided and he saw the wisdom of this advice. He contented himself with a few observations on Smyth's book which he forwarded to Archbishop Troy for his reading, "and that of those other reverend prelates who have, in a manner so obliging, prevented the intended bad effects of the malicious publication." [30] His own lengthy retort to Smyth he kept among his private papers where it remained unread while Carroll lived.

The ungrateful conduct of Smyth in Maryland, combined with the Whelan-Nugent troubles in New York, caused the superior growing concern, nevertheless. It was all very well for John Thorpe to ask from Rome, "What can you expect from vagabond priests?" [31] Carroll had to face the realities of his American domain where the need for priests was growing daily more acute. The Catholic population was increasing each year and, as the older families pushed west into Kentucky and beyond, the need for more clergy grew more urgent. Carroll knew that he must continue to rely on recruits from Ireland as well as elsewhere in Europe, but he wished he could convince the clerical emigrants that life inside the United States was not the priestly paradise they mistakenly anticipated. As he explained to Archbishop Troy:

> One thing must be fully impressed on their minds, that no pecuniary prospects or worldly comforts must enter into their motives for their crossing the Atlantic to this country. They will find themselves much disappointed. Labour, hardships of every kind, coarse living, and particularly great scarcity of wine (especially out of the towns) must be borne with. Sobriety in drink is expected from clergymen to a great degree.[32]

John Carroll had to suffer one more scurrilous attack from an unworthy priest before the Critical Period was over. This time the author of the pamphlet was a Frenchman whose activities centered in New England. In the fall of 1788, close on the heels of the Smyth affair, Claude Florent Bouchard de la Poterie arrived in Boston to be cordially received by the Catholics there. Like Father Whelan in New York, he had been a chaplain in the French forces during the Revolution and had stayed on in the United States after the war was over. Carroll gave Father La Poterie limited faculties in December after reading the fervent letters of the French priest and accepting in good faith the several letters of recommendations and testimonials which La Poterie had forwarded to him.

All too soon, however, La Poterie gave indications of falling far short of his superior's expectations. The Christmas holidays were still a vivid memory when the Boston priest began denying what he called the "false and scandalous aspersions" cast upon his reputation. Like most Europeans, La Poterie found the American freedom of the press an irresistible temptation, and he burst into print with an amazing list of credentials intended to silence his critics. The very items he included showed how little the befuddled fellow understood the temper of the American people, for he included among his other claims to reputation a patent of his election as a count of the Holy Roman Empire, and membership in "two learned academies in Rome." [33] Even before word came from Paris that La Poterie had been suspended there for conduct unbecoming a priest, Carroll was ready to admit that again he had been deceived in the confidence he had placed in a volunteer to his mission, and he confessed to Charles Plowden that La Poterie had turned out to be "a sad rascal." [34]

Since the death of Father Farmer in 1786, the mission had been without a vicar-general, and being unable to go to Boston himself, Carroll sent Father William O'Brien to investigate the true state of affairs in Massachusetts. It did not take O'Brien long to discover that La Poterie was unworthy of his post, and when Carroll heard this he suspended the French priest. The congregation was so glad to be rid of him that they assumed the numerous debts that La Poterie had contracted and breathed a sigh of relief when he left for Canada that summer.

And then came the public denunciation in pamphlet form. On his way back through the United States, en route to the West Indies, Father La Poterie stopped off in Philadelphia long enough to publish his burden of hatred and revenge. One more title was added to the growing literature of abuse; this time it was *The Resurrection of Laurent Ricci: or a True and Exact History of the Jesuits*. It was dedicated to "The New Laurent Ricci in America, the Rev. Fr. John Carroll, Superior of the Jesuits in the United States, also to the friar-inquisitor, William O'Brien." [35] The French priest was, of course, trying to summon up memories of the vituperative accusations levelled against the Jesuits at the time of their suppression in 1773. Lorenzo Ricci had been their last General. He was a man of profound piety and phenomenal courage, but La Poterie meant no compliment when he devised the title and dedication of his vindictive and incendiary pamphlet. The contents of his pamphlet belied any such connotation. By this time Carroll was convinced that enduring abusive language was to be a concomitant of his office and, emulating the true character of Lorenzo Ricci, he declined to dignify the absurd attack by a reply. Aside from an official report to Rome on the causes for the priest's suspension, he officially ignored the unsavory affair.

Only his closer friends like Thorpe and Plowden realized how heavily these scandals pressed upon the American superior. To the man of breeding, vulgarity is ever distasteful; to the man of impeccable virtue, vice is a perpetual anathema. Although his courtesy compels him to ignore rudeness, and charity constrains him to forgive the sinner, the offenses and the sins remain forever repugnant. John Carroll could willingly tolerate indignities which concerned himself alone. What the American mission needed were men willing to go where no missioners had gone before, men imbued with zeal for souls and little else. "It was thus that religion was propagated in every age of the Church," he told Archbishop Troy. "If clergymen animated with this spirit will offer their services, I will receive them with cheerfulness and direct their zeal where there is every prospect of success." [36] But he could not condone public scandals in a country where Catholics were detested enough already. For the welfare of the Church it was imperative that his powers be so enlarged that he might deal decisively with these recalcitrants. There were too many fine, hard-working priests making daily sacrifices in the performance of their duties to allow these occasional vessels of clay to complicate or retard the great work in which the Church was engaged. The time had come for Rome to re-assess the needs of the faithful in the United States. Carroll resolved to take action without further delay.

CHAPTER
VIII

ELECTION AT WHITEMARSH

THE times were changing. Over at Annapolis the state legislature was busy with plans to combine Washington College on
the Eastern Shore with a new foundation on the west bank into the
University of Maryland. James Rumsey was given the exclusive
privilege and benefit of making and selling the new boats of "a
model by him invented," the marvelous steamboat over which so
many later claimants would quarrel. Navigation was the topic at
the dinner tables in the 1780's, and the readers of the published
proceedings of the Maryland Legislature could tell how William
Paca, Thomas Stone, and Samuel Chase stood on the momentous
issue of making the Susquehanna navigable. Many a post-war dollar
went into the newly incorporated "Proprietors of the Susquehanna
Canal" while other restless funds found their way into the treasury
of the Potomac Company which George Washington and Charles
Carroll had encouraged in company with the superior's brother
Daniel. While Daniel Carroll presided at company meetings and
weighed the question of how many shares of stock he might wisely
acquire, Washington went to investigate the possibilities of locks,
dams, and subsidiary canals.[1]

But as one preoccupied Carroll bustled off to his meetings at
Wise's Tavern in Alexandria, or at John Suter's in Georgetown, his
brother in Baltimore had business with the birds. Lady Arundell in
England, after acknowledging her natural pleasure at her friend's
promotion to superior, sent a coaxing reminder that Father Carroll
had promised her a Virginia nightingale to be sent after his return
to America. The priest smiled ruefully at the memory of his
nostalgic rhapsodies at Wardour Castle. His partiality for American
warblers had led to this. Well, she should have her birds. He at

length secured a pair of the delicate creatures and sent them across the Atlantic. It was not his fault that they perished on the voyage, and Lady Arundell thanked him prettily for the little corpses. Lord Arundell, when he wrote, said that he was more concerned about the Virginia hams they had been promised.[2] The American superior reflected upon the evils of nationalism and wondered what else he might be expected to despatch to England as a result of his earlier enthusiasm. He wished, fleetingly, that he could be at Wardour once again. There were true friends of his order. He almost envied old Brother Joe Blyde.

And yet it was not a one-way traffic across the sea. Mary Christine Arundell's letter in February of 1786 was brought to John Carroll by Francis Beeston, one of her own *élèves*, as she called him. William Strickland at Liège told Carroll, "Mr. Beeston has been a very serviceable man at the Academy and I doubt not will prove a valuable recruit to your mission." [3] Father Beeston was to be for Carroll that special friend the priest must have—the sometimes younger confidant who shares the petty disappointments and the larger joys, the intimate who accepts the idiosyncracies as part of the natural burden of friendship, the companion at public functions, and the patient ear in the private study. Francis Beeston was sixteen years younger than the American superior, but their interests were almost identical. An ex-Jesuit and alumnus of Liège, Beeston became the most intimate friend that Carroll allowed himself in later life. Those closest to the prelate rarely closed a letter without sending warm regards to "Mr. Beeston." When difficulties came to Philadelphia in 1788 Father Beeston was relied upon to act as pastor at St. Mary's Church and he served there until his friend became bishop. But after 1793 Father Beeston was in Baltimore near Carroll. Together they went on St. Patrick's Day to dine with James and Joanna Barry. When the younger man died in 1809 it was the Archbishop of Baltimore, John Carroll, who wrote the Beeston sketch for the *New American Biographical Dictionary* which was published in Baltimore the following year.[4]

While Lady Arundell mourned the fragility of American songsters, and Father Carroll rejoiced in the acquisition of a new friend, the younger members of the Carroll family pursued the old pattern of going abroad to study, or acquiring by travel the desired polish and charm. William Strickland, who was now the new head of the Liège Academy, sent word by way of London to Father Carroll that his young kinsman, Master Charles, was receiving all the advantages of a gentleman's education. Dancing, lessons in music, drawing, and fencing or riding were all included for those who could afford the extras. Like earlier Marylanders abroad, young Charlie was a liberal spender and his extra items of *"Menues plaisirs"* were the common family topic. Carroll smiled reminiscently when he read, "Your young kinsman is said to be inclined to make this article pretty considerable, were he indulged." [5] The Carrolls were all hearty eaters.

It was pleasant to know that Carrolls were still received kindly in England and on the continent. Lady Arundell wrote from Wardour Castle in 1786 of her pleasure at receiving Father Carroll's two young cousins, and she commented on their lively spirits.[6] Carrolls were always welcome at Wardour, she said warmly. Later, in 1789, when Charles the Signer's daughter Kitty went abroad, too, the superior was pleased with Strickland's report which said:

> Your little kinswoman, Miss Kitty Carroll, arrived at Liège safe and in good spirits. Her brother is a fine boy and does not want talents. . . . The line of life he will probably be engaged in is that of Representative of his country or a magistrate. . . . He should possess a knowledge of the Law of Nations as well as of those of his own country.[7]

Vattel's *Law of Nations* was all the rage these days. Gentlemen in Congress were as apt to refer to him as to Blackstone, as they argued politics and international law in loud voices. There was no Carroll in the younger line to pore over Bellarmine or savor St. Ignatius. Theology seemed to hold few attractions.

But if the Carrolls were more interested in society and politics there were rumors that grace might be operating in other family circles. The papal nuncio in Paris wrote on July 5, 1787, that Mr. Jefferson was bringing back to the United States two daughters who had been brought up in a French convent at Panthemont. "The eldest," he said, "seems to have great tendencies toward the Catholic religion. She is only sixteen. Her father, without absolutely opposing her vocation, has tried to distract her." Thomas Jefferson hoped his daughter would wait until she reached eighteen before making a decision in regard to religion.[8]

After Jefferson returned to become Secretary of State under the new government of the United States, Paris remained interested in his daughter's inclination. "I am sure," the nuncio told Carroll, "that you will not neglect to profit from the favourable dispositions Miss Jefferson showed here for the Catholic religion. It is a very interesting subject and can only do honor to your zeal. I know how much delicacy and prudence this affair requires, but it could not be in better hands." [9] But there was a wider gulf between Monticello and Baltimore than mere physical distance, and all the delicacy in the world was valueless if Miss Jefferson did not choose to approach him. Youthful religious enthusiasms were only too apt to wane in the demanding, bustling American milieu, as John Carroll well knew from observation of his own young relatives. History would associate the name of Jefferson with the father's odd preference for a hodge-podge of Epicureanism and Christianity, and forget that the daughter Martha ever leaned toward the purest of Roman orthodoxy.

The superior at Baltimore could accept the changing society about him with a shrug of his massive shoulders. But one question ran deep below this surface preoccupation with friends and relatives. What of the episcopacy? When was the United States to have her own bishop? The need for ampler powers was not to be denied, nor solved by looking back over the shoulder of European history. The new nation in North America seemed to have sired a national church, and the annoying hobbles which present relations with Rome imposed made the vigorous creature restive.

In the first place, Rome seemed slow to grasp the implication of the Church's position in the United States. When he had received the news of his appointment as superior, Carroll had tried to explain to the Holy See how objectionable all foreign jurisdiction appeared to the average citizen. Catholics were anxious that no pretext be given their enemies for accusing them of submitting to a foreign authority. He called Rome's attention to the sixth article of the Confederation charter of government which expressly forbade the acceptance of "any gift, office, or title of any kind whatsoever from any king, prince, or foreign government." Never one to mince matters, the new superior had said clearly in 1785:

> We desire that the faith in its integrity, due obedience towards the Apostolic See and perfect union should flourish; and at the same time that whatever can with safety to religion be granted, shall be conceded to American Catholics in ecclesiastical affairs. In this way, we hope that distrust of Protestants now full of suspicion will be diminished and that our affairs can be solidly established.[10]

To John Carroll, and those of his friends who understood the American situation, the appointment of a Superior of the Mission in 1784 had been only a temporary and unsatisfactory solution to the problem. Strickland had pointed out that July, that the appointment was a deviation from the regular procedure of the Church which could only be justified by the necessity of the time. "This excuse has no place in America," he told Carroll. Diocesan bishops were the proper solution, and Rome ought to agree with Carroll on this point.[11] As a matter of fact, when John Thorpe in Rome had first forwarded the news of Carroll's appointment he had intimated that as soon as the Holy See received a report on the condition of religion in North America Carroll would be elevated to the dignity of a bishop. On the arrival of that report, Thorpe assured his friend, "You will accordingly be so nominated by the pope and the place determined for your consecration. Cardinal Borromeo sent for me to give me this intelligence, on the veracity of which you may entirely depend."[12] Benjamin Franklin, who had interested himself in his old companion's case earlier, assured the Paris nuncio that same summer that he personally preferred to see John Carroll made bishop at once. Congress, he told Doria Pamphili, would be most pleased and would not object to Carroll's going to Quebec for his consecration.[13]

It had been something of a shock then, when Carroll read his actual papers of appointment, to find that he was even less than full prefect, that he was limited by "cramping clauses" which bound him closely to the Sacred Congregation of Propaganda Fide. Thomas Talbot in London commiserated with him over his difficulties, and Thorpe wrote indignantly from Rome, "We have been deluded! What you have received is far from being what you were led to expect." It seemed to Thorpe, in his wrath at having been the bearer of misinformation, that Propaganda was trying to "fix the North American Catholics within their jurisdiction."[14] As time passed it became more evident to less partial observers like Strickland that a superior responsible to Propaganda was infinitely less desirable than a bishop. "The latter enjoys very extensive powers in the spiritual line, by virtue of his ordination," he said, "and I should apprehend that a jurisdiction of this sort, if properly understood by the ruling powers of the country, would be much less exceptionable than a state of dependence on the caprice of a Congregation, which for some years has not been distinguished by the purity of its motives or the disinterestedness of its views."[15]

John Carroll himself had been reluctant to accept the post on such confining terms, but his concern for the Church in America overruled his personal scruples. He did not hesitate, however, to protest to Rome, and he was eventually rewarded by Thorpe's news in the summer of 1785 that his authority would be extended. "Your faculties would be enlarged," Thorpe had heard, "and the cramping clauses, against which you had with so much reason remonstrated should be struck out." It now appeared that Rome had never meant them for Carroll, but through an oversight in the secretary's office they had been left in the first instructions sent over to America.[16] This time Thorpe was right. Cardinal Antonelli himself assured Carroll on July 23, 1785, that every risk of displeasure he hoped would now be removed. "I have seen to it that a new copy of faculties be enclosed for you, in which this clause has been removed, and the power has been granted you of selecting workers whom you judge suitable," were the cardinal's words.[17]

In 1785 this had seemed enough of a victory. Carroll himself had come to believe that there was no hurry about a bishop until the United States had some young men ready for ordination. His existing right to confirm, and his now clarified right to confer faculties where he liked, had seemed to answer the immediate needs of his mission. He was quite aware that among the American clergy there was some opposition to having a bishop in the United States. The first general chapter at Whitemarsh the year before had passed a resolution declaring a bishop unnecessary, and then had appointed a committee of three to notify Rome of their opinion in this regard. Part of this opposition sprang from the memory of colonial opposition in general. But the recent Episcopalian decision to have an American bishop hinted that there was more to the opposition at Whitemarsh than concern for tradition.[18] In their memorial to the Holy See the committee gave as their second reason, "We are not able to support a bishop in a manner becoming to his situation." It implied to anyone who cared to read the lines that the ex-Jesuits did not want to see their hard-won properties in the New World fall into the same hands which had despoiled their former comrades in Europe. John Carroll, himself an ex-Jesuit, could understand this reluctance to open new avenues to Roman intervention. He could appreciate, too, although he was less optimistic than his brothers, that a hope of restoring the Society of Jesus prejudiced their attitude toward the establishment of a bishopric.

But as the months went by and his visitations revealed the inherent weaknesses in his position, the superior came to believe that only a bishop could meet the American requirements. A single situation like the Nugent trouble in New York spoke volumes to him on the subject of the episcopacy. For, in spite of his tact and patience, Carroll was faced with worse troubles than ever after Father Whelan's departure up the Hudson River. As so often happens when a congregation takes a personal preference for pastors, the favorite turned out to be less bearable than his ousted predecessor. In October of 1787 Carroll was compelled to visit New York in person to listen to the charges now levelled against Father Nugent. Convinced of the justice of these accusations, Carroll suspended the priest's faculties and replaced him by the Dominican, Father William O'Brien, from Philadelphia.

What then happened would have humiliated a man of much less dignity than John Carroll. Nugent refused to submit to authority and on the Sunday morning that his superior offered Mass at St. Peter's in Barclay Street, the rebellious priest addressed the people in a vituperative tirade against Carroll. The superior, maintaining his self-control with difficulty, announced Nugent's suspension to the congregation, withdrew from the altar, and went over to the residence of Don Diego de Gardoqui, the Spanish *chargé d'affaires,* to offer his Mass in surroundings more conducive to worship and divine praise.

It galled him to realize what scandalous reports of the affair must be reaching the ears of the gentlemen of Congress who were then sitting in New York. His whole experience had been among men of courtesy and breeding, and he felt an instinctive, deep disgust for the behavior of these people who rioted in the very presence of the Blessed Sacrament. Nevertheless, Nugent was a priest, and his followers were as much a part of the Mystical Body as was the superior. There was no choice but to try to bring peace to this tumultuous congregation. Carroll decided against an oral appeal, distrusting his own emotions. Instead, he resorted again to the pen wielded in solitude and subject to discipline and correction. His address was the real Carroll speaking to his flock.

Addressing the people as "Dear Christians, and most beloved Brethren in Jesus Christ" the superior began by explaining his concern at seeing his holy religion endangered by dissensions, especially in a country where that religion was already viewed through the false coloring of prejudice. He called upon the congregation to preserve the faith of their forefathers in its purity in the face of every temporal discouragement or worldly interest. Once again he carefully explained the Church's position on the appointment of the clergy to their particular charges, and his own responsibility in this case to provide them with a worthy pastor. He concluded his painstaking appeal with a plea for perfect charity, well-grounded hope, and unshaken and active faith. "May these virtues rest with you for ever, and bring you to life eternal," he said in conclusion.[19]

It seems incredible that this appeal should have failed, but the Nugent schismatics turned deaf ears, and the following Sunday they broke down the door of the church and rushed in, followed by a curious crowd of non-Catholics. Carroll had no weapon against such stubborn resistance. He returned to Baltimore determined to make Rome realize that the time had come for a bishop. In March, 1788, he reported to Cardinal Antonelli the plain facts of the Nugent affair, and said forcibly that the necessity for episcopal authority was becoming more evident every day. He knew that he would be accused of ambition. It was a risk he was willing to take. Certainly with his existing powers the burden of his office was becoming unbearable. It was no longer a case of half a loaf being better than none.

The American clergy by this time were likewise in almost unanimous agreement with their superior that the time had come to ask for a bishop. That very month they sent a petition to the Holy See asking for an American bishop, citing the Nugent schism as one of their arguments. This petition, which was drawn up by John Carroll, Robert Molyneux, and John Ashton, suggested that the United States should be directly responsible to the Holy See, and that the bishop be elected by the priests of that mission.[20]

The American clergy were not the only ones aware of the advantages a bishop would offer. Catholics of other nations residing in the United States agreed that the new nation required such an official. As early as March, 1785, the French minister, Barbé-Marbois, had informed the Congregation of Propaganda that the elevation of John Carroll would be most advantageous to the Church. Diego de Gardoqui, the Spaniard, told Carroll in person that he saw little future for American Catholicism if a bishop were not soon appointed. He offered the services of his country's diplomat, Count Floridablanca, as a channel through which the clergy's petition could travel, and John Carroll accepted. Francis Beeston was given the task of seeing that Gardoqui got the petition,

and when the latter forwarded it to Spain he attached a letter of
his own urging the appointment of Carroll.[21]

That same year, too, Filippo Filicchi, the Italian merchant who
was in the United States on business, met Father Carroll and offered
him his services. Carroll wrote to Father Thorpe in Rome of
Filicchi's offer and recommended the Leghorn merchant to his
friend's attention. Filicchi did not reach Italy until late in 1788,
having been delayed in Barcelona, but he wrote Thorpe from Spain
of his interest in the American superior's case, and Thorpe reported
to Carroll that he certainly would be happy to take Filicchi up on
his offer to intercede.[22] After his arrival back home in Italy, Filicchi
sent word to Thorpe by a younger brother, Antonio, who was then
a law student at Rome, that Filippo desired to do what service he
could for the Church in the United States, and for John Carroll in
particular. He had consulted Monsignor Angebelli, the Bishop of
Gubbio, and had been advised to draw up a memorial representing
to the Holy Father the "absolute necessity for establishing a Catholic hierarchy" in the United States. The merchant was further willing to write to Cardinal Antonelli as well, he said, but not wishing
to make a false move that might harm the cause, he would wait
for Thorpe's approval.[23]

Thorpe began to suspect that in the Filicchis of Gubbio the
American Church had found valuable friends. When Antonio came
to see Thorpe he brought with him William Seton, a guest of their
house, and young Seton offered Thorpe the services of his father's
mercantile firm as an avenue of communication for Roman-Amer-
ican correspondence. After talking with the New York traveler
Father Thorpe was convinced that letters going through the Filicchi-
Seton route stood a much better chance of speedy delivery, and he
told Carroll, "This very amiable gentleman has had his letters in
a regular and expeditious course," and he added that he intended
to accept the young man's offer. After January, 1789, Thorpe sent
his mail from Leghorn to Messers William Seton and Company of
New York, and it was by this route that John Carroll eventually
received the favorable decision of Rome that the United States
clergy were to select their own see city and to nominate their own
choice for bishop.[24]

It was a signal victory for the American Church in their struggle
to establish a firm foundation free from outside intervention, this
right to choose their own bishop. When Strickland heard the joyful
news he congratulated Carroll that a regular hierarchy was to be

begun at last. But he warned his friend, "I can not suppose that the mode of appointing the first bishop will be continued for his successor. It will be, I should apprehend, one of the first duties of the new-elected bishop to constitute a chapter, or something equivalent to it, for future elections, and also to nominate a coadjutor for that extensive territory." [25] But John Carroll believed in facing one thing at a time. First, the good tidings must be conveyed to the other American priests. On March 25, 1789, a committee composed of himself, Molyneux, and Ashton, sent out a circular announcing the Roman decision. In May the jubilant priests assembled at Whitemarsh and, after celebrating Mass, cast their votes for the first bishop of the United States. John Carroll was elected by a vote of twenty-four to two. When Strickland heard the news in Liège he observed:

> I will not congratulate you on the choice which has been made of a Bishop for America because I am sure that you submit to it with reluctance. But you must give me leave to congratulate America and religion, who by that choice have gained an able pilot to conduct them through a dangerous sea.[26]

Rome was content. Having been reassured through Thomas Jefferson at Paris that Carroll's appointment as bishop would give offense to neither "our institutions or opinions," a general congregation of the cardinals of Propaganda ratified the Whitemarsh election and on September 14, 1789, Pope Pius VI confirmed the choice of John Carroll as first Catholic bishop of the United States. The apostolic bull was prepared and despatched to the United States with the words:

> Nothing more acceptable and pleasing could happen to us, than . . . that you should have nominated, by almost unanimous consent, John Carroll as the first Bishop of the new See of Baltimore. For since our Holy Father Pius VI was fully aware of the unblemished reputation of Mr. Carroll and of the remarkable zeal with which for many years he has strenuously laboured there for the salvation of souls, His Holiness has confirmed . . . this first election . . . which you have exercised with such rectitude and wisdom.[27]

The choice at Whitemarsh was vindicated. The United States had a bishop at last.

CHAPTER
IX

ANOTHER AUSTIN

ALTHOUGH he might have anticipated that when the Holy See had finally decided upon a bishop for the United States, the choice would devolve upon himself, John Carroll found the eventuality oppressive. His knowledge of himself, he confided to Plowden, convinced him that he was entirely unfit for the station. "The interest you take," he wrote to his friend, "proves the warmth of your friendship, but it proves likewise how blind and partial friends are liable to be. Your condolences would have suited better the situation of my mind." [1]

In his eagerness to insure the conditions most conducive to the progress of the Church he had temporarily ignored the implications for his own future. With the choice now irrevocably fixed, the bishop-elect faced the fact with deepest misgivings. He was henceforward, it seemed, deprived of all expectation of rest or pleasure; and, knowing full well the pitfalls laid by pride, he experienced "sudden terror with respect to eternity." It was difficult enough for a common priest to save his soul, but the temptations to which a bishop was exposed would test his reserves to the utmost. In a letter to Cardinal Antonelli he admitted, "My only consolation is that not by my own will, but in spite of my expectation, this portion of labour and solicitude has fallen to me. So that if it has come about by the wish of Divine Providence, He, as I truly hope, will aid me Who has destined me for such a heavy burden." [2]

Already expressions of congratulation were pouring in, couched in phrases verging on adulation and fulsome praise. The friendships which prompted them could not help but warm Father Carroll's heart, but the words themselves filled him with a vague distaste. He put the letters aside and turned his attention to more edifying concerns. John Carroll was not the only southern gentleman receiving congratulations in 1789. George Washington, the first citizen from Mount Vernon, had been unanimously elected to the presidency under the new Constitution. The various religious groups, not wishing to seem less appreciative *en masse* than they were as individuals, tendered President Washington a variety of formal testimonials from their respective churches. Washington had already replied to the Episcopalians in August, expressing his joy at the "fraternal affection" which seemed to increase daily among the friends of religion. In October he acknowledged the address of the Quakers with the expression of his firm conviction that religious freedom was the choicest of blessings, as well as the most valued of rights. It was high time the Catholics of the country went on record with respect to their own pleasure at George Washington's accession.

The "Address of the Roman Catholics" to the President which was forwarded in December represented both the clergy and the laity. The bishop-elect signed it for his priests, while the laymen were represented by the signatures of his brother Daniel, Cousin Charles of Carrollton, Dominick Lynch of New York, and Thomas FitzSimons of Philadelphia. The courteous elegance of the address not only testified to the great admiration Father Carroll personally felt for the President, but the sentiments expressed were representative of the combined joy and satisfaction of all Catholics throughout the nation. With deep sincerity they told their civil leader:

> Our congratulations have not reached you sooner, because our scattered situation prevented our communication and the collecting of those sentiments which warmed every breath. But the delay has furnished us with the opportunity, not merely of presaging the happiness to be expected under your Administration, but of bearing testimony to that which we experience already. It is your peculiar talent, in war and peace, to afford security to those who commit their protection into your hands.

Then the address went on with customary Carroll forthrightness to treat the subject of Catholic liberty within the new Republic's salutary environment. The prospect of national prosperity under President Washington, Carroll asserted, was peculiarly pleasing to his co-religionists.

While our country preserves her freedom and independence we shall have a well-founded title to claim her justice, and the equal rights of citizenship, as the price of our blood spilt under your eyes, and of our common exertions for her defence—rights rendered more dear to us by the remembrance of former hardships.

It was the voice of "Pacificus" ringing out in his plea for full and complete justice, for equal rights under the law. "We pray for the preservation of them where they have been granted," he continued, "and expect the full extension from the justice of those States which still restrict them." [3] The respectful yet positive reminder contained in a document bearing the names of three illustrious Carrolls denoted the confidence these eighteenth-century Americans placed in the democratic processes of government, confidence placed in leaders of high caliber, reliance upon the general will to mete out justice, conviction that desirable reforms could be achieved if those who perceived the need for reform were energetic enough to point the way. The address to Washington clearly bore the imprint of John Carroll's mind and hand. It augured well for the Church in the United States that its first bishop was a man of such candor and courage.

George Washington replied to the Catholics of the United States in a letter dated March 12, 1790. He was pleased at the compliment to his administration contained in their "affectionate address." While disowning undue credit for his country's felicitous condition, the President believed the national prosperity should excite in its citizens a more fervent desire to "establish and secure the happiness of their Country, in the permanent duration of its freedom and independence." He acknowledged the claims of the Catholic citizens to equality and he expressed the hope that as mankind become more liberal they would be more prone to allow the equal protection of civil government to all alike. Washington declared:

I hope ever to see America among the foremost Nations in examples of justice and liberality. And I presume that your fellow-citizens will not forget the patriotic part which you took in the accomplishment of their Revolution, and the establishment of their government, or the important assistance which they received from a nation in which the Roman Catholic Faith is professed.[4]

Washington did not hesitate, as Carroll had done in his letter to the *Gazette,* to mention the debt American liberty owed to Catholic France. It likewise augured well for the Church in the United States that the first President was a man of such liberality and honor.

Viewed in retrospect, this exchange of formal notes seems rather characteristic of the whole tenor of republican culture in the eighteenth century. Leaders in that day were men of stature and dignity. The times demanded, on the other hand, highly stylized conventions in private correspondence and public deportment. If the elaborate and formal exchanges lacked a certain spontaneity and individuality, they were at least free from the bald and ill-considered manifestations of a later era. Indeed, the very rigidity of the *mores* and general usages served the salutary purpose of shaping the more vulgar citizen to a gentler mold. It is not too much to say that an odor of something quite like nobility still clings to the papers of the Carrolls, the Washingtons, and the Jeffersons of that day. They were men nurtured on the grander concepts of political philosophy, men schooled in the politely precise expression of their ideas and ideals, and they had grown to maturity anticipating the responsibilities of adult leadership in a complex and rapidly changing world. They were at variance, it is true, in many respects: in regard to religious practice, foreign policy, economic interest, and a dozen minor matters as well. But they were all stamped with the same die, their undeviating belief in the dignity of man.

By April of 1790 Father Carroll received from Rome the official notifications which confirmed the earlier news from friends regarding his appointment. The time had come when he would have to reach a decision in regard to the place of his consecration. There were several possibilities. Havana was out of the question, since the see was without a bishop at the time. Cardinal Antonelli leaned toward Quebec, himself. Ireland, in the person of Archbishop Troy of Dublin, extended an invitation in January, 1790. But it was England which beckoned with irresistible appeal for Carroll. He had a promise made to Thomas Weld to keep.

The Weld family had been important in the history of the Catholic Church in England for centuries. Humphrey Weld had acquired Lulworth Castle in Dorset in 1641, and it had remained the ancestral home since that time. Thomas Weld, the sixth possessor of Lulworth Castle, was a personal friend of George III who occasionally stayed at the castle. When the first relaxation of the penal laws had come in 1780 Weld began to toy with the idea of building a proper church on his estate. Rumor had it that the king, hesitating to give formal sanction, had suggested that the building should appear to be a family mausoleum. In any case, on Candlemas Day, 1786, the foundation stone of the chapel was laid for the circular building which would be called St. Mary's. It was to this chapel, the first Catholic church built in England since the Reformation, that Father Carroll had been invited to come for his consecration. He diplomatically explained his acceptance to Archbishop Troy saying:

> When the subject of an American Bishopric was first started, I received so pressing an invitation from a most respectable Catholic gentleman in England, that I unwarily promised to be consecrated in his chapel, if the appointment should fall to my lot. Had it been otherwise I should have hesitated between Ireland, the land of my forefathers, and Canada. Though on the whole, I flatter myself that my going to England may be attended with some advantages to the cause of religion.[6]

And all of this was true. When Father Thorpe discussed Carroll's choice with Cardinal Antonelli in Rome he commented approvingly that it would be easier for his friend to provide for his Baltimore church by purchases made in England, or by gifts prompted by friendships there. Going to England would also give Carroll a chance to solicit volunteers so badly needed on the American missions. But going to Lulworth had personal enticements as well. The prospect of seeing Charles Plowden, who was now chaplain at Lulworth Castle, was an undeniable inducement. Carroll admitted to Plowden, "My inclination certainly leads me to accept of an offer not only so flattering, but which will afford me an opportunity of seeing some of those friends whom I shall ever honor and love." [7]

Before sailing for Europe the bishop-elect set his affairs in order. Some of his fellow ex-Jesuits had expressed their qualms that the presence of a bishop in the United States might lead to intervention in their property management. The brief *Ex hoc apostolicae* from Rome had empowered Carroll "to administer ecclesiastical incomes," and Father John Ashton, the procurator of the ex-Jesuit properties since 1784, evinced alarm. Carroll scotched these fears. On May 26, 1790, he wrote out a formal declaration for his uneasy colleagues to the effect that he did not consider himself in any way empowered to interfere in the former Jesuit estates. By July he was ready to leave for his second voyage to Europe.

It was forty-two years since that first trip to St. Omer with his cousin Charles, and there was little except the chain of memory to link that untried lad impatiently pacing the Annapolis wharf with the sober, half-reluctant traveler of 1790. That staid matron Annapolis was fast losing out to the lusty wench from Fells Point. Baltimore which in 1748 had scarcely two dozen houses scattered on her three streets now, in 1790, had 13,503 people crowding the busy thoroughfares which pushed up from Dugan's and McElderry's wharves, and pressed upon the wooded hill where John Carroll would soon consecrate the ground for his cathedral.[8] The summit from which anxious citizens had watched for British ships during the Revolution would lose its crown of sycamores and oaks, and raise its cross and dome to the skies above America's first see city. The United States was ready for bishops, and John Carroll had as his fellow-passenger in 1790 the bishop-elect of the Protestant Episcopal Church of Virginia, Dr. James Madison.

Carroll arrived in London on July 22, 1790, to find his friends there concerned because La Poterie's malicious attack on him in the *Resurrection of Laurent Ricci* had reached Rome that summer. Even on the eve of his consecration, it appeared, Father Carroll was not to be permitted to forget his trials at home. It had not occurred to him to bring along any documents relating to La Poterie's case, but they were unnecessary, as it turned out. Cardinal Antonelli wrote reassuringly that the Congregation of Propaganda Fide considered the Boston priest's charges without any foundation. Rome suggested tactfully that the American bishop might avoid these charges of prejudice in favor of ex-Jesuits by the simple expedient of securing new priests of other affiliation. France, Antonelli hinted, might be a source of priests for the United States.[9]

The chilling wisp of fog from the La Poterie scandal was soon dispelled in the warm sun of approbation and welcome from Carroll's friends. John Brewer, a former college friend, wrote from Shepton Mallet:

> I heard at Wardour that you were daily expected at Lulworth. It gave me pain to find that your appointment was to you an occasion of uneasiness and trouble. I will be bold to say you are the only one, either in Europe or America, who does not rejoice at it. The United States of America, I am sure, have every reason to return thanks to God for a disposi-

tion of his Providence, in their regard so peculiarly gracious. A virtuous prelate, in every respect equal to the great charge he is called to, and capable of supporting with zeal and dignity the interests of his flock, of religion, and of God, must be a signal blessing of every nation."[10]

Lord and Lady Arundell, too, were ready to rejoice with their old friend, and sent their family chaplain to participate in the ceremonies at Lulworth. Thomes Weld had already written to Bishop Charles Walmesley, O.S.B., asking him to consecrate the American candidate. "If this meets with your lordship's approbation," Weld suggested, "the less it is spoken of the better; the more private it can be done, the better. I suppose your lordship has seen Mr. Throckmorton's publication on the election of bishops."[11]

Charles Walmesley, Bishop of Rama, had been Vicar Apostolic of the Western District of England since 1764. He was the leader of one faction among the English bishops in a heated controversy which had developed the year before Carroll's arrival over an oath of allegiance which implied repudiation of the Pope's temporal power. Opposed to the Walmesley faction were the followers of the Northern Vicar Apostolic, Matthew Gibson. The bishops had scarcely reached an agreement to unanimously condemn the oath on October 19, 1789, when the death of James Talbot left London without a bishop, and the choice of his successor re-opened the controversy. Sir John Throckmorton in a pamphlet on the subject had offered as an eccentric solution that the people elect their own bishops without Roman authorization. A bitter war of pamphlets followed and thus upon his arrival Carroll discovered that the United States was not the only place where the topic of Catholic bishops was discussed in less than muted tones.[12] As a matter of fact, his own country seemed in advance of England in this matter, and more than once he was pleased to note the admiration that his nation's liberality aroused in English observers. "We all seem run mad," Brewer commented. "In America, I hope, it is not so."[13] At Lulworth Carroll's friends hoped none of the English acrimony would tinge the consecration of the first bishop of Baltimore. And it did not.

Sunday, August 15, 1790, found Lulworth Chapel full to overflowing. It was the feast of the Assumption of the Blessed Virgin, a fitting day for the consecration of the first bishop of the nation whose patron she was to be. The altar was a blaze of wax tapers and golden ornaments. The munificence of Thomas Weld had "omitted no circumstance which could possibly add dignity to so venerable a ceremony." The consecration took place during a solemn high Mass at which the bishop and bishop-elect were each attended by their respective priests and acolytes in solemn array. Charles Plowden and James Parter assisted Walmesley, and young Thomas Weld, the seventeen-year-old scion of Lulworth who was to be a cardinal in later life, held the missal over Carroll's shoulders during the ceremony. No one there that August morning would ever forget the richness of the vestments, the majesty of the choir's intonation, or the humble dignity of the priest who had come so far to be thus honored among his friends.

To the simpler hearts, touched by the beauty of the scene, Bishop Carroll's consecration was principally a cause for personal rejoicing in their friend's joy. To those like Lady Arundell it was a vindication of the hopes and expectations of many years. But to others the event held deeper implications. It symbolized a new era for the Church in the land across the sea, a land where Catholics enjoyed equal participation in human rights with their neighbors of every other denomination. As Charles Plowden, who preached on that memorable occasion, expressed it, "The very term toleration is exploded, because it imports a power in one predominant sect to indulge that religious liberty to others which all claim as an inherent right." In the United States, it was to be hoped, toleration was dethroned for freedom. Who could predict what this environment would mean to the universal Church? In his brief sermon Father Plowden elaborated upon this theme. Speaking of the American Revolution he commented:

> Although this great event may appear to us to have been the work, the sport, of human passion, yet the earliest and most precious fruit of it has been the extension of the kingdom of Christ, the propagation of the Catholic religion, which heretofore fettered by restraining laws, is now enlarged from bondage and is left at liberty to exert the full energy of divine truth.

As he listened John Carroll felt once more the old excitement course through his veins. His nation was, indeed, a land of promise, her greatest blessing, religious liberty. A faulty instrument he might be, but the exactions which his office required of him found him compliant. Yes, even proud of the opportunity thrust upon him.

Gone were the misgivings of the voyage over. He sat erect and waiting while Charles' prophetic sentences rolled over his head.

> Glorious is this day, my brethren, for the Church of God
> which sees new nations crowding her bosom. Glorious for
> the prelate-elect who goes forth to conquer these nations for
> Jesus Christ, not by the efforts of human power, but in the
> might of those weapons which have ever triumphed in this
> divine warfare.

He, John Carroll, would be the instrument. What was Charles saying? "Powerful in piety, powerful in zeal." Yes, these must be his
weapons. Piety and zeal. He lowered his eyes hastily to veil the
surging emotion which glazed them at Plowden's exhortation to the
congregation. "You will earnestly solicit," the preacher commanded,
"the descent of the Holy Ghost on the bishop-elect, that like another
Austin he may worthily fulfill the extent of his apostleship to which
he is called." [14]

Another Austin. It was challenge enough for any man. John
Carroll awaited the seven-fold grace that would be his armor.

After his consecration Bishop Carroll remained for a few weeks
visiting his friends at Lulworth and Wardour Castles. He was more
than ever impressed with the virtue which prevailed at these two
aristocratic households, and their pressing invitations to prolong
his stay tempted him strongly. But even stronger was his eagerness
to return to his bishopric in America. He remained in England only
long enough to accomplish what he could for the Church in the
United States. He declined the hearty invitation to cross the Channel
to Liège for a visit with his old friends there, but, using London
as his headquarters during the month of September, Bishop Carroll
accomplished much by letter and interview. He strongly urged the
case of his needy diocese to propertied English Catholics, and interested many benefactors in his dearest project, a school at George
Town. Men like Brewer assured Carroll that he would certainly
depend on all they could do for his academy, and many legacies
were eventually diverted to the American school's interests.

All in all, it was a stimulating sojourn, that month in London.
His opinion was frequently sought on the controversial issues of the
day, the opposition to Bishop John Douglass' appointment, the
notorious oath. But he refused to commit himself for the most part.
"When I see men of abilities and virtue engaged on both sides," he
explained to Lord Arundell, "I dare not venture to direct in a

matter of so much consequence without studying the question much more than I have had time to do." [15] It was pleasant, however, to be deferred to and consulted. Carroll admitted to Archbishop Troy that if he had seen any real prospects of bringing harmony on the question of the oath he probably would have formed a very decided opinion. As it was there were enough more relevant matters requiring his attention.[16]

There was the letter to the Holy Father, Pius VI, to be written. The new American bishop wanted to assure Rome of his gratitude for the honor thus bestowed, and to reaffirm his loyalty to the Holy See. Two months earlier, on his arrival in Europe, Carroll had asked Cardinal Antonelli to present his respects to the Pope; but, now in September, he wished to make his personal obeisance.

There was also the matter of a pamphlet commemorating Carroll's consecration. Plowden wrote from Lulworth that a printer named Coghlen wanted to publish a short account of the August rites. "Mr. Weld wished that what was done here on August 15 may not appear in print unless you should desire it," Charles said. Carroll saw little harm in giving his assent to a publication which would consist chiefly of his friend's sermon, and so, before the year was out, there appeared *A Short Account of the Establishment of the New See of Baltimore, Maryland, and of the Consecrating of the Right Rev. Mr. Carroll.* The most interesting events were those which related directly to Bishop Carroll's hopes for the Church in the United States.

From his temporary residence in King Street that fall Carroll relayed to Plowden the contents of two letters he had recently received from Paris, letters from the nuncio, Archbishop Antonio Dugnani, and Father Jacques André Emery, the Superior-General of the Society of St. Sulpice. "They both solicit my passage to Paris to confer with some gentlemen of the Seminary who wish to employ, in the rearing of young clergymen, that experience which is made useless by the revolution in their own country," he told Plowden. "They offer to bestow their services gratis." [17] The newly consecrated bishop, preoccupied as he was with other matters, was reluctant to cross the Channel. As he remarked to Charles, "We are certainly not ripe for a seminary. It would take some years before we have scholars far enough advanced to profit by this generous offer." To the papal nuncio at Paris he explained, "If our seminary were already opened or even if we had a youth sufficiently instructed to begin the life of studies and the exercise of the ecclesiastical life, I should regard the offer . . . as one of the greatest evidences of Providence toward my immense diocese."

Carroll was struck by another possibility, however. Until the time were ripe for a seminary, he shrewdly saw that some other use might be made of zealous French priests. When he replied to Father Emery he said as much. On the banks of the Wabash River in the United States there lived the remnants of what had once been a thriving congregation belonging to the Diocese of Quebec. "Up to now," the Bishop of Baltimore suggested, "I have been very unfortunate in the priests whom I have destined for those places. Would the gentlemen, of whose desires you have informed me, be willing to engage themselves in those missions?"

It seemed desirable to the French negotiators to talk to Carroll in person, and since the American would not cross the Channel one of the Sulpicians must go to London. Their choice for an emissary fell upon Charles François Nagot, then the vice-president of their major seminary. Nagot went armed with a list of questions formulated by Emery, and the discussion quickly took on a very practical tone. It became apparent that the French society had carefully considered the project of a seminary from every angle, and by the time Carroll had answered a few of the precise questions posed by Nagot he found himself considering the project as more immediately interesting than he had at first imagined.

The bishop discovered that the obstacles which seemed to bar the way for Nagot might be easily overcome. To the Sulpician's questions about living conditions and American customs he gave as accurate replies as he could. A house and grounds for fifty or more young men would cost, he believed, between 25,000 and 30,000 *livres*. The best location for a seminary, of course, would be near the bishop's church. He estimated that a year and a half at least would be needed to build a large house, but the Sulpicians could probably rent a house while waiting for its completion. No, the consent of the Congress was not needed for their entry into the United States, but they might want to become naturalized citizens under the provisions of the new Naturalization Act. Yes, they could publicly wear the clerical habit. As the discussion continued it seemed to Carroll as if there were no really insuperable obstacles. The two principal ones, money and seminarians, were overcome by Father Emery's offer to raise a sizeable sum to finance the undertaking, and the suggestion that four or five seminarians in France might go over to finish their training in the new school. Carroll found himself animatedly describing the healthy Baltimore climate and suggesting that he could be on the lookout for "a proper purchase."

The result of the September conference in London was that both the bishop and Father Nagot began to consider that the project could begin in the near future. Carroll told one of his friends enthusiastically:

> We have settled that two or three gentlemen selected by Father Emery shall come to Baltimore next spring. They are furnished with the means of purchasing ground for building, and, I hope, of endowing a seminary. . . . I believe they will bring three or four seminarians with them who are either English or know it. They will be amply provided with books, apparatus for a church, and professors of philosophy.

As he wrote it all down, in his carefully rounded letters, the shrewd Marylander became more certain of the excellence of his bargain. He concluded energetically, "I propose fixing them near my own home, the cathedral of Baltimore, that they may be, as it were, the clergy of the church and contribute to the dignity of divine worship. This is a great and auspicious event for our diocese." To Cardinal Antonelli he announced, "I have decided to establish the episcopal seminary of Baltimore." Nagot's mission had succeeded. To Lord Arundell Carroll confessed, "While I can not but thank Divine Providence for opening on us such a prospect, I feel great sorrow in the reflection that we owe such a benefit to the distressed state of religion in France." There was no denying, however, that Carroll's spirits rose as he contemplated this solution to the plaguing problem of priests.

Another improvement was imminent in this respect. After Cardinal Antonelli was made aware of the troubles caused by unworthy European priests whose false claims deceived Carroll, he advised the American prelate to require of these men recommendations from their bishops. Carroll was pleased to report the cardinal's advice to Archbishop Troy of Dublin, and in a letter written to Ireland just before his departure for home Carroll asked Troy to vouch for an Irish Capuchin who was a "postulant" for the American mission.[18] Perhaps this type of precautionary measure would put an end to the Nugents and La Poteries in his diocese. By the end of September Carroll was eager to be off, and with rising elation he watched his baggage being stowed on board the ship at London.

But the weather seemed determined to test the fortitude of the new bishop. For several days "contrary winds" kept the vessel anchored in the Thames, and when at last Carroll embarked at Gravesend for America it began to storm in earnest. Strickland reported later from London, "After you left us the weather became extremely tempestuous and at intervals ever since we have had some of the most tremendous storms ever remembered in this country." [19] At sea, Bishop Carroll and the returning Protestant Bishop Madison wondered if they would ever see their newly confirmed domains again. It was not until December 7 that Carroll was once more in Baltimore.

The *Maryland Journal and Baltimore Advertiser* notified its readers on December 10, 1790:

> On Tuesday last the ship Sampson, Capt. Thos. Moore, arrived from London. In this vessel came as a passenger the Rt. Rev. Dr. John Carroll, recently consecrated Bishop of the Catholic Church in the United States. On the landing of this learned and worthy prelate he was respectfully waited on by a number of his fellow citizens of various denominations who conducted him to his residence.

To the enthusiastic crowd of clergy and laymen, Catholics and non-Catholics, who were at the wharf when the long over-due vessel put in, this was their old friend and countryman, John Carroll of Rock Creek and Baltimore. But he was more. This stocky, ruddy man with the narrow, aristocratic face carried on his middle-aged shoulders the mantle of greatness. He was *Joannes, Episcopus Baltimorensis,* the first Catholic bishop of the United States, and they were his people, many of them the subjects of his see city. Their faces showed their curiosity and pride, and over all, their respect and veneration for the office he bore. It was quite proper that they should escort their bishop to his home, the unimposing small rectory attached to St. Peter's Church where he was to spend the remaining twenty-five years of his life.

That was on Tuesday. The following Sunday Bishop John Carroll took official possession of his pro-cathedral in traditional liturgical style. Five priests and the trustees of St. Peter's met him at the door of the church and led him in procession to the altar, where he knelt while the magnificent strains of the *Te Deum* filled the little edifice. As the last notes lingered on the stuffy air the bishop was conducted to the first episcopal throne ever erected in

Baltimore. The church was crowded with Catholics and non-Catholics alike, most of whom had never seen a bishop of any kind before. The pontifical Mass was begun. Clouds of incense rose, and the candle-light flickered on the gleaming vestments.

Turning to his audience, the Bishop of Baltimore addressed his first sermon to his diocese.

He spoke at first of the duties of bishops in general, of his obligations as their head, of his responsibility "to exhort, to conjure, to reprove, to enter into all your sentiments; to feel all your infirmities; to be all things to all, that I may gain all to Christ." These were his tasks, extensive, pressing and indispensable. But these were the duties of all his brothers in the episcopacy. As first bishop of the United States he, John Carroll, had other duties even more burdensome, taking office as he did in a region where everything had to be "raised, as it were, from its foundations." These duties included the establishment of ecclesiastical discipline where discipline was unknown, providing for the religious education of Catholic youth—"that precious portion of pastoral solicitude"—the establishment of seminaries for the training of priests, assisting the faithful to preserve their faith untainted amid the contagion of error in which they lived, and preserving in Catholics a warm charity and forbearance toward every other denomination of Christians while at the same time preserving them from that fatal indifference which views all religions as equally acceptable to God and salutary to men.

The enormity of his task was spread before them, and the people sat sober and impressed. Then the bishop cast himself upon their mercy. He said simply:

> In God alone can I find any consolation. He knows by what steps I have been conducted to this important station, and how much I have always dreaded it. He will not abandon me unless I first draw down His malediction by my unfaithfulness to my charge. Pray, dear brethren, pray incessantly that I may not incur so dreadful a punishment.[20]

Those who heard John Carroll preach that Sunday morning knew that the Church in the United States had been blessed with a great and good man. History would prove how great a bishop.

CHAPTER
X

JOHN, BISHOP OF BALTIMORE

UP IN New York City the federal Congress in December of 1790 was listening attentively to Alexander Hamilton who had come over from his house in Wall Street to read his second report on the nation's finances. Already the tariff of 1789 had consolidated some of the Secretary of the Treasury's schemes for supplying an income for the new government. The boom in American shipping during the past year was in no small part due to his Tonnage Act, and the gentlemen at Federal Hall were in a mood to listen to Mr. Hamilton's newest proposal, a Bank of the United States.

A month later, on January 22, 1791, Daniel Carroll, the bishop's brother, received President Washington's appointment to serve on the commission "to survey the District of Territory . . . for the permanent seat of government of the United States." A stickler for procedure, Dan refused to serve until his term of office as representative expired on March 4; but he accepted the new commission after that date, and became the most zealous and active of the three men delegated to deal with the contentious Major Pierre l'Enfant. President Washington wrote to Daniel Carroll on March 11 that he was looking forward to a "full meeting with the commissioners" by the end of the month, and asked him to notify former Governors Thomas Johnson of Maryland and David Stuart of Virginia. Daniel was in for a great deal of bickering with l'Enfant over his extravagant plans for the federal city. Lands belonging to Carroll's relatives, his brother-in-law, Notley Young, and Daniel Carroll of Duddington were involved, and the commissioner's patience was sorely tried on more than one occasion.

John and Daniel Carroll's sister Mary had married Notley Young and had gone to live in a mansion which now sat, it seemed, squarely in the middle of the area where the Frenchman proposed to open a street. Daniel Carroll of Duddington, Dan's father-in-law, was unfortunate enough to own the manor on the spot where l'Enfant intended to erect five grand fountains with "constant spouts of water" running all day. In the older Carroll's absence the engineer had presumed to have the house demolished, and the bishop's brother found himself in the unenviable position of trying to bring harmony between his wrathful relatives and the ambitious l'Enfant. The laying of a cornerstone of the Federal City at Jones' Point on March 15 was only the beginning of four years filled with difficulties for Daniel Carroll.[1]

Over in Baltimore John Carroll was having his own problems of authority and jurisdiction. It is one of the ironies of history that scarcely had one bishop been finally agreed upon for the United States when two more were proposed for areas which involved Bishop Carroll's jurisdiction. Although neither the Gallipolis colony nor the Oneida Indians ever secured separate bishops, their negotiations with Rome in this regard during Carroll's first months in office did not contribute to the Bishop of Baltimore's peace of mind.

The Gallipolis colony was one of the tragic experiments engendered by the land-fever of the 1780's. The speculators in the future of the Northwest Territory known as the Scioto Company were the less successful counterpart of the more famous Ohio Company for which the Reverend Manasseh Cutler of Ipswich, Massachusetts, had lobbied so successfully. The Ohio Company was primarily aimed at securing land benefits for the Massachusetts veterans of the Revolution, and when Cutler agreed to let in on the deal a group of Congressmen and their friends, the Congress voted to sell a million and a half acres of land to the Ohio Company. At the same time the Scioto Company was given an option on the purchase of an additional adjacent three and a half million acres, and Congress then chartered both companies while Cutler induced the Scioto Associates to advance several thousands of dollars for the Ohio Company's dealings.

Colonel William Duer, the head of the Scioto Company, sent Joel Barlow to France to sell land, and many French optimists were lured by the enticing picture presented of the blissful Utopia that would be theirs along the banks of the Scioto. A French *Compagnie du Scioto* bought up three of the three and a half million acres of the American company but by 1790, the year of Carroll's consecration, had sold out their rights to a third "Company of Twenty-four." It is not surprising that these transfers led to many defective land titles which contributed to the eventual failure of the French colonizing efforts. Nevertheless, in the spring of 1790 a group of better-class French immigrants were preparing to leave for the United States. The promoters of the colony approached the papal nuncio in Paris with a request for a French bishop to accompany the emigrants. The nuncio pointed out that the United States had just been given a bishop in the person of John Carroll, but the colonists persisted. Under the leadership of a Benedictine priest, Dom Pierre Joseph Didier, they argued that their projected settlement would be too far from Baltimore for practical purposes, and besides French people preferred to have their own bishop whenever possible.

The nuncio, thus prevailed upon, wrote to Cardinal Antonelli on March 22, 1790, explaining the nature of the Scioto project and informing him of the colonists' desire to have Didier serve as their bishop in the American wilderness. The nuncio said quite frankly that the Benedictine priest was unknown to him, but that he would inquire further about him. In keeping with this assurance, Dugnani requested Didier to give him more information about the Gallipolis project. When the nuncio learned at the end of March that several priests were on the verge of setting out for Ohio with Didier as their spiritual head he immediately informed Rome. The next month the Holy See made known its decision. Didier could go to the United States as vicar-general for a limited space of seven years, but only on the specific condition that his jurisdiction did not conflict with that of Bishop Carroll.

It was obvious that although Rome had no clear concept of the geographical picture beyond the Appalachian Mountains, Antonelli had no intention of derogating from Carroll's authority. The Roman brief definitely made Didier's faculties hinge upon Baltimore's confirmation, and Cardinal Antonelli immediately informed the American bishop of the progress of the Gallipolis colony. In May he notified Carroll of the colonists' departure from France, and his August letter inquired whether they had yet reached the United States. While Carroll was in London, following his consecration at Lulworth Castle, he told Antonelli that one group of colonists had arrived after his own departure, but that he had heard nothing from Father Didier.[2]

There was no difficulty when the Benedictine finally arrived. Once Didier learned that the Gallipolis settlement was within Bishop Carroll's jurisdiction, he went to Baltimore in person to obtain the necessary consent to use his faculties. Father Didier re-

mained with his colonists until 1792, when it became evident that
the project was doomed to failure. The colonists dwindled to eighty
by 1796, and by 1805 there were less than two dozen. Didier spent
his last days in St. Louis, puttering over his fragrant herbs in the
little churchyard, until his death in 1799. Although the colony was
so short-lived it brought to the middle west a superior type of
French Catholic who contributed many an honorable figure to the
Detroit Territory.[3] The failure of the Gallipolis venture was soon
classed as only another incident in the long list of Utopian projects
which enliven the history of the frontier; but it removed the earliest,
if the most ephemeral, threat to John Carroll's episcopal authority.

The second situation involving a possible rival to Carroll's position developed at the same time, and centered around the Indians
of New York State. The Oneida Indians of the central Mohawk
Valley represented three clans who had proved friendly to the early
Jesuit missionaries. They had gained a reputation as the most
civilized of the Iroquois Nations. After the American Revolution a
French agent, Peter Pênet, gained considerable influence among the
Oneidas, and it was he who persuaded them to ask for a French
priest in 1787. The appeal was made to the Count de Moustier,
then the French minister in New York, and a Father Perrot re-
turned with Pênet to minister to the Indians living around Oneida
Castle. Although very little is known about the French priest's stay
among the Oneidas, on April 25, 1789, the three clans wrote to
Rome begging for a bishop for the Six Nations of the Iroquois.
The petition went, as in the case of the Gallipolis request, through
the papal nuncio at Paris who, in turn, had received it from the
Indians' agent, Jean de la Mahotière. La Mahotière proceeded
meanwhile to organize a French company of four to handle the
financial matters attending the erection of a chapel for the Indians.
The agent wrote to the Holy See that he had six Capuchins ready
to go to the New York mission.

As in the case of Father Didier's designs, the Paris nuncio was
reluctant to commit himself to forwarding a plan so nebulous, and
Dugnani asked La Mahotière to offer fuller explanations. The
Indian agent seemed to be a man of character, and yet the nuncio
was not certain that his project was feasible. When Dugnani forwarded the Indian petition to Rome, therefore, he voiced his own
uncertainty and then merely stated the agent's request for a bishop
and an Indian see.

Cardinal Antonelli again went to the heart of the matter. Was

this Indian territory within the jurisdiction of the Bishop of Baltimore, or perhaps, that of Quebec? If the Indians lived in neither
of these dioceses he would be only too happy to consider the sup-
plication of the Oneidas. When it was made clear that Baltimore's
boundaries contained the Mohawk Valley, Propaganda informed
La Mahotière that all his applications for spiritual directors would
have to be made to Carroll, and by 1792 Bishop Carroll had despatched a priest to minister to the tribes and this second episcopal
scheme came to nothing.[4]

It was pleasant to feel the reassuring support of Rome behind
his episcopal authority, and Bishop Carroll was only mildly concerned with these agitations on the periphery of his domain. He
was more immediately interested in his plan to hold a synod of his
clergy. There were half a dozen matters crying for attention not the
least of which were the providing a successor for himself, the necessity for more uniformity in the administration of the sacraments,
and the ever-delicate question of clerical discipline. On October
28, 1791, he sent to all his priests official notices that a church synod
would be held in November of that year. He said something of his
plans when he wrote to Plowden that fall. "We shall discuss the
mode of preserving the succession to the episcopacy of the United
States. Instead of a coadjutor, I am much inclined to solicit the
division of my diocese and the creation of another bishopric," he
explained.[5]

And then he went on to another subject that troubled him. He
admitted to his friend that the distance of his see from Rome was
fraught with danger. He had begun to perceive that having no near
connections with an intermediary European metropolitan had its
disadvantages. "Our clergy will soon be neither Europeans nor
have European connections," he predicted. "There will be danger
of a propensity toward a schismatical separation from the center of
unity." As eager as he had been to keep the Church in the United
States free from the political interpositions of Europe, Carroll
meant to remain alert to any incipient tendencies to drift from the
spiritual guidance of the center of Christendom. He was perspi-
cacious enough to foresee the day when the clergy would be American in every sense of the word. It was characteristic of him that
while his priests were still all European in either birth or training
he was anticipating the problems of the future. Not that he felt
any dismay. As he told Plowden, "The Founder of the Church sees
all these things and can provide the remedy. After doing what we

can, we must commit the rest to His Providence."

Doing what he could meant to Carroll giving immediate attention to the present difficulties, and the opening session of the historic first national synod in 1791 found the Bishop of Baltimore not a little tense with anticipation and withal quite determined. The first session which began on the morning of November 7 brought to Baltimore twenty priests. After assembling at the bishop's house they marched to the pro-cathedral with their bishop in his mitre and cope, and carrying his episcopal staff. The first session was little more than an organizational meeting. Carroll spoke solemnly on the purposes of the synod, and set before his priests his own hopes for its success. Two promoters for the synod were named, and Father Francis Beeston was delegated to act as secretary for the rest of the sessions.

The real business of the synod began with the second session. At this time the first subject to come under discussion was the adoption of rules for the administration of baptism and confirmation. Because of the shortage of priests and the scattered location of so many Catholic families there was a great deal of uncertainty about these sacraments. Many people were not certain of having received them at all, while others had been baptized privately or by non-Catholic ministers. Rules, therefore, had to be made for conditional baptism, and the clergy were admonished in regard to the keeping of baptismal registers.

On November 8, the second day of the synod, discussions centered around the sacrament of the Holy Eucharist. Stress was laid on the care of the altar and the support of the house of God. It was agreed that in every parish two or three men of virtue might be chosen to act with the pastor as trustees for the parish church. Nothing was said directly of the difficulties which previous trustees had caused in New York and Philadelphia, but the stipulation that the pastor could choose the trustees was aimed at lessening the evils of trusteeism. The support of the church and the pastor was to come from the collections taken up on Sundays or holy days of obligation. One-third of these collections, however, were always to be reserved for the poor of the parish. The third session concluded with the adoption of rules regarding the admission of children to their first Holy Communion. Children were to receive full instructions in Christian doctrine, make a general confession of their lives up to that time, and were to have reached the use of reason before being admitted as communicants.

The fourth session of the synod which opened on November 9 was chiefly concerned with the sacraments of penance and matrimony. Having so recently been troubled by recalcitrant priests, Carroll wanted it clearly understood that confessions could only be heard by priests who had secured the bishop's consent to the exercise of this faculty. The faithful must be warned that confessions made to suspended or unapproved priests were invalid. Priests were also warned that they would suffer suspension if they left their congregations without the bishop's sanction. Although the synod by no means eliminated errant and erring priests in the Diocese of Baltimore, the decrees did remove future justification for the insubordinate pastor or assistant. Laws do not abolish wrongdoing; but they may define crime and provide for its punishment. After 1791 it would be easier to detect and deal with violations by malefactors.

The sacrament of marriage required a lengthy consideration, and the synod adopted rather stringent rules on this subject. The clergy present were well aware of the grave dangers attending the Church's position in a non-Catholic environment. Mixed marriages were obviously unavoidable; but the Church must take every precaution to prevent a loss of faith through these marriages. Slowly and carefully the fourth session enunciated the rules which should regulate mixed marriages. Catholics should be warned of the dangers inherent in such unions. Pastors must try to lessen the danger of "falling away." The non-Catholic party to the marriage should be required to promise that no obstacle to the practice of the faith, or the rearing of the children of the union in the faith, should be erected. Priests must take care not to drive the eager couple into a marriage by a non-Catholic minister. Rather, they should perform the ceremony themselves if they could be certain no true impediment to the union existed. The Catholic party who contracted such a marriage was to be made aware that in so doing he forfeited the nuptial blessing prescribed by the Roman ritual.[6] The care with which this first synod delineated the principles applying to mixed marriages set an important precedent for future generations of clergy in the United States, where the problem of mixed marriage remains a very present one today.

The subject of Christian marriage was so important in Carroll's opinion that he had been considering for some time issuing a pastoral letter on that sacrament. A few days after the adjourning of the synod he therefore sent to his priests a circular in which he deplored the sacrilege and profanation of improper marriage. The bishop commanded:

> You are desired to make known to all that whoever have lately, or hereafter shall be guilty of applying to be married by any other than the lawful pastors of our Church, cannot be admitted to reconciliation and the Sacraments till they shall agree to make public acknowledgment of their disobedience before the assembled congregation, and beg pardon for the scandal they have given.[7]

The words may have rung harshly in the ears of the congregations to whom the admonition was relayed, but John Carroll was not over-estimating the temptations which were anticipated. He himself was to face resistance within the ranks of his own family in the not too distant future.

When Charlie Carroll of the prodigious appetite grew to maturity he became engaged to Harriet Chew of Philadelphia. Harriet's sister, Peggy, was already married to John Eager Howard and there was little opposition to Charles' alliance with such good connections. But the Chews were Episcopalians and Harriet's religion precipitated a crisis on the eve of the wedding. Charles Carroll, the Signer, quite naturally expected that his son would be married by their eminent relative, the Bishop of Baltimore. John Carroll went to Philadelphia in July, 1800, with the young man's sisters, Polly Carroll Caton and Kitty Carroll who would marry Colonel Robert Goodloe Harper before another year elapsed. But the Catholic prelate was surprised to discover upon his arrival that the bride's family were now insisting that the marriage of Harriet and Charles should be performed by Bishop William White according to the ritual of the Protestant Episcopal Church.

Bishop Carroll wrote at once to his cousin at Carrollton, describing his predicament. He said:

> On my arrival I found arrangements made for the marriage, first by myself in the morning, and afterwards in the evening and in a more ceremonious style by Bishop White. I resolved immediately not to enter into this compromise because it would be a most hurtful precedent hereafter, especially when given by myself.

Polly and Kitty were determined not to be present if the marriage were performed by anyone but a Catholic priest, the bishop told their father. The girls thought it would be disrespectful not only to John Carroll but to their absent father as well. "Neither I nor any Catholic clergyman can perform the ceremony under the present conditions," he concluded.[8]

The upshot of the whole contest was that young Charles capitulated to his family's pressure, unable to resist the combined disapproval of his sisters and his episcopal relative, and the prospect of offending his father. The harassed bridegroom decided in favor of his own faith and Bishop Carroll presided at the ceremony in old St. Joseph's Church in one of the season's most talked-of marriages. Kitty Carroll's marriage to Colonel Harper at Annapolis the following May was serenity itself by comparison.[9]

Bishop Carroll could not foresee these precise events in 1791 but he was correct in anticipating the trials the clergy would face in their attempts to insure the sanctity of marriage. Indeed, the near future would bring a deluge of letters from the frontier clergy deploring the difficulties which hasty weddings left in their wake. "Désir de femme est un feu que dévore," Father Stephen Theodore Badin wrote from Kentucky as he urged his bishop to speed a decision in regard to one couple's matrimonial plight. After the Sulpicians settled in Baltimore Carroll was frequently relieved to be able to consult Messieurs Jean Tessier and Antoine Garnier on the canon law relating to the rehabilitation of these frantic frontier unions.

To return to the synod of 1791, however, there were still other decisions to be reached before Father John Ashton rose to preach the closing sermon. Carroll wanted an opinion from the assembled clergy on the urgent question of a successor to the see in the event of his death. In view of the distance from the Papal States to the United States, and the uncertainty of channels of communication, the appointment of a coadjutor seemed desirable to some. There was an alternative, of course, the one Carroll had already expressed a preference for in his letter to Plowden. The diocese could be divided with a second bishopric at Philadelphia or New York. As it turned out, Rome preferred the first solution. Cardinal Antonelli told Carroll that the Holy See felt that in the present state of affairs one authority was definitely to be preferred. It would be much easier to control the clergy and to maintain a uniform discipline. Two bishops of equal dignity and jurisdiction might produce dissension and distrust. The Holy See was willing, however, to allow the American clergy to select their own coadjutor and would not object if his residence were to be fixed in some other city than

Baltimore. That was a matter for Bishop Carroll to decide. It appeared that Rome had a rather accurate estimate of Carroll's abilities, and did not expect to find them equalled in his present colleagues. They had no intention of weakening his position.

The first national synod came to an end with a sermon by Father John Ashton who enjoined his brothers in Christ with the words of St. Paul to Timothy, to be vigilant, sober, and industrious. He warned them against idleness and worldliness, and exhorted them to fulfill their three-fold obligations to feed, to lead, and to cure their flocks. He finished with a glowing tribute to their bishop:

> We are happy in having a pastor whose whole solicitude is to preserve the flock which Christ has intrusted to him, and whose example will be a guide to each one of us. Let us therefore benefit ourselves from so great a blessing, that by imitating his virtues and cooperating with his zeal we may save the souls of many redeemed with the blood of Christ, and in reward of our virtues and labors, shine like stars in heaven for perpetual eternities.[11]

The synod of 1791 was a success beyond the bishop's fondest hopes. He sent a copy of its decrees at once to Rome, and later, on April 23, 1792, he sat down to write a more leisurely and full account of its proceedings to the Holy See. At a general congregation on American affairs held in August by the Congregation of Propaganda the decrees of the synod were examined and Carroll's letter was read. Cardinal Antonelli reported to the American bishop afterward that Rome was deeply impressed with the progress he had made in the short period of his office. He congratulated Carroll on the pastoral vigilance displayed by the clergy at this first national synod. He suggested that some further clarification might be made of the rules relating to baptism, matrimony, and burial, and he concluded with the announcement that Bishop Carroll's faculties were to be further enlarged.[12] There was good feeling on both sides of the Atlantic.

The accomplishments of the assembled clergy in 1791 did not diminish in luster as time passed. Bishop Simon Gabriel Bruté of Vincennes commented in later years:

> We must read over the Synod of 1791 for the form, and its authority will be a good standard. In every line you see the bishop. In all you see how extensively he studied. The spirit

of faith, charity, and zeal in that first assembly has served as a happy model for its successor.

Indeed, when the First Provincial Council of Baltimore met in 1829 the priests gathered on that occasion ordered that the statutes of 1791 be printed at the head of their own decrees. "When we look back upon the circumstances of the times and conditions which existed at the period that the venerable John Carroll of happy memory, Bishop of Baltimore, held the Diocesan Synod of 1791," they asserted, "we greatly admire the zeal, prudence, and learning with which so many laws for the benefit of the Church were passed." The laws thus formulated under Carroll's guiding genius were in a sense the Twelve Tables of the American Church.

The Catholic laity were generally informed of the regulations adopted in November, 1791, by a pastoral letter published by the bishop on May 28, 1792, and signed, "John, Bishop of Baltimore." A copy of this letter happened to fall into the hands of a non-Catholic minister of the city, and under the *nom de plume* of "Liberal" this gentleman published some scathing strictures on Carroll's pretensions. It had been some time since the bishop's pen had been allowed the luxury of newspaper controversy and John Carroll found the present opportunity irresistible.

With tongue in cheek, and a twinkle in his eye, he seized a new quill and leaned over his writing table to indulge in one of his characteristic retorts. "Liberal" had stated that Baltimore was a large place and contained many inhabitants who disowned the bishop's jurisdiction, "and some who do a good deal more." Carroll commented that he supposed "Liberal" meant that they rejected the episcopacy altogether. "Let them, if they please," he said equally, "disown the one and reject the other. They use their constitutional right—and if the bishop knows his own heart he will leave them in the full enjoyment of it." Catholics, to whom his letter had been solely addressed, knew the voice of their pastor and were at no loss to recognize him, he felt sure. And until Protestant, Methodist, "or if they will pardon the expression," he added wickedly, "Presbyterian bishops," profess to hold bishoprics under the same approbation of the Apostolic See, he saw no room for confusion.

The Bank of Maryland or the Baltimore Insurance Office surely did not infringe on the civil rights of any citizen or claim any monopoly because of their use of the words "Maryland" or "Baltimore." "I am sure," Carroll said, "that neither the holders of shares formed pretensions so extravagant nor was it the intention of the legislature which incorporated them to debar other adventurers from making similar speculations, or assuming the same name and title if they chose." He liked the analogy and continued gleefully:

> So, likewise, let who will in other religious professions call themselves Bishops of Baltimore. It will excite neither regret nor opposition in him who is now known by that denomination. Indeed, considering his line of episcopal jurisdiction, and source of spiritual jurisdiction, he will think his own the best founded. But if others judge differently, he will not accuse *them* of invading *his* civil rights.

The Bishop of Baltimore said that he had naturally written the pastoral letter for Catholics alone, but that since there seemed to be so much interest in it, he would see to it that extra copies for the curious were left at the office of the printer, Mr. Angell. He concluded neatly, "The subject of this contention is so trifling in itself, and it affords so much room for ridicule, that if *Liberal* take up his pen again he must appear with something more material to engage the farther attention of John, *Bishop of Baltimore.*" [13]

He wrote the date at the bottom of the page, November 21, 1792, and sat back contentedly. It had been a nice little diversionary exercise. He supposed he was guilty of pride—but it had been amusing. Besides, who could tell? It might do some good to call attention to the excellent legislation of the first national synod in the United States. It would surely do no harm. And even a bishop is entitled to his little joke.

CHAPTER
X I

ALL OUR HOPES

IN THE fall of 1791 William Gaston of North Carolina came to
George Town, the thriving port on the Potomac River, to enter
the Catholic school there as its first student. It was for Gaston the
beginning of a long and noteworthy career which eventually brought
him to the United States Senate in 1813, and to the Supreme Court
of his state in 1833. For the school, Gaston's matriculation was the
beginning of an illustrious history whose pages are still being written, year by year.[1] The opening of Georgetown Academy was for
Bishop Carroll of Baltimore the realization of a dream he had been
cherishing these last ten years.

As long ago as his Plan of Organization of 1782 Carroll had envisioned Georgetown. A letter to Charles Plowden during the Critical
Period confessed, "The object nearest my heart is to establish a
college on this continent for the education of youth, which might
at the same time be a seminary for future clergymen." [2] All of his
letters to old friends in England and France carried this recurring
theme, Carroll's dream of a school. William Strickland wrote from
Liège that his friend's aim had his heartiest approbation, but Strickland warned Carroll not to be too sanguine. "The Academy at
Liège," he pointed out, "was begun under much more favorable
circumstances in many respects, particularly in respect to Masters,
than your school in America can reasonably expect. And yet it is
still after thirteen or fourteen years of labor in its infancy." Liège
would help all it could, however, and Charles Plowden was suggested by Strickland as a possible headmaster.[3] Thomas Talbot in
England doubted if Liège could spare "grown up and trained
plants" to assist in commencing an American school. "You have not
hands for so much work nor proper ones," he told Carroll dis-
couragingly in 1784.[4]

At the time that he became superior in 1784 Carroll was aware that the education of young men to the priesthood for the United States had engaged the attention of many others besides himself. During the negotiations preceding his appointment Benjamin Franklin, Doria Pamphili, Vergennes, and Talleyrand had all discussed the possibility of educating Americans in French seminaries, with Bordeaux specifically mentioned. Rome's request for a report on conditions in America in 1784 had asked categorically if there were schools in which Latin was learned and "where those youths who wish to prepare for the ecclesiastic state may have studied the humanities before repairing to France or Rome for the study of philosophy and theology." The official announcement of Carroll's appointment on June 9, 1784, said that Rome had decided to take two youths from Maryland and Pennsylvania "to educate them at the expense of the Sacred Congregation" in the Urban College of the Propaganda at Rome. The American superior was to choose those of more promising talents and a good constitution between twelve and fifteen years of age. Rome would even pay their passage over if the young men were unable to defray the cost of the voyage.[5]

It was characteristic of John Carroll that he did not immediately jump at the chance to send seminarians to Italy. He told his friend Thorpe:

> With respect to sending two youths, I shall inform Propaganda that it would surely be very acceptable to have children educated gratis in so religious a seminary. . . . But, as I suppose they will not receive any into their College but such as shall afterwards be subject to their government, and it being yet uncertain what effect my representations may produce, I shall delay that measure till further information is forthcoming.[6]

He was thinking of the mission oath which students in the Urban College were expected to take. This oath bound the student to obey the college laws, to promise that upon leaving he would not enter an order or congregation before the end of three years without the consent of the Holy See, and to send every year a report to Propaganda if he remained in Europe. Students educated under such obligations might prove to be of little immediate value to the American mission; or, and this Carroll feared more, they might provoke more extensive foreign intervention in American affairs.

When he spoke of his "representations" he meant, of course, his persistent hope of establishing a seminary in his own domain. Failing that, he saw another possibility. So great was Carroll's faith in religious freedom in his own country that he believed he could send his boys in safety to the ordinary colleges which were springing up throughout the thirteen states. He said as much to John Thorpe when he wrote:

> By acquiring civil and religious rights in common with other Christians we are become a national Catholic clergy. Colleges are now erecting for giving general and liberal education. These colleges are open both to masters and scholars of every denomination.

He made no secret of his hopes when he told Cardinal Antonelli on March 1, 1785, "There is a college in Philadelphia and it is proposed to establish two in Maryland, in which Catholics can be admitted as well as others. . . . We hope that some educated there will embrace the ecclesiastical state." [7]

As a matter of fact, Father Ferdinand Farmer, along with Carroll's friend Franklin, was already a member of the board of trustees of the University of Pennsylvania,[8] and Carroll himself was one of those entrusted to solicit subscriptions for St. John's College in Annapolis. Neither of these projects, unfortunately, offered an immediate solution; and no one questioned that a Catholic college would ultimately be a necessity. The clergy, therefore, went ahead with their discussions of plans for a school. When the second general chapter of the clergy met in November of 1786 their plans began to take shape. Resolutions adopted between November 13 and 22 covered concrete proposals for raising money, procuring tutors, fixing student fees, locating and building the college. Carroll, James Pellentz, Robert Molyneux, John Ashton, and Leonard Neale were named directors for the institution which was to be located at "George Town in the State of Maryland." Then began the real task of founding the school.

Meanwhile, Rome's offer to educate two priests had not been forgotten. Carroll's first reluctance was soon dissipated when Cardinal Antonelli sent him a copy of the mission oath with the notation:

> You will see clearly that . . . each student shall return to his own province with the intention of devoting his labours to the apostolic ministry. . . . If, however, you discover anything in the oath which could afford displeasure under the

present conditions we will not be averse to accommodating the same form of oath to meet the needs of the students of those regions in whatever way shall seem more desirable.[9]

Only a very churlish fellow would quibble in the face of such generosity, and Carroll now accepted the Roman offer gratefully. By July 2, 1787, two lads were ready to leave for Italy. One was from Maryland, the other from Pennsylvania. Both were to be gone from the United States for ten years, yet neither one ever reached the original goal of ordination. By the time they returned from Rome in 1797 there was no longer any necessity for sending others, for Georgetown was then offering young gentlemen courses in the humanities and liberal arts, and Baltimore had its own seminary.

Getting Georgetown started took some time, however. After the clergy's vote to undertake the school there still remained two vital considerations: money and masters. When Carroll told Antonelli of their November decision he admitted that he would have to look to Europe for monetary support, and to Plowden he spoke of the other prerequisite, "a fit gentleman to open the new establishment." He wrote insinuatingly, "How often I have said to myself: what a blessing to this country my friend Plowden would be! What reputation and solid advantage would accrue to the academy from such a director." [11] Charles had an excellent reputation among the ex-Jesuits, and his friends all conceded him to be a "devout historian, a fine gentleman, a polite scholar, and an accurate critic." [12] But if the Maryland school were to start out as a simple academy, some felt Plowden's talents might be wasted. Father Strickland, the head-master at Liège, told Carroll:

> I can not entirely agree with you in your ideas of the school you wish to establish. In the schools established by other professions, the endeavour will be to place a man at their head whose universal knowledge, and brilliant talents may give as great an *éclat* to the establishment as possible. In your case, is such a man desirable?

Strickland said quite frankly that if he were starting the school he would attempt at first only a grammar school. "When this is brought to some degree of perfection," he observed, "it would, I think, be much easier to form a school of higher studies." [13]

Although John Carroll did not subscribe in theory to his friend's views, it began to appear that he might be unable to secure a head-

master of any degree of brilliance. He told Plowden soberly in
October, 1791:

> The Academy will be opened in a few days, but not so
> advantageously as I hoped. No president *pro dignitate loci.*
> I can hardly forgive my friends at Liège. Here was an oppor-
> tunity for infinite service to the cause of God and His
> Church.[14]

Then, where Liège had proved unwilling, Brussels provided a man.
Robert Plunkett, a graduate of the English College at Douay, and
a chaplain at the Benedictine Convent in Brussels, appeared to fill
the breach. More than two years before Plunkett had asked Rome's
permission to go to America. Cardinal Antonelli had told Carroll
of Plunkett's desire, and the superior had welcomed the arrival of
the priest from Belgium in July, 1790. The Bishop of Baltimore
now waited anxiously for some indication that Plunkett would
accept the post of president of the infant academy instead of remaining on the Maryland mission where he had been serving. Father
Plunkett did accept, and Georgetown had its first head. Plunkett
remained with the school until Robert Molyneux took over two
years later, and his tenure allowed the school to get fairly started
earlier than might otherwise have been possible.

Financing the infant institution was quite a different matter.
Back on January 25, 1787, Carroll had informed his friend Thomas
Sim Lee of the "flattering prospects" which the future academy
seemed to proffer. Two Maryland gentlemen had joined in granting a fine piece of ground for the purpose of building on the
"Potowmack" River.[15] But these flattering prospects were quickly
threatened. Although the clergy had approved the idea of a school
"for the education of youth and the perpetuity of the body of the
clergy of this country," when it came time to solicit subscriptions
for Georgetown it appeared that all of the priests in the Southern
District were not unanimously behind the project. News of this
opposition reached Carroll in letters from Fathers Leonard Neale
and Bernard Diderick. The chief objection seemed to center around
the old Jesuit fear of misappropriation of their property, but
Diderick went further and accused the clergy chapter of having set
up the school matter, of having "contrived the business before-
hand," and of keeping the resolution secret until they were sure
of rushing it through. Carroll was highly incensed at the latter

charge, and he reproved Diderick for insinuations so injurious to
the character of his colleagues. He referred the gentlemen of the
Southern District to the letter which John Ashton had sent convok-
ing the November meeting. "I beg you to recall," he pointed out,
"that the subjects of deliberation were so much known that Mr.
Pellentz, not being able to attend personally, wrote his opinion on
all these facts." [16]

Carroll was familiar enough by now with the old fears and cau-
tiousness of his colleagues. He knew that the hope of a restoration
of the society would always color the opinions of many ex-Jesuits.
As he explained to Plowden:

> They act from this laudable motive. . . . They fear that
> Georgetown will occasion some alienation of property for-
> merly possessed by the Society, which they wish to restore
> undiminished to her at her reestablishment. . . . They posi-
> tively assert that any appropriation to the school . . . is a
> violation of the rights of the Society; thus supposing a right
> of property can exist in a non-existing body, for certainly the
> Society has no existence here.[17]

The Society of Jesus had been suppressed in the western world since
1773. Carroll could not go on living in the past; and in this particular case, he had no desire to predict the future. The simple fact
was that the clergy of the United States, meeting in their regular
chapter, had resolved to undertake a school. He exclaimed, "Surely,
the resolutions of Chapter are binding in matters of this nature."

If any gentlemen of the Southern District had delicate con-
sciences Carroll would relieve them. He pointed out that they need
have no fears of violating justice in using their property for the
benefit of a school. In the first place, the Church taught that death
extinguishes property rights in such a manner that even if the
Society were revived, those rights would not be. In the second place,
the property to be applied to the school had never belonged to the
Society of Jesus. And finally, even supposing the society to exist at
the present time, it ought to find the erecting of a school most conducive to the ends of the society.[18] There was no need for the clergy
to fear any detriment to their society should it ever be restored,
Carroll assured them.

> Schools and seminaries have generally been encouraged and
> protected by the bishops, whether immediately under their

own direction, or the direction of the Society. And if she should be re-established in this country in our lifetime, there is no doubt but, with the other property, the government of the school will likewise be surrendered into her hands.[19]

His words were truly prophetic, but in 1787 the dissident clergy only knew that they had lost the argument. The business of raising funds went forward without further ado. The committee on subscriptions circulated printed forms to facilitate the work of the agents who bore such respected names as Carroll of Carrollton, Notley Young, John Darnall, and George Digges. In Philadelphia Thomas FitzSimons led the list, while in New York Dominick Lynch acted as agent. In spite of the character of the collectors and the "salubrity" of the advantages which the prospectus of the academy set forth, the responses were scanty. Carroll wrote in discouragement to Beeston in 1788 that he was afraid the project was doomed to failure. In Rome Thorpe commiserated with his friend and expressed his sorrow that "our own brethren" were so reluctant to encourage Carroll's academy and the project of an ecclesiastical seminary.[20]

Nevertheless, ground was broken on the lovely site overlooking the river, and Carroll reported to Cardinal Antonelli on April 19, 1788, "The building of the school was begun a few days ago. But if it is to be brought to a happy completion, our principal hope is in Divine Providence." Carroll knew that he had the approbation of the Prefect of Propaganda, for Antonelli had already persuaded the Sacred Congregation to vote an annual subsidy of one hundred *scudi* for a period of three years. The building which was just begun was expected to be three stories high, exclusive of the "offices under the whole." "From this beginning," the American superior told Antonelli, "I believe the conservation of religion in these lands depends, for without the school there will be no chance of establishing a seminary for the maintenance of the clerical body and the extension of our holy religion." [21]

It has already been seen how Carroll employed the time after his consecration in England to enlist the sympathies and financial support of his friends there. Plowden, Brewer, and Talbot each pledged their generous efforts.[22] Talbot said heartily, "I wish it to flourish and speedily. Religion will depend much on its success." [23] By the time Carroll embarked for Baltimore he believed the future of his *protégé* was for the first time assured. And, indeed, it was.

In 1791 the "Academy at George Town, Potowmack River, Maryland" began its long and worthy task of education, and the bishop who so many years before had received his own start at Bohemia Manor, viewed its progress with pardonable pride and paternal solicitude. The school would have lean years and stormy days, but it would endure.

If the Georgetown academy was the answer to the need for the "several branches of classical learning" which would prepare young men for the "study of the higher sciences in the university of this or of neighboring states," as the prospectus claimed, then St. Mary's Seminary in Baltimore was to be the major seminary for the final education of the men who meant to follow the ecclesiastical way of life. This second institution for learning within the Diocese of Baltimore was begun simultaneously with the national synod and the opening of Georgetown. The autumn of 1791 was not one the bishop was likely to forget.

In the spring following Carroll's consecration, in accordance with the plans he and Father Nagot had discussed in London, the Society of St. Sulpice was introduced into the United States. The first band of Sulpicians embarked from St. Malo on April 8, 1791.[25] The leaders of the group were Nagot himself, Jean Marie Tessier, Antoine Garnier, and Michele Levadoux. All were qualified teachers. Nagot was pre-eminent in philosophy and theology; Garnier, a much younger man, was a linguist; Levadoux and Tessier had had experience at Bourges and Viviers respectively. Accompanying the masters were five seminarians who had volunteered to become the first students in the Baltimore school. They came from England, Canada, France, and one was a recent American convert, John Caldwell of New Jersey. The journey was made on the same vessel which carried the author, Chateaubriand, and the details of their journey found their way into his now famous account of the *Voyage en Amérique*. It was a long and tedious trip for the anxious men, and it did not end in Baltimore until July 10, 1791. They had been three months en route, with delaying stop-overs at the Azores on one side of the Atlantic, and at St. Pierre and Miquelon on the other. It was a relief to clamber off the hot and stinking vessel at Baltimore.

They were more than a little disappointed to find that Bishop Carroll was away on a visitation to Boston, but the resident rector of the pro-cathedral, Charles Sewall, gave them a cordial welcome. Father Sewall told them that he had secured lodgings for them in a house on Baltimore Street, and it was here that they stayed until Father Nagot rented the "One Mile Tavern" off the Hookstown Road beyond the town.

The three-story red brick tavern which became the first permanent residence of the gentlemen of St. Sulpice was virtually in a forest and seemed an ideal spot for a seminary. After a month's trial of the place they purchased the tavern and several adjoining acres of the surrounding woodlands; St. Mary's Seminary had a home of its own. Upon his return from Boston Bishop Carroll was elated to find what a blessing the French priests were already proving to his church. He commented approvingly, "They attract a great concourse of all denominations by the great decency and exactness with which they perform all parts of the divine service." Before their first year was completed the Sulpicians had thoroughly convinced Carroll of the wisdom of his decision. He wrote glowingly to Cardinal Antonelli:

> The establishment of a seminary is certainly a new and extraordinary spectacle for the people of this country. The remarkable piety of these priests is admirable, and their example is a stimulant and spur to all who feel themselves called to work in the vineyard of the Lord. . . . But what is still more important . . . is that the clergy will be brought up in the purity of the faith and in holiness of conduct. All our hopes are founded on the Seminary of Baltimore.

"All our hopes." In 1788 he had said of Georgetown, "On this academy is built all my hope of permanency and success." Now, in 1792, St. Mary's in Baltimore was proving the perfect complement. On these two foundations the bishop envisioned the erection of a body of clergy well-grounded in the liberal arts and especially trained in the ecclesiastical subjects and state of life. Georgetown and St. Mary's, here were the remedies for past evils. In spite of its lack of dignity in size and adornment, the pro-cathedral was beginning to take on the aspect of an episcopal church; while over on the Potomac River and out at One Mile Tavern young men were free to choose the priestly vocation without a care for ocean voyages or the other costly items of a continental education.

And yet, as rosy as the prospect seemed in 1791 when both schools were founded, the next decade and a half brought to John Carroll unforeseen vexations emanating from these very institutions which he affectionately called his only hopes. Scarcely had either Georgetown or St. Mary's Seminary opened their doors when friction began to appear, friction which nearly precipitated in 1801 the complete removal of the Sulpicians from the United States and the closing of the Baltimore seminary.

The decade from 1791 to 1801 was fraught with difficulties for the whole nation, and in one sense the educational controversies which rose to plague the bishop were the product of the acrimonious and nationalistic jealousies spawned by the wars in Europe and the consequent foreign relations of the Federalist administrations. There can be little doubt that the Anglophobia of the Republicans and the antipathy of the Federalists for France colored the rivalries between Georgetown and St. Mary's.

The administration of John Adams which began in March, 1797, inherited the antagonisms generated during Washington's second term. In the campaign of 1796 Adams was accused of being a monarchist, an aristocrat, an enemy of the masses, and an English bootlicker; while Thomas Jefferson, his opponent, was branded a friend of anarchy, a French tool, an atheist, and an enemy of the Constitution. Adams, who won by the small electoral advantage of three votes, faced a French Directory government highly incensed by the Jay Treaty with England. From July of 1796 to June of 1797 more than 300 vessels registered in the United States were seized under the terms of the decrees issued by the five directors of France. The last Federalist envoy to France had been threatened with arrest, and the President had all he could do to avert war during his first year in office. After the canny Talleyrand became the French foreign minister he delighted in fanning the flame of the rising feud between the anti-French Federalists and the Democratic-Republicans in the United States.

The notorious X.Y.Z. Affair in 1798 produced a tremendous reaction against the French. French flags were yanked down from the coffee houses, and the black cockade of patriotism sprang to innumerable buttonholes. Joseph Hopkinson up in Philadelphia scribbled off his rousing "Hail Columbia!" which was soon being sung boisterously inside the grog shops. On June 18, 1798, Robert Goodloe Harper, Kitty Carroll's future husband, paraphrased Pinckney's retort in the more euphonious, "Millions for defense but not one cent for tribute!" Congress, as usual, meant to suit the popular clamor if it could, and abrogated the treaties of 1778 with France, enacted the Alien and Sedition Acts, created a Navy Department,

and generally countenanced an undeclared war with France. George
Washington from his uneasy retirement at Mount Vernon charged
the agents and partisans of France with conspiring against the peace
and happiness of the Republic and sourly expressed the hope that
the legislation of 1798 would undeceive the French Directory. He
told Charles Carroll of Carrollton, "I highly approve the measures
taken by the government. . . . I even wish they had been *more
energetic.*" [26] The Federalists enjoyed their heyday, and the pro-
French Republicans skulked furtively in the background for the
nonce.

It would have been strange if the French Sulpician seminary in
Baltimore had gone unscathed during these recriminations. Although Jefferson had received most of the southern vote in the
recent election, Delaware and much of Maryland had voted Federalist. Charles Carroll, the bishop's cousin, had already indicated
his attitude when he made it clear that he would never accept the
appointment as United States Minister to France. James Monroe,
who had held the office from 1794-1796, described Charles as "sensible and attached to Federal measures." Gentlemen of the opposite
persuasion labeled the Signer as "that hoary-headed aristocrat" with
"British monarchical and aristocratic policies." The old gentleman
himself admitted candidly to his son Charlie in 1800 that his appre-
hensions of Jefferson and the Republicans caused him to dread
"that in the course of a few years I might be driven into exile by
the prevalence of an execrable faction." Like Washington earlier,
the squire of Carrollton feared that the true interest and real independence of his country were on the verge of being sacrificed to
France. "The men, so far as I am informed, who style themselves
republicans," he asserted, "very generally wish success to France. In
other words, the friends of *freedom here* are the friends of Bonaparte, who has established by military force the most despotic
government in Europe." [27]

Many a Marylander held the same views and regarded all things
French as part and parcel of "execrable faction." Bishop Carroll
had reason to suspect that some of his own colleagues were chiefly
inspired by political and nationalistic prejudice in their growing
opposition to the Sulpician institution in Baltimore. Writing to
Plowden in 1798 he commented on the antagonism Georgetown held
toward St. Mary's:

National attachments, that bane of all communities where

they are suffered to exist, have been the original cause of the mischief. . . . The directors had too strong prejudices against everything which was derived in any shape from France; and in consequence thereof, their judgment had an involuntary bias. . . . God grant that every thing may turn out for the best.[28]

Again in 1800 he confessed to Plowden that there still existed a jarring note in his relations with the men conducting Georgetown. "An anti-Gallican spirit has engendered prejudices against the Sulpicians here," he told Plowden. "In consequence, the poor seven youths who were to come from Georgetown to begin their ecclesiastical life and studies, are detained there for philosophy. It is still my endeavour and hope to compose these differences." [29]

Back in France, Father Emery was also convinced that anti-French feeling lay at the bottom of his society's difficulties in Baltimore. He said: "I see a depth of rivalry and jealousy which I did not at all conceive. . . . They write that we are not proper for educating young Americans, and that may be the truth. Perhaps it is fitting that Americans be educated by Americans." [30] Undoubtedly many partial minds chose to forget that these French priests had originally been driven from their homes by the Revolution and republicanism in France and preferred to believe now that all French priests were imbued with republican principles.

Political faction and national jealousies were, of course, only one element in the antagonism which had come to exist between Georgetown and St. Mary's. More intensely provocative were the competition for students and masters, the difficulties of financing both schools, and to a lesser extent, the question of admitting non-Catholics. In the beginning, in 1791, it had seemed reasonable to expect that the academy on the Potomac would prepare candidates to study for the priesthood in Baltimore, as well as providing a general Catholic education for others. As it turned out, however, the academy furnished the seminary only one student in the first decade while it took from Baltimore four of the seminary's own students. True, the St. Mary's students went to Georgetown in the capacity of instructors, but this did not lessen the Sulpician resentment since so many of the young men who went to Georgetown to teach ended up with no vocation for the priesthood. Even greater bitterness was engendered by Georgetown's decision in 1800 to undertake some of the work of a seminary itself. Carroll gave his version of the development to Plowden, saying:

Six or seven young men who intend to embrace an ecclesiastical state were to have entered into the Seminary and
commence their philosophy this month, when a violent, and
to me expected, opposition broke out; and to counteract
the Seminary, a sudden resolution was adopted to open a
course of philosophy in the College. Though I find fault
with the time and manner of announcing this resolution,
yet I should not be opposed to it, if there was amongst us
a man fit to undertake a course of philosophy without dis-
gracing himself and the College. . . . I shall place in the
Seminary all those for whom I can make a provision.

Although Carroll was by his own testimony a Federalist in his
politics and a former Jesuit in his religious vocation, neither of these
predilections clouded his vision in the present situation. As bishop
his sole concern was the welfare of the Church. To him the state
of affairs was ludicrous. In Baltimore was a seminary without seminarians while over on the Potomac were philosophy students with no
philosophy teachers. He summed it up morosely for Plowden:

Georgetown is not flourishing. The reason is not merely want
of sufficient numbers of men capable of conducting that
establishment, but errors committed at the very outset; and
above all, national prejudices in my opinion very ill-founded,
against the worthy priests of St. Sulpice and the system of
education pursued in the seminary.

His opinion of the seminary was unqualified. He said emphatically:
"Never can candidates for Holy Orders be placed in better hands;
and I am sure that at the present, there are none others in the
United States to form their education." [31]

Meanwhile, thus deprived of any hopes of receiving students
from Georgetown, St. Mary's had decided to start an academy or
college of its own. In August, 1799, classes were actually begun in
St. Mary's Academy. It is interesting to find that at the same time
that the Sulpician seminary in Baltimore was found by Americans
to be too French, its secular branch conducted by the same men was
suspected by Frenchmen of being too American! The French consul
in Baltimore on September 4, 1801, reported to Paris that boys from
the French colonies in the West Indies might imbibe dangerous
doctrines should they attend the Sulpician academy or college in
Baltimore. Although he warmly praised the high calibre of the

faculty and their strong ties with France (the school was known, he said, to use the French tongue to the exclusion of the English), the consul, Jacques Levillain, feared the boys might be indoctrinated with notions of colonial independence.[32] John Carroll, on his part, was not particularly in favor of the school either. But for other reasons. It would be a threat to the Georgetown academy for which he had held such hopes for nearly twenty years. He gave a grudging consent since Spaniards and French exiles in San Domingo seemed eager to enroll. He tried at first to limit their numbers to a dozen students, but before the school was a year old there were already more than that number. Father Nagot agreed to accept only foreign boys, but he reminded the bishop that St. Mary's charter from the State of Maryland allowed the Sulpicians to take enough boys to fill the school. St. Mary's would limit herself to twenty-five students, Nagot told Carroll. "We agree to receive only foreigners. We make this double sacrifice in the desire of preserving union with your gentlemen of Georgetown."

Bishop Carroll's peculiar genius for preserving his own equanimity, and for meting out exact justice in spite of his personal preferences, shows in every phrase of his reply to Nagot. On October 16, 1800, he told the Sulpician evenly:

> Although I have always looked with displeasure on the establishment of your academy because it has become a subject of discord and jealousy, I have at the same time constantly recognized the right you have to establish it and to give it the form you please. . . . The limitation of twelve students having been passed, I have expressed to you frankly my sentiments. But if I insisted upon you consenting to a new limitation and engaging to take only foreigners, I repent of having done so. It would be more fitting to leave you in the full exercise of your rights which every inhabitant has in the United States, of opening a school and receiving students as he pleases.[33]

He had a tremendous pride in the equal protection of the laws which he conceived his government guaranteed. Nagot knew where the bishop stood. But the French priest should know that men trained in the Maryland tradition of legalism which was as old as the colony itself did not need to have the law explained to them. Anyone who cares to study the Carroll papers which pertain to this brief *contretemps* between Georgetown and St. Mary's at the turn of the century can see that John Carroll was neither prejudiced in favor of ex-Jesuits as the Smyths and La Poteries claimed, nor partial to the Sulpicians as the restored Jesuits on occasion might suggest. The Bishop of Baltimore was too big a man for bias or favoritism. His eyes roved beyond present disorders and rivalries to the ultimate good of his beloved Church. Let Georgetown and St. Mary's squabble if they must over the course each would teach or the students each would enroll. They were both needed. Above all, the Sulpicians must not be allowed to abandon their work in his domain.

It was no idle suspicion, either, this fear of losing the Society of St. Sulpice. Emery in Paris was beginning to suggest that the lack of seminarians in Baltimore removed any valid reasons for keeping the society in the United States. Conditions in France were improving since Napoleon's rise to power, and it was now safe to consider the re-establishment of their work there. In 1800 the superior-general notified Carroll that he was considering recalling the Sulpicians to France. The bishop was shocked at the suggestion and wrote at once to Emery: "I believe it would be one of the greatest misfortunes which could happen to this diocese if it should ever lose them. . . . I earnestly beg you to banish the idea from your mind." But Emery was not easily dissuaded. In 1801 he began his plans for a gradual withdrawal of the French priests. Carroll wrote more urgently than before, "I conjure you, Sir, by the bowels of Our Lord not to take them all away; and if it is necessary that I submit to the terrible trial of seeing the greatest number depart, I beseech you to leave at least a germ which can fructify in the season decreed by the Lord."

But Emery appeared adamant. He said bluntly. "At the end of ten years we are no farther advanced than in the first days. There is no question of abandoning the Seminary of Baltimore since in fact it has never existed. It is only the question of abandoning the project of a seminary." It was not Carroll's fault, he granted; but the vocation of the Society of St. Sulpice was to train men for holy orders. The external ministry or work of the missions was not their province. He felt that the talents possessed by Garnier, Levadoux and Maréchal could be put to better use elsewhere. In 1803 these three priests returned to France and Carroll began to dread the day when no single Sulpician would remain in Baltimore.

In the end it was Rome that intervened to preserve the American bishop's dream. When Pius VII went to Paris for the coronation of

Napoleon as Emperor of France, Father Emery discussed his intentions toward Baltimore with the Pope. When the subject of the seminary was broached the Holy Father said: "My son, let it remain. Yes, let that seminary exist; for it will bear its fruits in time." [34] St. Mary's was saved. Indeed, as if to validate the Pontiff's prophetic words, it began almost immediately to thrive. Between 1800 and 1810 nearly half a hundred young men entered the doors at Paca Street, and of these twenty-three were eventually ordained.

Georgetown, too, emerged during this decade as a permanent and successful institution. With the restoration of the Society of Jesus in the United States under the superior Robert Molyneux the many previous inadequacies were eliminated. The school on the Potomac passed into the hands of the Jesuits as Carroll had long since predicted; and the work of the academy and college went rapidly ahead. The bishop was not naive enough to hope that all rivalry between the two schools was completely removed. But both were now firmly established. Both were to endure.

Although Bishop Carroll was primarily interested in education under religious auspices, so deep was his conviction that education must flourish in this new Republic that he became famous in Maryland as a patron of schools of secular origins as well. When in 1784 the Maryland Legislature authorized the charter of St. John's College at Annapolis, Carroll was asked at once to serve on the board entrusted with soliciting subscriptions and donations for the new endeavour. Four years later he was unanimously elected president of the board of trustees of the college which offered a liberal education "to youth of every religious denomination." He told Plowden of the project:

> A college has lately been opened at Annapolis, under the protection of our state legislature, and amply endowed by them. It is erected on principles of perfect equality as to religion. The original agents appointed by act of the assembly to model and encourage it, were three clergymen and three laymen, one of whom were Catholic, Church of England, and Presbyterian. I had the honor of being the former.[35]

Meanwhile, in 1785, at the second annual commencement, Washington College conferred an honorary degree on Father Carroll even though he could not be present at the ceremony which George Washington attended. Carroll thanked the college with the words:

On this occasion I feel a very lively impression of gratitude for the favourable and indeed too advantageous opinion,
you are pleased to entertain of me; and at the same time, I
received additional pleasure from the diffusion of liberal
and tolerating principles overlooking diversity of religious
sentiment considered literary merit alone in the collashon
of academical honours. I flatter myself that your example
and influence will perpetuate this spirit in Washington College for the advancement of science and the happiness of
our State.[36]

Baltimore's leading Catholic was apparently gaining a reputation
for public-spirited zeal. The following year he was asked to preside
at a public meeting held on March 27, 1786, to discuss plans for the
first Baltimore academy. That July this institution dedicated "to
qualify youth for the ordinary business of manhood," began its
career.[37]

During the decade following his consecration as Bishop of Baltimore Carroll was preoccupied with the early struggles of Georgetown and St. Mary's, but in 1801 his name was again connected
with a non-sectarian institution. In that year the legislature chartered the Female Humane Association Charity School and the bishop
served on its first board of trustees. On January 7, 1802, he was
elected president of the board in a meeting held in his own rectory.
Catholics worked together with Presbyterians, Baptists, Lutherans,
Methodists, and German Calvinists to contribute money to educate
and maintain "poor female children of every denomination." [38]
Carroll must have made an excellent chairman, for the very next
year he was elected to preside over the thirty-seven trustees of the
newly-founded Baltimore College which opened its doors to youth
of every denomination "who shall be freely admitted to equal privileges." By 1810 a suitable building housed the college on Mulberry
Street, just opposite the Catholic pro-cathedral.[39] As the pastoral
duties of the Bishop of Baltimore increased during the years that
ensued he was compelled to relinquish these civic services, but his
reputation remained. After the University of Maryland was re-
chartered in 1812 Archbishop Carroll was elected provost, but age
and ecclesiastical burdens forced him to decline.[40]

Carroll's views on education, when considered in their entirety,
show him to have been a man of unlimited vision. Neither men nor
circumstance could modify his conviction that in the United States
the human mind and spirit might expand and flourish in a newer

and unparalleled freedom. He believed that Catholic colleges and seminaries should adapt their systems to the milieu in which they hoped to survive. The rigidity of old-world patterns was not suited to the new nation which he cherished. Speaking of Georgetown's difficulties in 1802 he commented to Plowden:

> Its president, my coadjutor, and his brother Francis . . . both of them as worthy men as live, deter parents from sending their sons thither by some rigorous regulations not calculated for the meridian of America. Their principles are too monastic and with a laudable view of excluding immorality, they deny that liberty which all here will lay claim to.[41]

He did not deny that it was difficult to decide what degree of freedom should be allowed in literary establishments, and he gave it much thought as his remarks to Plowden show:

> Theory and experience are constantly at variance in this case; for tho the principles of religion and morality command or seem to command the Instructors of youth to restrain their pupils from almost every communication with the men and things of the world, yet that very restraint operates against the effects intended by it, and it is too often found, that on being delivered from it, young men, as when the pin that confined a spring is loosened, burst out of confinement into licentiousness, and give way to errors and vices, which with more acquaintance with the manners and language of the world, they would have avoided.

After Robert Molyneux took over at Georgetown Carroll told him, "If the love and respect which you enjoy universally do not restore its credit, it must be certain that there is some radical defect in its constitution, so far as relates to its aptitude to suit the inclinations and genius of my countrymen." [42] And when Anthony Kohlmann succeeded Molyneux, Carroll expressed his hope to Plowden that Georgetown might benefit "when Mr. Kohlman has become more informed of the customs of this Country, and understands that a College, founded like that of George Town for the education of youth generally, must not be governed on the principles and in the system of a Convent." [43]

It was not only in discipline that Carroll favored greater liberality but in the area of intellectual activity as well. He was chagrined that the followers of St. Ignatius no longer led the field in moulding the minds of men. In 1803 he spoke freely of these matters to Plowden who would not willfully misunderstand him.

> It must be owned, that for more than a century, we have been greatly eclipsed by the Gentlemen of Douay; witness Hawarden Manning, Walton Challenor, Butler, and now Milner and Coombs. Sometimes I have reflected on the causes of it, and those I have suggested to myself, operate, it is hoped, no longer at present. It seemed to me that at Liège far from encouraging young men to extend the circle of their knowledge, the heads of the College esteemed no merit but that, of the study of their dictates. The little of Greek which had been learned at S. Omer or Bruges, was suffered to perish; the Hebrew lesson was a mere mockery; even the cultivation of Latin elegance was thrown aside; and as to our native language, there was scarcely a book of it in the Library worthy of being studied. No modern author of any science or in any language was introduced into it. Thus genius and talents were cramped, and a habit of inapplication was acquired, which few escaped.

He concluded his reflections with the fervent wish, "I long to hear of the revival of that spirit amongst the descendants of the Society which shone forth in its first ages, and still exists in the Constitutions of St. Ignatius!" [44]

A year later he broached the subject again saying:

> Strongly as my attachments are to the doctrine of our schools, yet I should regret very much, if, after the re-establishment, they should be fettered by any other restriction than that of the Orthodox doctrine of the Catholic Church. By allowing this liberty, and taking care that it be not abused to the detriment of true faith, it seems to me that our schools will be formed more agreeably to the maxims of St. Ignatius, and the axe will be laid to the root of that envy, contradiction, misrepresentation and hatred, which followed us amongst many Catholics heretofore. [45]

In the seminaries he did not want the study of theology to become fossilized, and only a few months before his death he told the Jesuit superior at Georgetown, "I am indeed anxious for an uniform system of Divinity amongst us, allowing however all the liberty of opinion granted by the Church, if on particular questions the Professor shall differ from his text book." [46]

On the subject of faculty members, Carroll held that virtue and piety were not enough. He criticized the Neales for lacking the necessary interest in "polite literature." "In this country," he told Plowden, "the talents of the president are the gauge by which the public estimates the excellency or deficiency of a place of education; to which must be added affability, address, and other human qualities, for which neither of the brothers is conspicuous." [47] Although he would have preferred to have schools conducted by the members of one religious society, maintaining that hired professors have an interest so different from that of a sacred attachment to the cause of God and His Church,[48] Carroll came to favor the employment of all talents whether possessed by the religious or otherwise. He said bluntly to John Grassi in 1813:

> My opinion has ever been, that when any body of men publicly profess to undertake the education of youth, they are bound in justice to provide suitable teachers tho they be not members of their own body, if they cannot be found amongst themselves. But previously to your coming to George Town, those who preceded you, were persuaded either that the young men employed under them were fully competent, or that every consideration was to yield to that of preserving the government of the college in the same hands . . . excluding every teacher who had not been trained in the same routine of servile imitation and narrowness of studies as themselves. This was not the enlarged system of St. Ignatius, as any one who reads his life may observe.[49]

It is not surprising that in the state where he was born and was to die Carroll had the veneration of all manner of men. After his death the journals commented that the multitude who crowded to his funeral seemed to indicate "that some great public ceremony was to be performed or some national calamity to be deplored." Devoted as he was to the faith of his fathers, he yet respected all men and worked untiringly with all creeds for the expansion of the nation's intellectual resources. "The extent of his knowledge and the enlargement of his mind fastened upon men of liberal science. The liberality of his character, and his Christian charity endeared him to his Protestant brethren with whom he dwelt in brotherly love," the contemporary press commented.[50] A present generation can stand in wondering admiration at the many institutions which still flourish a century and a half after the exertions of his fostering care.

CHAPTER
XII

OF HUMAN SORROW

ON SEPTEMBER 18, 1793, another of the cornerstones of the federal capital was laid, and Daniel Carroll, the bishop's brother, participated along with President Washington in ceremonies conducted by the Masonic lodges of Maryland and Alexandria.[1] When John Carroll heard of it he frowned irritably. Daniel had been a Mason since 1780, and of course the President was recognized as the nation's most illustrious Mason. But the Bishop of Baltimore could scarcely approve of an association that had borne Roman censure since the time of Clement XII's apostolic letter of 1738.[2] Daniel could do as he liked, but if anyone wanted the bishop's opinion he was willing to give it, as he did to Michael McElhiney on January 7, 1794.

Carroll said plainly:

> Severe and heavy censures, even that of excommunication, have been denounced by two successive Popes against all persons who continue in or join the Society and frequent the Lodges of Free Masons, and the reason alleged is that their meetings are found by experience to be destructive of morality and to diminish very much the habit of religious exercises. I do not pretend that these decrees are received generally by the Church, or have full authority in this diocese. But they ought to be a very serious warning to all good Christians not to expose themselves to dangers which the Supreme Head of the Church has judged to be so contagious.[3]

Daniel was within the law in the strictest sense. But his brother could see no point to his making a public spectacle of himself. The Bishop of Baltimore sniffed with his long Carroll nose and tried to think of pleasanter things.

There was the organ for St. Peter's, for example. Almost as soon as he was made bishop, Carroll had set William Strickland the task of finding him an organ for the Baltimore pro-cathedral. The head of the Liège Academy said that he doubted he could find one for the meagre sum Carroll was willing to pay, but Strickland would try. On November 11, 1791, Strickland had written complacently that one of Charles Carroll's old classmates had helped him get an organ. True, it was not a new one, but it was as good or better than the kind the bishop might have expected; and it was cheaper by a third. The Bishop of Baltimore was pleased. There was nothing he liked better than a good bargain, and £136.10.0 was a very acceptable sum for such an addition to St. Peter's Church.[4]

That new French priest from Cayenne could now enjoy his choir work, the bishop reflected. Father John Moranvillé had amused the bishop with his energetic attempts to improve the music at the pro-cathedral. The newcomer from the French colony of Guiana had formed a choir, for the most part composed of ladies, and had applied himself endlessly to rehearsing them for the Sunday services. Moranvillé sang with them himself during the high Mass and vespers, marking time for them with flourishes and grimaces. He and Father John David, the Sulpician, even composed hymns for the choir, and until Father Moranvillé went to St. Patrick's as pastor in 1804 his musical endeavors at St. Peter's were an accepted part of the pro-cathedral's services.[5]

Baltimore seemed to be growing more cosmopolitan with every passing day. The decrees of the National Assembly in France affected others beside the French Sulpicians in Paris. Father Moranvillé had fled Cayenne when the exactions of Paris reached France's South American colony, and other French immigrants continued to wend their round-about ways to the United States. Strickland wrote from London in 1792 that the city was thronged with French *émigrés,* 5,000 of whom were ecclesiastics who had "escaped with their lives but little else." And he then observed a trifle sardonically. "It is a pleasing thing to see Englishmen of all religious persuasions trying to exceed each other in generosity and charity to relieve their distress. If we do not excell in religion, we are not at least lost to feelings of humanity." [6] Many of these *émigrés* stopped in England only long enough to secure letters of introduction to the Bishop of Baltimore and then proceeded on their way to the United States. Father Francis A. Matignon was one of the first to arrive in this manner, but he only headed a long list of such priests.

Then, too, there was the descent of the Dominican refugees upon the city in 1793. The astonished inhabitants of Baltimore looked out one day in July to see a fleet of twenty vessels cast anchor off Fell's Point. The entire score of ships were from San Domingo, and as the fetid holds disgorged their human cargoes of whites and Negroes the news raced up from the waterfront and through the city that a massacre had taken place on the island, that Cape François had fallen, and that hundreds of other refugees were even now on their way to the United States. The generous citizens of Baltimore summoned an emergency meeting at the Exchange and appointed a committee of merchants to help care for the homeless exiles. It was decided to start immediate subscriptions for the relief of the sufferers, and within three days nearly $11,000 had been pledged. News of the crisis spread quickly throughout the state, and money was raised in Frederick Town, Hagerstown, George Town, Annapolis, and along the Eastern Shore.

Still the refugees poured in. By July 13, three dozen ships lay in the harbor, and within ten days fifty-three had arrived. The numbers exceeded 1,500. It was hoped that the French minister, Edmond Genêt, might take an interest in the plight of the Dominicans, but that gentleman was more concerned with activities destined to bring down the wrath of the neutral President upon his head than in assisting his colonial compatriots. By December the state's resources had been so taxed that it was decided to ask the United States Congress to come to the aid of the refugees. Congress consequently empowered the President in February, 1794, to distribute $15,000 of which Maryland received $2,000 as her portion.[7]

Baltimore was amply repaid for her generosity toward the newcomers. Widow La Combe opened a boarding school for girls in South Street where the refinements of a French education would be available to the young ladies of the better families. When James and Joanna Barry, the bishop's friends in Washington, heard of it they sent their oldest daughter, Mary, to Madame La Combe's where Carroll called from time to time to get reports on his young friend. Fathers William Dubourg and John Moranvillé both taught there for a while. A certain Jacques Pinaud advertised that he would instruct the sons of gentlemen in the graceful art of fencing. Some refugees opened coffee shops and tobacco manufactories; others founded great mercantile houses like that of the Marquis de Poléon. Dr. Pierre Chatard proved an inestimable boon during the constantly recurring plagues of yellow fever, and many a patient believed himself cured by the doctor's humane lancet. When Moreau de Saint-Méry visited the city in 1794 he was struck by the improved appearance of Baltimore, and he noted in his journal that the arrival of the colonists from San Domingo, "who to mention it while in passing have been received with open arms," had stirred neighboring gardeners to fresh activity. "As a result," he recorded, "a quantity of flourishing and attractive gardens have sprung up here and there." [8]

Bishop Carroll was probably more concerned by the influx than any other one person. His Catholic population in Baltimore was virtually doubled, if the parish registers could be believed. With the refugees from San Domingo came the former Superior-General of the clergy on the island, Abbé Adrien Cibot. The Maryland *Journal* on August 20, 1793, carried a report of Cibot's "elegant and affecting Discourse to his emigrated Flock," and the French priest made a good impression in other quarters. He went eventually to Bohemia Manor to minister in the area where his new bishop had begun his education so many years ago. Another Dominican refugee, Abbé Georges de Perrigny, went out to Doughoregan to act as chaplain to Cousin Charles' family, while Abbé Marcel-Guillaume Pasquet de Leyde went to Deer Creek. Naturally a little dross came in along with the gold, and the Bishop of Baltimore was not elated to discover that that anathema, Free Masonry, was brought in by other refugees. Former Dominicans came to compose the greatest part of *La Verité* Chapter of Baltimore. But the diocese on the whole received very healthful injections of culture and piety; and, as in the case of St. Mary's College, new schools were created in response to the needs of the exiles.

The cultural life of Baltimore was improving in other ways. Just before Christmas, in 1795, some of the city's leading citizens had held an informal meeting to discuss the possibility of beginning a public library. Bishop Carroll acted as temporary chairman of the meeting and Polly Carroll's husband, Dick Caton, took down the minutes of the day's decisions. In co-operation with the Presbyterian minister, Patrick Allison, and the rector of old St. Paul's, J.G.J. Bend, Carroll set in motion the project which became known as the Library Company of Baltimore. This preliminary meeting drew up some outlines for a constitution which the committee then submitted to various citizens of Baltimore who might be expected to take an interest in "so laudable an institution." The response was enthusiastic, and within only a few days fifty-nine patrons were secured.

After the holidays were over the committee went rapidly ahead with the organization of the project. On January 20, 1796, they convened at Bryden's Inn, and in company with Robert Gilmor, the founder of the first powder mill in Baltimore, lawyer Nicholas Brice, and merchant David Harris, they incorporated themselves. It was agreed that stock in the Library Company of Baltimore should sell at twenty dollars a share, and that members of the company should contribute annually an extra four dollars for each share of stock purchased. The enthusiasm of the founders was contagious, and in January and February the directors met nearly every week, such was the progress of their affairs. It was an undertaking after the bishop's own heart and he was unanimously elected president of the company, an office which he retained almost until the day he died.[10]

The Library Company flourished. Within two years of its establishment a sufficient number of books had been collected to warrant printing a catalog, and Carroll asked the company to investigate the cost of printing one. When it was found that John Hayes of Baltimore would do the job within reason, his press was given the commission. The Library Company took its work very seriously, and the directors went on record in the matter of book selection in 1802 as desiring to enrich the library "with those productions which are esteemed most conducive to encourage religion and morality, diffuse historical information, and advance the cultivation of the sciences and useful arts." Perhaps the bishop was influenced by the past, recalling the time when his reply to Wharton had been so hampered by a lack of library facilities, but the catalogs of the library under his direction showed that books on theology, religious tracts, and sermons out-numbered those of any other variety. The library was not unmindful, however, of the interests of the general reading public, and it assured its subscribers that a share of their funds would always be used "for gratifying the taste of genius and providing for the entertainment of those readers who seek amusement and instruction in works of a lighter and less durable kind."

The year of the founding of the Library Company of Baltimore was a heartbreaking one for its president, however. In 1796 John Carroll lost both his mother and his only brother within a few months of each other. In February Eleanor Darnall Carroll died at the age of ninety-two. She had been alert and quite herself almost until the very end. It was she who had meant a family home to the bishop. Her "holy life" had been a constant comfort to John Carroll, and his letters contained frequent references to "my saintly mother." Although Elizabeth Carroll, his unmarried sister, assumed many of the household burdens at Rock Creek, it was the indomitable old lady who remained mistress to the very end. She had husbanded her strength and her wealth carefully, and at the time of her death her household furnishings were valued at £2,500, and the estate employed thirty-nine slaves, twenty-four of whom worked at the "House Plantation" at Rock Creek. Her will was very simple. After her debts were paid the remainder of the property went to "my daughter Elizabeth Carroll." Daniel and John were appointed executors with their sister.[12]

Eleanor Carroll was laid to rest in the Carroll Chapel and a simple stone was erected "by her mourning children to testify their veneration for her eminent virtue." The mainspring of the family was gone. The bishop had lost the only person who could be relied on to care, year in and year out, what happened to him. They had been very close. Since his return from his consecration at Lulworth he had never missed a summer with her. It was many weeks before he could write to Plowden, "My good and venerable mother closed her long and may I add her holy life on the 3rd of February in full possession of her intellectual faculties, till she ceased to speak, an hour or two before her death. She was in the 93rd year of her age." [13] Daniel Carroll never recovered from the blow of her departure. Three months after Eleanor Carroll was buried her son died at the age of sixty-six. The Maryland *Gazette and Baltimore Daily Advertiser* marked his passing with the notice, "Last May 7, died at Rock Creek, Daniel Carroll, Esq., a gentleman of unbounded philanthropy, and possessed of all the esteem of all who had the pleasure of his acquaintance."

In Daniel Carroll Maryland had lost a valuable citizen. As a senator for his state, as Maryland delegate to the Continental Congress and to the Philadelphia Constitutional Convention he had served his state well. As a representative in the United States Congress, and as Commissioner of the Federal City he had served the nation. "To the American heritage Carroll had contributed his ardent belief in the value of a strong and centralized government, and his deep conviction that religious liberty was a proper attribute of the dignity of man." [14] His passing was a general loss; but to the

Bishop of Baltimore the death of Daniel Carroll was a more personal grief. Jacky Carroll had lost his brother Dan. In the presence
of death the mind hurtles back through time, and for a moment
the bishop was a lad again, grieving for his brother who had gone
across the sea.

The double loss of both his mother and brother left the bishop
with increased responsibilities. He was now the head of the remnant
of the family. He was executor for his mother's estate and bore the
responsibility of seeing that Elizabeth was never in distress. Dan's
will added to his duties as well. Having no children alive at the
time of his will-making, Daniel Carroll had bequeathed his properties to his grandchildren, William and George, with the stipulation that all management of the estate should be in the hands of
the bishop and his two brothers-in-law, Notley Young and Robert
Brent. To John Carroll as bishop Dan left "two acres of land comprehending and contiguous to the Roman Catholic Church" erected
on the Carroll estate, charming old St. John's Chapel. It was fortunate that John had inherited his father's business acumen. Young
Will and George Carroll, as it turned out, were his first wards, but
not his last. The bishop sometimes felt like a veritable *paterfamilias*
when he considered all the private transactions which required his
attention, as well as the increasing properties of the Diocese of
Baltimore. Just a few years earlier Alexius Elder of Emmitsburg,
Maryland, had deeded to the bishop a small piece of land near the
mountain for the purpose of building a church.[15] There were always
the details of English legacies, too, as well as the claims of the
American ex-Jesuit properties to be remembered. Whether he liked
it or not, the bishop's temporal responsibilities were growing more
extensive with every passing year.

And then, as if losses must occur in pairs, in 1799 Carroll was
faced with two more deaths, that of Pope Pius VI, the head of
Catholic Christendom, and that of George Washington, the former
chief executive of the nation. Once again the blows fell only a few
months apart. For some time the Holy Father had been in exile at
Valence, his last days saddened by the upheavals which followed in
the wake of the French revolutionary armies. Early in 1798 Pius VI
had been expelled from Rome at the command of the Corsican
adventurer, Napoleon, under humiliating circumstances. When
Napoleon's general had demanded his two rings the aged Pontiff
had replied with painful dignity, "I can give you one of them
because it is my own property. But the other will have to pass to my

successor." He was speaking of the Fisherman's Ring. On February 23 he crossed the frontier of his former domain and two days later reached Sienna where he stayed for three months as "the Prisoner of the Anti-Christ," as Napoleon was sometimes termed. The respite at Sienna was short-lived, however, and after miraculously escaping the earthquake which shook the ancient city about noon of May 26, 1798, the Pope journeyed to the Certosa near Florence. Although the French Directory talked of exiling him in Sardinia, for nine months Pius VI stayed on at the Carthusian monastery. When he was once more ordered to travel he was so paralyzed it required four servants to lift him into his conveyance. Across the snow-covered Apennines, in a fevered delirium, the tragic old Pontiff was carried, on through Bologna, Modena, Reggio, and Parma. On April 30 he crossed the border into France, and finally in July reached Valence where he was left to die.[16]

Meanwhile the rest of Christendom was uncertain from day to day of the Pontiff's condition, his whereabouts, or the means of communicating with him. On January 3, 1799, Strickland had written from London, "The situation of the Pope and of Italy has long been precarious, and it is now more so than ever. I do not apprehend that there can be any better way of communicating with him than by means of his agent in London, Mr. Erskine." He enclosed Charles Erskine's address in Edward Street, hoping in this way to facilitate Baltimore's communication with the papal court.[17] The old channels of correspondence through France were quite unreliable in the months preceding Napoleon's *coup d'état* which was to overthrow the Directory government in Paris. Carroll had been grateful for Erskine's services and wrote to him on August 20 of his previous difficulties in securing avenues to the Holy See. It had been nearly three years, he told the papal agent, since his request for a coadjutor for Baltimore had been approved, and yet neither the brief nor a duplicate had arrived to make the matter official. "My advanced age is a constant monitor to me of mortality," Carroll explained, in asking Erskine's indulgence in this matter of the brief.[18] He little suspected that within a fortnight the Holy Father would be dead.

On August 29, 1799, Pope Pius VI died, crying in a loud voice, "Father, forgive them." Two months later Erskine despatched the sad news to the Bishop of Baltimore.[19] It was not just the possibility of the Chair of St. Peter's remaining empty for an uncertain period which troubled Carroll. Eventually, on March 14, 1800,

Gregorio Cardinal Chiaramonti was elected Pius VII, and things would go on as usual in their slow, deliberate fashion, with the news of Roman decisions reaching America only after months or years had elapsed. The Bishop of Baltimore was depressed by the remembrance of things past. The Pope who had died in exile was the Holy Father who had confirmed the choice of John Carroll as the first bishop of the United States. It was Pius VI who had declared that "our beloved son, John Carroll," because of his faith, prudence, piety and zeal should head the Church in the new Republic. That had been ten long and arduous years ago. Now Pius VI was gone, and it seemed to the Bishop of Baltimore as if a little of himself had died with the news of the Holy Father's passing.

He ordered that a funeral service be held at once and that all priests of the diocese offer Masses of requiem as soon as convenient. His circular letter to the clergy carried Carroll's reflections on the Pontiff's death. "During the whole time of his pontificate," he reminded his priests, "irreligion and impiety never ceased from uniting their efforts to extinguish the faith and bring ruin to the Church of Christ." And yet Pius VI had never deviated in his fidelity, infused as he was, it seemed to Carroll, with divine wisdom and fortitude. His example, particularly to the clergy, encouraged others to imitate his zeal and constancy. No sense of danger to himself had ever diminished his pastoral solicitude. "If he committed any errors in his civil administration," Carroll continued, "it must be asserted for the honor of the Holy See that during such severe trials he maintained the doctrines of the faith in their integrity and as he received them from the successors of St. Peter." Persecuted and maligned, bending under the weight of years and infirmity, he had submitted his body to the power of his enemies but his integrity he had preserved forever before God and man.[20]

In Advent, that portentous season of beauty and longing, sorrow struck again. On December 14, 1799, after a short illness at his beloved Mount Vernon, George Washington died. No man was more generally mourned. In New York, his late capital, the silent cortege filed through the streets with the riderless horse, a poignant reminder of the absent hero. Congress hastened to proclaim that on the next anniversary of Washington's birth the nation would observe a day of general mourning, and the Bishop of Baltimore sent his clergy a letter requesting that they "bear public testimony of our high sense of his worth, and our sincere sorrow for being deprived of that protection which the United States derived from his wisdom, his experience, his reputation, and the authority of his name." [21] He would, of course, deliver the discourse at St. Peter's pro-cathedral himself. He set to work at once on the preparation of his sermon.

As he sat at his escritoire, quill in hand, frowning in deep thought, the great admiration Carroll had always felt for the first President came flooding back. Usually when great men die, he reflected, the mind leaps ahead to their possible successors and the talents they must possess to fill the void. But in Washington's case this was not possible. Never again, the bishop was certain, would one man unite so many splendid and useful virtues. The late leader had set such a pattern of public probity as had never been equalled in the eighteenth century. When the bishop contrasted the aftermath of the American Revolution with the years which immediately followed the French revolutionary convulsions, with their carnage and cruelty, he was convinced that it was the enlightened morality of Washington and his associates which had made the difference. It seemed incredible that Washington was now dead. True, when the bishop had last dined with the Washingtons that day in June of this very year, in company with his nephew's widow, Elizabeth Digges Carroll, and her brother, Washington's family physician had been present. But Dr. James Craig was a frequent guest at the Mount Vernon table, and neither the Bishop of Baltimore nor the other guests had any suspicion that these days of dining in such dignity and charm as always graced the general's table were numbered. That had been on June 11, the bishop recalled.[22] Now in December the great man was no more.

As Carroll went over his sermon, crossing out a phrase here, rearranging the sequence of modifiers there, inserting the semicolons he used to end his sentences, he reviewed in little spurts of recollection the relation George Washington had borne to his own career. They had both come into office at the same time—the President taking his oath of office on April 29, and the bishop being named by Pope Pius VI on November 6, 1789. Carroll had been delighted at Washington's election, and he had written elatedly to General Arthur St. Clair on January 29, 1789, "The cause of federalism is so fully triumphant in this state, that the whole federal ticket for Representatives and Electors of the President has been carried without the mixture of any other character." [23] That same year the Catholics had presented their address to Washington to which he had soon replied with his compliment on their part in the Revolution. At the synod of 1791 the bishop had initiated the custom of public prayer for the government to be said at the close of the Mass, a petition that asked that God would assist "the President of the United States, that his administration may be conducted in righteousness, and be eminently useful to Thy people over whom he presides; by encouraging due respect for virtue and religion; by a faithful execution of the laws in justice and mercy; and by restraining vice and immorality." [24] The bishop knew the words well. How many times since that November in 1791, he mused, had he uttered those words with George Washington's calm and chiseled features in mind, serenely confident that the prayer would continue to be answered.

It was in 1791, too, that the Carrolls had first interested themselves in Indian affairs in the west. In reply to a letter from Charles of Carrollton, Secretary of State Jefferson had written on April 15, 1791, "I thank you for the trouble you have been so kind as to take in this business. Our news from the westward is disagreeable. Constant murders committed by the Indians and their combinations threaten to be more and more extensive." [25] After the crushing defeat of General St. Clair on November 4 in the Ohio country, Bishop Carroll had felt compelled to offer the government his own recommendations. It was not presumption on his part. As early as July 7, 1789, Washington's Secretary of War, Henry Knox, had recommended to the President that missionaries of excellent moral character should be appointed to reside among the Indian nations since "such a plan, although it might not fully effect the civilization of the Indians, would most probably be attended with the salutary effect of attaching them to the interest of the United States." Since the President himself had opened the present session of Congress with the expressed sentiment that mild principles of religion and philanthropy might be the best system of conduct toward the Indians, Carroll felt it appropriate to direct a memorial to Washington on March 20, 1792, informing the chief executive that the Catholic bishop had priests "willing and desirous of devoting themselves to the charitable employment of reviving and continuing amongst those Indians the lessons of religion and morality." He suggested that since missionary work among the Indians could bring certain benefits to the United States the Congress might be asked to "make for a few years a small allowance for the necessary subsistence of clergy employed in disseminating the principles of Christianity among the natives of the Western Territory." [26]

Just at that time the President feared the situation in Ohio was too critical to risk needless martyrdoms, but he commented to Carroll:

Impressed as I am with an opinion that the most effectual means of securing the permanent attachment of our savage neighbors is to convince them that we are just, and to show them that a proper and friendly intercourse with us would be to our mutual advantage, I cannot conclude without giving you my thanks for your pious and benevolent wishes to effect this end upon the mild principles of religion and philanthropy.[27]

He said that when the proper occasion presented itself he would support such measures as might bring the blessings of society to what he termed the "untutored minds" of those fierce fellows. In the meantime, Washington had been too long a general not to be convinced that authority would have to precede enlightenment. Early in 1792 he sent General Anthony Wayne to subdue the northwestern Indians who had defeated St. Clair. Wayne's victory at Fallen Timbers in 1794 paved the way for the surrender of the British border forts from which much of the incitement of the Indians had emanated; and the Jay Treaty of 1795 did much to remove the British influence over the Indians in that region.

Washington had been as good as his word, too. He had gone before Congress with a request that a sum be appropriated for the Catholic priests who would minister to the Ohio Indians, and Carroll was able to report to Charles Plowden: "The president, as empowered by congress, has allotted a sum of money for the subsistence of two Catholic priests amongst the Indians of Illinois. I have sent two French emigrants thither." [28] In 1796 Bishop Carroll wrote to James McHenry, Knox's successor in the War Department: "You may rest assured that the persons appointed will make it their endeavour to reconcile the inhabitants to our Government and interests." At the same time Carroll told Secretary McHenry that if the War Department had any documents that might indicate enmity to the United States in appointees Carroll might name, the bishop would be very grateful to know of them. He had no intention of furthering the animosities of questionable priests, or of empowering any shepherd whose full loyalty to the United States was in doubt.[29] Now in 1800 the bishop reminded himself that he must write soon to the present Secretary of War, Mr. Samuel Dexter, to inquire if he intended to continue the sums to which the Reverend Mr. Rivet had become accustomed in the Illinois Country.[30]

Bishop Carroll had been most sympathetic toward Washington's foreign policy, too. He had viewed with repugnance the mushrooming of Republican clubs dedicated to French interests and swayed by Jefferson's avowal that the French Revolution was "the most sacred cause that man ever engaged in." Carroll told Archbishop Troy of Dublin:

> To oppose the mischief meditated by, and fomented through, the machinations of these societies we stand in need of the firmness, the undisputed courage, the personal influence and consummate prudence of that wonderful man, our President Washington. It is impossible for a person not thoroughly acquainted with our situation to know how much depends at this time on one man for the happiness of the nation.[31]

Like his cousin Charles, John Carroll had been deeply impressed by the wisdom he found in Washington's *Farewell Address* which was published on September 17, 1796. He told Plowden:

> You will see in the public papers an admirable address of our excellent president Washington to the people of this state on retiring from public life. He has far other principles of the necessity of Religion than the superficial French theorists on government. Tho I cannot help rejoicing at the prospect before him of enjoying some repose at the expiration of his quadriennium of service . . . yet I am fearful for this country when he is no longer the head of it to overawe the sowers of sedition and wild democracy.[32]

Charles Carroll had encouraged the Maryland Assembly to print the President's address as "a small testimony of the affection we bear." [33] The Bishop of Baltimore bore testimony to his own veneration for Washington's words when he pronounced his eulogy in St. Peter's Church that February day of general commemoration. Speaking of the late leader Carroll said feelingly:

> The last act of his supreme magistracy was to inculcate in most impressive language on his countrymen . . . his deliberate and solemn advice; to bear incessantly in their minds that nations and individuals are under the moral govern-

ment of an infinitely wise and just providence; that the foundations of their happiness are morality and religion; and their union amongst themselves their rock of safety.

The bishop's peroration was delivered from the depths of his sincerity and he concluded with the ringing words:

> May these United States flourish in pure and undefiled religion, in morality, peace, union, liberty and the enjoyment of their excellent Constitution, as long as respect, honor, and veneration shall gather around the name of Washington; that is, whilst there still shall be any surviving record of human events! [34]

At the close of his eulogy Bishop Carroll retired to his episcopal throne, exhausted but filled with satisfaction. It was one of his best sermons. He could tell by the solemn hush which persisted after his last words had died away. Well, that was as it should be. His greatest sermon for the greatest civil leader he had ever known. Men like Washington were not born any more. Or, perhaps, it was just that he was growing old. He held his lips rigid to prevent the wry smile that twitched at the corner of his mouth. No, he had meant what he said. "While he lived we seemed to stand on loftier ground. . . . He was invested with a glory that shed a luster on all around him." The Bishop of Baltimore did not expect to meet another man of Washington's stature in his life time.

CHAPTER XIII

CHOIRS OF VIRGINS

IT SOMETIMES seemed as if a bishop's work were never done. In spite of the aching adjustments to personal losses and grief, Bishop Carroll had to press forward, devise new plans, and meet the increasing burdens of his multiplying flock. Providing for a supply of priests through the agencies of Georgetown and St. Mary's Seminary was a solution to only half the problem. He was at no time blind to the compelling needs of the Catholic laity. General education must be provided. President Washington had been quite right when he said in his *Farewell Address* that whatever might be conceded to refined education both reason and experience demanded that religion and morality, those indispensable supports of political prosperity, be inseparably maintained. Certainly, the bishop could not neglect the foundations of his own flock's piety. Teachers for the young of both sexes must be secured.

Before Georgetown was ever opened John Carroll had contemplated the introduction of religious women into the United States. Father Thorpe in Rome quite agreed with his friend's conviction that nuns were invaluable, and he stated on January 16, 1788, "A house of Ursuline nuns, or of any other who by institute make a profession of educating female youth, might be of singular advantage in the provinces contiguous to your own residence." John Thayer, the Boston convert who was studying for the priesthood in Europe, was conversant with several convents in Paris and he tried to interest some English nuns there in an American establishment. Thayer was especially eager to introduce the contemplative "Theresians," as he called the Carmelites, into the United States; but Thorpe saw some disadvantages. He told Bishop Carroll: "If means can be procured for settling both Theresians and Ursulines, perhaps it would be advisable to bring in the latter before the others on account of their immediately visible utility." [1] If only Theresians were to go to the United States, Thorpe said, they would have to become temporarily in some fashion school mistresses. The bishop himself felt that the primary need at the time was for teachers; but, as it turned out, the first band of religious women to enter the Diocese of Baltimore were the Carmelites, a contemplative order.

The coming of the Carmelites in 1790 was quite natural. Many Maryland women in the eighteenth century had been drawn to the Carmelite vocation and had gone abroad to enter convents on the continent. Ann Matthews of Charles County, her two nieces from Port Tobacco, Ann Mills, as well as Bishop Carroll's cousin, Ann Louisa Hill, were all at Hoogstraet in Belgium in the English convent there. But the suppression of the Carmelite houses in the Low Countries during the revolutionary disturbances of 1789 made their future uncertain. Their confessor at Hoogstraet, another Marylander and old classmate of Carroll's at Bohemia Manor, was Charles Neale. Neale now offered the American Carmelites a farm at Port Tobacco, Maryland, as a refuge and the women gratefully accepted. Four of the nuns, accompanied by Father Neale, set out for the United States on April 19, 1790.

The travelers from Belgium could easily have passed their future bishop on mid-ocean, for Carroll was on his way to Lulworth Castle the very month that these Maryland Carmelites crossed the Atlantic. While he was in London Bishop Carroll heard from his cousin, Ann Louise Hill who had remained at Hoogstraet, that the four had left for America. "It is the subject of great joy," she wrote, "to hear our Holy Faith and religion flourishes so much in my native country. . . . I am glad our holy order is the first." [2] Although she was not going to the United States herself the bishop's cousin assured him that all his undertakings would be remembered in their constant prayers at Hoogstraet where she was now the superior.

The four nuns from Belgium, their confessor, and Father Robert Plunkett who was also on his way to Maryland, landed in New York City in July. They did not tarry in the northern port, but hastened to Norfolk and from there up the river to "Bobby Brent's Landing" on the Potomac. Ann Carroll Brent, the bishop's sister, welcomed the travelers to the Brent mansion, and Father Neale celebrated Mass for them in the Brent family chapel on the morning of their arrival. They spent a leisurely day at the Landing, enjoying the delicacies of a Virginia Sunday dinner. In the evening the nuns went on to the house of the Barrys, the bishop's Irish friends at George Town, and remained there for several days.[3]

There followed a brief period of uncertainty as to the permanent location for their convent. Father Charles Sewall at Baltimore in Carroll's absence advised the Carmelites to accept the house offered by Baker Brooke near Port Tobacco. On October 15, 1790, the feast of St. Teresa, the first Carmelite convent in the United States was dedicated. By the time the bishop returned to Baltimore the little group was quite at home in surroundings which, to Mother Bernardine at least, were sweetly reminiscent of her youth. Within two years John Carroll was able to write to Cardinal Antonelli that other women had been admitted for probation to the convent. "They are a salutary example to the people of the vicinity," he said gratefully, "and their singular piety has moved even non-Catholics to admiration." [4]

But the bishop's own purposes were still not served. He admitted to Rome that the convent would be of far greater benefit in the immediate future if a school for girls could be undertaken. The Congregation of Propaganda, comprehending the American bishop's needs, discussed the advisability of allowing the contemplative nuns to open a school. Cardinal Antonelli reported in September: "While they are not to be urged to undertake the care of young girls against their rule, they should be exhorted not to refuse this work which will be so pleasing to God and which is badly needed." Rome perceived that the great scarcity of workers and the lack of educational facilities made modifications of rules tolerable in this new diocese.[5]

It was a dilemma which John Thorpe had foreseen back in 1788 when he had advised against "Theresians." He was not at all sure that relaxing the rule of Carmel was a solution. If the Carmelites became school teachers, he told his friend, "After some time you will have neither good Theresians nor good school mistresses." [6] The nuns themselves did not believe their rule could be safely modified, and under the direction of Father Charles Neale they told the bishop they must refuse to become a teaching order. They had come to pray for the American missions, for the clergy, and for the Church in general, they explained. Carroll was momentarily irritated by this attitude on the part of the Carmelites and said as much to Plowden.

They have multiplied themselves considerably, and give much edification by their retirement, and total seclusion from the world, and I doubt not the efficacy of their prayers in drawing down blessings on us all; but they will not concern themselves in the business of female education, tho the late Pope, soon after their arrival, recommended it earnestly to them by a letter sent to me by Cardinal Antonelli. . . . As Mr. Charles Neale governs that house with absolute sway, I suppose, that the opposition arose chiefly from him.[7]

Plowden replied sympathetically that it seemed to him Neale was a "most unaccommodating" man.[8] In the end, of course, Carroll got over his pique. He could remember his own distress at the suppression of the Jesuits and could understand the ardent desire of the Carmelites to preserve the peculiar vocation to which these devout women had been called. The Diocese of Baltimore was dedicated to the Blessed Virgin. Had not the synod of 1791 prescribed that the litany in her honor, under the title of the Assumption, be said before Mass on Sundays and holydays? It was quite proper, indeed, that the first religious women in the diocese should be her devoted handmaids. The bishop was content.

Nevertheless, the need for teachers still persisted, and the Diocese of Baltimore waited hopefully for women who could devote themselves to this salutary work. A partial solution was not long in appearing. In 1792 three nuns of the Second Order of St. Francis, the Poor Clares, came to Baltimore to seek a place in Bishop Carroll's diocese. They first tried to locate in Frederick Town, north of the Monocacy River on Maryland's frontier, but they were unsuccessful. They next came to George Town where they acquired some property near the academy and proceeded to open a school for young ladies. Although the Poor Clares did not remain permanently at George Town, the spot which they had selected was destined to become later a lasting location for a girls' school.[9] This first attempt to establish Catholic education under the direction of religious women was continued under another group, the Visitandines, and it became eventually one of the most famous schools for women in the South.

The origins of the first convent of the Visitation Order in the United States are associated with the names of Miss Alice Lalor and Bishop Leonard Neale. While Neale was still a priest ministering in Philadelphia between the years 1793 and 1799 he had met Miss Lalor. This young woman from Ireland was already pledged to a life in religion, but she anticipated pursuing it in Ireland after

a brief stay in the United States. While she remained in Philadelphia, however, she and two widowed companions of her voyage
placed themselves under Father Neale's spiritual guidance.[10] It became Neale's task to persuade her to remain in this country and
assist him in founding a religious community so sorely needed.
When Neale went to Georgetown in 1799 he prevailed upon the
three "pious ladies" to come to the town on the Potomac to teach
at the convent of the Poor Clares. When Leonard Neale perceived
that the austerity of the life of the Poor Clares did not lend itself
to the needs of the times, he decided to organize his friends from
Philadelphia under a separate establishment. Thomas Betagh, in
Dublin, learned of it from Bishop Carroll in July, 1805, when the
latter wrote: "My coadjutor, the Rt. Rev. Bishop Neale, has formed
under the conduct of four or five pious ladies a female academy at
George Town and has acquired for them a handsome property of
lots and houses." After praising the nuns, he asked Betagh if he
could send two nuns to assist them in getting properly organized.
"One of them ought to be fit to become immediately the Superior
and mistress of novices," he suggested, "and the other to preside in
the female academy." [11]

Bishop Neale meanwhile formulated rules for the women based
on those of the Society of Jesus, and the women adopted a habit
resembling that of the Carmelites. When the Poor Clares gave up
their property in 1805 their superior, Celeste le Blond de la Roche-
foucault, transferred it to Neale. Within the library of books which
the Poor Clares left behind was contained a copy of the rules and
constitutions of the Order of the Visitation. In this chance circumstance the women of George Town found their directive. The Igna-
tian rule and the Carmelite habit were abandoned, and the women
under the direction of Bishop Neale adopted in practice and appearance the life of Visitandines.[12]

A decade or more passed, however, before the little group would
have the advantage of European example. Bishop Carroll tried in
their behalf to get women from Dublin and Brussels, but to no avail.
Both William Strickland and Charles Plowden were enlisted to
encourage Visitandines to come to the United States but English
nuns were not forthcoming, either. The *Gazetteer* of 1810 commented in its description of George Town, "The Roman Catholics
have established a college here, which is in a flourishing state," but
it made no mention of the women's academy. Indeed, the existence
of Leonard Neale's cherished institution for women remained very

precarious. Carroll himself grew dubious when he considered with Neale the uncertain canonical status of the prospective Visitandines. He asked Neale if a religious house of an order approved by the Holy See *could* be established without the concurrence of some authority of the Order of the Visitation. Was the convent on the Potomac capable of having religious bound by solemn vows while they remained unrecognized as a member of the order? He suggested that the ladies under Neale's direction might get around these difficulties by making simple vows after passing through such a novitiate as the rule directed, "to which might be added the vow *ingrediendi religionem*" and their consequent entrance into "a solid and perpetual engagement when this can be done regularly and consistently with the forms prescribed by the Church." [13] Carroll offered as alternatives a merging with the community Elizabeth Seton was about to found, or forming a community of Ursulines which a wealthy woman of Baltimore wished to endow. Still another proposal suggested a union with the Carmelites at Port Tobacco. But Neale remained optimistic and refused all these alternatives. And in the end he was vindicated.

On January 29, 1814, on the feast of St. Francis de Sales, the women finally pronounced their vows after a novitiate that had dragged on for fifteen years. After the coadjutor became Archbishop of Baltimore himself, one of his first acts was to petition Rome for recognition of his Visitandines, and on July 14, 1816, Pope Pius VII granted the request. On December 28, 1816, the rewarding event took place when Mother Teresa Lalor and the two oldest sisters received the white veil in the morning, and that afternoon, after pronouncing their solemn vows received the black veil and silver cross. By the end of January the community was permanently organized under their formal regime, and the new archbishop, serenely happy like Simeon of old, was ready to sing his *Nunc Dimittis*.[14] When he died the following year there were thirty-five nuns of the Order of the Visitation to pray over their patron's grave, which quite fittingly lay in the vault beneath their chapel.

But if Bishop Carroll owed his first teaching order to the persistence of his stubborn colleague at George Town, he was to acquire his second order of teachers through the unwitting generosity of Mr. Jefferson over at the Federal City. Thomas Jefferson, the most skillful exponent of the strict-interpretation-of-the-Constitution school of thought, found himself in a predicament as President of the United States. That vast, undefined region west of New Orleans carelessly labelled the "Louisiana Territory" had been virtually thrust into the hands of his commissioners whom he had sent to Paris to secure the city itself. Not having time to spare for amending the Constitution, and suspecting the inconstancy of the auctioneer, Napoleon, President Jefferson had taken refuge behind a convenient doctrine of expediency and, in 1803, had purchased Louisiana.[15] The treaty of April 30, 1803, had been quite a bargain for the new Republic, and with it Bishop Carroll found that he had acquired something himself.

Rome had defined the domain of the Bishop of Baltimore as containing "all the faithful living in communion with the Catholic Church . . . so long as they are subject to the government of the Republic, whether they dwell in the provinces of Federated America, or in the neighboring regions." The Louisiana Purchase thus made the whole Mississippi Valley a part of Carroll's jurisdiction. And with New Orleans and the valley he acquired another teaching order.

In 1727, the same year that Daniel Carroll of Upper Marlborough had married Eleanor Darnall and brought her to the Carroll house in Prince George's County, ten Ursuline nuns in France were planning a new beginning also. While the future bishop raced with his sisters down to the river's edge and back again, farther to the south, these French women were busy opening a school in the humid settlement which sprawled along the Mississippi toward Lake Pontchartrain. Successful from the very start, the French Ursulines conducted both a day school and a boarding academy for the girls of New Orleans and the plantations. While the young man from Maryland studied at Liège or taught at Bruges, and came eventually to his bishopric in the United States, the Louisiana community had seen several bishops come and go. From 1727 to 1803 they had belonged at one time or another to the Dioceses of Quebec, Santiago de Cuba, Havana, and most recently the Diocese of Louisiana and the Floridas.[16]

Although the treaty of cession was negotiated in 1803, all signs of previous French and Spanish dominion did not immediately disappear. In some places the flags of three nations were flown at the same time. Mother Thérèse de St. Xavier Farjon, the superior of the Ursulines, was not dismayed, but she experienced a natural curiosity as to the future of her order under the new regime of the United States. Accordingly, on November 1, 1803, she wrote to the Bishop of Baltimore.[17] John Carroll realized that the adjustments in property rights in a territory so transferred from one nation to an-other might properly belong to the Department of State, and so he sent Mother Farjon's queries to James Madison, Mr. Jefferson's secre-tary of that department, and recommended to Madison charitable consideration for the Ursuline establishment "which has hitherto provided a fund out of frugality and self-denial, sufficient to procure gratuitous education for nearly one hundred destitute female chil-dren." [18] The Ursulines themselves wrote directly to President Jef-ferson on March 21, 1804.[19] Before many months had elapsed the uneasiness of the Ursulines was dispelled. Secretary of State Madi-son presented Bishop Carroll's letter to the President who was favorably impressed by the bishop's explanation of the educational work of the nuns in Louisiana. Madison assured Carroll of Jeffer-son's "real interest" in promoting a pious and useful training in "this new portion of the American dominion." Governor William C. C. Claiborne in Louisiana had already been authorized to assure the ladies of the monastery of the "entire protection which will be afforded them." [20]

Meanwhile President Jefferson himself had written to Mother Farjon on May 15, 1804, in words of perfect courtesy, that the principles of the Constitution were a sure guaranty that their institution would be preserved without intervention from the civil authorities. He said:

> Whatever diversity of shade may appear in the religious opinions of our fellow citizens, the charitable objects of your institution cannot be indifferent to any; and its furtherance of wholesome purposes by training up its young members in the way they should go, cannot fail to insure it the patronage of the government it is under. Be assured it will meet with all the protection my office can give it.[21]

By May of 1812 Governor Claiborne was able to give the Ursulines a copy of the act of Congress which authorized the Secretary of War to facilitate the exchange of land with the Ursuline Nuns of New Orleans.[22]

The bishop now had three groups of religious women perma-nently established within the Diocese of Baltimore. Except in a general way he had had very little to do with the introduction of any of the three. The Carmelites had come while he was in England and were really the charges of Charles Neale. The Order of the Visitation was clearly the child of Leonard Neale's endeavors. The

Ursulines had been handed over, full grown, by the territorially ambitious hand of Thomas Jefferson. But one community which originated within Carroll's jurisdiction before his death was in a very special sense John Carroll's own. They were the daughters of Mother Seton, the Sisters of Charity of St. Joseph.

Bishop Carroll had first heard of Elizabeth Seton through the Filicchi brothers of Leghorn. Ever since Filippo had interested himself in the American prelate's affairs the Italian family had performed innumerable small services for the Diocese of Baltimore. When the younger brother, Antonio, came to New York in 1804 it was to be expected that he would carry letters of introduction to the Bishop of Baltimore. Before Antonio's business activities for the Leghorn firm permitted him to come to Baltimore, however, he was already corresponding with the bishop on a subject very close to his heart.

Antonio Filicchi was eager to see the completion of the conversion of Mrs. William Magee Seton, the widow of his friend who had offered the services of the Seton firm so many years ago to Father Thorpe in Rome. The firm of William Seton and Company had since been wiped out due to the reverses suffered during the undeclared war with France, and William had died in Italy in 1803 while trying to recover his health. When Antonio Filicchi accompanied his friend's widow to New York in 1804, therefore, he was in reality serving several purposes. Ostensibly, he traveled on business for the Leghorn counting house, and as a protector for the recently widowed Mrs. Seton; but he was in reality more concerned with Elizabeth Seton's spiritual dilemma. The thirty-year-old widow who faced the future with five small children and no visible means of support, had been attracted to Catholicism by the pious practices she had seen in Italy. It was Filicchi's hope that upon her return to New York she would enter the Church. Both he and Filippo had urged her to ask John Carroll for help and enlightenment, and when Antonio saw her reluctance to do so, he wrote himself on July 26, 1804, explaining Mrs. Seton's plight to the bishop and urging Carroll to send her some "invincible, direct reply." [23]

At the time the Bishop of Baltimore was spending his customary days of relaxation with his sisters at Rock Creek, and did not receive this first appeal before the worried Italian wrote again. Filicchi's second letter stressed the vital importance of Mrs. Seton's conversion, involving, as he pointed out, "the eternal salvation of six souls," the children's as well as the mother's. "From your in-

structions," he pleaded, "must depend the tranquillity of my conscience." The bishop wrote at once to Mrs. Seton after receiving
Antonio's letters, and his words were so encouraging to the confused
woman that she confessed to Antonio that she held them to her
heart while she went down on her knees to pray for guidance.
Filicchi gratefully told the bishop, "Your wise and holy instructions in such a delicate and interesting case . . . are certainly
the only adequate ones."

Salutary as Bishop Carroll's first letter had seemed, Elizabeth
Seton continued to wage her war with doubts and fears during the
fall and winter of 1804. When the new year was ushered in with
no decision on her part the Bishop of Baltimore warned Filicchi,
"She ought to consider whether the tears she sheds and the prayers
she offers heaven are purely for God's sake." Carroll suspected that,
perhaps, some "alloy of worldly respect or inordinate solicitude"
for temporal concerns might be her stumbling block. He was beginning to grow very interested in the outcome of this struggle going
on in the heart of Filicchi's friend. He experienced a pang of disappointment when in February Father Matthew O'Brien of St.
Peter's Church in New York informed him of several conversions
there, but added, "Mrs. Seton is yet in the scale." His pleasure in
May was great when he finally received Filicchi's announcement,
"Your learned remarks and advices have not been in vain. You will
certainly thank God and rejoice in the intelligence that at last Mrs.
W. M. Seton is numbered in your flock with her five children."

From that time on the Bishop of Baltimore continued to get
news of the New York convert from a variety of sources. His dear
friends, James and Joanna Barry, went north in 1805 to find a
climate more beneficial to their daughter Mary's health. In the
fall when Mary became worse the parents moved her to New York
City, and after her death in November they remained in New York
for some time. James had to make trips to Canada and Joanna
found one place as good as another for concealing an aching heart.
In the course of attending Mass at St. Peter's the Barrys met Mrs.
Seton and Carroll wrote to them commendingly, "I was most happy
to hear that you found an acquaintance with Mrs. Seton. Her situation and sacrifices have interested me so much." The Barrys and
the new convert soon became warm friends and Elizabeth Seton
caught her first glimpse of the bishop's patrician face in a picture
Joanna cherished of their old friend.

When Antonio Filicchi came to Baltimore in March, 1806, he

discussed with Carroll the matter of placing Mrs. Seton's two sons in a Catholic school. The bishop naturally felt that Georgetown would be more suited to the boys' requirements, but he advised Filicchi to visit St. Mary's, too. Touched by the valor of this widowed mother who had been willing to cut herself off from family and friends in order to become a Catholic, the bishop resolved to contribute something to her sons' education. When Filicchi returned from his inspection of the two schools Carroll told him of his intention, and to James Barry in New York the bishop wrote, "In concert with Bishop Neale, I provided means for their reception and education of her two sons at Georgetown for at least two years." Barry was to act for Mrs. Seton in arranging the other details with the college.

In late spring the bishop met Elizabeth Seton in person for the first time when he administered the sacrament of confirmation at New York on May 25, 1806. He liked her taking the name of "Mary" to add to her other two, and he insisted on addressing her thereafter as "Mrs. M. E. A. Seton." He was immediately charmed by the small gentlewoman's radiance and wit. The little Seton girls who clustered around their dark-eyed mother made him think in contrast of the young Carrolls and Catons out at the Manor. How different was their worldly portion! He resolved that these children should not suffer for their mother's courage, and after his return to Baltimore he made it a point to always inquire after Anna, Bec, and Kitty, and he begged Mrs. Seton to think of him always as their parent in God.

He discovered that he enjoyed indulging in a moment or two of light humor in his letters to New York, and occasionally he would relate to his Mrs. M. E. A. Seton the hazards of the episcopal office. He described the interruptions he suffered when a drunken sailor burst in upon his study to proclaim loudly that he was informed by inspiration or revelation that all his excesses had been forgiven. The bishop added drolly, "The same spirit which assured him of his conversion and forgiveness had ordered him to write and publish a book highly important to the United States. When it comes from the press you will allow me to send you a copy." The raillery never obscured the more profound understanding the wise old prelate possessed of his new friend's needs. He sensed an unusual yearning for sanctity in this small, energetic woman. He wanted to give her the guidance she sought so eagerly. "Whatever I learn of you," he told her encouragingly, "increases my solicitude, respect and admiration. But," he warned, "attribute no merit to yourself on this account. . . . It is beneath the dignity of a Christian, who has ever meditated on the folly as well as the criminality of pride, to glory in that which belongs not to him."

Carroll soon learned that his confidence in this convert's sincerity was well-founded. It began to appear that she had a vocation for the life of a religious and was seeking a solution that would not derogate from her children's prior claims upon her. She wrote asking him what he thought of her going to Montreal where she might be associated with a convent and have her daughters educated in a Catholic school. She would rely on his decision, she told the bishop. Carroll suggested that she consider some of the more practical aspects of the proposal. If the girls were unhappy in Canada, could she then return to New York? Could she get released from her present obligations to the boys who boarded with her while they attended St. Mark's School? While refusing to be responsible for her final decision, the bishop left Elizabeth Seton little doubt that he was not enthusiastic about the Montreal scheme. The next project with which she presented him was more to his liking. Through Father William Dubourg, who was now president of St. Mary's College in Baltimore, Mrs. Seton had begun to consider the wisdom of coming to Baltimore to open a school for girls within the very shadow of the bishop's wing. Dubourg had been in New York City on several occasions in 1807 and 1808, and he had been favorably impressed with the convert's piety. While he was in Boston he discussed her case with the Boston priests, Francis A. Matignon and John Cheverus. All agreed that it would be a pity to allow her talents to escape the country when the education of girls in the United States was so urgent. During the spring of 1808 Carroll was in poor health, and a painful inflammation of the eyes made writing sheer anguish. He begged Joanna Barry to apologize to Mrs. Seton for his neglect. When he received Elizabeth Seton's letter, however, and learned of the plan in a general way, he replied heartily, "Though I am entirely ignorant of all particulars . . . it is enough for me to know that it has the concurrence of Dr. Matignon and Mr. Cheverus." The die was cast, as far as Elizabeth Seton was concerned. If the bishop approved, then to Baltimore she would go.

The feast of Corpus Christi in 1808 was a dismal, dripping day. It very nearly spoiled the festivities out at St. Mary's Seminary and College. But the new chapel which Maximilian Godefroy had designed with such loving care was ready to be dedicated, and even if the bishop's seventy-year-old bones protested at the dampness, he was expected for the pontifical Mass and the rest of the rites. He did not hear the slight commotion during the singing of the *Kyrie Eleison,* nor did he see the four somewhat bedraggled travelers slip into a pew at the rear of the little church. And it is quite likely that he did not sense the fascinated stares of eight wondering eyes as they watched the Bishop of Baltimore perform the "awful ceremonies seen for the first time." But after the service was over and the crowds spilled out into the muddy yard which surrounded the brand-new building, John Carroll could see that Father Dubourg and his sister, Madame Victoire Fournier, were talking excitedly to a diminutive lady and three girls. Elizabeth Seton had arrived and was ready to move into the neat little house which adjoined the Sulpician grounds.

The bishop was satisfied that Mrs. Seton was in good hands there near St. Mary's, but he wanted her to feel that she had other friends as well. She must meet Robert Barry, James's nephew, who acted as consul for Portugal in Baltimore. The Barrys were quite willing to look after the Seton girls while their mother went to get the boys from George Town. Through the bishop, too, Mrs. Seton had access to the home of his younger relatives, Kitty Harper, Polly Caton, and their connections. It was apparent from the start, however, that Mrs. Seton had not come from New York to enter the whirl of Baltimore or Annapolis society. Although pupils were slow in coming to the house on Paca Street, she was determined to lead a life of regularity and discipline. She was in the chapel each morning at six and again at six-thirty in the evening. Bishop Carroll was enormously pleased with this newest addition to his diocese, and he saw to it that Judge Nicholson's niece entered her school and he enlisted Mrs. Seton's aid in preparing small children for their first Communion. He listened attentively as the earnest widow consulted him on the advisability of sending for her sister-in-law from New York; and Mrs. Seton wrote excitedly to Cecilia Seton, "Blessed Bishop Carroll . . . exhorts you not to enter in any engagement whatever." The bishop himself interceded with Father Anthony Kohlmann, Cecilia's pastor, asking that she be encouraged to come to assist Mrs. Seton.

It was evident to the Bishop of Baltimore that the Paca Street school was only a stepping stone for his young *protégée.* Elizabeth Seton had a vocation and was straining at the leash of worldly contacts. As early as October of 1808 she was telling close friends, "It is expected I shall be the mother of many daughters." Recruits appeared from widely separated places. One girl came from Philadelphia before the year was out and others appeared from New York and Baltimore. One even wrote from the hills of Emmitsburg, north of Frederick Town. Louisa Caton, the bishop's grandniece, whose beauty was already a portent of her later fame, considered briefly the possibility of following the magnetic little widow into the new community. Carroll told his sister, "She is resolved on renouncing the world altogether, and joining the most virtuous Mrs. Seton. . . ." Louisa Caton was only half in earnest, as it turned out, and a few months later the bishop admitted rather sheepishly to Mrs. Seton that his giddy young relative was in raptures over the social life in Washington, and particularly over what Carroll described as "the perfect freedom which reigns in our sister's family."

Louisa's inconstancy was the exception, however. Father Cheverus in Boston was more of a prophet when he told Elizabeth Seton in March, 1809, "I see already numerous choirs of virgins following you to the altar. I see your holy order diffusing itself in different parts of the United States." John Carroll cherished a similar dream. But the Bishop of Baltimore felt a special obligation toward Elizabeth Seton. When events began to point toward a mother house far from Baltimore, a community trying to take root on the Maryland frontier, the cautious bishop hesitated. What of the children? Could she fulfill her obligations as their mother? Mrs. Seton replied with characteristic simplicity that her daughters were eager to go to Emmitsburg, and that even were they to remain in Baltimore she could never provide the advantages which were thought so necessary in that environment. As for her sons, they could enter the Sulpician school for boys which was just getting started near Emmitsburg. She swiftly brushed aside the bishop's protests. He insisted, nevertheless, that when she took her vows in March she consider whether she should take a vow of poverty. "I have a doubt whether and how far you can keep that vow in your present circumstances," he said doggedly. It was respect for his wishes which led her to accept a dispensation from the vow insofar as it involved her freedom to handle her children's property for their own use.

Deep in his heart Bishop Carroll was vaguely disappointed at the turn events had taken. It had seemed to him at first that Elizabeth Seton's community had been meant for Baltimore, and he had not been loath to think of himself as their protector. Now in the spring of 1809 it appeared that Providence had designated the wilderness of northern Maryland to be the cradle of this infant community. The financial benefactor of Mrs. Seton's group, Samuel Cooper the seminarian at St. Mary's, had insisted on the Emmitsburg location and Mrs. Seton was convinced that Cooper had been divinely guided to this choice of location. It was only natural that the women should turn to the gentlemen of St. Sulpice as their protectors for they were already on the scene at Emmitsburg. The bishop was too old to contemplate that arduous journey more often than the regular episcopal visits demanded. He had learned the habit of graceful acquiescence, he hoped. Once the women had made their choice, he said, he surrendered "as much as a bishop can surrender," their government into the hands of Father Nagot and the council of St. Mary's. He did it with such good grace that Mrs. Seton was never reproached by his disappointment. She continued to pour out to him all her problems and woes, and he continued to send her his sage advice. The only way in which he ever betrayed himself was in his partiality for her side of the question when future differences arose between his ardent foundress and her Sulpician superiors. Whether in Baltimore or Emmitsburg, Mother Seton could rely on the unfailing support of the Bishop of Baltimore. The Sisters of Charity of St. Joseph were his first American sisters, founded by an American convert to meet an American need. They were just one more proof of what he had always believed, that the United States was a most congenial soil for the flowering of the Catholic faith.

CHAPTER XIV

DIFFUSION OF JOY

THE ladies who gathered about Mother Seton were not the only ones to be moved by the founding impulse as the nineteenth century began. Several religious orders of men attempted to plant communities in the rich soil of the American needs. Two groups, the Franciscans and the Trappists, met with little success in their first efforts to begin permanent establishments in an era of Jeffersonian democracy. Two others, the Augustinians and the Dominicans, were more happy in their endeavors. The most challenging development, however, was the restoration of the bishop's old society, the Jesuits, who emerged from the shadows of three decades with hesitant steps, frequently restrained by their prudent protector of those dark years of the suppression.

There is no way to account conclusively for the failures of the Franciscans and the Trappists to begin permanent establishments during the reign of John Carroll. The obvious difficulties which contributed to their discouragement were not insuperable. Where the Franciscans failed in Philadelphia, the Augustinians succeeded. Where the Trappists came to grief in Kentucky, the Dominicans triumphed. It is not consistent to say that the country was not ready for contemplative orders when the Carmelites were making progress at Port Tobacco, or to pretend that friars were not suited to parish work when the Dominicans were able to survive on the Kentucky frontier. Both the Franciscans and Trappists would succeed to an admirable degree in a later period within the boundaries of the United States. It is simply one of the facts of history that while Carroll lived neither of these orders became a permanent foundation within his jurisdiction.

Beginning in 1803, the Franciscans tried fruitlessly under the leadership of Michael Egan, O.F.M., for nearly a decade to establish a monastery in Pennsylvania. The Trappists led by Dom Urbain Guillet arrived in Baltimore in 1802 and likewise spent more than ten years in a succession of locations in Pennsylvania, Kentucky, Illinois, and New York, but to no avail. It was not until the middle of the nineteenth century that either Franciscans or Trappists were destined to begin lasting parent houses in the United States.

The Augustinians were more fortunate. On February 15, 1796, Archbishop Troy of Dublin notified Carroll that the bearer of his letter, Matthew Carr, was leaving Ireland permanently for the new world. Carr was an Augustinian and in the last provincial chapter in Ireland had been chosen superior of the Augustinian house in Dublin. Troy had known Carr for many years, and he told the Bishop of Baltimore he felt that Ireland's loss would be Carroll's gain.[1] The arrival of Father Carr in the early spring of that year marked the beginning of an attempt to found a branch of his order in Philadelphia. Matthew Carr and John Rossiter had been so commissioned by their brothers in Ireland, and they preferred an eastern city for their location. Carroll was somewhat disappointed that the frontier area had not appealed to them and he told Archbishop Troy, "I wished, indeed, that they would have directed their views for an establishment towards our great western country, because if able and apostolical men could be obtained to enter on that field it seems to me that it would become a most flourishing portion of the Church of Christ." [2] He was not insistent on his own preference, however, and left the men at full liberty to determine for themselves where they should locate.

The Augustinians settled quickly and efficiently in Philadelphia and by August of the same year Carroll was able to congratulate Carr on his initial success, and further notified him that he would serve as vicar-general for the northern part of the diocese.[3] Father Carr soon applied to the Holy See for permission to establish the new monastery and Rome replied on May 27, 1797, with an indult of consent. Bishop Carroll forwarded the good news to Philadelphia that the motherhouse for the Province of Our Lady of Good Counsel might become a reality. The cornerstone of St. Augustine's Church had already been laid in the September following Carr's arrival in the city, and with funds contributed by such generous Americans as President Washington, Governor Thomas McKean, Commodore John Barry, and augmented by gifts from the French and Spanish diplomats in the city, the monastery church was soon erected. Writing from Rome in May, 1797, the Prefect of Propa-

ganda, Hyacinthe Cardinal Gerdil, expressed the great consolation
that the Holy See felt at this mark of divine favor for the United
States. Contrasted with the darkness and the calamitous times which
then prevailed in Europe, the progress of religion in the new world
seemed like a beacon light of hope.[4]

Seven years later the Dominicans resolved to make a beginning
in the United States. On January 12, 1804, Father Edward D. Fenwick wrote from England that a long conceived project of founding
an establishment under Carroll's patronage was soon to become a
reality. "I now regard it as the will of heaven, since it is approved
and much recommended to me by our General at Rome," Fenwick
asserted.[5] In May Fenwick reported that although his immediate
superior in Carshalton, England, was raising some objections to
their going, three recruits were already offering their services for
the American venture.[6] It was actually October before Strickland
notified Carroll that he had learned that Fenwick and two companions had sailed from London. The English ex-Jesuit said, "I
sincerely hope they will succeed in their pious undertaking. The
field is large." [7] By November 29, 1804, Fenwick and one companion,
Father Robert A. Angier, had arrived in southern Maryland and
notified Carroll of their arrival. Fenwick added that he hoped the
other two recruits would be able to come in the near future.[8]

The new arrival from England, who was to become the founder
of the Dominicans in the United States, was a former Marylander
himself. Born in St. Mary's County in 1768, Fenwick had been sent
as a youth across the sea to study at Holy Cross College in Bornheim in Belgium. At the age of twenty he entered the Order of
St. Dominic and five years later was ordained to the priesthood.
The French Revolution had been no respecter of religious orders,
and the priests at Bornheim like others elsewhere found their properties confiscated, and Father Fenwick, in spite of his American
citizenship, had been arrested. After his release the Maryland Dominican crossed the Channel to England and sought refuge at
Carshalton in Surrey, outside of London. It was here that his decision to return to the United States was made.

All things considered, the negotiations preceding Fenwick's departure from England had encountered relatively little delay or
difficulty. His English provincial had given him permission to discuss the project with Rome and Baltimore. There happened to be
in Rome at this time a learned Irish Dominican, Richard Luke
Concanen, who was assistant to the master-general of the Domini-

cans; and it was Concanen who urged Fenwick to establish a distinct, independent province of the order instead of a branch of the English friary at Carshalton.

After his arrival at Norfolk, Virginia, Fenwick visited his relatives while waiting for Bishop Carroll to express himself on the steps to be taken next. At first the two men did not see eye to eye with regard to a permanent location for the enterprise. Carroll offered the Dominicans the Kentucky mission field as an area ripe for the harvest, but Fenwick explained that he had returned to the United States with the particular hope of locating the order in his native Maryland. This time the bishop would not be denied. Kentucky must be served. He could be stubborn if the occasion demanded it, and Carroll held out until Fenwick reluctantly agreed to surrender his dream of a college in his native state. Once the decision was made, the Dominican went west to inspect the field which he had agreed to till.

At the time of Fenwick's visit to Kentucky, Father Stephen T. Badin was in charge of that frontier region. Badin was a French *émigré* who had come to Baltimore in 1792 while still a seminarian. He completed his studies at the Sulpician seminary there and was ordained by Bishop Carroll on May 25, 1793, the first priest to receive holy orders at Carroll's hands. He had since been struggling valiantly on the mission and was sorely in need of assistance. Other priests had come and gone, but the French refugee persisted. His colleague of his first journey to Kentucky deserted Badin and went to New Orleans. Father John Dubois spoke frequently of his desire to come to Badin's aid, but he became absorbed in founding a college at Emmitsburg, Maryland.[9] The Boston convert priest, John Thayer did come to Kentucky in the summer of 1799 to be cordially received at Scott City, but before he had been there a year Badin began to suspect that he was quite unsuited to the Kentucky mission.[10] Thayer cherished some exotic theories that could only provoke trouble, Badin told Carroll. "I do fervently wish," he wrote to Baltimore, "that he may never become a follower of Raynald's false philanthropy in practice. As to the theory and discourse, he is evidently a disciple."[11] Badin himself had fled from France in 1792 when the worst fruits of Raynal's teachings had begun to ripen, and he had every reason to deplore the teachings of the ex-priest whose *Philosophical and Political History of the Indies* had argued that natural man was violated by civilization, and that religion was the invention of hypocritical priests. The Kentucky frontier was no place for attacks, however academic, on soldiers and governmental officials; and the Abbé Raynal had denounced such officials as existing for the sole purpose of victimizing peaceful citizens. Bishop Carroll himself had no sympathy for Raynal's theories. He had long since commented to Plowden on February 20, 1782:

> To me he appears the enthusiast, I had almost said the bedlamite of liberty. When a person, especially a Frenchman, born under an absolute government, has got his head full of sentiments of an English Whig, he is sure to extend them and push them to excess, like a spring which being bent too much one way recoils to the other with too great violence.

Thayer was also consorting with avowed Deists in Bardstown, and was talking recklessly of the emancipation of slaves in Kentucky where there were over 80,000. All too soon the convert priest erred in other directions as well and Carroll told Badin that scandalous rumors regarding his assistant were as prevalent in Baltimore as they were on the frontier. For the latter reason Thayer was ordered to refrain from saying Mass until an investigation could be made. On March 18, 1801, Carroll resolved to make Badin his vicar-general for the whole State of Kentucky and told Badin, "I empower you to assume that quality in all your official acts." [12] In the end, Thayer was ordered out of Kentucky and Father Badin again found himself overburdened with work. If it had not been for Father Michael Fournier who assisted him from 1799 to 1803, and Father Anthony Salmon, the new vicar-general would have been quite alone in his heroic efforts to serve the Catholics on the Kentucky frontier.[13]

The year 1805 was a brighter one for Badin. Father Fenwick's preliminary visit in the spring was an omen. Badin told Bishop Carroll gratefully on May 15,

> I have the happiness this day of enjoying the company of the Rev. Mr. Fenwick. . . . Many are the tokens of your goodness to me and my numerous congregations, and I have now to return heartfelt thanks for making Kentucky so effectually the first object of your pastoral solicitude upon the arrival of St. Dominic's family.[14]

On July 18 Father Charles Nerinckx, a Belgian priest, arrived to assist Badin. In the fall Fathers Thomas Wilson and William Tuite, two Dominicans, appeared to lay the groundwork for Fenwick's permanent arrival in 1806. In December the Dominicans purchased a house and 500 acres of land near Springfield, and St. Rose's Priory, the motherhouse of the order in the United States, was assured. Clearly a new era was opening in the Kentucky region.

Edward Fenwick was, quite naturally, the first provincial of the new province which had received official sanction from the Congregation of Propaganda Fide on March 11, 1805. Under his leadership the little nucleus went energetically ahead with their plans to start a college. Bishop Carroll gave his approval on April 25, 1806, and in 1807 the small school dedicated to St. Thomas Aquinas opened with twelve students, half of whom eventually became postulants in the Dominican order. The bishop felt a keen satisfaction when he contemplated this second successful attempt at founding orders of religious men, and he assured Father Concanen on November 21, 1806, "As long as my jurisdiction over that part of the Diocese of Baltimore lasts, nothing shall be wanting on my side to favour their object." [15] The faith was moving westward, slowly but surely. He marveled at the heroism of these frontier priests and he sometimes wished he were younger so that he, too, might labor more actively for the Church. The Badins and the Fenwicks were the real soldiers of Christ. But bishops were necessary, too, he knew. It was the old, old lesson to be learned anew each day. "Not my will, but Thine."

It was the restoration of the Jesuits, however, which most intimately concerned the Bishop of Baltimore. Many times during the interim of the suppression which lasted from August 16, 1773, to August 7, 1814, Carroll reflected on the mysterious ways in which Providence worked its miracles. The papal order which had decreed the suppression had been left up to the individual bishops to enforce, and oddly enough it had been in Russia that the only remnant of the society had been ultimately left to exist. This group of Jesuits in White Russia became as a matter of course the solitary hope of future greatness in the minds of ex-Jesuits elsewhere.

Scarcely more than a decade elapsed after the suppression in 1773 before vague hopes of a union with Russian Jesuits began to rise in American hearts.[16] The former members of the Society of Jesus in the United States as early as November 6, 1783, declared that they would "to the best of their power promote and effect an absolute and entire restoration of the Society of Jesus, if it should please Almighty God to re-establish it in this country," and Carroll had been one of the signers.[17] Father Thomas Talbot, hearing of the American dream of restoration, told Carroll that the United States ought to be an ideal place for the society since it was a "free State, independent of foreign potentates, where liberty of conscience is not controlled, where Catholicity was first planted by the Jesuits." He thought their affiliation with the Russian Province could be easily effected.[18] Plowden's letters in the spring of 1786 indicated that similar hopes were prevalent in England as well. Plowden sent Carroll a manuscript of an *Account of the Preservation and Actual State of the Society of Jesus in the Russian Empire Dominion,* and Carroll thanked him for it saying, "I have read it with great eagerness and infinite pleasure." [19] To Carroll the manuscript represented the history of a providential deliverance, and he passed it on to the other members of his clergy for their edification.[20] These gentlemen went on record in 1788 as having "come to a full determination of applying for this reunion, a determination not to be baffled by any attempts." But this time Carroll's name was not among the signatures.

The reasons for Carroll's reluctance to act hastily are not hard to find. As Superior of the American Mission he was responsible to the Roman Congregation of Propaganda Fide, and Rome had shown no signs of favoring a restoration as yet. Furthermore, the attacks upon him for alleged partiality toward ex-Jesuits by Fathers Smyth and La Poterie had reawakened old jealousies. The time was not ripe for aggressive action. He was placed in an unenviable position. He saw with misgiving that the old spirit of his beloved society was dying out and he confessed sadly to Father Beeston that he feared it would last no longer "than they live who have been trained under its discipline." [21] To Plowden he exclaimed, "O poor Jesuits! When shall we have you again?" It was not easy to be cautious. "It is singular enough," he commented, "that some of our own friends are blaming me for being too irresolute or indifferent, for not adopting their more intemperate councils with respect to restoring the Society; whilst, on the other hand, Smyth, the Abbé, and others, are accusing me of sacrificing to this intention the good of religion." [22] The great task, however, was the care of souls under his jurisdiction, and it was that work that Carroll was determined nothing should baffle. The need for priests attracted a veritable "medley of clerical characters coming from different quarters and various educations." He ruefully explained his dilemma to Plowden saying:

I cannot avoid employing some of them, and they soon begin to create a disturbance. As soon as this happens, they proceed to bring in Jesuitism, and to suggest that everything is calculated by me for its restoration; and that I sacrifice the real interests of religion to the chimerical project of reviving it.[23]

On the eve of his consecration as Bishop of Baltimore Carroll truly began to fear that restoration was indeed a dream. Perhaps they were only deluding themselves. And yet he could not help thinking that the society was never needed as at that very time. He told Plowden:

The late convulsions in Europe, when traced to their real sources, must discover to every thinking mind the necessity of a virtuous education, and of encouraging men, capable of conducting the rising generation through all the degrees of moral, religious and literary improvement. On whom then can the governing powers turn their eyes, but on those trained under the discipline of the Society? [24]

Nevertheless, he was compelled to restrain himself. At the very moment of his consecration at Lulworth Castle Cardinal Antonelli was being haunted by fears of the revival of the society in America, and Carroll admitted that it was fortunate that Propaganda's alarm had not preceded the issuing of the bulls for erecting the See of Baltimore, or the United States might still be without a bishop.[25] At least his caution had left Carroll free to reassure Rome that excessive devotion to Jesuit interests could not be imputed to himself. On September 27, 1790, he wrote to Cardinal Antonelli warmly praising his ex-Jesuit clergy and firmly stating that not one could be spared even to accommodate critics whose attacks were inspired by "cupidity, ambition, or hate." At the same time he refuted the charge of favoritism by pointing out that of the thirty priests he had commissioned as Superior of the Mission only seven were ex-Jesuits.[26]

By far the most cogent argument in favor of caution on Carroll's part was, however, his devotion to the true nature of the Society of Jesus itself. In 1795 when the other ex-Jesuits were eager to appeal to the Pope for a restoration of the society in the United States, Carroll stated his position clearly and beyond any possibility of misinterpretation. He said he was compelled to consider:

First, the precautions necessary in approaching the subject. Secondly, though it is so desirable a measure, yet I am far from an intimate conviction, that any considerable advantage would be derived from the reappearance of the Society with a mutilated and defective Constitution, instead of that one, complete in all its parts, by which the Jesuits were formerly governed. Indeed, I should have fears that such a restitution might be of prejudice by preventing a full and entire one, in some later period. The jealousies aroused by the Society's Constitution, and misrepresentations of it. Now, if for the sake of obtaining any kind of re-establishment we would submit to a breach of the Constitution a precedent would be obtained for never restoring the body in its original form.[27]

Although the Bishop of Baltimore could see, as he did on more than one occasion, some justification for modifying the rules and practices of some communities, if the Church and its needs in the new world were to benefit, he could never bring himself to conceive that anything but the original rule and constitution of his former society should prevail. The longer he studied them the more admirable he found them. As he said on a later occasion:

For those Constitutions I believe that no one feels more respect, or a higher estimate of their wisdom, not merely because I love the Society with the most filial tenderness, but because I have studied their excellence, and in various countries and circumstances have had the happiness of observing their effects. . . . Wherever these constitutions were observed in their letter and spirit, they raised men eminent in knowledge for defending the church, and illustrating its history, and doctrines; great masters of a spiritual life; zealous and disinterested labourers in all the functions of zeal and evangelical ministry . . . in whatever might conduce to the salvation of souls.[28]

He preferred to wait for a full and perfect restoration rather than be instrumental in divesting the society of one iota of its original virility. The same reasoning led him in 1800 to oppose affiliation with a pseudo-Jesuit society calling themselves the Paccanarists.[29]

The first substantial hope for restoration soon appeared, however. On March 7, 1801, a Pontifical Brief, *Catholicae Fidei,* granted canonical existence to the Society in Russia with the privilege of aggregating members from any part of the world. Carroll received the encouraging news from Father Strickland who added, "The Pope has also given it under his own hand that if any other sovereign desires to have the Society established in his dominions, he will concur with pleasure in the execution of that design." [30] The American ex-Jesuits were immediately interested, and Carroll begged Plowden, "Send me as early as possible, all the authentic information on this subject of which you are in possession;" while Leonard Neale at Georgetown wrote more poetically to the president of Stonyhurst in England, "We have heard of the re-establishment of the Society thro Mr. Strickland. But the clear light does not shine on us. You, who are nearer the sun, should not refuse to communicate its benign rays." [31]

When in 1802 Father Gabriel Gruber became general of the society in Russia, Bishop Carroll and his coadjutor Neale lost no time in appealing directly to him for further clarification. Had the Sovereign Pontiff permitted the erection of the society elsewhere than in Russia? Were only former members to re-enter or could new members be received? What probation was to precede the restoration of former members? Already their thoughts went racing ahead to the day when a general congregation would be held. How should the delegates be chosen? News came from England that the society there was partially restored under Charles Plowden by aggregation to Russia. Optimism mounted, and with it impatience for some word from Father Gruber.[32] A year passed without any word arriving in the United States from Russia. Nevertheless, Father Gruber had written on March 12, 1804, justifying American aggregation, and describing the means by which it could be accomplished; and when the letter finally arrived the ex-Jesuits in the United States speedily acted upon its directives. On June 21, 1805, Bishop Carroll named Father Robert Molyneux to head the restored Society of Jesus with the heartfelt prayer, "That God may bless this attempt to restore the Society in the United States, and all your efforts to effect it." [33] After his cousin Charles, Robert Molyneux was the bishop's oldest friend.[34] Together with Charles Sewall and Charles Neale, Father Molyneux was the last remnant of the old society. Neither Carroll nor his coadjutor felt that they dared risk the society's future by joining themselves at that early date. Both had given serious thought to resigning the episcopal office to resume their former status as Jesuits, but a second glance had showed the present state of affairs too uncertain. Carroll had voiced his fears to Strickland the previous year. "If after abdicating one's property another Pope should declare the re-establishment, in virtue of a mere verbal promise, void and contrary to ecclesiastical institution," he queried, where would they find themselves? "I sincerely hope that the Pope will soon be so unfettered," he continued, "as to be able to issue in full and authentic form a bull or brief for re-establishment." [35] But until such a time, the mystery and distrust which surrounded the restoration in England made him wary. The Bishop of Baltimore had no desire, after thirty years of patient waiting, to see the diocese fall into the hands of a bishop who might prove inimical to the society during this period of uncertainty.

Carroll was seventy years old that year, and he thought with longing of the joys of closing his life within the society which he had loved these many years since he "went up the hill to Watten." But he had been forced to sacrifice his personal preferences before, and it was too late to start pampering himself now. Robert Molyneux and his colleagues would have to bear the brunt of the work of revival. Meanwhile the bishop would bide his time. Until a full and canonical restoration was forthcoming from Rome Carroll would act as a buffer between the American Jesuits and their enemies both in the United States and elsewhere. He was not deceived. New recruits would quickly outnumber the few old men who were the only ones with any experience in the Jesuit way of life. The whole question of property rights would demand solution, and transfers of property were apt to be effected with noticeable shortness of temper.[36] Needless antipathy between the secular clergy and the Jesuits must be prevented. As he explained to a later superior of the revived society:

> You must not put it out of your mind that Bishop Neale and myself, as we are now the only prelates who were ever Jesuits, so probably we may be the last, who will ever be called to govern any of the Churches in this country. It is therefore of importance to establish a precedent, as will convince our successors of its being for the advantage of their dioceses to live in perfect intelligence with the Regular Clergy, and especially our Brethren.[37]

No, whatever his personal wishes might be, the bishop could serve the whole Church best by postponing his own re-affiliation.

In the end Carroll was rewarded. On December 7, 1814, as Archbishop of Baltimore, he had the supreme pleasure of receiving a copy of the bull *Sollicitudo omnium ecclesiarum* which restored the Society of Jesus throughout the world. He wrote joyfully to the Jesuit superior at Georgetown, *"Laudemus Deum et exultemus in eo!"* And to Charles Plowden he said from a full heart, "Your most precious and grateful favour of October 8, accompanied by a copy of the bull of restoration . . . diffused the greatest sensation of joy and thanksgiving." [38] The old archbishop had less than a year to live and he had paid dearly in the time between 1805 and 1814; but he had lived to see his beloved society fully vindicated. Anyone who had any memory of the former services of the Jesuits, who had heard of the unjust and cruel treatment they had undergone, or who had witnessed the terrible consequences of their suppression must now surely rejoice. It was too late now for John Carroll ever to take up his old vocation, but the awful pain of that suppression in 1773 was wiped out at last. Once more the Society of Jesus had come into its own.

CHAPTER
XV

ALARUMS, EXCURSIONS, AND SCHISM

THE test of greatness in a man goes beyond the coincidences of noble contemporaries and momentous occasions. His ultimate measure is taken by the shaping of events which in his absence would have taken quite a different course. It is only when one speculates on what the Catholic Church in the United States might have become without him that the true stature of John Carroll emerges. Silhouetted against the leaping flames of nationalistic prejudices, the lurid light of faction and revolt, the figure of the first Bishop of Baltimore takes on gigantic proportions. Perhaps no other man was so capable of adjusting the many disparate and warring elements within the country to that precarious balance which at Carroll's death not only insured its survival but also predicted the marvelous future of the Church in the Republic.

The Church in Carroll's time had two distinct modifying characteristics; it was in the first place a minority culture in a predominantly Protestant nation, and it was essentially English in its composition. Numerically speaking the Catholics in 1790 were scarcely 30,000 in three millions. From the point of view of national origins, although there were numbers of Irish, French, and German immigrants within the Church their proportion to English Catholics was no greater than the larger proportions of all non-English elements in the nation to the total English population.[1] Although within this Anglo-American minority nationalistic friction sporadically burst into flame, Bishop Carroll preserved substantially undiminished the unity of his flock. It was no small accomplishment. He had to combat quarrelsome priests, ambitious trustees, nationalist predilections, outright schism, and even the threat of an independent church. Resistance to authority cropped out from Boston to Savannah; querulous complaints poured in from the seacoast to the Mississippi Valley. Flagrant abuses were perpetrated by Irish, Germans, French, and English alike, while immigrants and American converts brought equal grief to the door of St. Peter's Rectory in Baltimore. If the whole sum of abuse, misconduct, and actual vice were to be presented it would seem as if Carroll must have been inundated by a floodtide of harassments. To recount only a few typical challenges to his leadership will serve, however, to suggest the genius of this father of the American hierarchy. Schism and trusteeism in Boston and Philadelphia, German nationalistic ambitions in Pennsylvania and Maryland, and the specter of an independent church in Charleston will suffice to show Carroll's greatness.

Carroll's troubles in Boston with Father La Porterie, of which we have already spoken, in the days preceding the bishop's consecration were a portent of things to come. Oddly enough, the bishop's difficulties in Boston after his consecration at Lulworth Castle were caused by an American, Father John Thayer, the Boston convert. Carroll had heard a great deal about Thayer during the years that the American convert was studying for the priesthood abroad. Strickland had said just before Thayer left Europe:

> He is a good man and though a little out of the common character of missioners has done much good in London and its suburbs. He has not quite so much deference to the opinion of his elders as I could wish on some occasions, but this I attribute to the want of education and the overgrown ideas of American Liberty.[2]

When Thayer arrived shortly afterward in Baltimore Carroll greeted him cordially and accompanied the convert on part of his journey northward. At the time Thayer was filled with apostolic zeal and was impatient to reach Boston where he could spread the blessings of his new faith. The bishop noticed a particular ignorance in the Bostonian on matters of authority and discipline. Like many another convert he seemed to wish to speed up the age-old cautious machinery of the Church. He was quite ready to be made superior of the New England area and found nothing presumptuous in the notion. Carroll was not unaware of Thayer's eagerness for power, but he was not given to random reproofs. He would wait and see. Heaven knew Boston needed zealous priests and Carroll could always stomach a little arrogance in others if the good of the Church would be served.

The bishop's toleration seemed at first to be wisdom. Thayer's arrival in Boston was accompanied by an almost immediate increase in the congregation.[3] Baptisms increased and Lenten devotions took on new meaning. Thayer encouraged the sale of Catholic books in the city, and circulated an account of his own conversion. He was an energetic preacher and made use of his talents twice during the week, as well as on Sundays. He reported to Carroll the cordiality which greeted him on all sides, and the bishop mused on the curious ways of Providence that chose such instruments.

And then Father Thayer's officiousness began to make trouble. Father Louis de Rousselet, the other priest in Boston, had come there in September, 1789, at Carroll's request. In prevailing upon Rousselet to go to Boston the bishop had said, "I know very well that you will meet with difficulties, but all first settlements have such." Neither Father Rousselet nor Bishop Carroll expected that the difficulties in Boston would stem principally from another priest. But in January, 1790, the first hint came. Thayer wrote to Baltimore that because of the poverty of his congregation there was great hardship in maintaining even one priest, and he said peremptorily, "I should, therefore, wish you to place Mr. Rousselet in another parish as soon as possible as he will be in some measure useless here on account of his language." A short time later he wrote again demanding what he called an "authentic paper in Latin" which would constitute him "superior of the mission in New England." Carroll replied coolly, "I was not edified with your first letters asking superior authority and ridiculing Father Rousselet's pronunciation." When Rousselet amiably offered to leave Thayer in command in Boston the bishop-elect objected. There were enough French parishioners in the city to make his stay desirable.

As Easter drew near, however, the rift in the Boston congregation became more apparent. With Rousselet's decision to remain, the Irish became apprehensive lest Thayer would then leave, and told Carroll so. Carroll at the time was preparing for the voyage to England for his consecration and was unable to visit Boston, but he wrote to both the French and Irish groups, "If harmony and subsistence cannot be had without my appointing one pastor exclusively of the other, Mr. Rousselet must be nominated on account of prior residence, age, and his having been desired of me in the name of the congregation to send him to Boston." Carroll exhorted his charges to lay aside all national distinctions and attachments. "Strive to form," he admonished them, "not Irish, nor English, or

French congregations and churches, but Catholic-American congregations and churches." On June 1, 1790, he named Rousselet as
sole pastor; if Thayer could remain with the Boston church, well
and good, but if he did he must be subordinate to Rousselet. The
bishop-elect then sailed for Europe.

During Carroll's absence Thayer and Rousselet continued their
rivalry and staid Boston was treated to the odd spectacle of their
respective adherents "bawling, threatening, vociferating, and brand-
ishing their clubs" in the old church on School Street while Father
Thayer screamed from the pulpit in vain efforts to appease the
tumult. In the course of the rioting the French faction removed
the church furnishings to Father Rousselet's house at 23 Union
Street and held Mass there; the Irish remained in possession of the
dismantled church building on School Street. Carroll's vicar-general
for the northern district, Father Francis A. Fleming, O.P., tried to
effect a temporary settlement pending Carroll's return by granting
the two Boston priests separate jurisdictions. And there matters
rested briefly.

On December 28, 1790, the Boston *Herald of Freedom* announced that "the Right Rev. Doctor John Carroll, lately consecrated Bishop of the Catholic See in America" had returned to Baltimore. Fleming summarized the Boston situation for the new prelate,
and told his superior that he believed Rousselet might be ready
finally to resign, and that for the good of all this might be the best
solution. The French priest in the later months of the schism had
descended to the use of indecent allusions and uncharitable expressions and Carroll was persuaded that he was no longer suited
to pastoral work in Boston. Accordingly he notified Thayer that he
would acquiesce to Fleming's promised appointment of Thayer as
pastor.

Scarcely had Carroll reached his decision when he received from
Rousselet's partisans letters which presaged further dissensions.
After congratulating the bishop on his safe return to the United
States the French faction reiterated a series of charges against
Thayer and invited Carroll to come to Boston to see for himself.
They were doomed to disappointment. On March 10, 1791, Bishop
Carroll told them:

> Though it gives great pain to me, as I am sure it will to you,
> I must send you notice that reasons of a most urgent nature
> demand of Mr. Rousselet the resignation of his pretensions

to the pastoral office of Boston. He himself will make this known to you. As I cannot, without the greatest inconvenience, set out for Boston before the end of Lent, I earnestly request you to use all your endeavours . . . to acquiesce in this necessary and indispensable measure, and to make use of the ministry of Mr. Thayer, notwithstanding all natural reluctance, till I can make a permanent establishment for that congregation.

What the bishop did not relate to the congregation was that he had just received from France letters revealing matters very prejudicial to Rousselet's character. He wrote privately to the priest of this information and begged him to resign before the public had a chance to hear of the scandal. He assured the Frenchman that he would never divulge the damaging information, but that Rousselet must now retire peaceably. "I feel great anxiety for you on every account," Carroll said soberly, but he went on to add, "As soon as you receive this you will understand that I revoke all powers and faculties which were granted by me." The bishop's heart was sorely troubled. He knew how the affair must look to the uninformed observer. Certainly Thayer's own conduct did not merit his emerging victorious. But the Catholic people must not be left bereft of all religious service, and his information concerning Rousselet made the removal of the French priest imperative. He could only hope that Father Thayer might reconcile the French now that their leader was gone from the scene.

In May the bishop went himself to Boston. He was the first Catholic bishop to visit that city, and the respectful and hospitable reception accorded him was impressive testimony to Carroll's dignity and worth. At the annual banquet of the Ancient and Honorable Artillery Company at Faneuil Hall he was invited to return thanks at the close of the meal at which the rector of Trinity Church had asked the blessing. The bishop also attended an annual service of the Humane Society at Trinity Church, and was a guest of honor along with Governor John Hancock. Carroll later thanked Hancock for the courtesies extended during his Boston sojourn, and he told the governor:

I knew that your Excellency was conspicuous for civility and politeness, as well as eminent for patriotism and public services; and I had always heard that the town of Boston was distinguished for its hospitality. But everything was far beyond my highest expectations.

Although a more skeptical observer of Carroll's triumph commented, "The cause which he meant to serve is not the foundation of this respect; it is wholly owing to his personal character," there is little doubt that Carroll's visit did much to dilute the harsh judgments of Catholicism which the conduct of Rousselet and Thayer had elicited. The sermon which he preached on the second Sunday of his stay was heard by a "crowded and very respectable audience," and his listeners were edified by what was described as the "charity, benevolence, and the piety" of this bishop which seemed to contradict previous notions that Roman priests were victims of "superstition and priestcraft." Carroll himself was very pleased with the deference accorded him and he commented to Charles Plowden, "It is wonderful to tell what great civilities have been done me in this town, where a few years ago a popish priest was thought to be the greatest monster in creation."

Carroll remained in Boston for three weeks, preaching on Sunday, confirming thirty people on Ascension Thursday, and conversing with leaders of both the French and Irish groups within the parish. He skillfully eluded the more persistent questions about the reasons for Rousselet's resignation, and he secured from Thayer a written promise acknowledging the bishop's authority and his own obligation to submit to possible removal in the future. To the congregation he made it clear that Father Thayer was to be accepted as their pastor as long as Carroll or his successors should judge it to be proper.

After the departure of the Bishop of Baltimore on June 16 the Boston *Herald of Freedom* was unstinting in its compliments to the city's distinguished visitor. It proclaimed enthusiastically:

> As a preacher, his talents were admired; as a companion, his society was sought; as a man, he was esteemed, revered, and honoured. The narrow prejudices entertained by the ignorant or the illiberal, vanished from the radiance of his candour, and shrunk from the test of his piety. Under his auspices, even the prejudiced view with more favorable eyes, a religion which he so truly adorned. . . . Boston would congratulate the hour of this Gentleman's return, and will remember with gratitude and pleasure, his visit to the State.

Bishop Carroll did not anticipate that his visit would heal all the wounds which the Thayer-Rousselet schism had inflicted; nor did he cherish the foolish hope that Thayer's nature would change. He was scarcely surprised, therefore, when he learned of subsequent violence of behavior on the part of the priest and resistance on the part of the French parishioners in the weeks following his episcopal visit. But relief of a permanent sort was in view. On June 6, 1791, Thomas Talbot had written from London that Providence had placed a very worthy man under his guidance. "He wishes much to put himself under your care," Talbot continued; "he knows English very tolerably already." The priest was Francis A. Matignon, a French *émigré* whom Talbot had quickly come to love and esteem. Talbot, who knew something of Thayer's past, commented that Matignon would make a most proper companion for Thayer since the Frenchman would be able to respect Thayer's zeal without being blind to the convert's "foibles," as Talbot called them.

Father Matignon sailed from Le Havre on April 9, 1792, in company with the Sulpicians, François Ciquart, Gabriel Richard, and Ambrose Maréchal. Four more valuable men to the Church in the United States probably never traveled together. Ciquart was to serve the Indians in Maine; Richard would do yeoman service in far-off Michigan; Maréchal became in time Archbishop of Baltimore, and Matignon brought lasting peace to the troubled Boston congregation. Soon after Matignon's arrival in Boston, John Thayer agreed to go south to work in the mission field of Virginia, bequeathing all his properties, ecclesiastical and personal, to Father Matignon, and explaining to his bishop, "My extreme love for the Boston Congregation made me desirous of retaining so valuable a man as the Doctor, and made me look out for another place for myself, knowing that both of us could not live there." [4] Thayer's belated concern for the Church's welfare was generously rewarded. In little more than a year Matignon had healed the schism, completely paid off the church debt, and substantially softened public hostility to the Catholic Church. From that time on the progress of the Church in Boston went steadily forward.

In Philadelphia a somewhat similar situation developed during the early years of Carroll's episcopacy, only this time the Germans rather than the French gave the temporary schism a nationalistic aspect. As early as 1787 the Germans in Philadelphia had expressed their dissatisfaction with Father Lawrence Graessl whom Carroll had appointed after the death of Ferdinand Farmer. They had suggested their preference for John Heilbron, a German Capuchin, and when Carroll refused to remove Graessl the discontented group raised money to build a new church and began work on Holy Trinity.[5] Philadelphia was growing rapidly and there was little doubt that another church would be useful. Carroll accepted the assurances of the German leaders that they were only concerned with the good of souls, and suppressed any stirrings of irritation that he might have felt at the original spirit which had prompted the undertaking.

On March 22, 1789, the builders of Holy Trinity Church elected John Heilbron as their pastor and announced their choice to Carroll. They believed that having built the church, and having pledged the support of its pastor they were entitled to elect their own man. The principle implied was too dangerous for Carroll to allow, as generous as he meant to be. He pointed out that the congregation had no authority in the selection of pastors, and he refused to accept Heilbron's election, stating categorically that the German Capuchin would be suspended if he did not acknowledge Carroll's authority. Heilbron expressed his willingness to submit to the superior and promised that he would never act anywhere "as an officiating clergyman without submission and dependence to the ecclesiastical authority," as he put it. He signed a document evidencing his good intentions, and Carroll then appointed him pastor of the new church. Seeming accord prevailed when Carroll visited Holy Trinity early in 1790 to administer confirmation there. After Carroll's consecration Father Heilbron left Philadelphia to travel in Europe in the hope of securing financial aid for his church. He never returned, and the first phase of the Philadelphia dissidence was over.

The next outburst of trusteeism came six years later. Father Peter Heilbron had succeeded his brother at Holy Trinity in the intervening years and was going about his pastoral duties in a generally uneventful way when Father John N. Goetz arrived from Austria to reopen the old issue of parishioner preference. Goetz quickly gathered about himself a faction who supported his arrogant demands for equality with Heilbron, and when the rightful pastor refused to accede to the trustees' demands the Goetz faction succeeded in deposing Heilbron and installing their favorite. When Bishop Carroll learned of the trouble he warned both Goetz and the warring trustees that they stood in danger of excommunication. Leonard Neale, the pastor at St. Mary's Church, was by this time bishop-elect, having been named Carroll's coadjutor in April of the preceding year, and he published a pastoral letter to the German Catholics of Holy Trinity explaining their errors. To their claim that they enjoyed the old *jus patronatus* or right to name their pastor Neale retorted with a lesson in church law, saying explicitly:

> You have no *Jus Patronatus.* You can have none, because your church has no fixed, permanent and unalienable fund for the support of a pastor. . . . Besides, though you really possessed the *jus patronatus,* it would entitle you merely to present, and not to appoint or discharge your pastor. For according to the practice and doctrine of the Catholic Church, from the Apostles's days down to the present time, all pastors are appointed by their respective bishops, without whose concurrence and approbation they can have neither mission nor jurisdiction.

Neale concluded bluntly terming Goetz and his adherents schismatical and heretical.

Unfortunately, the Goetz faction was not susceptible to logic. The rift widened perceptibly when Father William Elling, "a trouble-breeder" from southern Pennsylvania joined the Goetz party. In February of 1797 Bishop Carroll himself intervened. In a letter aimed at persuading the recalcitrant members to come to terms he explained that he had deferred addressing them until the present time in the hope that their attachment to their faith would have prevailed. "But my expectations have proved in vain," he said; and it was now imperative that he point out to them their grave danger. He spoke plainly of Goetz's insubordination and the fatal consequences their own actions must produce. The bishop's tone was calm, judicious, and charitable. He said:

> I am conscious of feeling every disposition, not only of good-will, but of tender solicitude to promote the welfare and respectability of your congregation, and the increase in all godliness; so I cherish the hope that a sense of religion . . . and an awful horror of the guilt of schism and apostasy will revive in all hearts and banish out of them discord and disobedience, and bring back again the pleasing prospects of extending the reign of Jesus Christ in truth and holiness.

The truth was that Carroll saw in the Philadelphia schism the gravest danger to the Church. He told Plowden in July, "I am afraid that the greatest part of the Congregation and a noble new Church built by them, will be lost to our religion." [6] The issue involved did not permit compromise. The German malcontents were putting forth the claim that dependence on Rome or submission to bishops appointed by Rome represented submitting to a foreign jurisdiction. It was an error common enough in the thinking of those outside the Church; but now to have it defiantly asserted by a group of supposed Catholics was unthinkable. All during his visitation in Virginia that summer he mulled over the question. The logic of his position seemed so irrefutable. He decided to make another attempt at enlightening the Philadelphia schismatics. On July 28, 1797, he put it all down in the admirable reasonableness which was his habitual mode of expression.

"I am responsible to God and men for the sacred trust," the bishop began; "permit me to specify some of the terms." Bishops have a divine right to govern their flocks in spiritual matters. This right is communicated to them either immediately by Christ Himself on their lawful appointment or mediately through the successor of St. Peter. All inferior pastors must receive their missions and spiritual jurisdiction from the bishop or persons exercising episcopal power in his name. Even if any person or group should possess a right of patronage or presentation of a priest to a vacancy, the priest must be presented to, approved and inducted by the bishop before he can exercise any spiritual jurisdiction. Once the clergyman is constituted the pastor of a congregation they have no lawful power or right to dismiss him, but only the right to complain of his neglect, immorality, or incapacity to the bishop who will then be bound to examine the validity of these complaints. Furthermore, there is no appeal from the bishop's decision in the case within his competency except to his metropolitan, if he have one, or in cases purely spiritual to the Holy See or deputies appointed by it. In the present case, Carroll pointed out, the Diocese of Baltimore had no metropolitan; and pending appeals from his judgments, the bishop's decision was not to be suspended. This was not only explicitly stated in the papal brief for the erection of the Diocese of Baltimore, it had been decreed by the Council of Trent and, as a matter of fact, was even a part of Anglo-Saxon law, "as may be seen in Blackstone concerning bishops and persons," he added.

When even this exposition produced no recantation Carroll was forced to excommunicate both Fathers Goetz and Elling. The schism was now a reality. Even though Goetz left Philadelphia soon after, the Germans under Elling's leadership continued in their disobedience. When Bishop Carroll went in person to Philadelphia in 1798 the trustees had him arrested and the counsel for one of the ringleaders, James Oellers, in open court denied the bishop's authority or jurisdiction over Holy Trinity Church, and foully abused the Church, its laws and doctrines, its government, the Pope, and the Council of Trent. It was the nadir of human respect, that John Carroll in all his personal and episcopal dignity should be exposed to such insolence. It seems inconceivable that any man subjected to such indignities could go on negotiating with his persecutors, but the Bishop of Baltimore was too big a man for them all. Submission to his authority was what must be achieved, and when the trustees made overtures to him in November, 1801, the bishop instructed Father Carr, the pastor of St. Augustine's Church, to treat with the schismatic group. It was this very James Oellers who on November 30 asked Carroll for a speedy reconciliation. The following January Elling submitted to his bishop saying, "I shall always acknowledge in you my common father and bishop. . . . I ask you one thousand times pardon, my dear Sir." Such was the magnanimity of the Bishop of Baltimore that all censures were removed from Elling and he was made the rightful pastor of the church to which he had formerly brought so much distress. On March 12, 1802, Carroll told Plowden in relief, "It gives me great pleasure to inform you that the German schism at Philadelphia is now extinct; and to my great satisfaction the abettors of, and its principal authors . . . have made to me the acknowledgement of their submission in the most satisfactory terms." [7] Elling remained as pastor of Holy Trinity until October 25, 1806, when he resigned to be succeeded by a Jesuit, Adam Britt. It was Britt who less than a year later informed Carroll that he needed an assistant who could speak English since so many of his congregation had forgotten their German mother-tongue. Not only was the schism healed, it appeared, but the first wave of German nationalism had spent its force.

Although the Philadelphia troubles were primarily those of trusteeism, two somewhat paradoxical elements emerge. The nationalistic bias of congregations and priests indicated a stubborn clinging to old world culture and customs. But the appeal to the civil courts in the midst of the controversy was decidedly American. This quality of the changeling in some of his people could not help but complicate the problems of the first bishop. Nor were these two contradictory elements confined to Philadelphia alone. In western Pennsylvania a German Franciscan from Mainz stirred up a similar hornet's nest. Again the right of bishops to name pastors was involved; again the civil courts were invoked. But in this case there was an added legal complication involving the validity of a will.

The year prior to Carroll's consecration a Dutch priest from the Danish West Indies came to Carroll for faculties, and having been granted them he proceeded to Westmoreland County in Pennsylvania. Father Theodore Brouwer was apparently a man of some wealth for he purchased in that area 165 acres of land in 1789, and the following spring acquired a farm called Sportsman's Hall. Having been in poor health from that time on, Brouwer made a will on October 24, 1790, bequeathing his extensive holdings to "the priest that shall succeed him to that place." Within a week Father Brouwer was dead.[8]

Father Francis Rogatus Fromm, the Franciscan from Mainz, arrived in the United States in 1789, as Carroll later stated, "unsolicited, unexpected, and unknown." Since Carroll was always willing to use priests if nothing were known against their characters, he appointed Fromm to reside at Conewago. Fromm did not remain at his post, however, but moved on to Westmoreland County where he took over the properties and pastoral duties of the late Father Brouwer. He notified Bishop Carroll in August, 1791, that he had been chosen by the congregation there and intended to serve them. Fromm's disregard for the bishop's authority resulted in Carroll's notifying him on May 13, 1793, that any and all powers formerly granted to Fromm were thereby revoked. Nearly a year passed before Fromm acknowledged his bishop's letter, and in the meantime Carroll learned that the congregation were dissatisfied with the German's pretensions. While the bishop was in Conewago in August, 1795, he resolved to write to both the congregation and their self-styled pastor. To the Westmoreland Catholics he said:

The Rev. Mr. Fromm as you know already, having never been commissioned to exercise pastoral functions amongst you, I now inform you that he is likewise suspended from celebrating Holy Mass; which if he shall presume to do in defiance of ecclesiastical authority, it is hereby enjoined on you not to attend at his Mass.

Carroll promised to secure a pastor for them as soon as possible, and asked them to sanctify the Sundays and feast days by private religious exercises at home until a pastor could be sent.[9] To Fromm he wrote less cordially:

> Though I have no reason to suppose that you will pay any more regard to the contents of this, than any of my former letters, yet I think it my duty to make known to you that you have incurred the penalty of suspension from every exercise of your order, even that of celebrating Mass, and that I hereby interdict you from that as well as every other function of your priesthood until you come before your Ecclesiastical Superior to answer the charges against you.[10]

Carroll's August letter brought an immediate response from Fromm, and the bishop believed he read in it some beginnings of a returning sense of duty. With his customary charitableness he told Fromm, "I promise to recommend you to be pastor of some Catholic Congregation . . . within as short a time as possible after I am convinced of the integrity of your principles and perfect morality of your life." He said that Fromm knew in his heart that he had acted contrary to every ecclesiastical rule. "Your resignation of Mr. Brower's property," Carroll suggested, "without any compulsory measures, would be one strong evidence of your sincerity." [11] When Carroll referred to compulsory measures he meant the action which the executors of the Brouwer property intended taking to recover it from the German usurper. Unfortunately, the bishop's hopes for any lasting reform in the Franciscan's conduct were immediately blasted. Before the week was out he learned from the priest himself that he had not only gone on administering the sacraments after having been forbidden to do so, but he had further secured a lawyer to defend his occupation of the Brouwer property. Pressure was put upon the bishop to excommunicate Fromm, but Carroll demurred, saying that it would give too much cause for anti-Catholic feeling. The case, as far as the civil authorities were concerned, would have to rest on its own merits.[12] If he understood the law, and he had always been much interested in it, he doubted that Fromm's counsel could have much "reliance on the real merits of his case." As he pointed out to the counsel for the executors:

> Though the authority of the Executors extends not to freehold, yet after Mr. Brower's death, the care of all his property devolved on them, till a priest was presented to be settled on the land, as the will directs. . . . The happiness of

Society and the constitution of the Commonwealth of Pennsylvania require that every religious denomination shall exercise the right of appointing their Ministers, according to their respective rules and discipline, if not repugnant to the laws of the State. Now the Roman Catholics having . . . their particular form and discipline for the appointment of the Ministers of Religion . . . it follows that the Executors have not yet performed that duty, which, as such, belonged to them, of surrendering Mr. Brower's property to a priest appointed agreeably to the discipline of their Church; and that Mr. Fromm, by holding possession, obstructs the execution of their duty; and therefore, that they rightly institute a suit against him.[13]

The reasoning of Carroll was soon vindicated in the Pennsylvania courts. Judge Alexander Addison's decision in 1798 said specifically:

The Bishop of Baltimore has, and before, and at the time of Fromm's taking possession of this estate, had the sole episcopal authority over the Catholic Church of the United States. Every Catholic congregation within the United States is subject to his inspection and without authority from him, no Catholic priest can exercise any pastoral functions over any congregation within the United States. . . . Fromm had no such appointment or permission, and is therefore incompetent to discharge the duties or enjoy the benefits, which are the object of the will of Browers.[14]

If the Bishop of Baltimore found any gratification in the civil authority's recognition of his spiritual powers in Pennsylvania he was not yet free from the kind of conniving which had precipitated this particular case. Indeed, under the bishop's very eyes, at St. Peter's pro-cathedral, a German priest was already plotting more resistance. A certain Father Cesario Reuter, after having been welcomed in Baltimore to assist the German Catholics there, began fomenting a plan for a separate church within the city to be distinctly German. Carroll was willing to admit the need for a new chapel within the parish, but he adamantly opposed an independent church. When his bishop's opposition and his congregation's poverty prevented Father Reuter's ambitions from materializing, he went to Europe and tried to ingratiate himself at Rome. There he complained that Carroll was not doing justice to the German Catholics, he recommended giving the Germans a Catholic bishop of their own, and he displayed a catechism he had prepared for the instruction of German-Americans. He succeeded in giving such a favorable account of himself that the Holy See relieved him of the censure under which Bishop Carroll had placed Reuter. Encouraged by his reception in Rome, the German priest returned to Baltimore in 1799 and resumed his ministry at St. John's Church in spite of Carroll's opposition. But Reuter over-estimated his power. When he attacked Carroll again in a letter to Propaganda in April of that year the cardinal-prefect replied rebuking Father Reuter for his insubordination to his bishop, and branding as false his accusations that Carroll had forbidden the use of the German language in his parish. Reuter was reminded that he himself had preached in German in Carroll's pro-cathedral. Rome saw no purpose in a separate church or bishop for the Germans of Baltimore; nor was there any need for a German catechism.

Reuter was not easily swayed, however, and by August 24, 1799, Carroll informed Propaganda that the recalcitrant pastor had carried his congregation into open schism. He hinted that Reuter had taken Rome's attitude as encouraging resistance to his bishop's authority. What the attitude of the Maryland civil authorities might be remained to be seen. Carroll said plainly:

> We live among non-Catholic sects, and there is no hope of civil magistracy or the secular powers putting these stubborn men in their place. Therefore, it seems to me that it is of grave importance to strengthen episcopal jurisdiction rather than lessen it by exemption; for if the power of the bishop fails, then all hope of regulating the moral conduct of the clergy and of the laity perishes.

He was heartened by the reply he received to his plain speaking. Hyacinth Cardinal Gerdil wrote on December 14, 1799, that Propaganda had no intention of abetting Reuter's actions. Carroll's reputation for prudence, piety, character, and learning was too high in Rome to permit any undermining of his authority. The following week Rome rebuked Father Reuter for his actions. But it was only after four more years of controversy, and a court action in which Carroll was again vindicated, that the bishop's authority over St. John's Church was finally recognized by the erring pastor, congregation, and trustees.[15]

There was never any question of Carroll's genuine concern for the spiritual welfare of the German-speaking members of his diocese. At the time of Reuter's dissidence there were only thirty Germans in Baltimore unable to speak English, and the children in these families already used English more fluently than they did the German. Carroll's conditions laid down for Reuter's submission said clearly that consent could be obtained for a German church providing the bishop's authority be recognized and that the church be considered as a chapel within the parish of St. Peter's Church. The Baltimore crisis was plainly one more of the sort which resulted from an exaggerated nationalism on the one hand, and an eagerness to invoke the courts in an attempt to gain lay control of church properties on the other. At the very outset, both of these tendencies are understandable. The assimilation of a minority group into a strange environment, a strange polity, and a strange culture is neither easy nor rapid. The Catholic Church was not the only institution that had to cope with the difficulties inherent in a "melting pot" national community. Nor were misunderstandings over property rights surprising. Although the right to administer Church property belongs to the Church, from the very beginning lay trustees had acted as assistant administrators of such property in the United States, property furnished and supported in many cases solely by the congregations whom the trustees represented. It was only when controversies over a particular pastor arose that national loyalties and the question of property rights became distorted. Resentment at episcopal appointments led to false claims on the part of congregations and their trustees, claims that since they furnished the church they had the right to select their pastor. As long as minorities remained within the Catholic population, as long as the trustee system prevailed, such controversies could arise; and since both factors did prevail long after Carroll's lifetime, later bishops were destined to face the unpleasantness which nationalism and trusteeism could produce. John Carroll's contribution consisted in his firm and undeviating insistence upon episcopal authority in spiritual matters and his forthright representations to the Holy See on this subject. Threat of schism could, and would, flare up again. But Carroll's successors were secure in the exercise of their episcopal powers.

But Carroll himself was never to enjoy the fruits of complete victory while he lived. One area he never succeeded in pacifying was the region of the South. The issues of trusteeism and independent churches reared their ugly heads in Norfolk, Virginia, in

Charlestown, South Carolina, and in Augusta, Georgia. Father Michael Lacy kept comparative peace at Norfolk while Carroll lived, but Father Simon Felix Gallagher at Charlestown and Father Robert Browne, O.S.A., at Augusta remained insubordinate and troublesome to the end. Through all of these trials the magnanimity of Carroll shows clearly. The patience, the charity, and the firmness of the founder of the American hierarchy never failed. The letters to the trustees of Charlestown in later years show the same lucidity, the same strict adherence to the principles of canon law, and above all, the same zeal for souls which permeated the earlier letters to Philadelphia, Boston, and Baltimore. Father Gallagher, like Father Fromm, was offered a chance to start anew in some other area.[16] No door was ever closed by Carroll's hand to the repentant priest or the reconciled congregation. No bishop coming after him would ever face such vast domains to govern spiritually, but every bishop thereafter could do no better than to model his judgments and actions upon those of the first Archbishop of Baltimore.

CHAPTER
XVI

ARCHBISHOP CARROLL

JUST before Easter, in 1808, the Bishop of Baltimore sat down to write a note to his coadjutor over in George Town. Easter was later that year, and the bishop was in a generous mood. After extending his fatherly solicitations to the ladies of the Visitation who were Neale's dearest charge, Carroll said, "With this you will receive one, and the most brilliant, of the two beautiful mitres which were presented to me last year by some of the benefactors in Flanders. . . . Du Cherrai has promised to take great care of it and deliver it safely before Easter Sunday." [1] He smiled in satisfaction. He liked to think Leonard would have the more elegant of the two mitres. Carroll was too old to care about such things anymore. And, perhaps, his conscience would feel less guilty over some of the criticisms of Leonard's intellectual abilities he had confided in Plowden. The coadjutor had certainly not proved to be the assistant the diocese needed; but Leonard Neale was a man of virtue. The Bishop of Baltimore was the first to say so. He hoped his coadjutor liked his new mitre.

But help was definitely needed in the administration of Carroll's domain. The diocese had always been enormous from the very start, including as it did the whole territory governed by the United States. He doubted if any bishop in Europe ruled a larger domain. But since the acquisition of that vast uncertain territory called "Louisiana" beyond the Mississippi, there seemed to be no end to the bishop's juridical trials. Something would have to be done, Carroll mused. Back in 1791 when he had first suggested to Rome a division of the diocese, the Holy See had demurred, preferring a coadjutor with the right of succession. True, at the time Lawrence Graessl had been named coadjutor-elect in 1794 Rome had admitted, "Should the Catholic Religion, under the Divine blessing, spread further and the harvest of the Faithful prove more plenteous, it may be necessary for the Apostolic See to appoint more labourers . . . with episcopal jurisdictions." But there it had ended. When Father Graessl died before he could be consecrated Leonard Neale was made coadjutor in his place, and that was how things stood for another decade.[2]

What a time they had had getting Leonard consecrated! Although the bulls for Neale's appointment were issued in April, 1795, it was more than five years before he was officially raised to the episcopal dignity. The brief from Pius VI had not arrived until September, 1800. Then yellow fever, "that new pest of our country," had broken out in August and continued to rage on into November. Baltimore had been no fit place in which to collect as many priests as were proper for such a ceremony. Then when they had finally fixed upon December 8, word came over from Washington that Joanna Barry was critically ill. The bishop had been at his wits' end to know what to do. Francis Beeston, the only possible substitute for Carroll in the Barrys' eyes, was away on the Eastern Shore at the time and the bishop was alone at St. Peter's. The arrangements of Neale's consecration depended solely upon him. He sent a hasty note over to James Barry, describing his plight, and assuring him that if Joanna really needed him he would get there somehow, but that otherwise he dared not stir from Baltimore.[3] Eventually they managed to get Neale consecrated, and Joanna recovered to outlive poor James and both the girls. Bishop Neale had taken his new splendor back to Georgetown College where he had been presiding since March 30, 1799. It was not that Neale was useless in Philadelphia. More than any other clergyman, Carroll knew, Neale had worked to reunite the warring factions in that city.[4] But Georgetown needed a president in 1799, and the serenity of the academic life was more suited to a man still weakened by the ravages of yellow fever. Neale, like Francis Fromm, had been caught in the ravages of the epidemic of 1798, only with less fatal results.[5] But between the college and the interests of his "pious ladies," whom Neale had brought from Philadelphia to teach in George Town, the coadjutor had not perceptibly lightened the burdens of the Bishop of Baltimore. Carroll could not repress a smile when he recalled James Barry's dry remark, "There's no danger of Neale setting the Potomack on fire." [6]

When Pius VII succeeded to the throne of St. Peter Carroll wrote to the Congregation of Propaganda asking that the division of his diocese be reconsidered. In June, 1802, Cardinal Borgia answered that he failed to see how a division of the diocese would really ameliorate conditions unless several new dioceses were created. Four or five, instead of one new diocese, should be erected if Carroll's burdens were to be substantially decreased. Carroll was invited to suggest possible boundary lines, episcopal cities, and candidates worthy to hold such high office. He told Plowden happily that at last relief seemed in sight. "Probably a multiplication of dioceses may be the means of multiplying priests," he added hopefully.[7] Heaven knew there was still a lamentable dearth of respectable clergy in the United States.

Once the Bishop of Baltimore put his mind to the practical aspects of sub-dividing his domain he soon reached the conclusion that four new sees would be the best solution. The first should be at Boston and would comprise the five New England States. New York City should have jurisdiction over the State of New York and east Jersey. Philadelphia could have control over the rest of New Jersey, Pennsylvania, and Delaware. The fourth diocese should embrace Kentucky and Tennessee, while Baltimore, of course, would continue to rule over Maryland and the South. It was not too difficult to decide upon limits for the jurisdictions or the see cities. He eventually agreed to Bardstown for Kentucky, instead of either Frankfort or Lexington which had first appealed to him. The concentration of Catholics in and around Bardstown, plus the urgings of Badin, his vicar-general, made that place the ultimate choice for Kentucky.[8]

But suggesting candidates to become the respective bishops in these areas was another matter. In some cases the decision was made difficult by the presence of several admirable candidates; in others it was necessary to choose between less worthy men; and in New York, as Carroll knew to his sorrow, there was simply no one at all. In Boston, for example, there were Matignon and Cheverus. Ever since his arrival in 1792 Father Matignon had worked tirelessly for the Church in Boston and in the surrounding country. In 1796 he had been joined by another excellent French priest, John Cheverus of Mayenne. Cheverus had come to Boston upon the urgent pleading of Matignon, and together the two men had worked marvels in the New England area. During the critical years of the trustee trouble in Philadelphia Carroll had considered moving Cheverus to that schism-ridden city, but both Cheverus and Matignon had dissuaded the bishop from separating them. In 1799 the two French priests had begun plans for erecting a church and had allowed neither legal nor financial difficulties to deter them. Carroll told Plowden in February of 1803 that this very handsome and large church in Boston, "formerly the hotbed of the most rancorous Calvinism," was nearly finished and that he expected to go to Boston in the summer to consecrate it. The ceremony had been planned for August 15, a date very dear to Carroll for many reasons, and the Bishop of Baltimore found himself hoping to combine business and pleasure. If James and Joanna Barry were still at Newport when he went north in August he might stop there to see them.[9] But between February and September the event was twice postponed and the bishop's plans had to undergo many a change.[10] Holy Cross was finally dedicated on the feast of St. Michael the Archangel, September 29, 1803, and it was quite an occasion for both Boston and Bishop Carroll. The bishop and priests vested in the house of the Spanish consul in Franklin Square, and went in procession to the church where the crowd of Catholics and non-Catholics over-flowed into the churchyard.[11] There were many who recalled the bishop's earlier visit to Boston and who wanted to catch a glimpse of the great man once more. Father Cheverus preached the sermon that day, and as the bishop listened to the stirring sentences he thought, "Here is a man of ability." Cheverus would bear watching.

Bishop Carroll was not the only one impressed with the Boston clergy. When the Italian merchant, Antonio Filicchi, spent the winter there in 1804 he exclaimed, "With what worthy clergymen are here Catholics blessed! Their countenance, their conduct, their doctrine are acknowledged almost with enthusiasm by most Prot-estants themselves." [12] The only question, then in regard to a bishop for Boston would be resolving upon one of two excellent men. Carroll was always prone to give first place to those who had served the longest, and his first choice naturally fixed upon Father Matig-non the pastor. While Carroll was in Boston for the dedication he alluded to the subject of the division of the diocese, and hinted at Matignon's selection. Men close to the pastor at Holy Cross sus-pected Matignon would be very reluctant to accept episcopal office; and they were right.[13] When James Barry came to Boston in Sep-tember, 1804, with the news that Carroll intended naming Matignon, that good man wrote beseechingly to Baltimore, "I even dare to conjure you, if only for the honor of the episcopal dignity, to put a peremptory end to some rumors which have spread on this sub-ject. When I compare them with what I am, they humiliate and mortify me more than I can tell you." He went so far as to say that if Carroll really meant him to be a bishop he would "flee to the other end of the world." [14]

As time went on Matignon's aversion to the episcopal dignity became more obvious. On April 6, 1807, he wrote at length to Carroll justifying his reluctance. "I am thoroughly convinced," he said, "that if the distance that I have always lived from you had not made it an impossibility for you to know me, you would never have thought of such a choice." He went on to say that the good that had been done in Boston was almost exclusively the work of Cheverus. "He it is who occupies the pulpit, who is oftenest in the confessional, and who is my counsellor in all that is to be done." Matignon listed his own incapacities: his poor memory, his failing eyesight, the rheumatism which prevented even short journeys. Cheverus was the more able man in every way. "The title of Doctor of Theology which is the one advantage I have over him, cannot assuredly," Matignon protested, "supply for the lack of all virtue." [15]

The Bishop of Baltimore sat in silent respect after reading this letter. What a contrast to Thayer, that self-seeking grasper after authority! Boston was truly blessed. But there was a great deal of sense in what Matignon had said. Physical weakness could be an overwhelming handicap to a bishop of a diocese that would comprise all of New England. When Carroll finally gave Rome his opinion he stated, after praising Matignon:

> If the Holy Father and the Sacred Congregation see fit to accept the objections of this excellent man, who for no reason of self-indulgence but out of a conviction of bodily infirmity refuses to take the burden, there is no one else to think of than . . . John Cheverus. He is not only in the flower of age and health to undertake any labor whatsoever, but enjoys the highest esteem among all the people because of his indefatigable zeal, his incredible facility and success in preaching, and his personality by which he marvelously draws people . . . to the practice of piety and the setting aside of prejudice to the Church.[16]

Rome agreed with Carroll. Cheverus should be bishop in Boston.

If naming a man for Boston was complicated only by the rival virtues of the candidates, finding someone for New York was in the end prevented by the opposite situation. Older accounts of the division of the Diocese of Baltimore found Carroll's failure to name a candidate "a strange omission" prompted by "secret motives" and pregnant with danger to the independence of the American Church.[17] The simple fact is that there was not one man who had served in New York City since Carroll's own consecration in 1790 who was worthy of the post at the time the division of the diocese became a necessity. This seemingly harsh indictment of the many priests who flitted in and out of St. Peter's Church in Barclay Street is amply attested by the correspondence which raced from New York to Baltimore, and proceeded more temperately from the bishop's residence back to the parish rectory in that thriving port. Carroll refrained from naming his preference for Bishop of New York because he had the welfare of that same American Church at heart. There was not one stable, trustworthy, active man available in 1807 when Carroll was making his recommendations. We have the bishop's own testimony. He told Plowden on December 5, 1808, "I had no one fit for that station because when I wrote amongst the clergy in that state there was none whom my judgment approved as fit for it . . ."

In the first place, neither of the two O'Briens, William or Matthew, turned out satisfactorily. In 1787 when William O'Brien had gone to New York to repair the ravages wrought by the Nugent affair, Carroll had been filled with high hopes. He told the newcomer:

> I beseech you not to lose courage, for if you should I candidly own that I do not know where to find a clergyman in the United States who could replace you. I really consider your arrival in America at so critical a period as a providential designation of you to repair so dreadful scandals and heal such dangerous wounds given to religion as its first introduction into New York.[18]

O'Brien had, indeed, seemed a providential arrival in 1787, and for two years he served in New York with general success.

In 1789 William O'Brien determined to go to Cuba and Mexico to solicit money for the support of the church, and for two years he traveled, collecting money and religious objects for St. Peter's of Barclay Street. After his return in the fall of 1792 Father O'Brien struggled valiantly to save his immigrant congregation from the recurring attacks of yellow fever. Carroll tried to send him an assistant from time to time, but no one suited both the pastor and his bishop. In 1796 the trustees suggested John Thayer, but O'Brien objected violently, telling Carroll that he hated the Boston convert above all men. O'Brien, in turn, mentioned a Norfolk priest to whom Carroll objected saying, "He does not come up to my idea of the person fit to be your vicar. New York is a city of too much consequence not to demand superior abilities." [19] Two Irish Dominicans, Michael Burke and Bartholomew McMahon, had stopped for brief sojourns in New York but it was not until the turn of the century that a more permanent assistant was obtained in the person of Matthew O'Brien, a priest formerly stationed at Albany. Carroll had really intended the second O'Brien for Natchez but he had to notify the gentlemen of that city on February 1, 1801, "Rev. Mr. O'Brien who has kept me long in uncertainty has finally declined going thither at all." [20] Sometimes Carroll wished that he had gone south, that New York might never have heard of him at all.

Matthew O'Brien entered into the work at St. Peter's with a great deal of zest. As early as January 5, 1801, he was writing to his bishop of his plans for an organ, an organist, and a choir which he hoped would be "on the plan of Baltimore and Philadelphia." He was teaching catechism twice a week, and attracting converts to the fold. There was no question about the brilliance of his preaching. Long after Matthew O'Brien left Albany the trustees there complained to Carroll that their present priests did not come up to the talented Dr. O'Brien. By the end of 1801 the younger O'Brien was enthusiastically telling Carroll of the erection of a steeple on St. Peter's Church, the purchase of a bell, plans for a new iron railing, and the possibility of opening a chapel in "the extremity of the city where most of the poor Catholics are thronged." [21]

As Matthew's star soared, William O'Brien's waned. Whether it was pique, a falling off of interest, or primarily ill health which caused it, by 1805 William was no longer active in St. Peter's.[22] When Elizabeth Seton entered the Church that year it was "the young Doctor" who received her and guided her steps those first months within the fold. There is no question that the O'Briens did not get along well. In the summer of 1804 William had complained to Carroll that Matthew was not only determined "to keep himself at the greatest distance from me, but what is worse, reports among his acquaintances that the fault is mine." William was living at Warren Street and said plainly to Carroll, "My namesake cannot and indeed shall not live with me!" He hinted openly that Matthew had a depraved nature and proceeded to quote Seneca to his bishop on the subject of the human desire for praise.[23] Carroll wondered morosely whether he would ever find two priests who could work together in harmony for more than a few months.

Whether the older man's opinions were distorted or not by the attacks of rheumatism which grew worse as he grew older, there is little doubt that Matthew O'Brien was not easy to live with. Through Thomas Betagh in Dublin Bishop Carroll learned that summer that an Irish priest, John Byrne, was on his way to New York. Byrne was recommended by Betagh as a devout priest whose "extreme zeal, his labors, and immoderate abstemiousness" had injured his constitution.[24] He seemed like an ideal assistant for New York. But before the end of January, 1805, poor Byrne had offended Matthew O'Brien and the latter reported to Carroll that the Rev. Mr. Byrne was in a "violent perturbation," and was threatening to leave.[25] Father Byrne apparently had become quickly O'Brien's rival in preaching at St. Peter's and expected, not unreasonably, a share in the subsistence. Byrne's threat to leave New York for Baltimore reflected on O'Brien rather than on himself; Elizabeth Seton spoke of her great delight on the days that Byrne appeared on the altar, and William O'Brien told Carroll that "Good Mr. Byrne is very well calculated for this city. No clergyman you could send would answer as well." [26] When Byrne returned to Dublin in the summer of 1805 Carroll told Betagh, "The impression and memory of Mr. Byrne's eminent services at New York is fresh in the minds of those who were benefited by his ministry." The Bishop of Baltimore felt that Byrne ought to regulate his mortifications. "The stomach of few men can bear so much fasting and abstinence as he joined to his incessant labors," he commented. But Carroll prayed sincerely for his return.[26]

In the end Matthew O'Brien's true character became all too apparent and even the Bishop of Baltimore, as charitable as he was, could not close his eyes to the public scandal in New York. Matthew wrote angrily of the "cowardly atrocious enemy" who complained against him, and protested bitterly of this "terrible attack" on his character. The rumors, he claimed, were the fruits of terror, stupidity, or "hot-headed ignorance." [27] Carroll was filled with a vast distaste. This was even worse than the Nugent troubles. He heard with some relief in November, 1807, that the priest wished to leave New York, but Carroll was soon disabused. On February 14, 1808, O'Brien informed him, "I have resolved to remain here with a few scholars who lodge and board with me and am promised a professorship in the College lately established in this city." [28]

O'Brien did not teach in New York. He did, however, make amends for his distressing behavior in that city by eventually resuming his priestly duties elsewhere. Bishop-elect Michael Egan of Philadelphia refused to accept him, protesting, "From the contiguity of New York to Philadelphia scarcely anything happens in one city that is not immediately known in the other; and as his conduct is well known among the congregation in New York, it could not remain long concealed from the members of this congregation." [29] Philadelphia had enough discord and dissension without taking O'Brien. The repentant priest came at last to Boston where the beautiful example of Cheverus and Matignon overwhelmed him and he wrote wonderingly to Carroll, "The more I consider their circumstances, the greater is my astonishment. Like Anthony and Paul, they had one loaf already, but another half has been added in favour of me. I know not whence it comes. And nothing is wanting on their side to spread happiness about them." [30] But that was in 1812. It must be obvious that Carroll could not have named Matthew O'Brien in 1807 as a fitting candidate for the Diocese of New York.

If William O'Brien was too inactive, too ill, and Matthew too unstable, the other priests who served New York showed other defects. Michael Hurley, O.S.A., who came to New York in July, 1805, during the crisis caused by the yellow fever epidemic, was only twenty-five years old. He was not at all polished or elegant in his preaching, and his youthful seriousness caused many of the congregation to feel him proud and forbidding. Some of the trustees disliked him and Andrew Morris accused Hurley of meddling in local politics. James Barry, the bishop's old friend who was now in New York, heatedly as was his wont, defended Hurley and told Carroll it was only right that he should keep his distance from "the non-lettered spalpeens" who thought their priests were in a class with tailors or shoemakers' journeymen. "In church duties he is solemn, dignified, and punctual," Barry asserted. "Without the least infringement of the truth, he is by far the first ornament of our church." [31] Hurley, young reformer that he was, wrote earnestly to his bishop, "I can only say we are not as we should be. I fear some of us seek ourselves and not God, our own convenience rather than the good of religion. . . . There is certainly a great field for exertion here." [32] Father Hurley might have accomplished much good in New York, but he belonged to the Augustinians, and his superior, Matthew Carr, recalled the serious young man to Philadelphia where his talents were equally needed. In any case, his youth alone would have barred him from Carroll's consideration for so large and tempestuous a diocese as New York.

Bishop Carroll's decision in the summer of 1807 to replace Father Hurley with Father Louis Sibourd produced a variety of reactions. Hurley himself told his bishop he felt that the arrival of the French priest presaged much good for the distracted congregation. Matthew O'Brien, who was thinking of leaving the city for reasons of his own, approved of Sibourd's appointment. But William O'Brien criticized Carroll for dispossessing him and giving his place to "a stranger, a Frenchman." Father John Byrne who was back in New York was pleased to have the sober and virtuous Sibourd as a companion and co-worker. The bishop had been impressed with Father Sibourd's abilities almost from the moment of the priest's first letter of inquiry in 1801 from Port Republicain, San Domingo. Perhaps, with the assistance of the ascetic Byrne and Matthias Kelly, who had come to New York on Byrne's recommendation in 1806, Father Sibourd could bring order and piety to the mushrooming Catholic population of New York.

But once again, hopes were blasted in the bud. Faction again appeared to destroy harmony in congregation and peace of mind in Baltimore. The faction this time was not the creature of either nationalism or of trusteeism; it was rather the product of weakness in the face of temptation. Father Kelly, unlike Father Byrne, was neither abstemious nor hard-working.[33] He took his example from Matthew O'Brien, instead, and added to the rumors that went the rounds of the city. Already in December Louis Sibourd was sorry he had accepted the New York City post and told Carroll as much.[34] Father Sibourd was never a good preacher, and he knew his French accent was distasteful to his Irish parishioners; but there were other reasons why he wanted to leave. His health was poor, and his eyesight was failing. But more than anything else, he told his superior in discouragement, he felt his presence in New York was futile. His efforts to bring back regularity to the discipline of the Church found little support in the priesthood.[35] When Kelly joined forces with the younger O'Brien and the city was given double occasion for shocked whispers Sibourd wrote frantically, "For God's sake be not dilatory! Remove this guilty clergyman to the Baltimore Seminary, send him back to his country, or to any other place but New York."[36]

In the midst of Carroll's worries over this latest recalcitrant from

Ireland word came from New York that James Barry, James of the
hot-temper and even warmer heart, had died. On January 7, 1808,
the bishop lost this good and loyal friend. Father Sibourd's letters
containing the sad news of James' passing, of Robert Barry's arrival
to handle his uncle's affairs, of the deep mourning of Joanna and
Ann Barry, depressed the bishop more than he cared to admit. When
Sibourd reported in February that Fathers Kelly and O'Brien were
every day causing fresh scandal Carroll's wrath was terrible. He removed all powers from O'Brien and wrote peremptorily to Kelly,
"You are, after receipt of this, to abstain from the celebration of the
Mass or performance of any ecclesiastical function till you shall
be otherwise directed." [37] He informed the trustees that both priests
were inhibited from performing any priestly functions. Enough was
enough. The recollection of Matthew O'Brien's meritorious service
in the past, and the persistent hope that the erring man would be
recalled to piety and virtue, had made Carroll reluctant to use
harsh measures with him. But now he could only agree with
Sibourd's sentiments: "It is a dreadful reflection to see the Church
distracted by the annointed of the Lord. May the Almighty interfere and prevent the utter destruction impending on this congregation." [38] What could be more bitter than to suffer the loss of a
friend like James Barry, a layman of purest virtue and inestimable
character, and to see the city in which he died contaminated by
the disgraceful conduct of men ordained to the sacred priesthood?
No wonder poor Sibourd could not stomach it. Pick a bishop from
among those rascals? Not while he lived, the bishop thought angrily.

Kentucky was more consoling to contemplate. Like Boston, the
frontier settlements offered a choice of more than one good man in
1808. There was Theodore Badin, the first priest ordained at Carroll's hands back in 1793. An austere and untiring missionary,
Badin's only fault was that his zeal had a little too much of the
French fervor to suit some tastes. There was Charles Nerinckx, the
former parish priest of Brabant, whose special delight in Kentucky
was to work among the children, preparing them for their first
Communions. Already the ardent Belgian had begun to earn his
later title of "church-builder" with the laying of Holy Mary's cornerstone on November 15, 1805. There was Samuel T. Wilson who
had recently been made the provincial of the Dominicans in Kentucky. They were all excellent men.

But particularly there was Father Benedict Flaget to consider.
Flaget had gained experience on the frontier soon after coming to

the United States in 1792. After only a few weeks at St. Mary's Seminary in Baltimore to learn some English, Flaget had been sent in May of that year to the Indiana country where he worked assiduously around Vincennes.[39] After three years in the northwest Flaget was called back to act as vice-president of Georgetown when he was not teaching classes in French and geography there. After a trip to Cuba to seek students for St. Mary's College, 1798-1801, Flaget joined the faculty of St. Mary's and remained in Baltimore for seven years. Flaget admired the Bishop of Baltimore greatly and said of him on one occasion, "This good man of seventy-five is still enjoying perfect health, hears confessions every day, preaches nearly every Sunday and visits the sick. . . . What a crown he will receive at the end of his days!" The bishop felt a reciprocal admiration for Flaget and told Rome that he possessed tender piety towards God, most bland manners, and a knowledge of theology suited to episcopal rank.[40] When Father Badin recommended Flaget to Carroll it only confirmed the high opinion already formed in Baltimore of the French Sulpician's fitness. When Rome chose Flaget from among the four names Bishop Carroll submitted, the latter said, "The nomination of Flaget to fill the see was of a man, who under present circumstances, seems destined by Providence to unite all differences of opinion in the diocese confided to his paternal solicitude." [41]

When it came to Philadelphia, Carroll recommended only one name, that of Michael Egan, the Franciscan who had tried to found the first province of the Friars Minor in the United States. Father Egan had had three years in Rome as a younger priest; he had been pastor at St. Mary's Church in Philadelphia since 1803; and he was a man whom Carroll could sincerely recommend as endowed with all the qualities necessary to a bishop.[42]

On April 8, 1808, Pope Pius VII created Baltimore a metropolitan see and named the four suffragan sees as Boston, New York, Philadelphia, and Bardstown as Carroll had desired. Boston got Cheverus; Philadelphia, Egan; Bardstown, Flaget; and for New York Rome named the scholarly Irish-born Dominican, Richard Luke Concanen. Bishop Carroll had anticipated leaving New York for a time under the aegis of Boston, since he had no one he cared to recommend for the see; but Rome had decided upon Concanen, the priest who had assisted in the formulation of the new Dominican province in Kentucky. In addition to the four bishops-elect Rome had named an administrator for the Louisiana territory in the person of Father Nerinckx.[43]

As it turned out, Bishop Concanen never reached New York and his successor, Bishop John Connelly, O.P., arrived in that city two days after the dying archbishop had received the last sacraments. Carroll was not destined to see that greatest of American cities under its own bishop. But better days were ahead for New York after 1808. When Father John David refused the bishop's plea that he go to the troublesome area, Carroll decided to appeal to the semi-restored Society of Jesus for help. To Father Molyneux he said urgently:

> I have recourse to you at present, as to a person on whose determination the honour, estimation and perhaps the very being of our holy religion depends at New York. It is become absolutely necessary to place at the head of that Church a priest of the most respectable character; this necessity is much more urgent now, than ever, and admits no delays . . . it is possible only by the most prompt interposition, to prevent the explosion of dreadful scandals there.

He wanted Father Anthony Kohlmann, he told Molyneux, and he hoped the Jesuits would not be as reluctant as the Sulpicians to send relief to that distressed city. "God forbid," Carroll exclaimed impatiently, "that you should imitate this spirit so far distant from that of St. Ignatius!" To Father Kohlmann the bishop spoke frankly. "There is now at New York a fair opening," he told the Alsatian. "Mr. Byrne alone remains there with the charge of that most numerous congregation, computed by some to consist of more than 12,000 souls. You know how inadequate are the efforts of any one man for such a task, and much more those of our zealous, but not very learned or very prudent friend." It was possible, of course, that Sibourd might return to help Kohlmann once his health was restored. But in any case, the Jesuit was sorely needed. "The crisis is as important to religion as can almost happen," Carroll declared. It was a challenge which appealed to Anthony Kohlmann. He accepted it. When Bishop Concanen suggested the appointment of a vicar-general for the Diocese of New York Father Kohlmann was quite naturally given the responsibility. Under his far-sighted administration order was restored and the Diocese of New York began to flourish.[44]

Although the division of the diocese was decreed in 1808 it was not until 1810 that Carroll had the pleasure of consecrating his three suffragan bishops at Baltimore. Concanen who was consecrated in Rome on April 24, 1808, had expected to bring with him when he came to the United States the pallium for Archbishop Carroll and the briefs for the other bishops. But the Napoleonic wars which raged in Europe delayed his departure month after month. Mother Seton in Emmitsburg learned of Bishop Concanen's disappointment from Antonio Filicchi who wrote also of the Dominican's "truly venerable, sweet aspect and manners." The American vessel on which Concanen had hoped to take passage in the fall of 1808 was prevented from putting to sea, and Concanen had to return to Rome. Filicchi forwarded Concanen's letters for Carroll by way of Mother Seton, and that was the last Baltimore heard from Italy for over a year.

As the time passed and the delay continued the American bishops-elect began to hope they might escape episcopal duties entirely. Cheverus in Boston confessed in 1809 to Mother Seton:

> Should Bishop Concanen arrive, I hope I shall be permitted to remain as I am and that we shall be placed under the jurisdiction of the Bishop of New York. This appears to me the best plan for the present and for many years to come. If there must be a Bishop in Boston, I ought not to be the man. This affair has given me more anxiety and grief than I can tell.[46]

Flaget in Kentucky, too, was reluctant to enter upon his new road of responsibility. "Let me enjoy forever unmolested," he begged Carroll, "the humble post I occupy. . . . I will prove more useful to your diocese in remaining in the college than in going to Kentucky as bishop." He even tried, while he was in France in 1809, to enlist the support of his superior, Father Emery, in his opposition to the post. But Emery reminded him, "The Pope has given you express orders to accept;" and in the end Flaget acquiesced.[47] It was Flaget who was destined to bring to Baltimore the duplicates of the briefs for the consecration of the reluctant bishops. Flaget brought as well the sad news that Bishop Concanen had died on June 19, 1810, at Naples without ever laying eyes on his diocese.[48]

Carroll now hastened to prepare for the consecration of the three remaining bishops. On October 28, 1810, at the pro-cathedral in Baltimore Michael Egan was consecrated; and on November 1 John Cheverus was consecrated in the same St. Peter's. Three days later at St. Patrick's Church in Fells Point Benedict Flaget was consecrated as first Bishop of Bardstown. Carroll himself was not

invested with the pallium until August 18, 1811. By that time
Cheverus was safely back in his Boston diocese, and he wrote to
Baltimore of his pleasure at learning that Carroll was at last officially the first metropolitan of the Catholic Church in the United
States. "It is not a little remarkable," he suggested, "that the British
minister should have been the bearer of it." [49] Cheverus was thinking of the growing strain between the United States and England
in 1811. The new archbishop himself commented to Plowden,
"Would you believe that your minister here, Mr. Foster, brought
me the pallium which was committed to the late Bishop Concanen?"
But it was really not so strange that Augustus John Foster should
bring the symbol of Carroll's new authority to Baltimore. Foster had
served previously at the British legation at Naples, and it was at
Naples that Bishop Concanen had died.

Carroll's friends in Europe were delighted with this new honor
he had received, and Strickland wrote feelingly, "Please to accept
my best compliments for the establishment of your ecclesiastical
hierarchy: an event which a few years ago would have been judged
chimerical. The ways of Providence are inscrutable. Almighty God
only knows how to draw good out of evil." [50] The seventy-six-year-
old Archbishop of Baltimore nodded in agreement as he read
Strickland's lines. Only two decades ago there was one bishop in the
United States. Now there were four besides himself: Neale, Cheverus,
Egan, and Flaget. Carroll sighed in satisfaction. It was truly a grand
place, this Republic, for the service of God. He must write to
Plowden of the progress being made. "When the Suffragan Bishops
of this metropolitan See were assembled here in November, 1810,
with my Coadjutor," he began, "they received Episcopal consecration; and for some days after we regulated some points for the
government of our respective Dioceses." What pleasant phrases those
were, suffragan bishops, metropolitan see, our respective dioceses.
Charles would discount his pride, he hoped. Then he wrote on:

Our new Bishops, now in their Dioceses, are zealously and
successfully employed in organizing them, and extending
the kingdom of Christ. Bishop Flaget of Bardstown, Kentucky, entered on a field well prepared for his coming by the
zealous clergymen who preceded him, and great is his encouragement there. The English Dominicans, who came
some years ago, are settled in that country, have built a
convent, large church, college, and have many novices. Besides four priests of that order, the Bishop found and car-

ried thither five other zealous labourers, is building a seminary, etc. Too much praise cannot be given by me to the priests of St. Sulpice here for their zeal and sacrifices to the public cause. They now maintain and educate at their own expense twenty-two Seminarians for the ministry.[51]

Yes, there were blessings enough, when he stopped to count them. The bad days in New York were things of the past. "On the contrary," he told Plowden, "the Rev. Mr. Kohlmann, with Mr. Fenwick . . . has succeeded surprisingly in establishing a literary academy, and sanctifying and increasing the congregation."

He and Plowden did not have many years remaining for these exchanges. They must anticipate, he told his friend, that period, "which considering my advanced age, will soon close our earthly correspondence." But it was very pleasurable to be able to sign his last letters to England, "John, Archbishop of Baltimore."

CHAPTER XVII

BEYOND THE MOUNTAINS

THE consecration of the new bishops in 1810 was a public testimony to the rapid growth of Catholicism in the United States, but to Archbishop Carroll the triple ceremonies were a forcible reminder of how much work remained to be done. In the beginning scarcely any place outside of Maryland and Pennsylvania could be thought of as flourishing centers of Catholicism. Now, the great frontier areas stretching to the Mississippi and beyond, the borderlands of former French and Spanish jurisdictions, furnished fertile soil for the "grain of mustard." Carroll was more than glad that Flaget's original reluctance had been overcome. The archbishop never thought of the West without feeling a vast excitement seize his imagination. Under its spell he could understand Thomas Jefferson's passion for expansion. It was all of ten years since the former President had made his seemingly presumptuous remark, "However our present situation may restrain us within our own limits, it is impossible not to look forward to distant times when our rapid multiplication will expand itself beyond these limits and cover the whole northern, if not the southern continent." [1] But since then Louisiana had been added, and not long after that William Clark and the "Sublime Dandy," Meriwether Lewis, had penetrated the far western wilderness to the very Pacific. Although thus far no new states had entered the Union from the Northwest, the Mississippi Valley already had six senators in the federal Congress. When Henry M. Brackenridge made his voyage down the Ohio River in 1808 he had exclaimed, "Peace, civilization, and the cheerful sound of the human voice have taken the place of the frightful savage wilderness, of the nightly howling of the wolf, and the mid-day terrors of the Indian scalping knife!" As far as Cincinnati, at least, the curtain of the wilderness had been lifted.

How times had changed since Jefferson first took office. Carroll still had the letter Father Badin had written protesting against a bishopric for Kentucky. Even though he admitted that religion would acquire "more firmness and respectability" Badin had warned gloomily, "He would be almost a mendicant bishop as I have really been a mendicant priest." [2] Only five years later when François André Michaux made his journey through Ohio, Kentucky, and Tennessee he was impressed by the thriving commerce of the area. Pittsburgh was the key to the western country, serving as it did as an *entrepôt* for the spring and fall shipments of merchandise from Baltimore and Philadelphia, and destined for Ohio, Kentucky, and Natchez. Vessels now made the 2,100 mile voyage to New Orleans in forty or fifty days, while an Indian *pirogue* could do it in half the time. Traders along the Ohio exchanged hams, salt pork, native brandies distilled from corn and peaches, butter, hemp, skins, and flour of every variety. Indian corn was raised everywhere.

Kentucky, where Bishop Flaget would reside, was already a great horse country. Scant attention was given the breeding of draft horses and the Kentucky work animal was scarcely better than those used by the French peasants on the continent. But coach and saddle horses, together with lawsuits, were the chief topics of conversation everywhere. The Kentucky horses had been brought out from Virginia whose emigrants formed the basis of the frontier population. The beautiful thoroughbreds were in great demand in South Carolina and the other southern states, and together with the horned cattle and hogs prodigal in Kentucky were the source of steadily growing profits. With her economic ties thus demanding a backward, eastward glance, it was little wonder that Kentucky remained essentially "Virginia's third frontier," and that Kentucky gentlemen, like their eastern cousins, were becoming famous for their tendency to carry their passion for gaming and spirituous liquors to an excess.

Bishop Flaget waited until the spring following his consecration before setting out for Kentucky. Then in May, 1811, accompanied by his close Sulpician friend, Father John David, he left Baltimore. At Pittsburgh they joined Father Edward Fenwick and his fellow Dominicans and the little cavalcade of clergy boarded the flatboat which David later called "the cradle of our seminary and of the Church in Kentucky." An altar was made from boxes and the Bishop of Bardstown offered his Masses from the moving sanctuary. The trip was uneventful and after thirteen days they arrived at Louisville, the settlement nearest Bardstown where Flaget was installed on June 9, 1811, by Father Badin.

Three developments of that year, 1811, were to bring even greater changes to the million people who now lived in the West. In that year operations were begun on the Cumberland Road for which Congress had appropriated $30,000 five years earlier. This highway to the West was built from Maryland, across Pennsylvania, and reached Wheeling by 1818. As it entered the Ohio Valley in the years after the War of 1812 new stagecoach lines appeared, inns and taverns mushroomed, and regular mail service began running between Wheeling and the federal capital. In October, 1811, the *New Orleans* left Pittsburgh for New Orleans, and with the voyage of the big side-wheeler which reached the mardi-gras city in January steamboating on western waters got under way. The third event of significance to the frontier was the defeat William Henry Harrison inflicted on Tecumseh at Tippecanoe Creek on November 7, 1811. Ever since the Treaty of Fort Wayne in 1809 by which the United States acquired some 3,000,000 acres of Indian land, Tecumseh and the Prophet had made war on the chiefs whom they blamed for the negotiations. The victory at Tippecanoe was regarded by the people of the West as a decisive step toward the pacification of that area.[4] Taken together, the three events of 1811 portended a tremendous flood of migrants to the trans-Allegheny lands and an increase in the flock under Flaget's care. The Diocese of Bardstown included, in addition to the blue grass country, Tennessee, the territory which came to be Ohio, Indiana, Illinois, Michigan, and Wisconsin, and even that portion of Minnesota which lies east of the Mississippi River. The Cumberland Road, steam navigation, and the pacification of the Indians were of immediate consequence to Carroll's western suffragan see.

To serve in this sprawling domain, the new bishop of the West had in addition to Theodore Badin two other secular priests, four Dominicans, and Flaget's Sulpician *confrère,* John David. The latter had left Baltimore full of zeal for two projects, a seminary and a sisterhood, and it was not long before Father David had achieved both St. Thomas Seminary and had founded the Sisters of Charity of Nazareth. Meanwhile, Bishop Flaget devoted himself to the task of visiting his great domain. The report which he sent to Rome on April 10, 1815, was a striking commentary on the progress of the West. By the year of Archbishop Carroll's death Kentucky had a bishop, ten priests, six subdeacons, four students in minor orders, and six tonsured clerics. Nineteen churches had been erected up to that time and more were being planned. Flaget's report noted the constantly changing composition of his flock saying, "It is difficult to give the exact number of Catholics living in each congregation on account of continual emigrations, either from the older states to Kentucky, or from one part of that state to another, or to the territories of Louisiana." But he estimated that at least 10,000 souls were ministered to by his ten priests.[5]

Archbishop Carroll realized that Flaget would meet with some difficulties upon his arrival in an area formerly supervised by Father Badin. Ever since the advent of the Dominicans to Kentucky there had been some friction between the clergy of English origins and those speaking French. The Belgian, Charles Nerinckx, who joined Badin in 1805, had sided with the latter in a disagreement with the Dominicans over property transfers. Carroll had been deluged with letters from the frontier.[6] Now he wondered what Badin's reaction would be upon the accession of the Bishop of Bardstown. Badin had, of course, changed his opinion about the financial support for a bishop, and had expressed his belief to Carroll that there were now sufficient revenues to nourish episcopal government. But the property was in Badin's name. Was there to be more difficulty over property rights?

Carroll was not left long in doubt. Flaget found that Badin refused to transfer to his bishop the lands which the vicar-general held in trust for the Church. Flaget threatened penalties, saying that he feared that great scandal might arise if Badin's "boldness and contumacy were known." But, again encouraged by Nerinckx, Badin resisted. It was up to the archbishop to mediate. In the fall of 1812 both Badin and Flaget came to Baltimore to discuss their grievances. Bishop Flaget offered to be content with an unconditional deed to the seminary property and the bishop's residence, and the right of supervision over the other revenues. In the archbishop's presence Father Badin appeared conciliatory and signed an agreement satisfactory to his bishop. It was only later, when Flaget received the deed to the properties in question, that the Bishop of Bardstown discovered that the vicar-general had signed over only half of the stipulated land.

The Archbishop of Baltimore was more than a little annoyed when Badin's deception came to light. But Carroll understood his motives, even while deprecating his action. The missionary priest had almost single-handed wrested a living for the Church from the frontier wilderness, and he had contracted debts whose liquidation depended upon the proper use of the properties held in his name. He had never abused his authority in this respect, nor had he alienated an inch of land from the uses for which it was intended. It was unfortunate that he could not gracefully submit to the new situation which was created simultaneously with the See of Bardstown. Well, it was Flaget's problem now, and even though it was vastly irritating, it would not materially hamper the work of the Church.[7]

Bishop Flaget was too busy, as a matter of fact, to devote much time to the idiosyncrasies of his subordinates. Before he ever went to Baltimore in 1812 he had spent a year visiting part of his diocese and after his departure once more for Kentucky on April 22, 1813, he began the visitation of the other parts of his domain. For the first time since his own consecration in 1790 Carroll began to feel more confident about the care of souls in the Northwest Territory, the area north of the Ohio River and surrounding the Great Lakes. How that region had preyed upon Carroll's mind. The year that the new dioceses were created he had told Plowden:

> My heart bleeds so much for the Catholics of the State of Ohio, of Vincennes, Detroit, etc., places bedewed with the sweat of Jesuits and first established by their labours, that I feel a strong impulse to send other sons of St. Ignatius to cultivate the same soil.

But while sons of Loyola were in the making at Georgetown, he fervently prayed Bishop Flaget would bring consolation to those far-off congregations.

Not that Carroll had ever done less than he could humanly do for the Northwest Territory. When the Jay Treaty had been concluded with England in 1795 the jurisdiction of the Bishop of Baltimore had been extended in that region. Jean Hubert, then Bishop of Quebec, had courteously notified Carroll that according to the treaty, "the missions of Upper Canada are to be restored and will in consequence become a portion of the Baltimore Diocese." [8] The order for the evacuation of Detroit was signed at Quebec, and on July 7, 1796, Colonel Francis Hamtrack sent a detachment of soldiers to receive the surrender. At noon, on July 11, 1796, the British flag was hauled down and the Stars and Stripes unfurled. Carroll realized that the transfer involved more than the mere addition of Catholic members to his flock. Not only was the change one from French to American cultural dominance, but politically it involved a transfer of loyalties of former British subjects to the new Republic then testing its democratic ideology. A letter written by him to the trustees of St. Anthony's Church in the Detroit country shows Carroll's concern. After explaining that he had charged Father Michael Levadoux, his vicar-general in that area, to report on the condition of religion in the territory recently ceded, Carroll said hopefully:

> The principles of your religion, your behavior, your industrious habits, and your love of order are to me a real assurance that you will be peaceful citizens, obedient to the laws of the government and the state of which you are a part; and that you will never abuse the liberty in which you participate to make it a pretext for living without the restraints of religion, or of civil authority.[9]

Carroll knew only too well the problems posed by lingering loyalties in the more settled East, and his qualms about the frontier regions were not figments of his imagination. Father Levadoux in the years immediately following the acquisition of the Detroit country suffered doubly, from his former Sulpician colleagues' criticisms in Montreal, and from the congregations under his supervision. By the former he was attacked for the zeal with which he had embraced American ideals, while by the latter he was made unhappy by parish wardens who insisted on remaining British subjects, or by French parishioners who cherished a nostalgia for monarchical forms of government. But in his French vicar-general Carroll had a man after his own heart. Father Levadoux said firmly, "I am a member of the United States. I would be a wretch to abandon their interests to sustain those of a crown whose yoke they have thrown off." [10] The Sulpician priest followed the precepts of his bishop in Baltimore and worked to promote the best interests of both religion and civil authority. He was esteemed by General Wayne, Colonel Hamtrack, and the other officials of the government. Like Carroll, he was devoted to the leadership of President Washington, and on the occasion of the latter's birthday in 1797 Father Levadoux shared energetically in the first patriotic celebration ever held in Detroit. A special Mass was celebrated at St. Anne's, with places of honor reserved for officers and officials, and at the close of a long eulogy on the President Father Levadoux exclaimed:

Pardon, O Great One, the temerity of a stranger who has undertaken to eulogize you. Although born on foreign soil, he is no less an admirer of your virtues. O! that he could implant in the hearts of every one of his hearers the sentiments of admiration and veneration with which his own is filled! O that he could inspire them with the highest degree of attachment to the government which you have created, and which you have directed to the present with such wisdom and glory.[11]

When another Sulpician, Gabriel Richard, replaced Levadoux later he too proved a loyal American and was, in his turn, likewise criticized by the Canadian clergy for being extremely Republican and anti-British. Father Richard encouraged the mingling of civil and religious authority and allowed Protestants to hold some of the ribbons of the canopy in a Corpus Christi procession, while the militia of the civil government marched under arms as a military escort for the Blessed Sacrament. But the Church and the military forces were two of the most powerful forces for the preservation of order on the frontier, and both the Bishop of Baltimore and President Washington had from the start shared the belief that Christian principles and good government went hand in hand. Father Richard had remained to perform wonders in and about Detroit.[12] Beginning in 1802, he established a primary school for children, separate secondary schools for boys and girls, and a normal school for the training of teachers. The fire of 1805 which destroyed the city left Richard undaunted and Carroll learned that he had moved his pupils temporarily to a government warehouse. Not content with supporting formal education, the dynamic missionary then purchased a printing press and in 1809 began publishing what may be regarded as the first Catholic newspaper in the United States which he called the *Michigan Essay or Impartial Observer*.

While Detroit flourished under Richard, however, Vincennes languished. Fathers John Rivet and Peter Janin, who had been the two priests to benefit from the Congress's generosity, had gone to the West in 1795. Early in that year Samuel Hodgdon, the commissary of the army had been informed that the priests were ready to set out, and the War Department had authorized the transportation of their baggage. In the years that followed Father Rivet had kept both the War Department and Bishop Carroll informed of his progress in the Wabash territory.[13] For eight years he had worked heroically against the forces which vitiated the work of civilizing the Indians: liquor, the avarice of traders, and the landhunger of the white settlers. But ever since Rivet's death in 1804 the Indiana Catholics had received only occasional visits from Badin and Nerinckx in Kentucky, or from Father Donatian Olivier of Illinois. Carroll had been very depressed by the gloomy reports Nerinckx sent to Baltimore in 1806 and 1807. The Belgian priest was doing all he could to coax his friends in Europe to come to the frontier, but Indiana was in desperate straits at that time. Briefly, Carroll considered sending out three Jesuits, Fathers Malevé, Wouters, and Henry, to "renew the seed of the Society in the Western Country;" but unless replacements from Europe were forthcoming, the priests could not be spared from their eastern duties. Indiana would have to wait until her new bishop could devise some solution.

Benedict Flaget, himself, had a very personal interest in Vincennes. It was here that he had first been stationed by Bishop Carroll in 1792, after his arrival from France. For two years he had seen at first hand the desperate needs of this wilderness settlement. But it was not until May, 1814, that the Bishop of Bardstown could set out on horseback for the Old Post. From Vincennes Flaget reported with emotion, "The joy I felt to see once more these old parishioners was unalloyed. I remember their names and faces with astonishing facility. . . . They had not as yet lost their faith, and a zealous priest in their midst would bring them back without trouble." [14] The longer he stayed at Vincennes, hearing confessions, baptizing, and confirming, the more he was persuaded that his presence throughout that country was essential. Archbishop Carroll could rest content with his choice for the Bishop of Bardstown.

Anyone could see that Flaget's was the region profitting the most from the rising tide of immigration. The Church must make heroic efforts to keep pace with the thousands who poured into Ohio, Indiana, Michigan, and Illinois. But now with Father Richard continuing his labours in the environs of Detroit, with Bishop Joseph A. Plessis, Hubert's successor at Quebec, willing to exercise some of the powers of a vicar-general in the borderlands, and with Bishop Flaget penetrating farther into the area from the south, the Archbishop of Baltimore had less to weigh upon his conscience in the matter of the Northwest Territory.

Carroll wished he could feel as sanguine about the Mississippi Valley and New Orleans. Ever since the Louisiana territory with its twenty-one parishes and the Cathedral of St. Louis had been made a part of Carroll's jurisdiction in 1803 he had confronted a variety of problems there. The previous vicar-general, Patrick Walsh, left behind him a heritage of insubordination and schism. Carroll discovered that a trouble-making Capuchin named Antonio Sedella had even involved the civil government in his resistance to authority. A second problem facing Carroll had been the matter of approaching the United States government regarding church discipline in Louisiana. Rome had suggested such a course, and Bishop Carroll had complied in 1806 when he wrote to Secretary of State Madison on the subject. He spoke of his reluctance to make ecclesiastical appointments which might jeopardize the newly asserted authority of the United States over this Spanish-French population. In view of the disorders which had grown up during the relaxed state of civil and ecclesiastical authority, Carroll said, he felt that only a man of virtue, of prudent conduct, and particularly of "sufficient resolution to remove the disorders gradually," ought to be appointed to Louisiana. If such a man happened to be a native of France, would the President approve? [15]

Madison replied on November 20, 1806, that Jefferson greatly appreciated Carroll's delicacy in the matter, "but as the case is entirely ecclesiastical it is deemed most congenial with the scrupulous policy of the Constitution in guarding against a political interference with religious affairs to decline" making any suggestions in the case of Louisiana.[16] It was precisely what Carroll had anticipated. Mr. Jefferson's enthusiasm for the French was only too well known. Carroll smiled briefly as he read Madison's assurances that the President had "perfect confidence" in the bishop's patriotism and the purity of his views. Enclosed with this official reply of the government Madison sent Carroll a private opinion of his own. Speaking for himself Madison commented:

> It affords me satisfaction to find you, as might well be presumed, so fully in a disposition to admit into the stations for which you are to provide as little of alienage of any sort. . . . I will not conceal my wish that instead of a temporary subordination of the Roman Catholic Church at New Orleans to the General Diocese the subordination had been permanent.[17]

The Secretary of State was apparently fully aware of Carroll's loyalty to his government's interests. After he became President himself James Madison remained interested in the progress of this southern portion of Carroll's jurisdiction and he told the Ursulines of New Orleans:

> In a country where all rights, religious as well as civil, are protected by the laws, and guaranteed by an enlightened public opinion, the best securities exist for the tranquillity and esteem of those whose labors are devoted to the conscientious pursuit of laudable objects. . . . However inferior to my predecessors in other merits, my dispositions are equally friendly to the task of training youth in the paths of virtue and useful knowledge.[18]

Meanwhile, in 1806, Carroll had gone ahead with a clear conscience in appointing Father John Olivier for the time being. Two years later, when Propaganda further clarified Baltimore's powers over Louisiana and named Nerinckx as administrator, Carroll hoped briefly that the problem of the South was solved. But Father Nerinckx had refused to go to New Orleans, believing he was too much needed in Kentucky. After the consecration of the bishops was over in November, 1810, Carroll determined to force some kind of a solution in the matter of that area. On December 17 he wrote to Pius VII of his difficulty in persuading anyone to accept the task of administrator. He then proposed the name of William Dubourg, the Sulpician president of St. Mary's College in Baltimore. Dubourg had excellent qualifications for the position. He spoke the three languages then prevalent in Louisiana; he was a man of quick enthusiasms; and he was young enough still to have the energy such a task required. Carroll had been thinking for a long time that a man with Dubourg's facility with languages would be vastly useful in the southern Mississippi Valley region. Dubourg was finally prevailed upon to accept, and on October 18, 1812, he left Baltimore for his new position as Administrator Apostolic of the Diocese of Louisiana and the two Floridas. Dubourg's arrival in New Orleans brought temporary order by forcing Father Sedella into the background. But when Dubourg departed for Rome at the close of the War of 1812 this was a signal for fresh rebellion on the part of the Capuchin priest. Although William Dubourg was to return with a bishop's powers over the southern diocese, the last year of Archbishop Carroll's life was one of renewed misgivings over the future of the Mississippi Valley.[20] He died before reading Propaganda's suggestion that Upper Louisiana be made a separate bishopric with its see city at St. Louis. Only his persistent faith in the destiny of the West predicted the later greatness of that metropolis as a center of Catholicity.

The frontier was to leave its mark on the Church in many ways, and Carroll astutely apprehended that the modification might not be always beneficial. François André Michaux had found in 1804 that although the trans-Allegheny region was inhabited by many different sects the people lived "in the greatest harmony." [21] Theodore Badin had spoken quite charitably of a governor who was a Baptist minister "of a gentle character" and the missionary priest had been delighted to make use of the library of Transylvania Seminary, a Presbyterian school. He told Carroll, "If my finances would have permitted it I would have subscribed to furnish that library with orthodox books." [22] One Presbyterian minister had lent Badin a treatise of St. John Chrysostom which Badin hoped might make him as much a friend to Catholic doctrine as he was to the Catholic priest. No one approved more sincerely than John Carroll of the brotherly intercourse of all Christians and he was not concerned over this aspect of frontier life. But living in harmony frequently led to mixed marriages among the laity, and it was particularly true of the frontier areas that religious differences were never considered an obstacle to an alliance of families. Too often these mixed marriages were adulterous as well. In the original French or Spanish settlements such unions would have called down both religious and social ostracism on the heads of the erring parties. But now, in the presence of an Anglo-Saxon, Protestant population which wielded the civil authority, the old sanctions had lost their force. [23] Henry Brackenridge who visited the Louisiana Territory in 1810-1811 noticed that Catholics were less strict than formerly in their observance of the rules and discipline of their Church. "Of late," he commented, "this attention to the ceremonies of their religion is considerably relaxed, since other objects of pursuit and interest have opened to their view." [24]

In the Indiana territory the problem of mixed marriages was further complicated by the prestige given to the civil ceremonies by the officials of the territorial government. Father Richard had had a controversy with Judge Cownel J. Edgard over the necessity for a religious ceremony and the priest had told Carroll:

> I have explained to him our opinion. . . . I have distinguished the Sacrament from the contract and moreover the civil contract from the ecclesiastical contract, so that the civil

contract could have all its effects, though at the same time
the ecclesiastic contract might be invalid before our church.[25]

But even when both the clergy and the civil officials understood the
technicalities involved, the layman was usually more apt to take his
cue from the general practices he saw on every hand.

The problem was a vexing one, without question. At the first
synod Bishop Carroll and his clergy had faced it squarely. Mixed
marriages were unavoidable in the state of society prevailing in
the United States. The rules proscribing these unions, however, had
been drawn up with meticulous care. The legislation of the synod
had been sent to Rome, and the Holy See had congratulated Carroll
on the wisdom displayed in this first legislation of the clergy in the
United States. Nevertheless, Carroll was in advance of his times,
and one Canadian bishop said to him plaintively:

> I should like to confer with your Lordship about the norm
> to follow in regard to marriages contracted between Catho-
> lics and Protestants, which your missionaries, it is said, have
> permission to witness. Without doubt you have been thus
> empowered by the Pope, and he has refused similar powers
> petitioned by my predecessors.[26]

It was a matter which weighed heavily on Carroll's mind; his solution to the problem was only expediency, as he knew. He told
Charles Plowden:

> Here our Catholics are so mixed with Protestants in all the
> intercourse of civil society and business public and private,
> that abuse of intermarriage is almost universal and it sur-
> passes my ability to devise any effectual bar against it. No
> general prohibition can be exacted without reducing many of
> the faithful to live in a state of celibacy. . . . Tho' sometimes
> good consequences follow these marriages, yet often, thro' the
> discordancy of the religious sentiments of parents, their
> children grow up without attachment to any, and become an
> easy prey to infidelity or indifferentism, if you will allow
> the word.[27]

Another aspect of life on the frontier complicated the work of
its Catholic missionaries. Although the Methodists, Presbyterians,
and Baptists were all numerous in the land beyond the mountains,
a new flavor of emotionalism was creeping into frontier services.

Ministers grew more vehement in their discourses and the congregation vocally approved with shouts of "Glory!" and "Amen!" Michaux commented, "This species of infatuation strikes chiefly the women, who are carried out of the crowd and put under a tree, where they lie a long time, heaving the most lamentable sighs." There were instances where two or three hundred in a congregation were simultaneously affected, "so that one-third of the hearers were engaged in reviving the rest." [28] One of the most famous of the frontier preachers noted in his *Travels,* "I have seen Presbyterians, Methodists, Quakers, Baptists, Church of England, and Independents, exercised with the *jerks:* Gentleman and Lady, black and white, the aged and the youth, rich and poor, without exception." [29] What could the overworked priest, who had ridden miles on a gnawing, empty stomach, offer to compete with such drama? Often he did not even speak the same language as a majority of his listeners, and his sermon was apt to be nothing more than a halting, broken commentary on the catechism that fell on unlistening ears.

Life on the frontier tended to wipe out the restraints and refinements of convention or inhibitions, and more than one priest complained to Carroll, as Badin and Richard did, of the "quarrels, blasphemies, imprecations, violences, and drunkenness" of his people. The freedom of the frontier also seemed to oppose vocations to the religious life. In Baltimore the archbishop grieved that American youth seemed to have "an almost invincible repugnance to the ecclesiastical state," while Fenwick commented disgustedly in Kentucky, "What can you do or expect from hare-brained Americans . . . intoxicated with the sound of liberty and equality?" [30]

But the West was a challenge to the Church. In spite of its crudity, its raw newness, and its blatant vigor, the land beyond the mountains evoked the heroism latent in many a cultured European. Prince Demetrius Gallitzin, gentle Simon Bruté, gallant Gabriel Richard, and the rest bore hardships that would have killed lesser men, and persisted to wrest a Christian kingdom from the wilderness. Frail women like Elizabeth Seton and Catherine Spalding went to the fringes of the back country and beyond to care for the sick and to educate children. The frontier generated a vitality of its own. Before Archbishop Carroll died Bardstown was already planning her own cathedral, and numerous chapels raised their simpler crosses to the western skies. The Church in the United States was only beginning her gigantic work.

CHAPTER XVIII

WINTER WINDS

ARCHBISHOP CARROLL soon discovered that even the sharing of responsibility with his brother bishops did not remove all of his troublesome problems. His elevation to the office of archbishop was, instead, accompanied by increasing administrative burdens not the least of which involved the two religious establishments closest to his heart. His little foundress, Mother Seton, embarked upon a series of difficulties with her Sulpician superiors the year following the division of the diocese, while the Jesuit superior who was appointed in that same year embarked on a policy which frequently irked the Archbishop of Baltimore and led to increasing friction between Carroll and the superiors of the Society of Jesus. Worst of all was the fresh outbreak of trusteeism in Philadelphia involving, this time, insubordinate Irish priests. Mother Seton's difficulties were all resolved by the end of 1814, and a working agreement was achieved with the Jesuit superior by the summer of 1815; but the old archbishop went to his grave grieved at the Philadelphia situation and the legacy of distress he would leave to Leonard Neale.

When Elizabeth Seton went to Emmitsburg in 1809 Father William Dubourg, who was then the president of St. Mary's College in Baltimore, was appointed to direct the new community. One of his first policies in regard to spiritual advisors and confessors brought distress to the women and in the crisis which ensued Dubourg resigned.[1] Chagrined at having offended Father Dubourg, Mother Seton pleaded with Archbishop Carroll to intercede and effect his restoration. "The truth is," she admitted to Carroll, "I have been made a Mother before being initiated." But the archbishop felt that this was a matter between Mother Seton and the Sulpicians. "If Mr. Nagot or the Council of the Seminary see fit to restore Mr. Dubourg to the place he filled," Carroll told her, "you may depend upon my concurrence." But he saw formidable objections, he added.

Dubourg was not restored, and Charles François Nagot, the head of the Sulpicians in Baltimore, sent a sharp reprimand to Mother Seton saying, "I am persuaded it is God's holy will that Mr. David be superior of your house." Nagot was aware that she had talked the whole matter over with Archbishop Carroll, and he told her that he would have preferred to have Carroll make the decision. Since, however, the archbishop refused to meddle in Sulpician affairs, Nagot intended that Father John David should control her community. "Conform," he admonished her, "with all the simplicity of a humble servant of God, docile to His commands." Mother Seton confided in Carroll later:

> I have had a great many very hard trials, my Father, since you were here, but you will of course congratulate me on them as this fire of tribulation is no doubt meant to consume the many imperfections and bad dispositions our Lord finds in me. . . . I determine, dry and hard as my daily bread is, to take it with as good grace as possible. When I carry it before our Lord sometimes He makes me laugh at myself and asks what other kind I would choose in the valley of tears than that which Himself and all His followers made use of.[2]

The archbishop folded the letter carefully and put it away for safekeeping. Unless he were much mistaken, there was a woman marked for a great future. He had never been sure that he approved of the priests of St. Sulpice being made her superiors. But apparently she could take their peculiar brand of discipline in her stride.

Both the archbishop and his little friend in Emmitsburg were to meet great sorrows that December. Father Francis Beeston, the friend and confidant of twenty years, was lost to Carroll; Harriet Seton, Mother Seton's sister-in-law and companion at Emmitsburg, died three days before Christmas. When the archbishop received the news of Harriet's death he sensed what Mother Seton must be experiencing, and wrote consolingly:

> It seems to be the order of divine providence to lead you to perfection through the road of sufferings, interior and exterior. May you always correspond with the graces be-

stowed on you and walk the way of the cross with resignation and consequently with much spiritual profit.[3]

In the poignancy of his own grief over Father Beeston's death Carroll felt particularly close to the valiant little woman in her Emmitsburg wilderness.

Her troubles were by no means over. Mother Seton's new superior, Father David, assumed the duties of his office with an aggressive determination to rule. He treated her with cold firmness, and overrode her own preferences in regard to the establishment of the school which was to be the community's chief work during their early years. Carroll got some inkling of David's methods from Mother Seton's letter in January. Their new house was almost ready, she told the archbishop, but she herself was greatly in need of advice. She was all in the wrong, she said in discouragement. "Not from discontent with the place . . . nor with the intention of our institution," she added hastily, "but circumstances have all combined to create in my mind a confusion and want of confidence in my superiors which is indescribable." There was something about David that simply closed her heart. "An unconquerable reluctance and diffidence takes the place of those dispositions which ought to influence every action, and with every desire to serve God and these excellent beings who surround me I remain motionless and inactive." She asked Carroll if he thought she were being tempted.[4]

Carroll perceived in her letter a very real discouragement, and he was disquieted at the thought that this foundation which was so dear to him might be on the verge of disintegration. He must act quickly. He wrote at once, "Let it be your only concern to progress more and more towards the union of your soul with God, and an entire disengagement from the things of earth." He reminded her that it would be a triumph for heterodoxy and irreligion if anything should happen to shake the stability of their institution. "I declare an opinion and belief," he said strongly, "that its ultimate success under God depends on your sacrificing yourself, notwithstanding all the uneasiness and disgust you may experience, and continuing in your place as superior." She must make every effort to meet David halfway. It was unthinkable, Carroll told himself as he sealed the letter, that Elizabeth Seton should not continue as mother of the community she had founded.

Father David was by no means as certain as his archbishop that Mother Seton was irreplaceable. He had a preference for Sister Rose,

the former Rose Landrey White of Baltimore, and he was considering the idea of making her the head of the community, or as an
alternative, forming a Baltimore branch with her in charge. Mother
Seton told Archbishop Carroll in April that she had been warned
to prepare herself for Sister Rose's replacing her. Carroll was incensed. He had not wanted her to go to that forsaken valley in the
first place. If anyone were to return to Baltimore as head of a community it should be Elizabeth Seton. When he met her daughter,
Anna Maria, in Baltimore that spring he said as much, and the girl
wrote excitedly to her mother, "The bishop told me the other day,
though as in secrecy and you will keep it such, that you would
probably be down in the fall again and still more probable not to
go back. At least he said you would be down before October with
a few." Mother Seton told Carroll at once that if it was God's will
that she should be called a little nearer she had some money which
could be used in promoting "any plan our Adored may please to
suggest."

As spring turned into summer and the archbishop heard nothing
from the Sulpicians on the subject of replacing Mother Seton he
came to believe that good sense must be causing their hesitation.
He told Mother Seton that although he had briefly thought it might
be better for her personally not to have both a school and a community of sisters to administer he could never approve of her
giving up the community. "It would be in my opinion a fatal
change to the prosperity of the institution of the Sisterhood," he
said. "If therefore it should be again proposed to me, it is my
determination to resist the proposal." While David continued in
his considerations regarding changes in the Emmitsburg leadership
the situation remained very difficult for Mother Seton, and the
archbishop did not discount the unhappiness she was experiencing;
but Carroll remained firm in his own conviction that she must stay.
"If you should ever be permitted to resign your maternal charge
over your community, I would rejoice on your own individual
account," he wrote understandingly. "But my hope for the continuance of the establishment would be very much weakened." He told
her that although these trials might seem heavy, she could expect
even heavier ones. "Never lose sight of the consoling words of Christ:
Take courage, for I have overcome the world," he concluded.

The archbishop was very accurate in his prediction that Elizabeth Seton would have heavier trials as time went by, but at least
she was never replaced as head of the community which she had

founded at such sacrifice to her own interests. When Bishop Flaget
went out to his Kentucky diocese in the spring of 1811, he took
with him John David with Carroll's ready permission. Father John
Dubois of Mount Saint Mary's at Emmitsburg was then named to
succeed Father David as Sulpician director to the women at St.
Joseph's, and from that time on all friction between Mother Seton
and her superiors vanished. Dubois had the full confidence of
Mother Seton, and under his direction all faction within the community was eradicated. Sister Rose became Mother Seton's most
valued assistant and the good work of the community and school
went steadily forward.

Father David's departure for Kentucky did not quite end his
influence on Emmitsburg affairs, however. He precipitated one more
crisis requiring Carroll's attention to Mother Seton's daughters, only
in this latter affair the archbishop found himself much more in
sympathy with David's position. Almost as soon as he had reached
the frontier region Father David determined to form a society of
women for the education of young girls. He had originally thought
of trying to get Ursuline nuns for the purpose, but once he saw the
situation in Kentucky he decided that cloistered sisters would be
less suitable than Sisters of Charity. He therefore wrote to Emmitsburg for a copy of the rules of his former charges.[5]

During the summer of 1812 the Kentucky experiment was begun,
and soon David came to believe that if he could have some Emmitsburg sisters to guide his infant community his work would be
vastly accelerated. Accordingly he wrote to Mother Seton, asking
for a few sisters for the Kentucky project. He stipulated particularly
that he wanted Sister Rose, and someone else fitted to teach. When
these sisters could not be spared from Emmitsburg David next proposed that the Kentucky sisterhood should be united to Mother
Seton's community but with alterations to the Emmitsburg rules.
He disapproved of the name "Sister Servant" which was the superior's title in conformance with the French rules which the
women there had adopted. He wanted Kentucky to train its own
novices in Kentucky; and finally he demanded that the superior of
the community as well as the confessors should be named by the
bishop.

By this time John Dubois, who had succeeded David as superior
of the Emmitsburg women, was aroused. If the Kentucky sisters
were to be considered part of the Emmitsburg group, then the original community should have something to say about the qualifica-

tions of the candidates to be admitted. In France, where the rules of Sisters of Charity originated, only one motherhouse existed; separate novitiates were not permitted. Furthermore, the Kentucky group were not sure of financial success; if they should fail, St. Joseph's community would be financially responsible for the sisters over whose qualifications they had had no control. David's suggestion that the rules be altered could only be effected, Dubois pointed out, by the consent of Archbishop Carroll, the superior of the Sulpicians in Baltimore, and Dubois himself acting in concert.

Both Dubois and David appealed to Carroll, presenting their respective arguments. Dubois was particularly prolific in his letters on the subject, and he continually used the illustration of French custom to reinforce his case. The Archbishop of Baltimore began to grow irritated at the constant reiteration of what was done in France. After all, this was the United States. He could understand Father David's disapproval of the word "servant" in an area where it was virtually synonymous with "slave." Mere distance and the hardships of travel to and from Kentucky made David's request for a Kentucky novitiate reasonable enough. On the financial side, naturally, the St. Joseph Sisterhood had every right to protect their hard-earned security and he told David, "It should be a matter of agreement between the house of St. Joseph and your establishment how far should extend the intercommunity of property." But the fact was that Carroll did not believe that Dubois' stubborn insistence on preserving the French rules of St. Vincent de Paul in their original purity was compatible with the conditions with which Bishop Flaget and Father David had to cope on the frontier. They were developing institutions to fit the American needs. As he said to David:

> At the very institution of Emmitsburg, though it was strongly contended for its being entirely conformable to . . . the Institutes of St. Vincent de Paul, yet this proposal was soon and wisely abandoned for causes which arose out of the distance, different manners, and habits of the two countries, France and the United States.

As for the primary purposes of the Sisters of Charity, in France they tended to hospitals and the sick; what the United States needed was school sisters. Carroll found himself leaning toward John David's views in the matter.

But Father Dubois was adamant as far as the community at

Emmitsburg was concerned. He said bluntly, "The constitution of the Sisters cannot be modified according to the various opinions of each bishop. Each of them is at liberty to approve or disapprove of our constitutions for his diocese. If he does not approve of them, he can establish another community according to his own ideas." This ended the discussion for all practical purposes. The community of sisters which grew up in Flaget's Diocese of Bardstown was the work of Father David and had no administrative connections with the Maryland community under Father Dubois. The rules followed in Kentucky were based largely upon those of St. Vincent de Paul, but they were modified to serve better the area in which they were to be practised. The Archbishop of Baltimore was just as well pleased.

None of these minor irritations attending the progress of Mother Seton's work involved anything more than Carroll's sympathies or personal preference. In the case of the Jesuits, however, he sensed a threat to episcopal authority if not to the continued existence of the very society itself. The years between the quasi-restoration and the complete restoration of the Society of Jesus were ones in which the men within the society and their archbishop did not always view things with the same perspective; and now that the patina of a century and a half has glossed over the old acerbities it may be admitted that John Carroll possessed the larger view.

In the first place, the years had brought to the old archbishop an enormously enlarged veneration for the contribution of St. Ignatius and the true meaning of the Jesuit way of life. He had thought he loved the Society of Jesus when he had protested in anguish against its suppression in 1773. In the years immediately following he had seen everything through the jealous eyes of an ex-Jesuit. Even his pleasure at the prospect of the opening of St. Peter's Church in New York had been colored in those days by his sensitivities. He had written at length to Plowden:

> A very handsome church is built, and was to be opened the 4th instant in honor of the King of Spain, who has been a considerable benefactor, and whose minister to Congress laid the first stone. I received a most pressing invitation from the Trustees to attend and perform the ceremony of the day; but I was then in our frontier countries, and received their letter too late. . . . I should not be surprised to hear that my non-attendance was the effect of disrespect to his Catholic Majesty.[6]

He and Charles had both been suspicious in the days preceding Carroll's appointment as Superior of the Missions that the American clergy were being ignored because they had been Jesuits.

But as the years passed and the pain of the suppression became less acute Carroll began to meditate over the causes for that suppression and the possible implications for the future of the sons of St. Ignatius. Could it be that in the years that lay between the founding of the Society of Jesus and its suppression by papal brief that imperfections had crept in that hindered the fullest practice of their founder's purposes? Had the suppression perhaps been providential? Would a restored society be able to start afresh, closer to the true rule of St. Ignatius? He said something of this to Thomas Betagh in 1805 at the time of the partial restoration. After speaking of the novitiate which was to begin that winter he went on:

> But I must say with you that tho I lend my cooperation, yet I wish much to see a firmer foundation, than any yet known here. . . . If the Society be destined to rise again, my prayer is, that it may renew, as in its first origins that fervent spirit of religion, those solid practices of piety, and that sound knowledge, sacred and profane, which rendered it the ornament of the church and its best defence. To produce these happy effects, we must have more men endowed with its genuine spirit and capable of inspiring it into others.[7]

With Plowden he shared all his speculations on the subject of their beloved society. "The dissolution and our separation from each other gave us an opportunity," he suggested, "of examining more coolly whence arose not only that virulence, which animated against us the avowed and secret enemies of religion, but likewise the bitterness and animosity of many Catholic prelates, priests, religious, and laymen." One of the causes for the hatred of the Jesuits by other Catholics, he thought, might have come from "the obligation to which our General Father Aquaviva subjected our schools of combatting constantly the doctrine of the powerful body of Thomists, instead of leaving us, as St. Ignatius, bound to the maintenance of no particular opinions, but only to the Doctrine of the Catholic Church."[8] He felt, too, that more cordial relations with Rome should be preserved by the society in the future. He told Plowden:

> If my advice could have any weight in the councils of the Society it would be in favour of a most cordial cooperation

and understanding with the Directors and alumni of the College of Propaganda, and other establishments of similar nature, instead of wrapping up ourselves in our own plans, without endeavouring to profit by the experience, lessons or influence of men engaged in pursuits similar to our own. The more I study the life of St. Ignatius, the more I am convinced that such was his spirit. . . . Those men who seek always the glory of God, must meet with opposition . . . yet by inspiring into, and bestowing confidence on good men a great deal of jealousy and heartburning would be avoided.[9]

He always came back to the same theme, however. The original precepts of St. Ignatius were the only true guide. Whoever was to govern the society, its provinces, and its houses, must "study the Institute, as it came out of the hands of its founder, and his spirit." It was one of the great regrets of Carroll's life that he had not studied the collections of the Bollandists relating to St. Ignatius. He said sadly, "When I had the opportunity of consulting these, in my younger days, I neglected and made little account of them; and thus lost the opportunity for ever." [10] Sometimes when the archbishop was feeling his age he wondered if there were any men sincerely devoted to St. Ignatius and capable of instilling this devotion in others. As he told Father Betagh:

The provincials of England were not in the habit of sending hither many of their best subjects—and of those who were in America, many are dead and the others are generally too far advanced in years, too inactive of course, for those employments and that constant vigilance, which the first beginnings of such an important undertaking require.[11]

The men who came from Europe, claiming to have been trained in the Jesuit rule, were apt to be like Father Nicholas Zocchi of whom Carroll told Plowden:

From this sample of the new order, I am induced to believe that they are very little instructed in the maxims or institute of our venerable mother, the Society. Tho they profess to have no other rules than ours, he seems to me to know nothing of the structure of our Society, nor even to have read the *regula communes,* which our very novices knew almost by heart.[12]

But it was not characteristic of the archbishop to remain in gloom, and he was more apt to speak cheerfully of the young men who joined the restored society with "magnanimous reliances" on the protection of heaven which Carroll found highly gratifying, or to list for Plowden the names of the excellent European recruits like Britt, Henry, Épinette, Kohlmann, Malevé, Bechster, and Wouters.[13]

Then there were canonical as well as ideological matters raised by the partial restoration of the society. The position taken by Carroll remained consistent from the first days of possible quasi-restoration until the full and unqualified restoration. For a decade his views on the precise status of the society in the United States were given clearly, and dispassionately, to any one interested in those views. He never ceased studying the matter, particularly during the months when the society accused him of stubbornness and error, but his conclusions were always the same. First, "that the effects of the publication of, and express submission of the Jesuits themselves to Clement XIV's destructive brief could not be superseded but by an instrument of equal authority and authenticity." [14] Second, that a *viva vocis oraculum* or oral permission for restoration "cannot abrogate a public and acknowledged instrument, such as the brief of destruction," and therefore the distinction of simple and solemn vows, so essential to the Society of Jesus, did not exist.[15] Third, that until the fatal brief of destruction should be formally revoked no bishop could ordain priests *titulo religionis,* and that the members of the quasi-restored society were "precisely in the state of secular priests, and cannot claim any privileges or exemptions to which religious bodies . . . were entitled." [16] Fourth, that Carroll's brief of consecration, the erection of the See of Baltimore, the bulls for the consecration of the suffragan bishops, the oaths of office required of them, these all placed the bishops in the United States under obligation to obey the Congregation of Propaganda Fide. The archbishop told the Jesuits at Georgetown:

> The authority of the Congregation of the Propaganda is greatly [fixed] here for the government of church affairs. . . . And I know that my delicacy and embarrassment between inclination and attachment on one side, and duty confirmed by oath on the other has induced some . . . to impute to me disaffection to the Society, which I am confident that I love more than you, because I knew it much better.[17]

There is no doubt that Carroll was uncomfortable in his unenviable position. He did not wish to see his old society hobbled. He tried to get the Pope to "derogate at least for these States, by an express brief from the penalties and censures of the Ganganellian Brief, which had its full execution in this country." [18] But those were the years when the Napoleonic decrees kept the ports of Europe virtually closed and when Bishop Concanen died without bringing any direct messages from the Pope, Carroll's hope was deferred. He went back to his perusal of the Church law on the subject. As he told an English Jesuit just prior to the full restoration in 1814:

> I have sometimes hoped that these researches would lead to a different conclusion, but I am sorry to say that they all ended in confirming the opinion already expressed. Wherever the brief was executed, the Society was extinguished, and to revive it, the same authority was requisite as for the creation and approbation of a new Order.[19]

It is only to be expected that, once having made certain to his own satisfaction of the law of the case, John Carroll would conform his actions and decisions with precision and justice to that law. He made his position clear to Father Molyneux, the first American superior of the society, when he said, "For we bishops, though we allow you to keep control over the members of the Society, must not admit of your assigning to them their Congregations." [20] Unfortunately, Molyneux's successor did not agree with either Carroll's interpretation of the society's status or the archbishop's insistence on control of all clergy. If Charles Neale was correct in his belief that the society possessed full canonical rights in the years 1806-1814, then he was quite justified in placing his colleagues in the locations where they would be most valuable to the Jesuit work. If, on the other hand, John Carroll was right in the logic he pursued, then he was justified in his annoyance at Father Neale's derogation from his episcopal jurisdiction.

Archbishop Carroll's first cause for irritation came in 1810, when he tried to find an assistant to replace the late Father Beeston. In the spring of that year Carroll decided to move Father Enoch Fenwick from Alexandria, Virginia, to Baltimore. The congregation at Alexandria protested to the archbishop against the loss of their pastor and Carroll understood their distress. But he explained to the trustees:

> It is now indispensably required for my necessary individual

aid and comfort to have with me a clergyman not only pos-
sessing my entire confidence, but young enough to act on
many occasions as copyist and even draughtsman of letters
which can only be committed to priests. . . . Besides, which,
since the death of my ever lamented companion Mr. Beeston,
the whole attention to housekeeping devolves on and fatigues
me beyond my ability. I am entitled to relief, and I cannot
find it but in Mr. Fenwick.[21]

He told the Virginians that he would try to do without Fenwick
until the middle of August out of respect and attachment to them.
He was therefore surprised and displeased when Father Neale at
Georgetown refused to let Fenwick come to Baltimore. Neale stood
upon what he considered his prerogative as Fenwick's superior, and
gave as reasons for keeping Fenwick that he was needed not only
to serve the Alexandria congregation but to act as vice-president
of the college as well. August came and went, and the archbishop
was still without any assistant at Baltimore. He wrote to Neale:

Necessity, which urges on every side, is most imperious
on that which impels me to call Mr. Enoch Fenwick to live
with me at Baltimore. . . . At the age of 74 I cannot any
longer act the part of Curate of the Rectory of a parish,
and at the same time undergo all the drudgery of my episcopal duties. You know that the General has committed to me
the disposal of the members of the Society for their minis-
terial functions.[22]

In the end, of course, Fenwick came to Baltimore; but the archbishop meant to have matters clarified. After the bishops were consecrated in November they met and passed a resolution to the effect
that priests belonging to either the diocesan clergy or to regular
congregations, once they were entrusted with the care of souls in a
particular area, could not be recalled against the will of the bishop.
There were still too few priests in the United States to make any
other alternative possible, they believed. The superiors of the various
orders would be consulted, of course, and their wishes, when reasonable and respectful would be met. But the assigning of clergy
for pastoral duties was the function of the bishops.

Father Charles Neale then, in defiance of this regulation, removed Father Adam Britt, S.J., from Holy Trinity Church in Philadelphia without "writing a line of civility to Bishop Egan," and
then, in spite of reproof from Carroll, adamantly refused to grant

Bishop Egan's request for a German priest to serve a Philadelphia German congregation. Carroll's patience was severely strained. He reminded Neale of the bishops' resolution and of the concern of the bishops for their own episcopal prerogative and the rights of the heads of religious orders. "If this mutual harmony be not preserved," he demanded of Neale, "and the fault lies on the side of the Superior, what hope is there of the Society being cherished, and its full re-establishment being perfected here?" The enemies of the Jesuits would be only too glad to carry tales to Rome and picture the society as desirous of war against the rest of the Church. "It was not by such harshness," Carroll reprimanded Neale, "that the Society heretofore obtained the confidence of the Prelates of the Church and was enabled by them to render such eminent services." [23] To Thaddeus Brzozowski, the General of the Jesuits in Russia, Carroll suggested that someone more amenable to American exigencies might be preferable in Neale's place. Father Brzozowski, who had already warned Neale against resisting episcopal jurisdiction, replaced Neale by Father John Grassi, an Italian Jesuit.

The advent of Father Grassi raised yet another vexing question relevant to the uncertain status of the society during the years of the quasi-restoration; this was the problem of property rights. During the War of 1812 fears of British attacks led the Jesuits to move their novitiate to a succession of locations. In March, 1813, Carroll learned that Grassi intended moving the novices from St. Inigoes to White Marsh. Although the archbishop did not believe the English would carry on a predatory war against private property, as they had when the Americans were rebels, he told Grassi that he would not withhold his consent to the removal.[24] Carroll was thinking in terms of the spiritual exercises of the novices, hoping that there would be no permanent interruption because of the war. He did not anticipate trouble from the quarter in which it actually arose. The White Marsh plantation was at the time under the care of Father Germain Bitouzy who had been there for over a decade. He was one of the trustees of the Corporation of the Clergy which had handled the ex-Jesuit properties ever since its conception in 1784. Father Bitouzy was not one of those enthusiastic about the quasi-restoration of the Jesuits in the United States, and he now refused to turn over the White Marsh plantation to the society. Father Grassi, in turn, insisted upon the society's right to repossess all former Jesuit houses. Angry protests poured into the archbishop's house, and the innocent novices were kept in great confusion. Carroll said to Grassi, "As things are now, it is unfortunate that the novices were not left at St. Thomas's where there is room enough, till everything was ready at White Marsh. . . . I dread its continuance at George Town for even a few weeks." [25] Toward the end of May the novices were taken to Frederick Town, Maryland, where they were certainly far enough from British attacks.[26] But the main quarrel between Grassi and Bitouzy was not over.

Carroll perceived in this new quarrel a danger to the existence of the Society of Jesus. Until the full restoration of the Jesuits was confirmed by papal decree, all caution must be exercised to prevent antagonism to the society on any score. He warned Grassi, "Let me beseech you to recommend to the members of the Society to follow the instructions of the Very Reverend Father-General, and convince themselves that they have not, and cannot have yet, any corporate right in the ecclesiastical property of this country." He went on to say he thought he saw a cloud gathering over the society. There were always anti-Jesuit priests about, who could and very well might threaten the society. "Their enmity would give me little alarm if it were not vitiated more and more by the presumptuous language and premature pretensions of some of your subjects." This was plain speaking, and a week later Carroll followed it up with a second warning to Father Grassi that his impetuous desire for immediate control of the former Jesuit properties could cause resentment against the society to break out afresh. Until Rome spoke the Archbishop of Baltimore could only collaborate with a semi-official restoration in the United States; but, meanwhile, he intended to prevent if he could any rash action by the Jesuits themselves which could delay or permanently prevent a full restoration in the future. He could still remember after all these years the bitter animosity aroused by their critics like La Poterie and Smyth. The accusations of Grassi and the others with him who possessed a narrower view fell heavily upon the old archbishop's ears. The poet spoke truly when he compared man's ingratitude to the harsh blasts of winter winds.

The implication of unfriendliness to the society, these latest innuendoes that he wished to prevent the Jesuits from the full possession of their lawful properties, seemed too much to be tolerated in silence. Carroll seized his forthright pen and addressed himself to the Jesuit superior. He began:

I must do myself justice to say that if ever any measures

were taken to organize a system for the preservation of the property which formerly did, and now again does, belong to the Society; to prevent it from being liable to waste and individual usurpation; if the College over which you preside obtained existence and legal capacity to acquire property and receive donations; if the very spot on which it stands, as well as the church, is now vested in the representations of the College these were originally my acts alone.

His mind went back to his Plan of Organization of 1782, devised in those times of lethargy and lassitude when his was the single voice raised to plead for action and incorporation. Grassi and his foreign colleagues from Russia, Germany, and Flanders had not lived in the United States during that critical period. They were all good religious men, it was true. But they were all possessed of limited points of view; not one was discerning enough to see the difference between the American scene and the countries they had left. They arrived now that the bitterest years of the struggle were over, and expected to enter into full participation of the benefits that the archbishop and his older colleagues had sacrificed so much to achieve. It was high time they were told the facts. He picked up his pen and resumed:

My journeys, year after year, my attendance on the general assemblies, my solicitations, my care and watchfulness over the wording of the different acts of the legislature which were necessary to erect corporations for the clergy and the College, so that they might not be a bar against the Society in case of its revival; these were done by me alone.

Indeed, the archbishop reflected, he had ample proofs of the opposition of his colleagues to almost every one of his protective acts, proofs in these scores of letters which had accumulated in his episcopal residence year after year. As a matter of fact, the society would not even now have a quasi-official existence in his domain were it not for his own efforts. "I alone," he informed Grassi, "opened up and continued the correspondence with the General in Russia and with his concurrence gave all the existence to it which it could receive without a full and authentic repeal of the destructive brief of Clement XIV."

He supposed it was too much to expect others to see the whole panorama of the Church in the United States as he did. It was only natural that each congregation, each college, each community, should see the Church's work through its own partial eyes. Each strove for the greatest good for the Church through its own particular institution. It was the bishops who must weigh and balance all of these convulsive, violent enthusiasms: restraining here, giving impetus there, until all working together produced the great general progress which must be the history of the Church. "I am ashamed," he told Grassi, "for having said so much of myself, which nothing should have extorted from me but the undeserved insinuations of my unfriendliness for not adopting the suggestions of a zeal which appeared to me so precipitate as to endanger the harmony of our fellow-labourers."

The old habit of conciliation was too strong to be foresworn. The aging archbishop was as generous to Father Grassi as he had been to any other priest with whom he had disagreed. Writing the next month to his confidant of many years, Charles Plowden, he said charitably, "My only apprehension is that some of our Brethren, and perhaps even Mr. Grassi himself, may be too impatient to effect at once what will be done better gradually by the helping hand of time." Patience came only with age. Men newly come to power and newly arrived on the American shores did not grasp the complexities which presented themselves to the mind of an octogenarian who had lived through the first quarter-century of the Republic. Jealousy and party spirit must not be allowed to estrange the secular from the regular clergy. He wrote tactfully to Father Grassi in May, "It is a comfort to me amidst these reflections to know that there is at the head of the College a person of your understanding, capable of estimating the consequence of such disunion, and therefore anxious to prevent all measures which tend to create it." [27] The full restoration of the Society of Jesus at the end of 1814 removed all the grounds for differences of interpretation in regard to the status of the Jesuits and in that full restoration the Archbishop of Baltimore had his full reward.

The most wintry blasts of the archbishop's closing years blew from Philadelphia and chilled the rectory in Baltimore with suspicions of Irish intervention in affairs American. Although the old notion that Archbishop Troy of Dublin influenced the nomination of Bishop Concanen in 1808 seems without foundation, Carroll himself had briefly suspected it to be true.[28] After the death of Bishop Egan of Philadelphia on July 22, 1814, Carroll felt the old suspicion flaring up again. Egan's last days had been made sorrowful by the disturbances created by two Irish priests, Father William Vincent Harold, O.P., and his uncle, Father James Harold. The two newcomers from Ireland first quarreled with the trustees of the pro-cathedral, St. Mary's, and then, having gained the support of some of the trustees, revived the old issue of a separate church. It was a repetition of the former German troubles in Philadelphia, but Bishop Egan was too old and frail to bear the scandals, and he died, as one of his loyal priests said, "The first victim of episcopal rights." [29]

Although both Harolds were out of the city at the moment of Egan's death, concern for Philadelphia's future was uppermost in Archbishop Carroll's mind the rest of the summer. He lost no time in consulting with his other bishops and the vicar-general of Philadelphia on the subject of Egan's successor, and soon a list of excellent candidates was compiled. There were plenty of good men if one of them could be persuaded to assume the heavy burden of bringing peace to Philadelphia. David of Kentucky, Dubourg of New Orleans, Gallitzin of Loretto, Benedict Fenwick the Jesuit, Dubois of Emmitsburg, there were men of proven abilities. Even Michael Hurley the Augustinian could not be overlooked.[30] Carroll told his coad-jutor, Leonard Neale, on September 27, 1814, that he had David, Dubourg, Hurley, and Gallitzin particularly in mind.[31] David was the first choice of all those consulted except Bishop Flaget, who protested bitterly against the loss of his greatest support in Kentucky.[32] But before Flaget's protests or Father David's own reluctance could influence the outcome Archbishop Carroll was incensed by a rumor that the Archbishops of Dublin and Bordeaux had intervened at Rome to recommend the younger, trouble-making Father Harold as bishop for the see city to which he had brought such dissension. Carroll did not learn until later that the recommendations of the American hierarchy which had been forwarded in November had not yet reached Rome, and it was infuriating to believe that arch-bishops abroad were meddling in the Church in the United States. Bishop Cheverus in Boston sympathized with Carroll, saying, "It is certainly astonishing that prelates in France and Ireland should recommend subjects for the mission here and be listened to, rather than you and those you are pleased to consult." [33]

Nor was it idle rumor. Archbishop Troy admitted that certain Irish prelates, himself among them, had indeed recommended Father William Vincent Harold for Philadelphia. Before Carroll could be appeased by Troy's apology, "I regret exceedingly an irregular act of mine should afford a moment's uneasiness to your Grace," he wrote indignantly to Plowden, "How any of these prelates . . . could determine themselves to interfere in an affair so foreign to their concern, and to which they are so incompetent, is a matter of surprise. Intrigue must have been very active." At the same time he told Plowden that letters from Troy had also informed Baltimore that another Dominican had been nominated for the vacant See of New York in September of 1814, and had already been consecrated in November. The new bishop of New York was John Connolly, and Troy had said, "He prays me to say that he would have written to your Grace if the war had not prevented him." This remark, however well-intentioned, did not soothe Carroll. Plowden shared his old friend's wrath and replied:

> I must assure you of the interest which I take in your very grounded and just complaints of undue interference in the nominations to your new American sees. I have long known the wonderful activity of Irish Friars to get their heads into mitres, and I have often been amazed at the success of their paltry intrigues.[34]

Although a letter from Cardinal Litta in Rome assured Carroll in June that Harold was not yet appointed, the following month fresh rumors reached Baltimore from Philadelphia that Harold had truly been appointed. The old archbishop was never to see another summer, but his strength could be rallied for one last valiant defence of the principles he held so dear. On July 17 he wrote a strong letter to Cardinal Litta, mustering with his old skill the arguments against Harold's nomination. The next day he despatched an urgent letter to his coadjutor in which he said, "No time should be lost in giving directions to Mr. Debarth to repair to Philadelphia, maintain the mastership of the house, the old chapel and premises." The vicar-general of Philadelphia, Father Louis De Barth, was a firm man and would execute the orders. Father Harold might come back to Philadelphia, but he would not easily take over church property if Carroll could help it. He even allowed himself the satisfaction of a last retort to the Archbishop of Dublin. "Would it not be resented," he asked pointedly, "as a very proper interference if the Bishops of the United States should presume to suggest to the Holy See the persons to be appointed to fill the vacant Sees of Ireland?" [35] To Bishop Flaget he commented rather acidly on August 11:

It is probable you will not experience the loss of Mr. David so much dreaded by you. It seems that several Irish bishops have interfered with a matter which concerns them not. . . . But as I still hope that some copy of my dispatches to Rome has been at length received, it is still uncertain what will be its effect comparatively with that of the Irish prelates.[36]

He had done all he could. If he had failed, then he had failed. But he told Plowden on October 13, 1815, "I do not and probably shall not hear of Harold's appointment." [37] And he did not. Although the See of Philadelphia remained vacant for five years after Carroll's death, Father Harold would never occupy it. The Archbishop of Baltimore had prevented that particular evil.

The old archbishop was not just charging windmills or suffering simply from pique. True, he did confess the wound he suffered from Archbishop Troy's part in the affair, telling Flaget, "I did not expect that my friend the Archbishop of Dublin, Dr. Troy, would be at the head of that interest." But a deeper insight into his actions can be gained from a sentence in his letter to Plowden written in the middle of the Harold episode. To Plowden he had always spoken frankly of the things nearest his heart; and on June 25, 1815, he explained:

> As to my personal feelings on this subject, I am almost indifferent but for the sake of the clergy and congregations of Pennsylvania, and especially Philadelphia, I deprecate his appointment which would be a signal for rancour, religious and political: religious, between the friends of the holy deceased Bishop and the partisans of Harold; political between the opponents of furious democracy and innovators upon established governments, or rather, those who are always ripe for innovations, glossed over with the fair pretexts of the *rights of the people*.[38]

In that admirable exposition can be discerned the two persistent objects of Carroll's devotion: the good of his flock and the welfare of his nation. The care with which he tried to keep nationalistic bias from undermining the unity of the Church has already been noted in an earlier chapter. In these last three cases another facet of his vigilant concern is presented.

John Carroll had a profound veneration for his nation's place in history. She was a new nation requiring modifications of older European institutions to meet the exigencies of her growing domain and the variety of her mission fields. American ideas and ideals required an enlightened intellect capable of exploring beyond the limitations of the old world. His objection to Grassi's procedures had stemmed from that conviction. He said to Plowden:

> Your friend Mr. Grassi is doing his best . . . here, but it seems to me that he consults chiefly, if not exclusively, foreigners . . . all of them good religious men, but not one of them possessing an expanded mind, discerning enough to estimate the difference between the American character and the countries which they left.[39]

On the other hand, the new nation was not a laboratory for frenzied experiments. The excesses of violent republicanism that had ripped France wide open had no place in the United States. Liberty was a dogma to be defined with care and judicious calm. Rash individual flaunting of the general order could not be "glossed over with fair pretexts of the rights of the people." No man ever perceived more clearly nor loved more devotedly the American belief in liberty within the law. His fight to prevent the accession of Father Harold rose above any human jealousy over his own ecclesiastical powers and property, or petty vindictiveness against an insubordinate priest. The consistency of his whole life would have been violated had he not protested. Only a glance at the feebleness of his writing during that last summer will eloquently attest how valiant that protest was. The spidery writing of those letters of 1815 was the work of Carroll's last earthly summer, the characters of a failing hand; but the undeviating firmness of the tone of those letters was the mark of a dogged devotion to an ideal which had persisted throughout his episcopal lifetime. In every line of the old archbishop's last aggressive act there is the distinctly recognizable mark of John Carroll. It is the mark of greatness.

CHAPTER
XIX

NO LASTING MONUMENT

AS THE termination of his earthly sojourn approaches a man begins to look back over his career with an evaluating eye. He is often preoccupied with uneasy speculations and dissatisfaction, as was the Archbishop of Baltimore. What had he done that would endure after him as a lasting monument to the high hopes with which he had begun? Some men, of course, could take comfort from the thought of their numerous progeny who would carry on the family name and bring to fruition the unfulfilled dreams. Others might spend these latter days in proud accounting of material wealth and worldly possessions. Cousin Charles of Carrollton could number with pride his many children and grandchildren, and his prosperous landed estates. Like a patriarch he presided at Doughoregan, watching the family life ebb and flow beneath his complacent gaze.

True, there was a falling off in faith among the younger branches of his family, and the archbishop had commented on the occasion of Mary Caton's marriage to William Patterson that the alliances of Charles' line of Carrolls seemed to prognosticate the loss of their religion. He had said to James Barry in 1806:

> Mary's uncle, mother, and aunt have all formed connections, as you know, out of the Church. I endeavour while I live to save the children, but cannot hope much from my weak endeavors. The most that can be said for the young people now coming forward is the scarcity of suitable matches of their own professions, which is a ruinous evil.[1]

But all was not lost. The Harper girls went to Mother Seton's school in Emmitsburg, to be shaped in the gentle mold of Christian womanhood. The Caton girls were not immune to religious influences, either. Archbishop Carroll was pleased to have occasion to write to Bishop Plessis of Quebec in 1815 that Richard Caton and his three unmarried daughters were planning a visit to that Catholic center.

> I have no doubt of their improving the opportunities which your Lordship may afford them of receiving deeper impressions of piety and religion from the examples they will find in your Lordship's diocese, and particularly if they be allowed to converse (for they know French) with the ladies of the different convents.[2]

The old archbishop was not without hopes that the Canadian visit would inspire in the hearts of his "very dear relations" more respect and attachment for their religion. Harriet Chew Carroll was doing her duty, too, in rearing young Charlie's girls in their father's faith. Cousin Charles seemed content on that score and congratulated Hattie later on her attitude. "Being persuaded that there can be but one true religion taught by Christ," he said, "I conceive it my duty to have my grandchildren brought up in it. . . . God bless you, dear Harriet, and by His grace enable you to bear up under the trials you have undergone."[3] When all was said and done, Cousin Charles had ample reason to feel contentment in old age. His accomplishments were many. His life had been worthwhile.

But when John Carroll surveyed his own life he saw nothing but a succession of forlorn hopes, unsolved perplexities, and half-finished institutions. In a quarter of a century he had not even been able to erect a cathedral to the honor and glory of God. Lately when he read the psalm at the *Lavabo* his heart shrank at the words, "I have loved, O Lord, the beauty of Thy house." This crowded old brick chapel on Saratoga Street was little more than a hovel to house so generous a Master, whose lavish hand had poured such blessings on this Republic. The harsh rod of his own inadequacy smote the old prelate's heart.

He had tried. Heaven knew how hard he had tried. At the very first meeting of the trustees of the Baltimore Catholics after their incorporation in 1795 a resolution had been adopted to open subscriptions for a cathedral. James Barry and David Williamson had come forward with enough to buy some lots from George Gale the following year. At the time the Gale property at Pratt and Exeter Streets had seemed an excellent site, being adjacent to the then fashionable section of Baltimore. But as the years passed the city expanded northwestward, and by 1805 the old "Cathedral Square" site was abandoned. Colonel John Eager Howard of Revolutionary fame consented to sell a full block of land to the Roman Catholic trustees in 1806 for $20,571 to be paid in five installments. Colonel Howard had proved a lenient creditor and had agreed to reduce the price to an even $20,000 in 1810, cancelling the interest due on the old amount at that time. The property had received some damage when Charles Street was graded after 1806, and Howard was a just man.[4]

After the deeding of the property on April 19, 1806, the bishop began to look eagerly ahead to the day when the cornerstone would be laid. The day was fixed for July 7, and Carroll laid his plans with care. This would be the first Catholic cathedral erected in what had been the original United States and he was anxious to have the ceremonies conducted with all the splendor appropriate to the undertaking. At half-past eight in the morning the ritual began. The Bishop of Baltimore in his episcopal robes, wearing the mitre and grasping his staff, walked in a procession of a score of priests and minor ecclesiastics all garbed in surplices and stoles according to their rank. Through the streets they proceeded in solemn dignity, up the hill to the wooden cross which marked the location where the future high altar would stand. Baltimore in July was stifling and the bishop's robes were hot and heavy. He was well past seventy and his heart beat heavily with the exertion of the climb. But Carroll was oblivious to his discomfort. He raised his voice in the sonorous tones of blessing over the chosen spot. Then, moving in slow procession to the west front, he blessed the first foundation stone and sprinkled it with water while the clergy chanted, "Unless the Lord build the house . . . unless the Lord keep the city. . . ." The consecrated stone was then put in place and the clergy circled the entire foundation chanting the 50th Psalm while the bishop invoked God's blessing on this noble undertaking.

Returning at last to the cornerstone, the assemblage sang the *Veni Creator Spiritus,* and the bishop addressed his flock. The copper plate which commemorated that morning's ceremonies bore the inscription: "The first stone of the Cathedral Church, to be erected for the honor of Almighty God, under the title of Jesus and Mary, was placed this 7th day of July, 1806, by the Right Rev. John, Bishop of Baltimore."[5] Hope soared, and Carroll descended the slope to old St. Peter's Church tired but happy. His friends all knew what this day had meant to their bishop. Joanna Barry wrote from New York:

With real pleasure I congratulate you on the commencement of the Cathedral. Yes, with heartfelt satisfaction I perused the exact account given in the paper of the ceremony. . . . May the building progress without interruption and earnestly do I pray Heaven that you may live to consecrate it and long officiate within its walls.[6]

But money was slow in accumulating. In the spring of 1803 the bishop had appealed publicly to his people to give evidence of their attachment to episcopal government by supporting a lottery which would be used to raise funds.[7] Lotteries were common enough in Baltimore in those days. St. Paul's Episcopal Church and the First Presbyterian Church had both used lotteries for money-raising, and the Baltimore Market had been completed with proceeds from one. Even Massachusetts had legalized lotteries for the benefit of Harvard College. The bishop could not guess, of course, that he would draw the first prize himself, giving Matthew O'Brien occasion to say, "I beg leave to congratulate you on the event announced in one of our papers this day which gives to your Cathedral 20,000 dollars and to all our people here abundant satisfaction." [8] In August of 1803 the bishop had also appealed to Napoleon Bonaparte, the First Consul of France, to assist in financing the cathedral as "a fresh proof of your devotion to the good of the Church." [9] But the bishop's part in an event of December of that same year was not destined to endear himself or his church fund to Napoleon's heart. The event was the marriage of the First Consul's brother in a ceremony at which Bishop Carroll presided.

On November 4, 1803, President Jefferson notified Robert R. Livingstone in Paris that reports from Baltimore indicated that Mr. Jerome Bonaparte was to marry Miss Elizabeth Patterson of that city. The President commented:

The effect of this measure on the mind of the First Consul is not for me to suppose; but as it might occur to him, *prima facie,* that the Executive of the United States ought to have prevented it; I have thought it advisable to mention the subject to you. . . . You know that by our laws all persons are free to enter into marriage, if of twenty-one years of age, no one having the power to restrain it, not even their parents; and that under age no one can prevent it but the parent or guardian. The lady is under age, and the parents, placed between her affections, which were strongly fixed, and the considerations opposing the measure, yielded with pain and anxiety to the former.

Jefferson went on to say that Mr. Patterson, the father of the bride-to-be, was the wealthiest man in Maryland, perhaps in the United States, after the cousin of Bishop Carroll. Mrs. Patterson, the mother, was a sister of the wife of General Samuel Smith. Consequently, said the President, "the station of the family in society is with the first of the United States. These circumstances fix rank in a country where there are no hereditary titles." [10]

While the President in Washington was perplexed by the possible political repercussions of such a match, the Bishop of Baltimore was more concerned over the religious aspects of the proposed alliance. Miss Patterson was not a Catholic, but Mr. Bonaparte was. There were the sensitivities of the Presbyterian Pattersons to be considered as well as the regulations imposed by the Church upon the Catholic party. William Patterson, while surrendering to the romantic desires of his daughter, meant to protect her if he could. He engaged Alexander J. Dallas, Jefferson's recent appointee to the office of United States District Attorney for the eastern district of Pennsylvania, to draw up a special marriage contract.[11] The contract was then witnessed by Carroll, the French consul in Baltimore, John Comegys and Joshua Barney, and acknowledged before James Calhoun the first mayor of Baltimore.[12] The Bishop of Baltimore recorded his own part in the affair on December 24, 1803, with the notation:

> With license, I this day joined in holy matrimony, according to the rites of the holy Catholic Church, Jerome Bonaparte, brother of the First Consul of France, and Elizabeth Patterson, daughter of William Patterson, Esq., of the City of Baltimore, and his wife.

The ceremony had taken place on the Saturday before Christmas at the Patterson home on South and Gay Streets. It can only be guessed what the bishop thought privately of the wedding of an eighteen-year-old bride and a nineteen-year-old groom on the vigil of Christmas. Carroll's letter to James Barry on December 26 simply noted tersely that on the preceding Saturday he had married Jerome Bonaparte to Miss Patterson.[13]

History leaves no doubt, however, as to the opinions of the First

Consul on the subject of his brother's precipitous action in Baltimore. He summoned Jerome home, commanding that he leave his
wife behind, and when the reluctant husband came to Lisbon after
a year's delay he found the ports of Europe closed to his American
wife. Jerome parted from Elizabeth at Lisbon, and she eventually
found haven in an English port. It was in England that Jerome
Bonaparte the second was born. When it became obvious that Napoleon, who was now the Emperor of France, had no intention of
recognizing the American marriage of his brother, Elizabeth Bonaparte came back to Baltimore with her infant son, and the Bishop
of Baltimore baptized the little boy who would never know his
father, in the presence of his abandoned mother, the Caton girls
(who were relatives of both the bishop and Elizabeth Patterson's
brother), and Father Beeston. When Pope Pius VII refused to annul
the marriage of Jerome Bonaparte, it was not likely the emperor
would forget that it was the Bishop of Baltimore who had made it
valid. Although the French Senate annulled the marriage and
Jerome consequently married Princess Catherine of Württemberg
on August 22, 1807, the munificence of the Emperor of France was
not apt to endow a cathedral in the city where the youthful Jerome
Bonaparte had so briefly forgotten to reckon with his imperious
brother.

Carroll knew that the burden of financing the church must rest
on his flock, and two years after the laying of the cornerstone he
issued a second appeal to the people, urging them to support as "a
monument of general gratitude" a cathedral which would afford to
the other churches in the diocese an example of the majesty and
solemnity of the divine service when conducted in truly liturgical
form. He had this appeal printed in circular form, and sent a copy
to his coadjutor in George Town with the sly remark, "I cannot
harbor a doubt of your concurrence to give efficacy to this address
in behalf of a monument of religion wherein I hope you are destined to preside." [14] Leonard Neale would be pleased at the picture
of himself as Bishop of Baltimore officiating in his new cathedral.

Meanwhile, designs for the edifice were being drafted. Benjamin
Henry Latrobe, the Yorkshire engineer and architect who was already engaged in planning the national capitol at Washington, was
asked to submit plans for the Baltimore church. Latrobe had originally been asked in 1804 to comment on a sketch of a proposed cathedral of another designer, but after pointing out its major faults
Latrobe had asked Carroll:

Permit me to propose that you will have the goodness to furnish me with the size, the form of the building you would prefer . . . also the amount of your present or probable funds and a plot of the place in which it is to be built and the other avenues leading to it. . . . I will then take the liberty of offering you a plan.

The Bishop of Baltimore accepted Latrobe's offer with alacrity and in less than a year the architect had submitted two designs, one Gothic and the other Roman in style. In theory, Latrobe admitted, the Gothic was to be preferred; but, he went on to say, "The Gothic style of cathedral is impracticable for the uses of common life, while the Greek and Roman architecture has descended from the most magnificent temples to the decoration of our meanest furniture." The grandeur and beauty of the Gothic deserved to be reserved for Christian churches without question; but in practice the Roman church would be cheaper to build. Latrobe confessed, "My habits incline me to the latter while my reasonings prefer the first." [15]

Anyone who knew Latrobe could have predicted, of course, that the cathedral would be classical in design, for he and Thomas Jefferson were the chief exponents of the classical revival in America. While Jefferson was a decided Romanist in architecture and Latrobe told the President emphatically, "I am a bigoted Greek in condemnation of the Roman architecture . . . subsequent to Hadrian's reign," the two men were more in harmony than otherwise.[16] It was Latrobe who in the end suggested the rotunda at the end of the campus which became the Pantheon-like library of the University of Virginia. It was Jefferson who admitted to Latrobe that he hoped the architect would be given the opportunity of finishing the center of the national capitol by "embellishing with Athenian taste the course of a nation looking far beyond the range of Athenian destinies." [17] The designs for the cathedral of Baltimore were drawn up during this resurgence of classicism, and although neither Carroll nor Latrobe ever saw the completed edifice it was their collaboration which envisioned the Ionic portico so reminiscent of the Erectheum, and the octagonal drum which rose into a Roman dome over the juncture of the transepts and nave. There is no way of knowing whether the bishop ever recognized how closely his architectural tastes coincided with those of the President whose political ideas he sometimes deplored. The first Catholic cathedral in Baltimore still stands, however, as an example of those powerful aesthetic impulses which permeated the culture of the early Republic. The

nobility, grandeur, and simplicity of the architecture of the era symbolized the purposes of the men who shaped its destinies. And in a
very special sense the cathedral of the premier see still testifies to
the greatness of the man who lies beneath its high altar, John
Carroll, the first Archbishop of Baltimore.

But none of this was apparent in 1811. The work on the church
had to be abandoned in that year and was not resumed until after
Carroll's death. The causes were obvious. When the British minister,
Augustus Foster, brought Carroll the pallium in the summer of 1811
his courtesy was only incidental to the main purpose of his mission.
He had been instructed by his government in London to offer full
satisfaction for the recent *Chesapeake* affair, but he was to remain
adamant on the subject of those British commercial restrictions so
obnoxious to the United States unless France showed herself ready
to rescind hers. When Foster arrived he found the Americans stirred
up over a new incident, the *President's* retaliation against the *Little
Belt*. The English vessel had been forced to strike her colors, and
proud rumors in the states fixed the number of killed and wounded
English seamen at over three dozen. The American public seemed
to view this second incident as simple justice after the *Chesapeake*
affair, and Foster found that his instructions were outmoded by the
current circumstances. Talk of war was in the air, and by fall the
War Hawks would be in control of Congress. It was only a matter
of time, people said, before England would have another war on her
hands. Conditions in Baltimore that year made it folly to hope for
the completion of the cathedral.

The archbishop had seen it coming. As far back as 1808, when
Mr. Jefferson's embargo had commenced to cripple Baltimore's commerce, it was plain that the Republicans were making a ruin of
the country's business. The Federalist Party which had practically
vanished after Jefferson's re-election in 1804 now revived in protest
and nominated Charles C. Pinckney. James Madison who won the
election seemed as inept as Jefferson in solving the commercial co-
nundrum which was posed by the French and British in their cut-
throat competition. More ships than ever lay idle in the Basin, and
Baltimore hoped that David Erskine, the new English emissary,
would talk some sense into Mr. Madison. There was a brief flurry
of anticipation. Perhaps under the influence of his American wife,
Erskine succumbed to the temptation to reach an agreement pleasing to the United States and he exceeded his instructions. He promised that England would rescind her decrees in exchange for a

pledge that the United States would reopen her trade with the British while still refusing to trade with France. But Canning in England repudiated Erskine's terms and sent Francis James Jackson to replace him. Carroll wrote in disappointment to Charles Plowden on September 19, 1809, "The raising here of our embargo and the subsequent convention with Mr. Erskine set all our American shipping afloat, but disavowal of that convention has very damped the spirit of enterprise." [18]

Carroll believed that the political intrigues of the French and the Irish in the United States were largely to blame for his country's growing animosity toward England. He could sympathize with the Irish, feeling as he did that they had "been goaded by their suffering into madness." But he was quite out of patience with the partisans of the French, those inveterate foes of England and of all orderly government, who used the newspapers to inflame the passions of the public. The old archbishop firmly believed that England was the last bulwark of security against Napoleon—the *spes ultima mundi* as he expressed it. Upon the arrival of Francis Jackson he told Plowden, "After the disappointment caused by the rejection of Mr. Erskine's treaty, we lovers of peace hope that he has brought terms of conciliation." Carroll did not want war, and certainly not a war with England.

As the year 1809 ended Baltimore was rife with rumors that the Holy Father had died, a victim of Napoleon's persecution. Pierre Babade at the Sulpician seminary said pessimistically that Pius VII had probably by now "gathered up the palm of Martyrdom," while Mother Seton up in Emmitsburg told friends, "Probably there is now no Pope, or if there is it is a relation of Bonaparte." The Sulpicians in Baltimore were trying to promote a novena to the Sacred Heart for the necessities of the Church, naming the second Sunday in January as the opening day. The Pope in his hasty passage through France as a prisoner had been heard to say, "*Orate et nolite timere.*" Pray and fear not. It seemed the least his loyal children could do for this man who was possibly already dead of his confinement on the Island of St. Margaretta near the coasts of Provence.[19]

The Pope was not dead, of course. But the feeble old man had seemed more dead than alive after his abduction by the rough soldiers who had taken him from Rome, through Florence and Turin, and thence to Grenoble. Strickland wrote from England in April, 1810, that little was known there about the Holy Father. "Of his Holiness, Pope Pius VII, we know nothing certain," he said. "Many contradictory reports are spread concerning him, fabricated by his enemies on purpose to conceal the truth. Whether he be alive or dead we know not." [20] But later in the year he was able to report, "By the last accounts he was a prisoner at Savona where he was lodged in a good house with liberty to see anyone who desired it, but always in the presence of French and German officers. I fear that he is now treated with greater severity." [21] Napoleon had found it uncomfortable, it seemed, to have the stubborn prelate on French soil, and he had transferred Pope Pius VII to Savona in Italy where the Pontiff remained until January, 1812. By the time the American bishops met in Baltimore in 1810 confirmation of the Holy Father's situation had reached them, and one of their first joint actions after their respective consecrations was to draft a solemn protest against the captivity of Pius VII. This document which was signed by Carroll, Egan, Cheverus, and Flaget on November 15, 1810, denounced the treatment of the Vicar of Christ who had been "first made a prisoner within the walls of his own palace, and then . . . forcibly dragged from the chair of St. Peter," to be detained a prisoner in a foreign land. The bishops decreed that on every Sunday and festival the 120th Psalm should be recited and followed by a special prayer for the Pope.

The American hierarchy had already received from Ireland a circular letter expressing the official sorrow of the Irish prelates over the "calamitous state of the Pope and the Church," and the American bishops resolved to reciprocate with a letter of their own. Consequently on November 26, 1810, the four men forwarded a joint message to the Archbishop of Dublin and the bishops of Ireland. Archbishop Carroll explained to Plowden later that "on account of the infancy of our hierarchy we felt a diffidence. We were more reserved than our Irish Brethren, not daring to anticipate the specific course to be pursued hereafter in the future contingencies of the Church, humbly trusting to the guidance of the Holy Ghost." [22] But the letter of the hierarchy of the United States made a good impression and was printed in both Ireland and England. Once more Carroll's friends across the Atlantic were edified by the wisdom and good taste of the Archbishop of Baltimore.

Although the Pope was not dead, political affairs in the United States were bad enough to depress the Catholics for some time to come. On January 27, 1812, Carroll told Plowden:

Our American cabinet, and a majority of Congress seem to

be infatuated with a blind predilection for France and an unconquerable hostility to England. This last is nurtured by the unaccountable impolicy of the latter in still maintaining the orders of council so detrimental to itself, and so irritating to us. Every day seems to bring us nearer to open hostility, in which we have everything to lose, and nothing to gain.[23]

While he was in Washington that spring Carroll felt war to be imminent. He told his young assistant, Father Enoch Fenwick, "My opinion remains the same as that of almost every one here, federal or democratic, that we shall go to war with Great Britain." And because it happened to be a rogation day he added fervently, "From which however may the Lord deliver us! A prayer suited to this *dies rogationum.*" [24] His fears were all too soon proved accurate. On June 18 the Congress of the United States declared war on England just three days after Governor Robert Bowie of Maryland called the general assembly to get an appropriation for troops. At Fort McHenry the guns were mounted and excitement raged down at the Basin where Baltimore speeded up the construction of her small, swift privateers which would prey upon the British vessels with such deadly efficiency.

Mr. Madison's government did not have the wholehearted support of the city, however. The *Federal Republican* editorially denounced the war efforts and precipitated such a riot that for days more timid souls dared not venture into the streets. When Carroll returned from his visitation at Deer Creek the violence of the two-day disturbance was waning, but he was appalled at the condition of the city and told Father Maréchal that Baltimore had certainly forfeited its character for good order and respect for laws. The only good thing he could say of the affair was that "few if any members of our Congregations have had a share in these turbulent proceedings." The archbishop privately considered the declaration of war "most unfortunate," but he could not tolerate resistance to the orderly democratic processes. It seemed to him a sad reflection on the "vigour, decision, and capacity" of the Baltimore magistrates that the city had reacted so infamously in the national emergency.[25]

Although the archbishop may have deprecated some of the policies which had led his nation into war, once that war was declared he put the full force of his influence on the side of the government. When President Madison called for a day of prayer in the national crisis Carroll responded with a charge to his pastors on August 6 that the Thursday of August 20 be set apart for that purpose. The members of the Catholic Church, Carroll reminded them, were greatly indebted to their nation for the past and present blessings they enjoyed, and they ought now to feel "an equal interest in the welfare of these United States during the awful crisis now hanging over them." As much as he deplored war as a means to settle grievances, John Carroll was always a patriot. In the sermon he himself delivered on August 20 he admonished his flock that they must all contribute to the preservation of their nation. Theirs was a just war, he asserted.

> We have witnessed the unremitting endeavours of our chief magistrate to continue to us the blessings of peace; that he has allowed no sentiments of ambition or revenge, no ardor for retaliation . . . to withhold him from bearing in his hands the olive branch of peace; We have seen him . . . renewing overtures of perfect friendship and cordial union, after his first proposals were contumeliously rejected. The ministers of peace, commissioned by him, . . . left no means untried to effect his salutary and benevolent purposes.

After defending the conduct of President Madison and the government in general Carroll went on to praise the President for his solid religious principles. "He never loses sight himself of the intimate connexion between the protection of heaven, and the happiness of nations," he asserted; and then he quoted the words of the presidential proclamation:

> The safety and prosperity of nations ultimately and essentially depend on the protection and blessing of Almighty God; and the national acknowledgement of this truth is not only an indispensable duty, which the people owe to Him, but a duty, which is favorable to the promotion of that morality and piety, without which social happiness cannot exist, nor the blessings of a free government be enjoyed.

The Archbishop of Baltimore could only heartily approve such views. "These are the maxims of wisdom," he commented, "confirmed by the experience of all ages, and the unanimous suffrages of all wise legislators."

The war in which they were now engaged might be viewed, Carroll suggested, as a war against the impious faction which had risen, and still prevailed, over the nation that now excited their alarms. He concluded with St. Paul's epistle to the Ephesians.

As to the rest, Brethren, be strengthened in the Lord, and in the power of his might. Put ye on the armour of God, that ye may be able to stand against the snares of the Devil. For our wrestling is against principalities and powers, against the rulers of the world of darkness. Wherefore take unto you the armour of God, that ye may be able to resist in the evil day, and to stand in all things perfect.

If in the deepest recesses of his heart John Carroll believed that Napoleon and his forces were the more impious of the European forces in the struggle, he would keep these convictions buried. Privately and publicly he would pray for the return of peace, "a happy peace in this life, and above all that peace which the world cannot give." [26]

But peace seemed far off as the year 1812 ended. The day after Christmas the British declared the ports and harbors of the Chesapeake and Delaware Bays to be blockaded. Marylanders were furious when the federal government refused their plea for protection against the harassing expeditions sent out from Admiral George Cockburn's fleet. The *Niles Register* commented bitterly that if the British squadron remained six months as near Baltimore as it was in the spring of 1813 the inhabitants of the city would have to seek refuge in the back country. As the year wore on St. Mary's County suffered particularly from the marauding raids of the enemy, but Carroll told Plowden that conditions were dreadful everywhere. "This and all other ports of the Chesapeake, and generally all from Rhode Island on the South and Southwest coast of the United States, are completely blockaded and of course no vessels for any foreign country sail hence." They could only hope for some ship flying a flag of truce to carry any news to Europe.[27]

The effects of the war on the Church were severe. Not only was Baltimore cut off from communications with Rome and with the Pope in exile, but the anticipated collaboration of Carroll's suffragan bishops had to be postponed. At the bishops' meeting in 1810 it had been intended that they should reconvene two years later; but after the declaration of war all was changed. Cheverus in Boston said he could see neither the necessity or even the utility of a provincial council being held in 1812. The Sees of New Orleans and New York had no bishops yet, and Cheverus was opposed to the long, tedious journey to Baltimore to discuss what seemed to him to be a few minor questions which could be answered just as easily by the professors at St. Mary's Seminary. The truth was that the expense of the trip was an insuperable obstacle. In Boston, as elsewhere, the poor were out of work. "We live from day to day," the Bishop of Boston said, and he confessed that he did not know whom he could ask for the ten dollars needed for the trip.[28] As time went on things grew worse, and Cheverus said gloomily, "The unhappy war into which we have been plunged has changed our flourishing cities into poorhouses. Unless God gives us peace, the commerce which was our sole means of support is destroyed." [29] It was sheer folly to talk of a meeting of bishops in the midst of such calamity.

The year 1814 had two faces for American Catholics. Events in Europe brought great joy. In January Napoleon had given orders that the Pope should be sent back to Rome. Pius VII had been at Fontainebleau from January, 1812, until the beginning of 1814 when he had been returned to Savona. With the defeat of Napoleon in 1814 the Holy Father was freed and he set out for Rome where he arrived on May 24. In March when Carroll learned of the delivery of the Pope from his imprisonment at Fontainebleau he had written joyously to Mother Seton, "If this should be confirmed our prayers for our captive Pontiff will be exchanged for a *Te Deum.*" [30] It was several weeks after the Pope's arrival in Rome before Baltimore got the news, but on July 3, 1814, Archbishop Carroll issued a pastoral to his people appointing July 10 as a day of general jubilation. The hymn of praise and thanksgiving was solemnly sung, followed by benediction of the Blessed Sacrament. On July 12 Carroll despatched a letter to the Secretary of Propaganda expressing the great joy diffused throughout the Catholic population of the United States for the liberation of His Holiness.[31]

Scarcely more than two months later seventy enemy ships lay off North Point, only twelve miles from Baltimore, and on Monday morning, September 12, the British under General Robert Ross landed and headed for the city. The war was pressing at the very gates of the episcopal city. John Carroll's heart ached for his people and he spoke to them in the words of surest consolation that he knew. He said:

> It is hereby recommended to our Catholic Brethren in this city, during the present state of alarm and danger often to implore the powerful aid and protection of our heavenly Father over ourselves and fellow citizens, and those particularly who must not leave their homes and families for the common defence. Let them be recommended to Divine mercy through the intercession of the Blessed Virgin Mary, as the

chosen Patroness of the diocese, not doubting of her readiness to intercede for those who have recourse to her in time of their need.[34]

The first force of the British attack was valiantly resisted. On September 19 Major General Samuel Smith, the uncle of Elizabeth Bonaparte, issued a general order of congratulation to the citizens of Baltimore for their heroic defense of the city. But no one was able to relax for weeks to come. Father Moranvillé who was overworked at St. Patrick's down at Fell's Point, frantically trying to care for his wounded almost single-handed, wrote apprehensively to the Sisters of Charity in Emmitsburg that he feared the British would "try once more the carrying off this place." He begged the good women not to forget Baltimore at this critical moment. At the Sulpician seminary on Paca Street rumors were rife that a numerous English fleet had returned to the bay, and Father Babade exclaimed, "God knows what will happen! *Pour nous* our lot is prayer and confidence." [33] The fall of the capital and the narrow escape of Baltimore in September left everyone uneasy, and the old archbishop shook his head in disgust at the deplorable conditions to which the ignorance and lack of perception of their leaders had brought the nation. Nevertheless, he issued another pastoral designating October 20 as a day of thanks for the city's deliverance and once more *Te Deums* rose from the pro-cathedral and St. Patrick's Church on the Point.

The memory of Baltimore's days of terror lingered long after the danger had passed and Carroll wrote to Plowden on January 5, 1815,

> The visit of your countrymen last summer to Washington has nearly ruined several of my nearest connexions. They came next to this city. . . . It was an awful spectacle to behold—before us at least forty vessels great and small and for about twenty-five hours fire bomb ketches, discharging shots on the fort upward 200 lb. weight each. You may suppose we did not sleep much. Heaven preserve us from another such visitation.[34]

Even then no one in Baltimore was aware that across the Atlantic the peace commissioners were arranging a treaty at Ghent. President Madison shared the general gloom and set aside January 12 as a day of fasting, humiliation, and prayer.

And then in February came the marvelous news of the treaty.

All through the nation there were fireworks and illuminations, and in Baltimore "every demonstration of joy." Peace had come at last. John Carroll was eighty years old, and he hoped now to live out his days in tranquillity. It was too late to accomplish the larger plans he had cherished in 1810, but it was good to have lived to see the restoration of peace to Europe and to his own dear country. He wrote contentedly to Plowden, "Having lived through God's providence to witness the return of peace. . . . I resume with pleasure and, whilst I can, propose to continue that correspondence which for so many years has been so delightful and beneficial to me." [35]

He knew now that he would never live to see the cathedral of Baltimore completed. There would be no lasting monument to remind men of his fond hopes for the Church. Indeed, when he reflected on the failures of the past, he felt like the man in the Gospel who had buried his talents in the ground. And yet it was something to have lived through these days of decision. The Napoleonic era which was over had rendered the times "uncommonly eventful and fruitful of serious reflection." England, a nation he had always admired, was at the height of her glory. To have stood alone against the overwhelming might of Bonaparte which had compelled submission from every power in Europe until it was met by British arms, and to have at length reanimated the trembling nations of the continent to shake off their yoke, that was the exclusive merit of Englishmen. He quite agreed with the words of the Holy Father's compliments to Great Britain.[36]

The archbishop chuckled suddenly. The United States had not done badly against these very paragons. He had never favored war against England, believing as he did that Napoleon was the true menace of the western world. But the Americans had proved themselves able to resist the recognized superiority of the British. Jackson at New Orleans had shown Pakenham a thing or two, and Carroll could still recall with a shudder the incessant pounding of the guns of old McHenry as they held off the English siege. The country had come through the crisis in spite of the muddle-headed leadership at the capital. It was consoling to reflect that the Church, too, would endure in spite of the personal inadequacy of John, Archbishop of Baltimore. His disappointment over the cathedral was, he mused, probably only vanity anyway. He began his sermon for April 13 which was to be the national day of thanksgiving for the restoration of peace and the signing of the Treaty of Ghent.

CHAPTER
X X

NOR TIME ENOUGH

THERE was very little time left for John Carroll in 1815, and
to the archbishop it seemed as if there were still less energy.
He confessed to Plowden at the beginning of the year, "I am the
only sluggard and do no good;" and to Father Grassi he said,
"There are now but a few hours of the day during which my mind
is fit for any serious application." [1] He was ashamed of the lassitude
which eroded his meagre store of strength, washing away each day
a few more grains of his dwindling estate. But he kept going as
best he could. In March when young George Ticknor called on the
venerable archbishop he found the old man busy writing a letter
to Bishop Cheverus in Boston, and by his side a beautiful copy of
Tasso's *Jerusalem Delivered* open on a frame. Ticknor was impressed by this union of letters and official duties, and was even
more flattered by the lively interest the archbishop took in his remarks on Mr. Jefferson's library, and the patriarchal benediction
Carroll bestowed on the budding New England litterateur when he
left.[2] Carroll found time, too, to draw up for Cousin Charles at Carrollton a list of books on religion suited to a study of comparative
religions.[3] A waste of time at Charles' age, the archbishop thought.
He ought rather to be enjoying the contentment a man derived
from approaching the grave on the warm bosom of Holy Mother
Church. But Charles apparently had no intention of dying yet.

But as spring turned into summer the archbishop found his own
strength fading more rapidly. He was too feeble to accept the nation's invitation to give the oration at the laying of the cornerstone
of the Washington Monument on July 4. It was painful to have to
decline this last opportunity to do homage to the man whose virtues
he believed would remain "undefaced and imperishable in the
hearts of his fellow citizens." But Carroll's voice was by now half

extinguished, as he put it, and he would not allow the occasion to fall short of the solemnity which it merited.[4] Even the cooler air at George Town, where he had gone in the vain hope of recouping his losses in health and energy, failed to produce the salutary benefits which usually accompanied a change of scene, and he returned to Baltimore in July to live out his days in the city which had been his home these many years.

The summer was a cruel one for the Archbishop of Baltimore. One after another his failures returned to plague him. Philadelphia, that city of schism and controversy, was in worse straits than at any time previous; and heaven alone knew whether his protests to Rome would prevent Harold's accession in the end. Certainly the nomination and consecration of Bishop Connolly for New York without consulting any one of the American bishops was a bad omen, and Carroll told Plowden he feared it set "a very dangerous precedent fruitful of mischief by drawing censure upon our religion, and a false opinion of the servility of our principles." In thirty years of correspondence with Rome he had still not succeeded in presenting the American sensitiveness to anything which smacked of foreign interposition in a strong enough light to be read by Italian eyes. Charleston to the south did not bear thinking of, either. Memory balked at the succession of unsavory rivalries, the questionable conduct, the complaints to Rome, which were ushered in by Father Simon Felix Gallagher when he had come bearing his letter from Archbishop Troy in Dublin in 1794. French and Irish names had punctuated the history of that area, Le Mercier, Sibourd, Ryan, Browne, Gallagher, and Clorivière; yet none had brought lasting peace to Carolina. Father Pierre Picot de Clorivière, whom Carroll had known as a divinity student in the class he taught at Liège, had been the first strong hope the archbishop had had for the South; but Clorivière had gone to France and Carroll had no idea when he would return. There was no one to stop Gallagher from keeping Charleston in confusion.[5] Trusteeism had never been scotched. There was no denying it. His intentions had been of the purest in those early days when he had tolerated lay trustees in the belief that the system could expedite the erection of parishes. Now he perceived the tragic results: dissensions and schism, and even the threat of an independent church. He told Bishop Neale that he regretted the day he had ever given his consent, even by implication, to the insidious system. He should have anticipated that the American ardor for civil liberty, when coupled with the Protestant example of congregational control, would produce these disruptive forces which now threatened his flock.

In a sense, the very blessings which had led to the wonderful progress of the Church in the new Republic contributed to her dangers. Religious liberty and the government's unshakable belief in the protection of private property had been misinterpreted by the Irish, the Germans, the French, the clergy and laity alike. They came to the United States without experience in democratic procedures, devoid of the heritage which the colonists had preserved during the American Revolution. Loosed from their former bonds of poverty, political subservience, and religious proscription, these immigrants in the excesses of their joy read into the American plan a much greater degree of freedom of action than actually prevailed in the early nineteenth century. They glibly mouthed the shibboleths of the Republic without the vaguest notion of the precise limitations which the heirs of the Revolution read into their Constitution and their laws. It was small wonder that in church affairs they were unable to make the distinctions which seemed so obvious to Carroll. All his expositions on the exact relation of parishioners to pastor had failed to instruct. These gaping wounds in the Church in Philadelphia, Charleston, and elsewhere immeasurably saddened his declining years. He tried in vain to summon the strength necessary to heal them, but it was not possible. His days were numbered and the old man knew it.

In July Carroll was overjoyed to learn that his old friend Father Strickland was still alive and in good spirits. "I likewise am now in my 80th year," he wrote to England, "and know the soothing consolations of old friends." [6] Charles Plowden, William Strickland and John Carroll: they had proved to be a hardy trio. It was a deep satisfaction to the Archbishop of Baltimore to muse over the long years they had known and shared each other's joys and sorrows. In spite of the summer heat the old prelate began to look forward to the ordinations which must take place in the fall. He sent word over to George Town that he would be pleased to have the company of his coadjutor on the trip to Bohemia the first week in September since he had two priests to ordain besides several who were to receive minor orders. [7] Bohemia, there was a name to conjure with. That had been the beginning. Bohemia, St. Omer, Liège, Bruges, Rome, London, Baltimore—and now Bohemia again. Who could have told that young Jacky Carroll, struggling over his rudiments at the Manor school in 1745, would be coming back seventy years later to ordain fresh recruits for the mission fields in a new and separate nation? There was something eminently fitting that this last conferring of holy orders by the first Catholic bishop in the United States should have taken place at Bohemia.

In October Mother Seton in Emmitsburg received a letter from Baltimore which wrenched her heart. Although he could scarcely hold a pen John Carroll had taken time to send her fifty dollars from Mary Patterson, and to forward a letter from Europe concerning her son who had recently departed for Italy.[8] As ill and as feeble as her friend in Baltimore was that fall, he could still summon these last spurts of energy to perform the acts of courtesy and love which were habitual to him. No one knew how hard his loss would press upon her, she thought, as she looked at the scrawling words of the archbishop's last letter.

On November 22, 1815, when Leonard Neale came over from George Town to visit Carroll he knew at a glance that his old friend was not long for this earth. The very next day, in fact, the Archbishop of Baltimore received the last sacraments at six o'clock in the evening with the clergy of his household and the seminarians from St. Mary's in attendance. The table near his bed was covered with the snowy linen cloth and the two candles and the crucifix were placed upon it. Father Enoch Fenwick who had succeeded Carroll's beloved Beeston went into the pro-cathedral for the Blessed Sacrament, and with the others attending him, brought back the Host to Carroll. Afterwards, as the archbishop's rheumy eyes roved over the faces of the good men who stood about his bed, Moranvillé who loved his music, Babade whose mysticism had inspired Mother Seton, Tessier whose theology had been his very staff, the solemn young faces of the seminarians who had never seen a bishop die, Carroll was overwhelmed with his own shortcomings. "My Reverend Brethren," he said earnestly,

> To all appearances I shall shortly appear before my God and my Judge. Entreat His infinite mercy to forgive me my sins, the abuse I have made of His graces and the bad example I may ever have given, the sacraments I have received without sufficient respect, the days of my life which I ought to have consecrated only to the promotion of His honor and glory.

Those who stood nearest him could see the archbishop lift his eyes toward heaven, and his veined hands moved as if in petition.

"Ah, if any one should be lost through my fault, beg Heaven to forgive me." Then in a serene, low voice he asserted:

I repose all my confidence in the goodness of God and the merits of our dear Lord Jesus Christ. I recommend myself to the powerful intercession of His Blessed Mother and of all the saints, in the hope that they will obtain for me the pardon of my offenses.

He then received the Blessed Sacrament, and after receiving Extreme Unction he put on his stole and gave his blessing to the men around him. The effort was almost too much and he was close to fainting before the room was finally cleared.[9]

Carroll lingered for another week, and during the last days of his life he saw countless men and women come to pay the respect they felt for Baltimore's grand old prelate, and to receive his last blessing. Daniel Brent, his nephew, commented in admiration to a friend, "His mind is as vigorous as it ever was and whenever any person goes to his room you would be pleased and astonished at his readiness in adapting his conversation and questions to the situation and circumstances of the person introduced." [10] He never showed any noticeable impatience or fretfulness, and flashes of his old humor made him seem quite gay on occasion. His memory served him to the very end.

Elizabeth Carroll came over from Rock Creek to be with her brother. She marveled at his tranquillity, at his consideration for all who entered his room. He was as interested in the young girl from St. Joseph's School as in the non-Catholic ministers who formed part of the steady stream which flowed to the rectory on Saratoga Street. Juliana White wrote to Mother Seton that she had seen the archbishop a few days before he died, and that he had spoken to her for about five minutes. "What I understood," she said humbly, "was beautiful." [11] To the Protestant minister who observed that Carroll's hopes must now be fixed on another world, Carroll said simply, "Sir, my hopes have always been fixed on the cross of Christ." [12] John Grassi knew his secret. Carroll had told him in quiet reverence, "One of those things that give me most consolation at the present moment is that I have been attached to the practice of devotion to the Blessed Virgin Mary, and that I have established it among the people under my care, and placed my diocese under her protection." [13]

It was a long time since that consecration on the feast of the

Assumption at Lulworth Castle, but not a day had passed since that John Carroll had not been sensibly convinced of the blessings of her intercession. It would be sheerest ingratitude to give way to uneasiness now. Even the day Father Fenwick stole quietly in to look for the book of ritual for the burial of a bishop, Carroll had not been distressed. Instead, sensing almost at once what his devoted assistant wanted, the archbishop told him precisely where to find it. It was not only an evidence of the remarkable clarity and precision of his memory; it was also a testimony to the sublime tranquillity of his spirit which faced mortality and death as if they had already been met and conquered. Elizabeth, his sister, did not know how he remained so thoughtful of them all. Just before he died he had asked anxiously if the carriage was ready for her, had urged them all to get a little rest, to eat something. Then, making the sign of the cross over them all, he had turned his head aside and died.[14] It was Sunday, December 3, 1815. The heart of the whole city was heavy with mourning.

The body of the Archbishop of Baltimore lay in state for two days at St. Peter's where he had so often addressed his flock. On Tuesday, surmounted by his mitre and his pastoral crozier, John Carroll was placed in his coffin. The solemn Mass of requiem was sung, and then the procession began to move slowly through Saratoga Street, up Franklin, to the chapel of St. Mary's Seminary on Paca Street where the first dignitary of the Church of the United States was laid to rest.[15] The windows along the way were thronged with spectators, and distinctions of rank and wealth, of religious opinion, were laid aside as the impressive cortege wound its way through the silent streets. He lay in the vault of the beautiful little seminary where Mother Seton had first appeared in the habit of the Sisters of Charity of Saint Joseph, and there he stayed until the cathedral of Baltimore was ready to receive him, and then in 1824 John Carroll was taken to his present resting place.

For nine days the people of St. Peter's offered prayers every night for the repose of their lost shepherd. The church was kept in mourning long after that, and many a parishioner thought it looked "lost without him." The papers were full of glowing tributes which called Carroll "a model of clerical character, dignified yet simple, pious but not austere," commented on the beneficence and tenderness of his heart, the purity of his doctrines and precepts, and pronounced, "His Church may well mourn, for his loss is inculculable." [16] The men who had best reason to appreciate Carroll were unstinting in their praise. Bishop Flaget wrote from Kentucky, "This holy man has run a glorious career. He was gifted with a wisdom and prudence which made every one esteem and love him." [17] Bishop Dubourg of Louisiana said, "He has certainly finished a beautiful and glorious career." [18] Bishop Cheverus of Boston had long since called Carroll God's charioteer in the sermon he preached at Baltimore in 1810, and on the first anniversary of Carroll's death he preached such a sermon of praise as would have beguiled the late archbishop himself. One listener in Cheverus' audience, the future Bishop of Vincennes, whimsically remarked, "I could see him stretched out at the bottom of his tomb, listening with pleasure, and smiling." [19]

The passage of time did nothing to diminish the great man's reputation. Grassi, the head of the Jesuits who had caused Carroll some pain in the months before the restoration, wrote in his *Memorie* in 1818, "To his courtesy of demeanor was joined a rare goodness of heart, qualities which won him the merited esteem and respect of the public." [20] Young Robert Gilmor remembered Carroll as a thoroughbred. "He never lost his dignity," he said. "It was impossible to treat him with disrespect or even levity, for he had spirit enough to resent any improper liberties taken with him and awed by his manners any approach to impertinence." [21] No one thought of Carroll without thinking of him as a great American, and Robert Walsh, whom Carroll had once recommended to Plowden as the "equal in extent of literature to any youth I ever knew," remarked of the archbishop:

> His patriotism was as decided as his piety. . . . He had joined with heart and judgment in the Revolution. He retained, without abatement of confidence or favor, the cardinal principles and American sympathies and hopes upon which he then acted.[22]

John Carroll died as he had lived, in humility. His failures oppressed him in his last years, yet without ever threatening his complete reliance upon God's will. To the very end his mind was active, trying to devise ways to further the interest of the Church he loved so selflessly. He seemed quite oblivious to his own part in the enormous progress Catholicism had made during his quarter of a century of episcopal control. The laity had increased four times over, the clergy had been more than doubled. He left three seminaries for the training of priests, three colleges for men, and several academies for young women. There were three convents for women, and three religious orders of men well established, and the Sisters of Charity were spreading all through the East and springing up along the frontier. These were some of his tangible accomplishments.

But far more important than these signs of physical growth, which was bound to come as the Republic prospered, the age of Carroll in the American Church firmly fixed the traditions which were to ennoble and to augment the prestige of that organization. Carroll's unabating devotion to religious freedom put the Catholic Church squarely on the side of justice and civil liberties in the public mind. His careful delineation of the relations of the Church with Rome in spiritual matters dispelled, for those who cared to listen, any doubt about the Catholic's loyalty to his nation in political affairs. Carroll's personal patriotism and his repeated defense of his nation and her great leaders put his own loyalty above question. He was the *beau ideal* of patriot and priest to all who knew him. He defined and gave proof of the eternal compatibility of Catholic Christianity and human freedom under democratic forms.

Within the Church itself he further demonstrated the wisdom of adjusting the various elements to that precise balance which is the ultimate test of great leadership and administrative capacity. He achieved collaboration rather than competition between the clergy and laity at great cost at times to his own pride and patience. He preserved harmony among the various orders of religious men and women in spite of accusations of prejudice here or partiality there. And above all, he demonstrated that the Church needed the special talents of each of the nationalities within the United States. He endured the stubbornness of the Germans, the occasional follies of the Irish, and the frequently impractical mysticism of the French. He bore the disagreements with Neale and Grassi that the restoration of the Society of Jesus might be effected to the best advantage of the whole Church. He listened calmly to the acrimonious debates between David and Dubois over the Sisters of Charity in order that each area might have a community of women suited to the exact needs of the locality and the times. His equable eye surveyed the whole scene and measured each crisis by the ultimate and common good.

His charity was an ever-welling font. "Some may impute to me too easy credulity," he once remarked to Plowden. "But I have great difficulty in persuading myself that men whose lives have been devoted to the service of religion. . . . can be acting a false or dishonorable part." He accepted the surliest of apologies and recognized the most reluctant of capitulations if only in the end the Church might be served. And yet no one ever hinted that the Archbishop of Baltimore was a weakling or an equivocator. Caution and delicacy might have been his check-reins, but courage and frankness were his spurs.

John Carroll lived to see his country's independence declared, won, and again preserved from the threats of Europe during the wars of the Napoleonic Era. He lived to see his flock multiplied, watered, and fed. After 1815 the United States would enter a period of expansion and as the population moved westward so would the parishes. But the patterns for future greatness had been designed before he died, and like Washington whom he had so greatly admired, Archbishop Carroll would be remembered by later generations of Americans as a true father of his country's greatness. He was the *pastor bonus* of the American Church in the days of its infancy; he helped to lay the foundations for that public morality which must always be the basic ingredient of a great and democratic nation.

James Cardinal Gibbons, writing on his great predecessor a century after Carroll's death said:

> The dominant idea in the mind of Bishop Carroll, who was as great a statesman as he was a churchman, an idea that has remained the inspiration of the Church, and has dictated all her policy of the last century . . . was absolute loyalty to the letter and the spirit of the Constitution of the United States.
>
> Bishop Carroll did not wish to see the Church vegetate as a delicate exotic plant. He wished it to become a sturdy tree, deep-rooted in the soil, to grow with the growth and bloom with the development of the country, inured to its climate, braving its storms. . . . His aim was that the clergy and people should be thoroughly identified with the land in which their lot is cast; that they should study its laws and political constitution, and be in harmony with its spirit. From this mutual accord of Church and State there could but follow beneficent effects for both.[23]

While example and inspiration count for anything in the history of the American people the career of John Carroll will remain a very present reminder that love of civil justice, when predicated upon love for God, and accompanied by unfailing charity toward fellowman, is as infallible a recipe for political happiness as our founding fathers intended to predict.

BIBLIOGRAPHY

I. ARCHIVAL SOURCES

Archives of the Archdiocese of Baltimore, Maryland.

Archives of Mount Saint Mary's College, Emmitsburg, Maryland.

Archives of Mount St. Vincent, New York.

Archives of St. Joseph Central House, Emmitsburg, Maryland.

Department of Archives and Manuscripts, Catholic University of America, Washington, D. C.

For a description of the Carroll papers in these archives cf. "Report of the Committee on the John Carroll Papers," *The Catholic Historical Review*, XXXIX (April, 1953), 40-43.

United States Archives, General Records of the State Department, Washington, D. C.

II. PRINTED SOURCES

Burnett, Edmund C. *Letters of the Members of the Continental Congress*. 5 vols. Washington, 1921-1931.

Carroll, John. *Eulogy on George Washington*. New York, 1931.

Eddis, William. *Letters from America, Historical and Descriptive: Comprising Occurrences from 1769-1777, Inclusive*. London, 1792.

Field, Thomas Meagher, ed. and comp. *Unpublished Letters of Charles Carroll of Carrollton and of his Father, Charles Carroll of Doughoregan*. New York, 1902.

Fitzpatrick, John C., ed. *The Diaries of George Washington, 1748-1799*. New York, 1925.

Force, Peter. *American Archives, A Documentary History of the English Colonies of North America. Third Series*. Washington, 1860.

Griffin, Martin, I.J., ed. "Last Illness of Archbishop Carroll," *Researches of the American Catholic Historical Society*. Philadelphia, 1905.

Handlin, Oscar, ed. *This Was America*. Cambridge, 1949.

Hughes, Thomas, S.J. *History of the Society of Jesus in North America: Documents*. 2 vols. New York, 1910.

Moran, Patrick Francis. *Spicilegium Ossoriense: Being a Collection of Original Letters and Papers Illustrative of the History of the Irish Church from the Reformation to the Year 1800*. Dublin, 1884.

Plowden, Charles. *A Short Account of the Establishment of the New See of Baltimore, Maryland, and of Consecrating the Right Rev. Mr. Carroll*. London, 1790.

Riley, Elihu S., ed. *Correspondence of "First Citizen"—Charles Carroll of Carrollton, and "Antillon"—Daniel Dulany, Jr., 1773*. Baltimore, 1902.

Robin, Abbé Claude C. *Nouveau Voyage dans l'Amérique Septentrionale en 1781 et compagne de l'armée du Conte de Rocheambeau*. Philadelphia, 1782.

Tryon, Warren S., ed. *A Mirror for Americans*. 3 vols. Chicago, 1952.

Washington, H. A., ed. *The Writings of Thomas Jefferson*. 4 vols. Philadelphia, 1854.

Wharton, Charles. *A Concise View of the Principal Points of Controversy Between the Protestant and Roman Churches*. New York, 1817.

III.   SECONDARY WORKS

Baisnée, Jules A. *France and the Establishment of the American Catholic Hierarchy: The Myth of French Interference, 1783-1784*. Baltimore, 1934.

Barker, Charles Albro. *The Background of the Revolution in Maryland*. New Haven, 1940.

Brent, John Carroll. *Biographical Sketch of the Most Rev. John Carroll*. Baltimore, 1843.

Cordell, E. F. *The University of Maryland, 1807-1907*. Baltimore, 1891.

Coupland, Reginald. *The Quebec Act*. Oxford, 1925.

Cross, Arthur L. *The Anglican Episcopate and the American Colonies*. New York, 1902.

de Courcy, Henry and Shea, John Gilmary. *The Catholic Church in the United States: A Sketch of its Ecclesiastical History*. New York, 1856.

Delaplaine, Edward S. *The Life of Thomas Johnson*. New York, 1927.

Dignan, Patrick J. *A History of the Legal Incorporation of Catholic Church Property in the United States, 1784-1932*. Washington, 1933.

Féval, Paul. *Jesuits*. Baltimore, 1879.

Fox, Sister M. Columba. *The Life of the Right Reverend John Baptist Mary David, 1761-1841*. New York, 1925.

Geiger, Sister Mary Virginia. *Daniel Carroll, A Framer of the Constitution*. Washington, 1943.

Gerard, John. *Memorials of Stonyhurst College*. London, 1881.

Gibbons, James Cardinal. *A Retrospect of Fifty Years*. 2 vols. Baltimore, 1916.

Glenn, Thomas Allen. *Some Colonial Mansions and Those Who Lived in Them.* Phliadelphia, 1899.

Godecker, Sister Mary Salesia, O.S.B. *Simon Bruté de Rémur, First Bishop of Vincennes.* St. Meinrad, 1931.

Gosse, Edmund. *A History of Eighteenth Century Literature, 1660-1780.* New York, 1929.

Griffith, Thomas W. *Annals of Baltimore.* Baltimore, 1824.

Guilday, Peter. *A History of the Councils of Baltimore, 1791-1884.* New York, 1932.

———. *The Life and Times of John Carroll, Archbishop of Baltimore, 1735-1815.* 2 vols. New York, 1922.

Gurn, Joseph. *Charles Carroll of Carrollton, 1737-1832.* New York, 1932.

Harlow, Vincent T. *The Founding of the Second British Empire, 1763-1793.* London, 1952.

Hughes, Philip. *The Catholic Question, 1688-1829.* London, 1929.

Kingston's New Biographical Dictionary. Baltimore, 1810.

Lehmann, Karl. *Thomas Jefferson, American Humanist.* New York, 1947.

Link, Eugene Perry. *Democratic-Republican Societies, 1790-1800.* New York, 1942.

Lord, Robert H. Sexton, John E., and Harrington, Edward T. *A History of the Archdiocese of Boston, 1604-1943.* 3 vols. New York, 1944.

McAvoy, Thomas T., C.S.C. *The Catholic Church in Indiana, 1789-1834.* New York, 1940.

McCormick, Leo J. *Church-State Relationships in Education in Maryland.* Washington, 1942.

MacDonald, Fergus, C.P. *The Catholic Church and the Secret Societies in the United States.* New York, 1946.

MacDonald, William. "American Political Writing, 1760-1789," *The Cambridge History of American Literature.* Volume I. New York, 1917.

Madelin, Louis. *The Consulate and Empire.* New York, 1936.

Melville, Annabelle M. *Elizabeth Bayley Seton, 1774-1821.* New York, 1951.

Metzger, Charles H., S.J. *The Quebec Act: A Primary Cause of the American Revolution.* New York, 1936.

Morse, Jedidiah. *The American Gazetteer.* Third Edition. Boston, 1810.

O'Daniel, Victor F., O.P. *The Right Rev. Edward Dominic Fenwick, O.P., Founder of the Dominicans in the United States.* New York, 1920.

Paré, George. *The Catholic Church in Detroit, 1701-1888.* Detroit, 1951.

Parrington, Vernon L. *The Colonial Mind, 1620-1800.* New York, 1927.

Pastor, Ludwig. *The History of the Popes.* Volume XL. St. Louis, 1953.

Riordan, Michael J. *Cathedral Records from the Beginning of Catholicism in Baltimore to the Present Time.* Baltimore, 1906.

Rowland, Kate Mason. *The Life of Charles Carroll of Carrollton, 1737-1832*. 2 vols. New York, 1898.

Ruane, Joseph William. *The Beginnings of the Society of St. Sulpice in the United States, 1791-1829*. Washington, 1935.

Ruskowski, Leo F., S.S. *French Émigré Priests in the United States, 1791-1815*. Washington, 1940.

Russell, William T. *Maryland: The Land of Sanctuary*. Baltimore, 1908.

Ryan, Leo R. *Old St. Peter's*. New York, 1935.

Scharf, John H., ed. *The Bicentenary Celebration of the Birth of Charles Carroll of Carrollton, 1737-1937*. Baltimore, 1937.

Scharf, Thomas J. *History of Maryland*. 2 vols. Baltimore, 1879.

Schauinger, J. Herman. *Cathedrals in the Wilderness*. Milwaukee, 1952.

——. *William Gaston, Carolinian*. Milwaukee, 1949.

Semple, Henry C., S.J., ed. *The Ursulines in New Orleans and Our Lady of Prompt Succor, A Record of Two Centuries, 1727-1925*. New York, 1925.

Shea, John Gilmary. *The Life and Times of the Most Rev. John Carroll, Bishop and First Archbishop of Baltimore*. New York, 1888.

Smith, Ellen Hart. *Charles Carroll of Carrollton*. Cambridge, 1942.

Sperry, Willard L. *Religion in America*. New York, 1946.

Spooner, Walter W., ed. *Historic Families of America*. New York, 1907.

Stockett, Letitia. *Baltimore, a Not Too Serious History*. Baltimore, 1936.

Tourscher, Francis E., O.S.A. *Old St. Augustine's in Philadelphia with Some Records of the Work of the Austin Friars in the United States*. Philadelphia, 1937.

Van Doren, Carl. *Benjamin Franklin*. New York, 1938.

Wallace, Willard M. *Appeal to Arms*. New York, 1951.

IV. PERIODICALS

Antony, C. M. "Lulworth Castle: Its History and Memories," *Catholic Historical Review*, I (October, 1915), 250-251.

"Archbishop Carroll of Baltimore, and the Irish Church," *Irish Ecclesiastical Record*, XV (December, 1865), 123-138.

Brislen, Sister M. Nernetta, O.S.F. "The Episcopacy of Leonard Neale," *Historical Records and Studies*, XXXIV (1954), 20-112.

Campbell, B. U. "The Life and Times of Archbishop Carroll," *United States Catholic Magazine*, III (1844), 32-41; 98-101; 169-176; 244-245; 363-379-662-669; IV (1845), 249-260; 782-791.

"Charles Carroll's Plan of Government," *American Historical Review*, XLVI (April, 1941), 588-596.

Conway, Bertrand C. "John Carroll, First Archbishop of Baltimore," *Catholic World*, CXVI (1922), 583.

Devitt, E. I., S.J. "Bohemia," *Records of the American Catholic Historical Society,* XXIV (June, 1913), 97-139.

Gilmor, Robert. "Recollections of Baltimore," *Maryland Historical Magazine,* VII (September, 1912), 236-242.

Hartridge, Walter C. "The Refugees from the Island of St. Domingo in Maryland," *Maryland Historical Magazine,* XXXVIII (June, 1943), 103-123.

Hoyt, William D., Jr. "Land for a Cathedral: Baltimore, 1806-1817," *Catholic Historical Review,* XXXVI (January, 1951), 441-445.

Jenkins, M. C. "The Most Reverend Leonard Neale, Second Metropolitan of the Catholic Church in the United States," *United States Catholic Magazine,* III (1844), 505-512.

Lanctot, Gustave. "Un Sulpicien Récalcitrant," *Moorsfield Antiquarian,* I (February, 1938).

McAvoy, Thomas T., C.S.C. "The Catholic Minority in the United States, 1789-1821," *Historical Records and Studies,* XXXIX-XL (1952), 33-50.

Moreau de Saint-Méry. "Baltimore as Seen by Moreau de Saint-Méry in 1794," *Maryland Historical Magazine* XXXV (September, 1940), 225-230.

Naughten, Gabriel J., O.F.M. "The Poor Clares in Georgetown," *Franciscan Studies,* XXIV (March, 1943), 63-72.

O'Daniel, Victor F., O.P. "Concanen's Election to the See of New York," *Catholic Historical Review,* I (January, 1916), 400-421; II (April, 1916), 19-46.

Parsons, Reuben. "The Suppression of the Jesuits," *Studies in Church History,* IV (1897), 439-503.

Purcell, Richard J. "The Education of the Catholics in Maryland," *Catholic Educational Review,* XXX (December, 1932), 586-588.

Quynn, Dorothy M. "Dangers of Subversion in an American Education," *Catholic Historical Review,* XXXIX (April, 1953), 28-33.

Rusk, William S. "Benjamin H. Latrobe and the Classical Influence," *Maryland Historical Magazine,* XXXI (June, 1936), 126-151.

Sherman, Stuart C. "The Library Company of Baltimore, 1795-1854," *Maryland Historical Magazine,* XXXIX (March, 1944), 6-17.

Smelser, Marshall. "George Washington and the Alien and Sedition Acts," *American Historical Review,* LIX (January, 1954), 322-334.

Smith, Sidney F., S.J. "The Suppression of the Society of Jesus," *The Month,* XCIX-CII (1902-1903), 48-62; 259-278; 383-404; 498-517; 604-624; 20-35; 126-153; 258-274; 366-377; 517-537; 581-592.

Steiner, Bernard C. "Maryland's Religious History," *Maryland Historical Magazine,* XXI (March, 1926), 1-20.

Sturges, Walter Knight. "A Bishop and His Architect," *Liturgical Arts,* XVII (February, 1949), 53-64.

FOOTNOTES FOR CHAPTER I

1. Charles Carroll to Countess Auzouer, September 20, 1771, *Maryland Historical Magazine*, XXXII (September, 1937), 203-208. This journal will hereafter be designated *MHM.*

2. Daniel Carroll's will was probated on May 22, 1751. For its contents cf. Sister Mary Virginia Geiger, *Daniel Carroll, A Framer of the Constitution* (Washington, 1943), pp. 16-18.

3. The best study of eighteenth-century Maryland is *The Background of the Revolution in Maryland* by Charles Albro Barker (New Haven, 1940).

4. Carroll to Carroll of Carrollton, October 6, 1759, *Unpublished Letters of Charles Carroll of Carrollton*, ed. Thomas M. Field (New York, 1902), pp. 33-34 hereafter designated *Unpublished Letters;* Carroll to Carroll of Carrollton, December 29, 1762, Ellen Hart Smith, *Charles Carroll of Carrollton* (Cambridge, 1942), pp. 52-53; Barker, *op. cit.,* p. 41.

5. *MHM,* XXIV (December, 1929), 316.

6. Carroll to Carroll of Carrollton, July 26, 1756, Kate M. Rowland, *Life of Charles Carroll of Carrollton, 1737-1832* (New York, 1898), I, 24; Bernard C. Steiner, "Maryland's Religious History," *MHM,* XXI (March, 1926), 10.

7. James Sterling, *A Sermon Preached Before His Excellency the Governor of Maryland and Both Houses of the Assembly at Annapolis, December 13, 1754* (1755), pp. 41, 45.

8. Carroll to Carroll of Carrollton, July 14, 1760, October 13, 1760, *American Catholic Historical Researches*, XXV (1908), 276, hereafter designated *Researches.*

9. Carroll to Carroll, May 15, 1753, *MHM,* XXVI (March, 1931), 51-52.

10. *MHM,* III (December, 1908), 364-368.

11. Richard J. Purcell, "The Education of the Carrolls in Maryland," *Catholic Educational Review*, XXX (December, 1932), 587-588.

12. One Jesuit historian states that "it was whilst he was pastor that the school or academy was begun in 1745 or 1746." An old account book of the school showed the same uncertainty when it billed the Carrolls for the first time: "May 20, 1745-1746, Daniel Carroll to your son's board." Cf. E. I. Devitt, S.J., "Bohemia," *Records of the American Catholic Historical Society of Philadelphia,* hereafter referred to as *Records,* XXIV (June, 1913), 97-139.

FOOTNOTES FOR CHAPTER II

1. Carroll of Carrollton to Carroll, December 19, 1761, *MHM,* XI (June, 1916), 187.
2. Purcell, *op. cit.,* p. 589.
3. Carroll of Carrollton to Carroll, March, 1750, *MHM,* X (June, 1915), 145.
4. Carroll of Carrollton to Carroll, c. March 22, 1750, E. H. Smith, *op. cit.,* p. 31.
5. For a detailed account of life at St. Omer cf. John Gerard, *Memorials of Stonyhurst College* (London, 1881), pp. 2-38.
6. Rowland, *op. cit.,* I, 63.
7. Geiger, *op. cit.,* pp. 16-17.
8. Charles Carroll of Annapolis wrote to his son, Charles of Carrollton, on October 10, 1753, "Jacky I suppose is gone up the hill." Rowland, *op. cit.,* I, 21.
9. Carroll to Carroll, February 8, 1759, *MHM,* X (September, 1915), 233.
10. Carroll of Carrollton to Carroll, November 11, 1762, *MHM,* XI (September, 1916), 277.
11. Carroll of Carrollton to Carroll, August 8, 1763, *MHM,* XI (December, 1916), 343.
12. Carroll of Carrollton to Carroll, April 29, 1763, *Ibid.,* p. 331.
13. Daniel Carroll to James Carroll, December 20, 1762, Peter Guilday, *The Life and Times of John Carroll, Archbishop of Baltimore, 1735-1815* (New York, 1922), pp. 3-4.
14. Carroll to Carroll, May 24, 1764, *Ibid.,* p. 32.
15. *Unpublished Letters,* p. 31.
16. Carroll of Carrollton to Carroll, July 15, 1761, *MHM,* XI (March, 1916), 71-72.
17. Carroll of Carrollton to Carroll, October 22, 1761, *MHM,* XI (June, 1916), 182.
18. *Unpublished Letters,* p. 54.
19. Carroll of Carrollton, October 22, 1761, Cf. note 17.
20. *Unpublished Letters,* p. 65.
21. Carroll of Carrollton to Carroll, March 17, 1762, June 14, 1763, *MHM,* XI (September, 1916), 262; XI (December, 1916), 336. For older treatments of the suppression of the Jesuits in monograph form cf. Reuben Parsons, "The Suppression of the Jesuits," *Studies in Church History* (Philadelphia, 1897), IV, 439-503; Sidney Smith, S.J., "The Suppression of the Society of Jesus," *The Month,* XCIX-CII (1902-1903). For a later treatment cf. Ludwig von Pastor, *History of the Popes* (St. Louis, 1952), XXXVIII, *passim.*
22. Carroll to Carroll of Carrollton, September 3, 1763, *Unpublished Letters,* p. 77.

23. Carroll to Carroll, May 24, 1764, *Researches,* XIII (1896), 26-27; Guilday, *op. cit.,* p. 32.
24. Geiger, *op. cit.,* pp. 32-33.
25. Carroll to Carroll, May 24, 1764, Transcripts of the Carroll Papers in the Department of Archives and Manuscripts of the Catholic University of America, hereafter referred to as CUA Transcripts.
26. CUA Transcripts, April 15, 1764.
27. *Ibid.*
28. Carroll of Carrollton to William Graves, November 7, 1767, Rowland, *op. cit.,* I, 86.
29. John Carroll Brent, *Biographical Sketch of the Most Rev. John Carroll* (Baltimore, 1843), pp. 27-29.

FOOTNOTES FOR CHAPTER III

1. Carroll's journal is printed in Brent, *op. cit.,* pp. 223-276. All references to this journal which follow are to be found therein.
2. It is possible that at Bologna Carroll may have met his Jesuit friend, Charles Plowden, for he speaks later of "renewing the memory of those happy days I spent with you in Bologna." Cf. Carroll to Plowden, February 28, 1779. Another time he refers to the numerous and kind friends he and Plowden shared in Italy: the Scottis, Rozaleses, Signorettis, and Canonicis. Cf. Carroll to Plowden, February 20, 1782. If Plowden and Carroll were together in Bologna it must have been early in 1772 for by the fall of that year Carroll speaks of Plowden as being at Liège and by January of 1773 Plowden was at Bruges. Cf. CUA Transcripts.
3. They probably left Rome on October 27, 1772. Cf. CUA Transcripts Carroll to Ellerker, October 22, 1772.
4. In a letter to his brother Daniel, September 11, 1772, Carroll stated, "After spending part of the autumn of 1772 at Naples, and its environs, we returned to pass the winter at Rome where I stayed till near the end of March." Cf. Brent, *op. cit.,* pp. 25-26.
5. Carroll to Carroll, February 2, 1769, Brent, *op. cit.,* pp. 27-28.
6. CUA Transcripts, Carroll to Ellerker, January 23, 1772; Guilday, *op. cit.,* pp. 36-37. Although this letter is clearly dated 1772 it seems that Carroll may have neglected to note the passing of the old year. Since by his own account he first arrived in Rome in October, 1772, it appears that he must have misdated this letter to Ellerker.
7. CUA Transcripts, Carroll to Ellerker, February 3, 1773; Guilday, *op. cit.,* pp. 39-40.
8. *Ibid.*
9. CUA Transcripts, Aston to Carroll, February 1, 1786.
10. Brent, *op. cit.,* pp. 25-26.

11. Paul Féval, *Jesuits* (Baltimore, 1879), pp. 326-327.
12. Brent, *op. cit.*, p. 27.

FOOTNOTES FOR CHAPTER IV

1. CUA Transcripts, Carroll to James Earle, June 15, 1809. Anthony Carroll, son of a Daniel Carroll and nephew of James Carroll of Maryland, acted as tutor for Carroll of Carrollton during his student days at St. Omer, Rheims, and Paris. (Cf. E. H. Smith, *op. cit.*, pp. 31-33; 42.) The will of James Carroll dated February 12, 1728, had left legacies to nephews Anthony and James, sons of Michael Carroll. Charles Carroll of Annapolis and Charles Carroll, the surgeon, were made trustees. Dominic, a cousin of James, Senior, was bequeathed 500 acres of land lying at Pipe Creek, and it was this legacy that Anthony Carroll was investigating for Dominic's heirs in 1774. (Cf. Thomas Hughes, S.J., *History of the Society of Jesus in North America: Documents* [New York, 1910], I, Part I, 249; 251-253.) In 1790 the question of this property still hung fire and was discussed by John Carroll and Anthony in London when the former was in England for his consecration as bishop. After the death of Anthony Carroll the heirs of Dominic still pressed their claims. (Cf. CUA Transcripts, Strickland to Carroll, September 3, 1795.) On February 28, 1798, Carroll wrote to Strickland, "Prepare to pay the money left Antony C. to one of Domc. Carroll's heirs." This seems to be the last reference to the matter.
2. CUA Transcripts, Carroll to Plowden, February 28, 1779.
3. *MHM*, II (December, 1907), 354-362; Archives of Georgetown University, J. A. Walter to John Gilmary Shea, April 23, 1888. Exports for the year ending September 30, 1794, amounted to $128,924, and shipping owned there in 1805 reached 2110 tons. Cf. Jedidiah Morse, *The American Gazetteer* (Boston, 1810).
4. Carroll of Carrollton to Carroll, September 12, 1774, *MHM*, XVI (March, 1921), 42.
5. The *Peggy Stewart* incident is described in the *MHM*, V (September, 1910), 235-245; William Eddis, *Letters from America, Historical and Descriptive: Comprising Occurrences from 1769-1777 Inclusive* (London, 1792), pp. 180-182; E. H. Smith, *op. cit.*, pp. 124-127.
6. The most comprehensive treatment of the Quebec Act is to be found in Reginald Coupland, *The Quebec Act* (Oxford, 1925). For a more recent estimate of its later importance cf. Vincent T. Harlow, *The Founding of the Second British Empire, 1763-1793*. Volume I (London, 1952). The place of the Quebec Act in American religious history is treated in Charles H. Metzger, S.J., *The Quebec Act: A Primary Cause of the American Revolution* (New York, 1936).

7. Guilday, *op. cit.*, pp. 76-78.
8. Worthington C. Ford (Ed.), *Journals of the Continental Congress* (Washington, 1904), I, 81-89; 115-120.
9. *Ibid.*, IV, 148.
10. Charles Lee to John Hancock, February 27, 1776, *Researches*, XXIV (July, 1907), 225.
11. Edmund C. Burnett, *Letters of Members of the Continental Congress* (Washington, 1921), I, 352.
12. Guilday, *op. cit.*, pp. 96-97.
13. Maryland *Gazette*, October 27, 1774; William T. Russell, *Maryland Land of Sanctuary* (Baltimore, 1908), p. 602. The address as it appeared in the *Gazette* was dated September 22, 1774, and was signed by "John Oliver, Bishop of Quebec, H. F. Graves, Superior of the Seminary, Louis Aug. de Glapion, Superior General of the Jesuits, and Emmanuel Cerspel, Superior of the Recollects."
14. Burnett, *op. cit.*, pp. 356-416.
15. Carroll to Elizabeth Carroll, May 1, 1776; Brent, *op. cit.*, pp. 40-43.
16. Carl Van Doren, *Benjamin Franklin* (New York, 1938), p. 543.
17. E. H. Smith, *op. cit.*, p. 140.
18. The details of the journey are found in the letter John Carroll wrote to his mother from Montreal on May 1, 1776, and in the journal kept by Carroll of Carrollton. Cf. E. H. Smith, *op. cit.*, pp. 140-145.
19. Willard M. Wallace, *Appeal to Arms* (New York, 1951), pp. 84-85.
20. Henry de Courcy—John Gilmary Shea, *The Catholic Church in the United States* (New York, 1856), pp. 47-49. Pierre R. Floquet had been superior of the Jesuits both at Montreal and Quebec prior to Carroll's visit. On June 15, 1776, he wrote to Briand, "I was complaisant to the Americans out of human respect. . . . I was the only Jesuit in Montreal. . . . Father Carroll did not lodge with me, and dined with me but once. He said Mass in our house by M. Montgolfier's permission."
21. E. H. Smith, *op. cit.*, p. 147.
22. *Ibid.*, p. 149.
23. Van Doren, *op. cit.*, p. 546.
24. *Ibid.*, p. 547.
25. CUA Transcripts.
26. *Records*, XXIV (June, 1913), 115.

FOOTNOTES FOR CHAPTER V

1. CUA Transcripts, Carroll to Plowden, February 28, 1779; Hughes, *op. cit.*, I, Pt. II, p. 650.
2. *Ibid.*
3. *Ibid.*

4. Philip Hughes, *The Catholic Question, 1688-1829* (London, 1929), pp. 147-150.
5. Carroll to Carroll of Carrollton, November 11, 1783, *Unpublished Letters,* pp. 159-160; Joseph Gurn, *Charles Carroll of Carrollton, 1737-1832* (New York, 1932), p. 112.
6. Guilday, *op. cit.,* p. 143.
7. CUA Transcripts, Carroll to Plowden, February 20, 1782; Thomas Hughes, *op. cit.,* I, Pt. II, 609; Guilday, *op. cit.,* p. 615.
8. *Ibid.*
9. CUA Transcripts, Carroll to Plowden, September 26, 1783; Thomas Hughes, *op. cit.,* I, Pt. II, 615-616; Guilday, *op. cit.,* p. 167.
10. *Ibid.*
11. Guilday, *op. cit.,* p. 170.
12. The date and address of this letter are not identifiable but the text may be found in Guilday, *op. cit.,* pp. 172-173, and in John Gilmary Shea, *The Life and Times of Most Rev. John Carroll* (New York, 1888), pp. 211-212.
13. CUA Transcripts, Propaganda Fide to Doria Pamphili, January 15, 1783; Guilday, *op. cit.,* p. 180.
14. Arthur L. Cross, *The Anglican Episcopate and the American Colonies* (New York, 1902).
15. The best treatment of these negotiations is to be found in Jules A. Baisnée, *France and the Establishment of the American Catholic Hierarchy: the Myth of French Interference, 1783-1784* (Baltimore, 1934). This study supersedes the treatment found in Guilday, *op. cit.,* pp. 178-201. Unless otherwise noted, Baisnée is the source for the account here given.
16. This is the conclusion, at least, of Samuel Flagg Bemis, the dean of American diplomatic historians. Cf. Samuel Flagg Bemis, *Diplomatic History of the United States* (New York, 1950), pp. 60-61.
17. CUA Transcripts, Plowden to Carroll, September 2, 1784; B. U. Campbell, "The Life and Times of Archbishop Carroll," *The United States Catholic Magazine,* III (1844), 376-377.
18. *Ibid.,* pp. 363-364.
19. *Ibid.,* p. 377. This letter is incorrectly dated "September 15" in B. U. Campbell's account. The original is dated September 18, 1784.
20. *Ibid.,* p. 376. Plowden to Carroll, September 2, 1784.
21. *Ibid.,* p. 379. Thorpe to Carroll, June 9, 1784.
22. *Ibid.,* p. 377. Carroll to Plowden, April 10, 1784.
23. CUA Transcripts, Thorpe to Carroll, July 2, 1784. The friend in Paris was John Thayer, a Boston convert, then in the Seminary of St. Sulpice.
24. The complete text of the letter is printed in Guilday, *op. cit.,* pp. 203-204.
25. CUA Transcripts, Marbois to Carroll, October 27, 1784.

FOOTNOTES FOR CHAPTER VI

1. CUA Transcripts, Strickland to Carroll, October 10, 1789.
2. E. H. Smith, *op. cit.*, p. 218.
3. CUA Transcripts, Marbois to Carroll, October 27, 1784.
4. At the request of Daniel Carroll, Charles of Carrollton prepared a plan of government in July, 1787. For an analysis of The Signer's views on central government cf. "Charles Carroll's Plan of Government," *American Historical Review*, XLVI (April, 1941), 588-596.
5. The report said simply, "There is properly no ecclesiastical property here: for the property by which the priests are supported is held in the names of individuals and transferred by will to devisees. This course was rendered necessary when the Catholic religion was cramped here by laws, and no remedy has yet been found."
6. CUA Transcripts, Carroll to Plowden, June 29, 1785; Guilday, *op. cit.*, pp. 236-237.
7. *Ibid.*
8. Leo R. Ryan, *Old St. Peter's* (New York, 1935), p. 37; Guilday, *op. cit.*, pp. 247-248.
9. Guilday, *op. cit.*, pp. 250-251.
10. CUA Transcripts, Farmer to Carroll, November 8, 1784.
11. *Ibid.*, Farmer to Carroll, May 10-16, 1785.
12. *Ibid.*, Carroll to Plowden, December 15, 1785; Guilday, *op. cit.*, p. 263.
13. *Ibid.*, Carroll to Trustees, January 25, 1786.
14. Pierre Huet de la Valinière had been deported from Canada during the American Revolution for his anti-British sentiments. Carroll sent him to Illinois as his vicar-general in 1788. Cf. CUA Transcripts, Carroll to Hubert, May 5, 1788.
15. CUA Transcripts, Carroll to Antonelli, March 13, 1786; Guilday, *op. cit.*, p. 269, states that this letter was not sent until August.

FOOTNOTES FOR CHAPTER VII

1. The "Junius" letters may have been the work of Sir Philip Francis, but the identity of Junius is still conceded to be one of the best-kept secrets of journalistic history.
2. William MacDonald, "American Political Writing, 1760-1789," *The Cambridge History of American Literature* (New York, 1917), I, 124-125.
3. MacDonald, *op. cit.*, p. 130; E. H. Smith, *op. cit.*, p. 80.
4. Elihu S. Riley, *Correspondence of "First Citizen," Charles Carroll of Carrollton, and "Antillon," Daniel Dulany, Jr., 1773* (Baltimore, 1902).

5. E. H. Smith, *op. cit.*, p. 114.
6. *Columbian Magazine,* December, 1787; *Researches,* XV (1898), 62-63.
7. Guilday, *op. cit.*, pp. 113-114.
8. Brent, *op. cit.*, pp. 97-105; *American Museum,* June 10, 1789.
9. Geiger, *op. cit.*, pp. 163-164. Daniel Carroll also exerted an influence on the wording of the tenth amendment to the Constitution.
10. There is no certainty regarding the exact relationship, but Wharton referred to Carroll as "my venerable relative" in a letter to Simon Gabriel Bruté, April 20, 1816. Thomas Hughes calls Wharton Carroll's "own relative" in Hughes, *op. cit.*, I, Pt. II, 722.
11. CUA Transcripts, Carroll to Plowden, September 26, 1783.
12. Charles Wharton, *A Concise View of the Principal Points of Controversy Between the Protestant and Roman Churches* (New York, 1817). This volume contains Wharton's *Letter,* Carroll's *Address* to Wharton, and Wharton's reply to Carroll. Unless otherwise noted, all subsequent references to the Wharton letter or to Carroll's reply are based on this book.
13. Guilday, *op. cit.*, p. 119.
14. Hughes, *op. cit.*, I, Pt. II, 631.
15. CUA Transcripts, Thomas Talbot to Carroll, September 21, 1784.
16. *Ibid.,* Talbot to Carroll, January 26, 1785.
17. *Ibid.,* Talbot to Carroll, August 20, 1785. Carroll wrote to Berrington on September 29, 1786, "Wharton made a reply to me, of which I never took notice for this reason, as well as because it really did not deserve any. I thought, for a time there began to be a sourness in the minds of our protestant brethren, which might, if irritated break out into violence, and perhaps a renewal of those shameful and barbarous laws, under which we groaned so long, and you still groan. Thank God! the remembrance of the controversy has now died away, and I see no symptoms remaining of an intolerant spirit. We are approaching to that happy term when in the appointment of men to offices of public trust, it will never be considered what religion does he profess but only whether he be honest, and able to fulfill it."
18. Guilday, *op. cit.*, p. 127.
19. CUA Transcripts, Thorpe to Carroll, August 31, 1785.
20. *Ibid.,* Plowden to Carroll, September 29, 1786.
21. *Ibid.,* Thorpe to Carroll, December 2, 1786.
22. *Ibid.,* Badin to Carroll, June 3, 1799.
23. In a letter from Simon Gabriel Bruté to Charles Wharton dated March 30, 1816, Bruté told Wharton, "At Mr. Carroll's death I was struck with the desire of writing to you. . . . He has borne before God the testimony of scandal, which your renunciation of his church and of your sacred priesthood, has occasioned in his diocese." This letter may be found in Wharton, *op. cit.*

24. CUA Transcripts, Carroll to James Frambach, April 20, 1787. Smyth was sent to Frederick owing to Father Frambach's illness.
25. *Ibid.*, Smyth to Carroll, March 15, 1788.
26. *Ibid.*, Carroll to William O'Brien, May 10, 1788.
27. Guilday, *op. cit.*, pp. 309-310.
28. Smyth's *Present State* was published in Dublin in 1788. Carroll's full reply, reprinted in Guilday, *op. cit.*, pp. 313-321, offers an ample summary of Smyth's theses.
29. CUA Transcripts, Strickland to Carroll, April 18, 1788.
30. Patrick Francis Moran, *Spicilegium Ossoriense: Being a Collection of Original Letters and Papers Illustrative of the History of the Irish Church from the Reformation to the Year 1800* (Dublin, 1884), p. 506, Carroll to Troy, July 2, 1789.
31. CUA Transcripts, Thorpe to Carroll, January 11, 1789.
32. Moran, *op. cit.*, p. 505, Carroll to Troy, August 11, 1788.
33. Guilday, *op. cit.*, p. 284, note 24.
34. CUA Transcripts, Carroll to Plowden, May 8, 1789.
35. The pamphlet was published in 1789.
36. Moran, *op. cit.*, p. 507, Carroll to Troy, November 9, 1789.

FOOTNOTES FOR CHAPTER VIII

1. *Votes and Proceedings of the House and Senate (1775-1795)*, January 22, 1787; Geiger, *op. cit.*, p. 81. An excellent account of the Potomac River enterprise and Rumsey's efforts to get the machinery for his boat cast is given in Edward S. Delaplaine, *Life of Thomas Johnson* (New York, 1927), pp. 384-414.
2. CUA Transcripts, Lady Arundell to Carroll, February 22, 1786; Lord Arundell to Carroll, September 10, 1790.
3. *Ibid.*, Strickland to Carroll, February 25, 1786.
4. Kingston's *New American Biographical Dictionary* (Baltimore, 1810), pp. 40-41.
5. CUA Transcripts, Thomas Talbot to Carroll, October 10, 1784. Charles was the son of Charles the Signer of Carrollton. E. H. Smith, *op. cit.*, p. 220, suggests that young Charles went to Liège first in 1785, but this letter seems to fix an earlier departure.
6. *Ibid.*, Lady Arundell to Carroll, February 22, 1786. These two young men remain unidentified.
7. *Ibid.*, Strickland to Carroll, August 9, 1789.
8. *Ibid.*, Papal Nuncio to Carroll, July 5, 1787.
9. *Ibid.*, June 28, 1790.
10. *Ibid.*, Carroll to Antonelli, February 27, 1785; Guilday, *op. cit.*, p. 220.
11. *Ibid.*, Strickland to Carroll, July 7, 1784.
12. *Ibid.*, Thorpe to Carroll, June 9, 1784.
13. Guilday, *op. cit.*, p. 239.

14. CUA Transcripts, Thorpe to Carroll, July 2, 1785.
15. *Ibid.*, Strickland to Carroll, March 21, 1787.
16. *Ibid.*, Thorpe to Carroll, August 26, 1785; August 31, 1785.
17. *Ibid.*, Antonelli to Carroll, July 23, 1785. The text of this letter is reproduced in Guilday, *op. cit.*, pp. 269-271.
18. The opposition to bishops in the Protestant churches seems to have been largely political before the Revolution. Certainly afterward the objections vanished, for Samuel Seabury of Connecticut was consecrated in Scotland on November 14, 1784. That same year at a conference of Methodists in Baltimore Francis Asbury assumed the title of bishop, although not actually consecrated as such according to formal standards. William White of Philadelphia and Samuel Provoost of New York were consecrated on February 4, 1787, at Lambeth Palace in England as Episcopalian bishops of their respective cities, and when Carroll sailed for England in 1790 his ship carried Virginia's bishop-elect, James Madison.
19. CUA Transcripts, Charge to the Catholics of New York; Guilday, *op. cit.*, pp. 279-281.
20. *Ibid.*, Memorial to Pope Pius VI, March 12, 1788; Guilday, *op. cit.*, pp. 347-348.
21. *Ibid.*, Carroll to Gardoqui, April 19, 1788; Guilday, *op. cit.*, pp. 346; 350-351.
22. *Ibid.*, Thorpe to Carroll, October 8, 1788.
23. *Ibid.*, Thorpe to Carroll, January 31, 1789.
24. *Ibid.*, Thorpe to Carroll, March 6, March 7, May 13, 1789.
25. *Ibid.*, Strickland to Carroll, May 13, 1789.
26. *Ibid.*, Strickland to Carroll, August 9, 1789. Ignatius Matthews and Henry Pile each received one vote. Three electors did not send their votes, either through choice or neglect. Cf. Guilday, *op. cit.*, p. 353.
27. *Researches*, XVII (October, 1900), 162, Jefferson to Maréchal, January 17, 1820. Writing to Maréchal on the subject of the death of Cardinal Dugnani Jefferson said, "I sincerely regret his loss, having been consulted by him while at Paris by instruction from the Pope previous to his making the appointment of Bishop Carroll to the See of Baltimore and given an assurance that he was perfectly free to make such an establishment without offence to our institutions or opinions." Guilday, *op. cit.*, pp. 353-354.

FOOTNOTES FOR CHAPTER IX

1. Owing to the frequency of citation from CUA Transcripts, subsequent Carroll correspondence cited may be presumed to be from that source, unless otherwise noted. Carroll to Plowden, October 23, 1789; Brent, *op. cit.*, pp. 109-110.

2. Carroll to Antonelli, February 6, 1790.

3. Guilday, *op. cit.,* pp. 365-366.

4. *Ibid.,* p. 366.

5. *MHM,* XXII (December, 1927), 317.

6. Carroll to Troy, July 23, 1790; Moran, *op. cit.,* p. 507.

7. Carroll to Plowden, May 8, 1789.

8. "Baltimore's Centennial," *MHM,* XXIV (September, 1929), 238-239; Robert Gilmor, "Recollections of Baltimore," *MHM,* VII (September, 1912), 236-242.

9. Antonelli to Carroll, August 14, 1790.

10. Brewer to Carroll, August 8, 1790. In a letter to Charles Plowden on March 7, 1798, Carroll noted, "The death of my ancient, & steady & honest friend Mr. Jn. Brewer was a sorrowful piece of information. . . . In a few years more there will be no living vestige of our dear Society."

11. C. M. Antony, "Lulworth Castle: Its History and Memories," *Catholic Historical Review,* I (October, 1915), 250-251. On July 11, 1953, the work of restoring historic Lulworth Chapel was completed when the Apostolic Delegate to Great Britain, Archbishop William Godfrey, consecrated the high altar assisted by the Bishops of Plymouth and Northampton. Monsignor Ronald Knox preached the sermon on that occasion. The restoration, based on two sketches by the original Georgian architect, John Tasker, was carried out under the guidance of H. S. Goodhart Rendel, a former president of the Royal Institute of British Architects, and was sponsored by Colonel Joseph Weld, the present squire of Lulworth.

12. Philip Hughes, *The Catholic Question, 1688-1829* (London, 1929), pp. 161-172.

13. Brewer to Carroll, August 8, 1790.

14. Charles Plowden, *A Short Account of the Establishment of the New See of Baltimore, Maryland, and of Consecrating the Right Rev. Mr. Carroll* (London, 1790).

15. Carroll to Arundell, October 4, 1790.

16. Carroll to Troy, October 3, 1790; Moran, *op. cit.,* pp. 508-509; *Researches,* XIII (October, 1896), 161-162.

17. Joseph W. Ruane, *The Beginnings of the Society of St. Sulpice in the United States, 1791-1829* (Washington, 1935), pp. 23-32, carries a detailed account of these negotiations.

18. Carroll to Troy, October 3, 1790; Moran, *op. cit.,* p. 509.

19. Strickland to Carroll, February 10, 1791.

20. Guilday, *op. cit.,* pp. 384-385.

FOOTNOTES FOR CHAPTER X

1. Geiger, *op. cit.,* pp. 166-180.

2. Guilday, *op. cit.*, pp. 394-403.
3. George Paré, *The Catholic Church in Detroit* (Detroit, 1951), p. 278.
4. Guilday, *op. cit.*, pp. 407-416.
5. Carroll to Plowden, October 27, 1791.
6. Guilday, *op. cit.*, p. 431.
7. *Ibid.*, p. 442.
8. Carroll to Carroll, July 15, 1800.
9. Catherine Carroll married Robert Goodloe Harper on May 23, 1801. Cf. E. H. Smith, *op. cit.*, p. 264.
10. Badin to Carroll, August 13, 1798. Carroll's note on the back of this letter indicates that it was carried to Tessier and Garnier for their advice.
11. The text of Father John Ashton's sermon is printed in Guilday, *op. cit.*, pp. 434-441.
12. Antonelli to Carroll, August 10, 1794.
13. This was published November 29, 1792. Brent, *op. cit.*, pp. 129-135 reproduces this retort.

FOOTNOTES FOR CHAPTER XI

1. Joseph H. Schauinger, *William Gaston, Carolinian* (Milwaukee, 1949), pp. 9-12.
2. Carroll to Plowden, September 23, 1783.
3. Strickland to Carroll, July 7, 1784.
4. Talbot to Carroll, September 21, 1784.
5. Antonelli to Carroll, June 9, 1784.
6. Carroll to Thorpe, February 17, 1785.
7. Carroll to Antonelli, March 1, 1785.
8. According to the charters of this institution the "College of Philadelphia" was chartered on July 13, 1753. On June 16, 1755, it was named the "Academy and Charitable School of the Province of Pennsylvania" or the "College and Academy of Philadelphia." On September 27, 1779, these titles were voided and the institution became known as the University of the State of Pennsylvania. It was at this time that Farmer, "the senior minister in standing in the Roman Catholic Churches" of Philadelphia was made one of the trustees. On September 22, 1785, another act confirmed the University of Pennsylvania. By 1791 Father Farmer was dead but a Catholic layman, Thomas FitzSimons, was on the board of trustees.
9. Antonelli to Carroll, July 23, 1785.
10. The two students at Rome were Ralph Smith of Maryland and Felix Dougherty of Pennsylvania.
11. Carroll to Plowden, January 22, 1787.
12. Ashton to Carroll, August 13, 1787.

13. Strickland to Carroll, October 11, 1788, May, 1789.
14. Carroll to Plowden, October 12, 1791.
15. Carroll to Thomas Sim Lee, January 25, 1787. Guilday has erred in citing this letter, *op. cit.*, p. 453. The two men were "Colonel Deakins and Mr. Threlkeld."
16. Thomas Hughes, *op. cit.*, pp. 673-675.
17. Carroll to Plowden, February 28, 1787; T. Hughes, *op. cit.*, p. 672. The principal opposition came from Bernard Diderick who seemed to be acting from motives of personal antagonism to John Ashton. Carroll told Plowden he had heard that Diderick was noted for turbulence in the Walloon province from which he had come. John Thorpe, however, reassured Carroll on this point in a letter dated July 7, 1787, in which he said, "A very respectable priest of his Walloon Province yesterday gave me his character which is entirely conformable to the good qualities which you notice in him. The other part has perhaps been overcharged or mistaken by them who related it to you."
18. Carroll to [?], February 7, 1787; T. Hughes, *op. cit.*, pp. 673-675.
19. *Ibid.*
20. Thorpe to Carroll, no date.
21. Carroll to Antonelli, April 19, 1788.
22. Brewer to Carroll, September 24, 1790.
23. Talbot to Carroll, December 5, 1792.
24. Strickland to Carroll, May 10, 1798.
25. Ruane, *op. cit.*, p. 24. The story of the foundings of St. Mary's Seminary which follows is based upon Ruane's account, pp. 24-36.
26. Washington to Carroll, August 2, 1798. For a good treatment of Washington's attitude during this period cf. Marshall Smelser, "George Washington and the Alien and Sedition Acts," *American Historical Review*, LIX (January, 1954), 322-334.
27. Gurn, *op. cit.*, pp. 163; 174-177.
28. Carroll to Plowden, December 11, 1798.
29. Carroll to Plowden, December 15, 1800; Ruane, *op. cit.*, p. 47.
30. Ruane, *op. cit.*, pp. 50-51.
31. *Ibid.*, p. 45; Carroll to Plowden, September 3, 1800, December 15, 1800.
32. Dorothy M. Quynn, "Dangers of Subversion in an American Education," *Catholic Historical Review*, XXXIX (April, 1953), 28-33.
33. Ruane, *op. cit.*, pp. 106-107.
34. For a fuller story of the threatened removal of the Sulpicians cf. Ruane, *op. cit.*, pp. 44-54.
35. Leo J. McCormick, *Church-State Relationships in Education in Maryland* (Washington, 1942), pp. 54-55. The committee to raise funds included besides Carroll, Rev. William Smith, Rev. Patrick Allison, and several laymen. Carroll to Plowden, February 24, 1790.

36. Carroll to Washington College, no date. "Collashon" meant, of course, collation, or presentation. Brent, *op. cit.*, p. 106, states that Carroll "had been made Doctor of Laws by the University of St. John's of Annapolis, in Maryland, and afterwards received the same degree and that of D.D. from other universities in the United States."

37. McCormick, *op. cit.*, p. 94. The first Baltimore Academy lasted about eight years.

38. *Ibid.*, p. 155.

39. *Ibid.*, p. 126; Thomas W. Griffith, *Annals of Baltimore* (Baltimore, 1824), p. 177. Griffith describes the building as having "a plain but convenient style." Baltimore College, like the other institutions to which Carroll contributed his services, was sponsored by both the clergy and laity of several denominations.

40. Griffith, *op. cit.*, p. 206; E. F. Cordell, *The University of Maryland, 1807-1907* (Baltimore, 1891), I, 45. Griffith states, "Archbishop Carroll in 1813 was elected provost of the University created in 1812 but declined the office. Instead Robert Smith, Esq. was chosen." The University of Maryland had been nominally in existence since 1784, but in 1806 the legislature had repealed the act which constituted the university from St. John's College on the Western Shore and Washington College on the Eastern Shore. Cf. McCormick, *op. cit.*, pp. 63-65. Robert Smith was the former Secretary of State of the United States.

41. Carroll to Plowden, March 12, 1802.

42. Carroll to Molyneux, May 22, 1807.

43. Carroll to Plowden, April 2, 1808.

44. Carroll to Plowden, February 12, 1803.

45. Carroll to Plowden, August 14, 1804. It is in this letter that Carroll deplores what he termed the former obligation of the Jesuit theologians "of combatting constantly the doctrine of the powerful body of Thomists, instead of leaving us, as St. Ignatius, bound to the maintenance of no particular opinions, but only to the Doctrine of the Catholic Church."

46. Carroll to Grassi, August 25, 1815.

47. Carroll to Plowden, April 2, 1808.

48. Carroll to Plowden, December 11, 1798.

49. Carroll to Grassi, September 24, 1813.

50. Brent, *op. cit.*, pp. 214-216.

FOOTNOTES FOR CHAPTER XII

1. Geiger, *op. cit.*, pp. 179-180.

2. Fergus MacDonald, C.P., *The Catholic Church and the Secret Societies in the United States* (New York, 1946), p. 2.

3. Carroll to McElhiney, January 7, 1794.
4. Strickland to Carroll, November 11, 1791.
5. Michael J. Riordan, *Cathedral Records from the Beginning of Catholicism in Baltimore to the Present Time* (Baltimore, 1906), p. 17.
6. Strickland to Carroll, November 15, 1792.
7. Walter C. Hartridge, "The Refugees from the Island of St. Domingo in Maryland," *MHM*, XXXVIII (June, 1943), 103-123.
8. "Baltimore as Seen by Moreau de Saint-Méry in 1794," *MHM*, XXXV (September, 1940), 225-230.
9. Hartridge, *op. cit.*, pp. 122-123.
10. Stuart C. Sherman, "The Library Company of Baltimore, 1795-1854," *MHM*, XXXIX (March, 1944), 6.
11. *Ibid.*, pp. 11-17.
12. Geiger, *op. cit.*, p. 11.
13. Carroll to Plowden, May 23, 1796.
14. Geiger, *op. cit.*, pp. 180-182.
15. Letterbook I, Emmitsburg, October 24, 1793.
16. Ludwig, Freiherr von Pastor, *The History of the Popes* (St. Louis, 1953), XL, 354-388.
17. Strickland to Carroll, January 3, 1799. Erskine was living at Number 4, Edward Street, London, at the time.
18. Carroll to Erskine, August 20, 1799.
19. Erskine to Carroll, October 29, 1799.
20. Eulogy on the death of Pius VI, no date.
21. Letterbook I, December 29, 1799. Carroll recommended that the priests pattern their sermons on that of St. Ambrose on the death of Emperor Valentinian who died before entering the Catholic Church, "but who had discovered in early age those extraordinary qualities which expanded themselves in Washington, and flourished with as much lustre, during a life of unremitting exertions and eminent usefulness."
22. John C. Fitzpatrick (Ed.) *Diaries of George Washington* (Boston, 1925), IV, 306.
23. Library of Congress, Division of Manuscripts, Carroll to St. Clair, January 29, 1789.
24. For the text of the prayer cf. Guilday, *op. cit.*, p. 432, note 21.
25. Gurn, *op. cit.*, p. 149.
26. General Records of the Department of State, Miscellaneous Letters, Carroll to Washington, March 20, 1792.
27. Gurn, *op. cit.*, p. 150. Washington suggested at the same time that in regard to the Indians living in Maine Carroll might apply to the state legislature of Massachusetts for a subsidy for priests working among those Indians. In 1798 the General Court of the State of Massachusetts awarded an annual allowance of two hundred dollars for a Catholic missionary. Cf. Guilday, *op. cit.*, pp. 613-614.
28. Carroll to Plowden, November 13, 1795.

29. Carroll was thinking particularly of Father Edmund Burke who was rumored to be obnoxious to General Wayne. Burke had expressed a desire to leave the Diocese of Quebec and to work under Carroll's jurisdiction. For an account of Burke and the Detroit country cf. Paré, *op. cit.*, pp. 244-253.

30. Thomas T. McAvoy, C.S.C., *The Catholic Church in Indiana*, 1789-1834 (New York, 1940), p. 78; Paré, *op. cit.*, p. 585; Carroll to Dexter, September 15, 1800. McAvoy states that priests were permitted to reside among the Indians under an act of Congress of March 1, 1793, which provided agents for their welfare. According to Paré Father John Francis Rivet was fortified by an official commission as "Missionary to the Indians." In January, 1795, both Rivet and Father Peter Janin were promised a yearly allowance of $200.00, and by June of that year Rivet was in Vincennes ready to begin his work under the auspices of the United States. Transportation for the missionaries and payment of their allowance was arranged by the War Department.

31. Moran, *op. cit.*, p. 514, Carroll to Troy, July 19, 1794. For a treatment of the Republican clubs cf. Eugene Perry Link, *Democratic-Republican Societies, 1790-1800* (New York, 1942).

32. Carroll to Plowden, September 24, 1796.

33. Gurn, *op. cit.*, pp. 162-163.

34. John Carroll, *Eulogy on George Washington* (New York, 1931); Brent, *op. cit.*, pp. 158-188.

FOOTNOTES FOR CHAPTER XIII

1. Thorpe to Carroll, October 18, 1788.
2. Guilday, *op. cit.*, pp. 375-376; *Records*, XX (1909), 251-253.
3. Guilday, *op. cit.*, pp. 488-489.
4. Carroll to Antonelli, April 23, 1792.
5. Antonelli to Carroll, September 29, 1792.
6. Thorpe to Carroll, October 18, 1788.
7. Carroll to Plowden, September 3, 1800.
8. Plowden to Carroll, January 26, 1801.
9. Gabriel J. Naughten, O.F.M., "The Poor Clares in Georgetown," *Franciscan Studies*, XXIV (March, 1943), 63-72.
10. The two widows were Mrs. McDermott and Mrs. Sharpe. Guilday, *op. cit.*, p. 494, says these two women died of yellow fever in Philadelphia, but the biographer of Leonard Neale disagrees. Cf. Sister M. Bernetta Brislen, O.S.F., "The Episcopacy of Leonard Neale," *Records and Studies*, XXXIV (1945), 41-42. In a letter to Leonard Neale on January 26, 1807, Carroll refers to Mrs. McDermott being with Miss Lalor.

11. Carroll to Betagh, July 14, 1805.
12. Brislen, *op. cit.*, pp. 42-43.
13. Carroll to Neale, March 27, 1808.
14. Brislen, *op. cit.*, pp. 43-44.
15. *The Writings of Thomas Jefferson* (New York, 1854), IV, 500-501. Writing to John C. Breckinridge on August 12, 1803, Jefferson said that neither the executive nor legislature had constitutional authority to make the purchase, but that they "throw themselves on their country for doing for them unauthorized what we know they would have done for themselves had they been in the situation to do it. It is the case of a guardian, investing the money of his ward in purchasing an important adjacent territory; and saying to him when of age, I did this for your good; I pretend no right to bind you; you may disavow me, and I must get out of the scrape as I can; I thought it my duty to risk myself for you."
16. For the early history of the Ursulines in America cf. Henry C. Semple, S.J., *The Ursulines in New Orleans* (New York, 1925), pp. 9-53.
17. Mother Farjon to Carroll, November 1, 1803.
18. National Archives, General Records of the Department of State, Miscellaneous Letters, January to July, 1804, Carroll to Madison, January 14, 1804.
19. Semple, *op. cit.*, pp. 60-61.
20. *Ibid.*, p. 59; Guilday, *op. cit.*, p. 482.
21. *Ibid.*, pp. 61-62. Guilday, *op. cit.*, p. 483, dates this letter August 22, 1804, but Semple reproduces a facsimile of the letter signed by Jefferson and clearly dated May 15, 1804.
22. Semple, *op. cit.*, p. 64.
23. For a fuller account of Mrs. Seton's conversion cf. Annabelle M. Melville, *Elizabeth Bayley Seton, 1774-1821* (New York, 1951), pp. 87-97. The account of the Carroll-Seton relations which follows is based upon this life of Mother Seton.

FOOTNOTES FOR CHAPTER XIV

1. Troy to Carroll, February 15, 1796.
2. Moran, *op. cit.*, p. 520, Carroll to Troy, May 25, 1796.
3. Carroll to Carr, August 26, 1796.
4. Gerdil to Carroll, May 27, 1797. For further reference to the period cf. Francis E. Tourscher, *Old St. Augustine's in Philadelphia* (Philadelphia, 1937).
5. Victor F. O'Daniel, O.P., *The Right Rev. Edward Dominic Fenwick, O.P.* (Washington, 1920), p. 83.
6. *Ibid.*, p. 86. The three recruits were Fathers Wilson, Angier, and Tosi.

7. Strickland to Carroll, October 4, 1804.

8. O'Daniel, *op. cit.*, p. 87. Fathers Wilson and Tosi were unable to leave Europe in 1804.

9. Badin to Carroll, April 11, 1796, June 18, 1796, August 4, 1796.

10. Badin to Carroll, June 3, 1799. For a life of Badin cf. J. Hermann Schauinger's forthcoming biography.

11. Badin to Carroll, March 13, 1800. "Raynald" was Abbé Guillaume Thomas François Raynal. Raynal had been educated by the Jesuits and was ordained, but he apostasized in 1747. His history of the Indies was banned in France in 1779 and Raynal's arrest was ordered but he escaped to Germany. Guilday, *op. cit.*, p. 86, asserts that Raynal was in the colonies during the American Revolution. By 1787, in any case, he had returned to France and apparently repented his earlier theories, for he addressed the Constituent Assembly on May 31, 1791, deprecating the violence of its reforms.

12. Carroll to Badin, March 18, 1801. Carroll wrote to Thayer ordering him to leave Kentucky on July 13, 1801. The *American Gazetteer* (Boston, 1810), gives the population of Kentucky as 406,511 with slaves numbering 80,561.

13. Father Anthony Salmon was with Father Badin less than a year. He arrived in January, 1799, but was mortally wounded in a riding accident on November 9, 1799. Cf. J. Hermann Schauinger, *Cathedrals in the Wilderness* (Milwaukee, 1952), pp. 22-26.

14. O'Daniel, *op. cit.*, p. 91.

15. *Ibid.*, p. 115.

16. A Russian proposal to this effect dated October 14, 1783, is in AAB, 2-V-8.

17. Resolution of the General Chapter, November 6, 1783; Hughes, *op. cit.*, I, Pt. II, 628.

18. Talbot to Carroll, September 21, 1784.

19. Carroll to Plowden, July 11, 1786; Hughes, *op. cit.*, I, Pt. II, 682-683.

20. Carroll to Plowden, November 13, 1786.

21. Carroll to Beeston, March 22, 1788.

22. Carroll to Plowden, May 8, July 12, 1789.

23. Carroll to Plowden, October 23, 1789.

24. Carroll to Plowden, March 16, 1790.

25. Carroll to Plowden, September 13, 1790.

26. Carroll to Antonelli, September 27, 1790.

27. Hughes, *op. cit.*, pp. 818-819, note 13.

28. Carroll to Charles Neale, September 11, 1810.

29. For a brief treatment of the Paccanarist movement cf. Guilday, *op. cit.*, pp. 542-544.

30. Strickland to Carroll, September 29, 1801.

31. Carroll to Plowden, March 12, 1802; Neale to Stone, April 21, 1802, Hughes, *op. cit.*, p. 762.

32. Carroll to Strickland, November 21, 1803. Carroll indicated in this letter that a letter to Gruber of May, 1803, had apparently not reached Russia.
33. Carroll to Molyneux, June 21, 1805; Hughes, *op. cit.,* p. 820.
34. Carroll to Plowden, December 9, 1808; Guilday, *op. cit.,* p. 553.
35. Carroll to Strickland, August 4, 1804; Guilday, *op. cit.,* p. 553.
36. The long and complex story of the difficulties over property rights is documented in Hughes, *op. cit.,* pp. 824-844. Bishop Neale felt that Molyneux's successor, Grassi, showed a "suspicious intemperateness and agitation of mind," and that Grassi's consultors betrayed "Tumultuous precipitancy" in some of their negotiations. Carroll himself commented to Father Gruber of the precipitancy of the newest Jesuit arrivals in demanding that property be resigned to the Society, and he admitted that he feared that intense jealousy might be fomented.
37. Carroll to Grassi, December 17, 1814; Hughes, *op. cit.,* p. 847.
38. Carroll to Grassi, December 10-11, 1814; Carroll to Plowden, January 5, 1815; Hughes, *op. cit.,* p. 846; Guilday, *op. cit.,* pp. 560-562.

FOOTNOTES FOR CHAPTER XV

1. Thomas T. McAvoy, C.S.C., "The Catholic Minority in the United States, 1789-1821," *Historical Records and Studies of the United States Catholic Historical Society,* XXXIX (1952), 37-41.
2. Strickland to Carroll, May, 1789.
3. The story of Thayer's career which follows relies upon the account given in Lord, Sexton, and Harrington, *op. cit.,* I, 420-477.
4. Thayer went to Kentucky in 1799 and spent about four years there, but he was no more suited to the frontier than he had been to New England. In 1804 he went to London and eventually passed from Carroll's ken. For an account of his life in London and Ireland cf. Lord, Sexton, and Harrington, *op. cit.,* I, 678-681.
5. The account of the Philadelphia difficulties which follows is based on Guilday's treatment, *op. cit.,* 647-657.
6. Carroll to Plowden, July 7, 1797.
7. Carroll to Plowden, March 12, 1802.
8. Shea, *op. cit.,* II, 448-450. Brouwer was also spelled "Browers."
9. Carroll to Westmoreland Catholics, August 5, 1795.
10. Carroll to Fromm, August 5, 1795.
11. Carroll to Fromm, October 18, 1795.
12. Carroll to Phelan, October 23, 1795.
13. Carroll to (?), August 24, 1798.

14. Shea, *op. cit.*, II, 450. Judge Addison was president of the Court of Common Pleas of the 5th Circuit of the State of Pennsylvania. Fromm seems to have intended to appeal the decision to a higher court, but he died in Philadelphia of yellow fever in 1798.
15. Guilday, *op. cit.*, p. 742.
16. Carroll to Gallagher, September 1, 1814.

FOOTNOTES FOR CHAPTER XVI

1. Carroll to Neale, April 12, 1808.
2. Carroll to Plowden, April 15, 1795; Guilday, *op. cit.*, pp. 573-575.
3. Carroll to Barry, November 27, 1800.
4. Carroll to [Carr?], July 27 or 28, 1797.
5. Brislen, *op. cit.*, p. 33.
6. Barry to Carroll, June 10, 1807.
7. Carroll to Plowden, December 7, 1804.
8. The *American Gazetteer* for 1810 describes Bardstown as "a flourishing place of 579 inhabitants situated on the head waters of Salt River, 50 miles SE Louisville, 619 miles from Washington." The spelling at that time was given as either "Bairdstown" or "Beardstown." Schauinger, *op. cit.*, pp. 39-40, discusses the choice of Bardstown. Badin also mentioned Danville and Lexington as possible choices.
9. Carroll to Barry, June 15, 1803.
10. Carroll to Barry, August 25, 1803.
11. Sexton, Lord, Harrington, *op. cit.*, I, 585.
12. Melville, *op. cit.*, pp. 91-92.
13. Sexton, Lord, Harrington, *op. cit.*, I, 633.
14. *Ibid.*, p. 634.
15. *Ibid.*, pp. 635-636.
16. *Ibid.*, p. 637.
17. Guilday, *op. cit.*, p. 631. The interpretation of Guilday has been generally accepted by writers since 1922.
18. Carroll to O'Brien, December 9, 1787. In a letter to Plowden on November 7, 1787, Carroll had said he was replacing Nugent with "A Mr. O'Brien, Dominican, well recommended by Archbishop Troy of Dublin."
19. O'Brien to Carroll, April 14, 1796; Carroll to O'Brien, Thayer, and Trustees, July 5, 1796.
20. Carroll to the Gentlemen of Natchez, February 7, 1801. The Pinckney Treaty with Spain, 1795, had fixed the 31° line as the southern boundary of the United States. Spain was slow to evacuate the land

north of the line and it was not until 1798 that the residents of that area felt any real change in their situation. In September of the following year Bishop Carroll received a request from the Roman Catholics for a pastor "qualified by education and exemplary manners to instruct and revive among us the religion of our ancestors." General James Wilkinson also wrote on behalf of the Mississippi Catholics, asking that a priest be sent. Carroll, on September 23, 1799, wrote to Matthew O'Brien who was then in Albany that if he wished to go to Natchez there were two good churches "plentifully provided with necessary furniture and utensils for divine service."

21. O'Brien to Carroll, January 5, 1801, November 6, 1801.
22. O'Brien to Carroll, February 19, 1805; Hurley to Carroll, March 20, 24, 1806.
23. O'Brien to Carroll, June 9, 1804.
24. Betagh to Carroll, June 3, 1804.
25. O'Brien to Carroll, January 7, 1805.
26. O'Brien to Carroll, July 27, 1807; Melville, *op. cit.*, p. 100; Carroll to Betagh, October 22, 1805. At Byrne's departure for Ireland in 1809 Carroll said of him, "He has laboured at New York both indefatigably & with extraordinary efficacy, edifying all at the same time by his most exemplary conduct and mortified life. That vineyard stood greatly in need of such a cultivator." Cf. Carroll to Betagh, May 6, 1809.
27. O'Brien to Carroll, February 3, 7, 23, March 7, 1806.
28. O'Brien to Carroll, November 26, 1807, February 14, 1808.
29. Egan to Carroll, January 30, 1809.
30. Sexton, Lord, Harrington, *op. cit.*, I, 643. O'Brien came to the Diocese of Boston permanently in May, 1812. For his last days cf. *Ibid.*, pp. 665-667.
31. Barry to Carroll, June 10, 1807.
32. Hurley to Carroll, January 2, 1806.
33. Hurley to Carroll, October 7, 1806, July 15, 1807.
34. Sibourd to Carroll, December 7, 8, 25, 1807.
35. Sibourd to Carroll, January 7, June 27, 1808.
36. Sibourd to Carroll, December 8, 1807.
37. Carroll to Kelly, February 5, 1808.
38. Sibourd to Carroll, March 1, 1808.
39. Ruane, *op. cit.*, p. 152.
40. Schauinger, *op. cit.*, p. 45. Flaget's remark was probably made in 1810 since Carroll was seventy-five in that year.
41. *Ibid.*, p. 41.
42. Guilday, *op. cit.*, p. 583.
43. Carroll to Plowden, December 5, 1808.
44. Carroll to Molyneux, February 25, 1807; Carroll to Kohlmann, April 15, 1808.

45. ASJCH, X, 38, 39, Filicchi to Seton, November 30, 1808; Plunkett to Carroll, September 3, 1810.
46. ASJCH, I, 10, Cheverus to Seton, April 13, 1809.
47. Schauinger, *op. cit.*, pp. 46-48. Carroll seems to have been unaware of this aspect of Flaget's trip for he wrote to Charles Plowden on September 19, 1809, "The Rev. Mr. Flaget . . . now the Bishop elect of Kentucky, has gone within the last fortnight to France in order to obtain some of his Brethren to go with him into his Diocese."
48. Carroll reported the death of Concanen to Bishop Plessis on October 15, 1810, saying, "After many fruitless endeavours to obtain a passage to America, he thought at last that he had succeeded, & fortified by a passport, he went from Rome to Naples, intending to embark on board an American vessel, which was allowed to bring home the unfortunate American seamen whose vessels had been so treacherously confiscated in Naples. But Mr. Concanen, on his arrival in that city, was instantly put under arrest & prohibited from going out; which disappointment made such impression on him, that he fell ill, & died in a few days. June 19."
49. Cheverus to Carroll, October 3, 1811.
50. Strickland to Carroll, March 15, 1811.
51. Carroll to Plowden, January 27, 1812.

FOOTNOTES FOR CHAPTER XVII

1. H. A. Washington (ed.), *The Writings of Thomas Jefferson* (Philadelphia, 1854), IV, 420-421, Jefferson to Monroe, November 24, 1801.
2. Badin to Carroll, October 9, 1799.
3. Schauinger, *op. cit.*, pp. 55-57; Guilday, *op. cit.*, p. 693.
4. For details of Harrison's relations with the clergy and the Indians during this period cf. McAvoy, *Catholic Church in Indiana*, pp. 116-121.
5. A translation of this report by Rev. Victor F. O'Daniel, O.P., appears in the *Catholic Historical Review*, I (January, 1916), 305-319. A summary of its contents appears in Schauinger, *op. cit.*, pp. 129-131.
6. For a comprehensive treatment of Badin's relations with the Dominicans cf. O'Daniel, *Fenwick*, pp. 127-165.
7. Flaget's difficulties with Badin over property are discussed in Schauinger, *op. cit.*, pp. 84-87; Guilday, *op. cit.*, pp. 696-698.
8. Hubert to Carroll, January 14, 1796.
9. Carroll to Trustees, October 19, 1796; Paré, *op. cit.*, pp. 273-274.
10. Levadoux to Carroll, February 8, 1797.
11. Paré, *op. cit.*, pp. 276-277.

12. *Ibid.,* pp. 316-319.
13. McAvoy, *Church in Indiana,* pp. 78-81.
14. Sister Mary Salesia Godecker, *Simon Bruté de Rémur, First Bishop of Vincennes* (St. Meinrad, 1931), p. 176.
15. Carroll to Madison, November 17, 1806; Guilday, *op. cit.,* pp. 707-708.
16. Madison to Carroll, November 20, 1806; Guilday, *op. cit.,* p. 708.
17. Madison to Carroll, November 20, 1806; Guilday, *op. cit.,* p. 709.
18. Semple, *op. cit.,* p. 64.
19. Carroll to Pope Pius VII, December 17, 1810; Carroll to Marechal, February 12, 1812; Carroll to Emery, January 2, 1801.
20. Dubourg was consecrated in Rome on September 24, 1815.
21. François André Michaux, *Voyage a l'ouest des monts alleghanys dans les états de l'Ohio, du Kentucky, et du Tennessee,* cited in Oscar Handlin, *This Was America* (Cambridge, 1949), p. 119.
22. Badin to Carroll, March 2, 1797.
23. Paré, *op. cit.,* pp. 279-280.
24. Warren S. Tryon (ed.), *Mirror for Americans* (Chicago, 1952), III, 484.
25. Paré, *op. cit.,* pp. 279-280.
26. Pierre Denaut to Carroll, October 10, 1798; Paré, *op. cit.,* p. 286.
27. Carroll to Plowden, October 10, 1798; Guilday, *op. cit.,* p. 780.
28. Handlin, *op. cit.,* p. 119.
29. Lorenzo Dow, *Travels,* cited in Tryon, *op. cit.,* III, 471.
30. Guilday, *op. cit.,* p. 772.

FOOTNOTES FOR CHAPTER XVIII

1. For a full account of this misunderstanding cf. Melville, *op. cit.,* pp. 167-170.
2. *Ibid.,* p. 171.
3. *Ibid.,* p. 173.
4. *Ibid.,* pp. 174-181.
5. *Ibid.,* pp. 190-194.
6. Carroll to Plowden, November 13, 1786.
7. Carroll to Betagh, October 22, 1805.
8. Carroll to Plowden, August 14, 1804.
9. Carroll to Plowden, June 2, 1809.
10. Carroll to Plowden, August 14, 1804.
11. Carroll to Betagh, October 22, 1805.
12. Carroll to Plowden, February 12, 1803.
13. Carroll to Plowden, April 2, 1808.

14. Carroll to Plowden, August 14, 1804.
15. Carroll to Plowden, December 4, 1804.
16. Carroll to Neale, September 11, 1810.
17. Carroll to Neale, November 5, 1811.
18. *Ibid.*
19. Carroll to Stone, January 3, 1814.
20. Carroll to Molyneux, December 11, 1807.
21. Carroll to Cleary and Robinson, July 5, 1810.
22. Carroll to Neale, September 11, 1810.
23. Carroll to Neale, November 5, 1811.
24. Carroll to Grassi, March 15, 1813.
25. Carroll to Grassi, April 30, 1813.
26. Carroll to Fenwick, May 28, 1813.
27. Guilday, *op. cit.,* pp. 557-563.
28. Shea, *op. cit.,* II, 664-665, argued that the nomination of Concanen was chiefly on Troy's recommendation but this view is refuted by Victor O'Daniel, O.P., in his article, "Concanen's Election to the See of New York," *Catholic Historical Review,* I (January, 1916), 400-421; II (April, 1916), 19-46.
29. Kenny to Carroll, July 21, 1814.
30. Carroll to Neale, September 27, 1814.
31. These names all appear in correspondence addressed to Baltimore in the fall of 1814. Cf. Barth to Carroll, September 7, 1814; Cheverus to Carroll, October 24, 1814.
32. Schauinger, *op. cit.,* p. 111.
33. Cheverus to Carroll, May 11, 1815.
34. Troy to Carroll, March 22, September 1, 1815; Carroll to Plowden, June 25, 1815; Plowden to Carroll, September 1, 1815.
35. Carroll to Litta, July 17, 1815; Carroll to Neale, July 18, 1815; Carroll to Troy, August 4, 1815.
36. Schauinger, *op. cit.,* p. 111.
37. Carroll to Plowden, October 13, 1815.
38. Carroll to Plowden, June 25, 1815.
39. Carroll to Plowden, June 25, 1815.

FOOTNOTES FOR CHAPTER XIX

1. Carroll to Barry, April 8, 1806. Mary Caton married Robert Patterson, May 1, 1806.
2. Carroll to Plessis, July 9, 1815; *Records,* XVIII (1907), 304-305.
3. *Researches,* XVII (October, 1900), 148-149.
4. William D. Hoyt, "Land for a Cathedral: Baltimore, 1806-1817," *Catholic Historical Review,* XXXVI (January, 1951), 441-442.

5. Riordan, *op. cit.*, pp. 19-20.
6. Barry to Carroll, August 20, 1806.
7. Pastoral Letter, June 23, 1803.
8. O'Brien to Carroll, February 19, 1805.
9. Carroll to Bonaparte, August 26, 1803; Guilday, *op. cit.*, pp. 730-731.
10. Washington, *op. cit.*, IV, 510.
11. Alexander James Dallas was appointed by Jefferson on March 10, 1801. Dallas subsequently became Secretary of the Treasury under James Madison, 1814-1816.
12. *MHM*, XVII (March, 1922), 95-96. The original marriage contract is in the possession of the Maryland Historical Society.
13. Carroll to Barry, December 26, 1803.
14. Carroll to Neale, June 19, 1808.
15. Latrobe's connection with the cathedral at Baltimore can be traced in the original documents at the archdiocesan archives in Baltimore. These documents have been amply discussed in Riordan, *op. cit.*, pp. 30 ff.; *MHM*, XXXVII (December, 1942), 349-351, XXXI (June, 1936), 126-151; Walter K. Sturges, "A Bishop and His Architect," *Liturgical Arts*, XVII (February, 1949), 53-64.
16. William S. Rusk, "Benjamin H. Latrobe and the Classical Influence," *MHM*, XXXI (June, 1936), 140.
17. Karl Lehmann, *Thomas Jefferson: American Humanist* (New York, 1947), p. 162.
18. Carroll to Plowden, September 19, 1809.
19. Melville, *op. cit.*, pp. 195-196.
20. Strickland to Carroll, April 17, 1810.
21. Strickland to Carroll, no date.
22. The texts of these documents are reproduced in Guilday, *op. cit.*, pp. 589-599.
23. Carroll to Plowden, January 27, 1812.
24. Carroll to Fenwick, May 4, 1812.
25. Carroll to Maréchal, July 30, 1812.
26. Pastoral Letter, August 6, 1812.
27. Carroll to Plowden, November 11, 1813.
28. Cheverus to Carroll, August 31, 1812.
29. Sexton, Lord, Harrington, *op. cit.*, I, 644.
30. Carroll to Seton, March 29, 1814.
31. Carroll to Propaganda, July 12, 1814.
32. Letter to the Catholics of Baltimore, no date.
33. ASJCH, I, 70, Babade to Seton, October 19, 1814.
34. Carroll to Plowden, January 5, 1815.
35. Carroll to Plowden, March 20, 1815.
36. Carroll to Plowden, October 13, 1815. Carroll paraphrased the Pope's compliment which was expressed in a letter to the Irish hierarchy.

FOOTNOTES FOR CHAPTER XX

1. Guilday, *op. cit.*, p. 825; Hughes, *Documents*, I, 853.
2. Gurn, *op. cit.*, p. 195. George Ticknor (1791-1871) was one of the most brilliant of Boston's literary circle in the age Van Wyck Brooks characterized as the "flowering of New England." Ticknor was only twenty-three when he called upon Carroll during his trip to the South to "see the men the cities contain." He was equally impressed by the archbishop's cousin Charles, and described him as "a monument of the best bred and best educated among our fathers."
3. E. H. Smith, *op. cit.*, p. 271.
4. Carroll to Fenwick, July 4, 1815.
5. For a recent account of the life of Clorivière cf. David Darrah, *Conspiracy in Paris. The Strange Career of Joseph Picot de Limoelan, Aristocrat, Soldier, and Priest, and the Gunpowder Plot against Napoleon on 3 Nivose, Year IX* (New York, 1953). A more accurate account of Clorivière's life in the United States is found in "Joseph Pierre Picot de Limoelan de Clorivière (1768-1826)" an unprinted master's thesis by Richard C. Madden (The Catholic University of America, 1938).
7. Carroll to Grassi, August 25, 1815.
8. Archives of Mount St. Vincent, I, 21, Carroll to Seton, October 27, 1815.
9. From Maréchal's account of Carroll's death in the Archives of the Archdiocese of Baltimore, reprinted in Guilday, *op. cit.*, pp. 826-827.
10. Brent, *op. cit.*, pp. 207-208.
11. Melville, *op. cit.*, pp. 243-244.
12. Brent, *op. cit.*, p. 218.
13. Guilday, *op. cit.*, p. 831.
14. Brent, *op. cit.*, p. 218.
15. *Ibid.*, p. 214.
16. *Ibid.*, p. 220.
17. Schauinger, *op. cit.*, p. 135.
18. Guilday, *op. cit.*, p. 829.
19. Melville, *op. cit.*, p. 247.
20. John Grassi returned to Europe after serving at Georgetown for five years. He described his American sojourn in *Notizie varie sullo stato presente della repubblica degli Stati Uniti dell'America settentrionale scritte al principio del 1818* (Milano, 1819).
21. Robert Gilmor or Gilmour was a wealthy Baltimore collector who acquired after Carroll's death the valuable autograph of Sir Walter Raleigh which John Carroll had picked up in London prior to his return to America in 1774. Cf. Campbell, *op. cit.*, p. 365.

22. Robert Walsh, like George Ticknor, was to earn a reputation as a man of letters after Carroll's death. Carroll recognized Walsh's capabilities as early as 1809 when he described the young man to Charles Plowden in a letter of June 2, 1809. He said, "If you should see him you will be very much gratified by his conversation. Having been much with Mr. Pinckney, the American minister, and in his confidence he has formed an acquaintance with many of your leading characters, and acquired an insight into public affairs. . . . He received the elements of his education at George Town College; his taste and improvement in the higher sciences from two most worthy priests of St. Sulpice . . . and he has continued to raise the superstructure of his variegated knowledge on these foundations." On Walsh cf. Sister M. Frederick Lochemes, *Robert Walsh, His Story* (New York, 1941).

23. James Cardinal Gibbons, *A Retrospect of Fifty Years* (Baltimore, 1916), I, 248-249.

INDEX

Acquia, 75.

Adams, John, hopes for Canada mission, 44; peace commissioner, 64; pamphleteer, 84; President, 145.

Addison, Judge Alexander, 210, 314, n. 14.

Alexandria, Virginia, 100, 156, 253, 254.

Alien and Sedition Acts, 145.

Alsace, Carroll's visit, 27.

American Gazetteer, 174.

Angier, Rev. Robert, O.P., 187.

Annapolis, Abbé Robin visits, 5; John Carroll sails from, 10; *Peggy Stewart* affair, 40-41; Confederation Congress meets at, 72; Lafayette visits, 73; Carroll drafts reply to Wharton, 91; Catholics attacked, 96; legislature meets, 100; surpassed by Baltimore, 115; Harper-Carroll wedding, 132; St. John's College, 138, 151; aids refugees, 158.

Antonelli, Leonardo Cardinal, receives reply from Paris nuncio, 63; requests report from Luzerne, 68; on Carroll's appointment as superior, 69; Carroll's report to, 73-75; confirms Whelan's faculties, 78; removes cramping clauses, 105; learns of Nugent schism, 107; Filicchi considers writing him, 108; learns of Carroll's misgivings over election, 110; prefers Quebec, 113; discounts La Poterie charges, 115; presents Carroll's respects, 119; advises Carroll on selection of priests, 121; and Scioto project, 126; and Oneida Indians,

127-128; on division of diocese, 132; congratulates Carroll on synod, 133; modifies mission oath, 138-139; on Plunkett, 140; gives money to Georgetown, 142; Carroll praises Sulpicians to, 144; on Carmelites, 172; on Jesuit revival, 192.

Antwerp, 16.

Arnold, Benedict, 43, 49-50.

Arundel, Lord, offers Carroll chaplaincy, 36; desires Virginia ham, 101; gets Carroll's view of bishop-oath controversy, 118-119; learns of Sulpician seminary plans, 121.

Arundel, Lady Mary Christine, wants birds, 100; and Beeston, 101; on young Carrolls, 102; at Carroll's consecration, 117.

Ashton, Rev. John, petition to Rome, 107; circular committee, 109; procurator of properties, 114; sermon at synod, 132, 133; director of Georgetown, 138; convokes clergy, 141.

Aston, William, 35.

Augsburg, 30-31.

Augusta, Georgia, 213.

Auzouer, Countess, 1.

Azores, 143.

Babade, Rev. Pierre, S.S., 271, 277, 282.

Baden-Baden, 29.

Badin, Rev. Stephen Theodore, on Wharton, 94; on frontier marriages, 132; on Kentucky frontier, 188-190; vicar-general, 216; untiring mission-

riet Carroll, 264; interest in comparative religion, 279.

Carroll, Charles IV, son of Charles of Carrollton, at Liège, 101-102; marriage, 131-132; learns father's views on Jefferson and France, 146; his children reared as Catholics, 264.

Carroll, Daniel of Duddington, father of Eleanor W. Carroll, 11, 124-125.

Carroll, Daniel of Litterlouna, 1.

Carroll, Daniel of Rock Creek, brother of John, signer of Constitution, 2; returns from Europe, 9; at St. Omer, 11; marriage, 14; letter to Ireland, 16; death of wife, 20; rents house, 20; visits John in Europe, 20; and Jesuit suppression, 35-36; wills chapel to John, 55; in government, 73; and Constitution, 89; president of Potomac Company, 100; signs Address of Catholics to Washington, 111; on District of Columbia commission, 124-125; a Mason, 156; death, 161; will, 162.

Carroll, Daniel of Upper Marlborough, father of John, 1; marriage, 2; inventories, 3; educates sons, 9; death, 10, 14; brings wife to Prince George's County, 176.

Carroll, Dominic, 38, 298, n. 1.

Carroll, Eleanor Darnall, wife of Daniel of Upper Marlborough, mother of John Carroll, 1; marriage, 2; relationship with son, 6; provides for son, 54; death, 160-161; comes to Prince George's County, 176.

Carroll, Eleanor W., Mrs. Daniel Carroll of Rock Creek, 14, 20.

Carroll, Elizabeth, sister of Bishop Carroll, at Rock Creek, 54; inherits mother's estate, 161; Carroll's responsibility, 162; at Carroll's deathbed, 283-284.

Carroll, George, grandson of Daniel of Rock Creek, 162.

Carroll, Harriet Chew, Mrs. Charles Carroll IV, marriage, 131-132; congratulated by father-in-law, 264.

Carroll, Henry, 6.

Carroll, James of Ann Arundel, 38, 298, n. 1.

Carroll, Bishop John, born, 1; childhood, 6; at Bohemia Manor school, 9; sails for St. Omer, 10; life at St. Omer, 12-14; inheritance, 14; enters Society of Jesus, 14-15; at Liège, 15-16; in Antwerp, 16; ordination date in question, 20; on death of Pompadour, 21-22; spirituality, 22; tours Europe, 26-34; fears of Jesuit suppression, 33-34; prefect of sodality at Bruges, 35; on suppression of Jesuits, 35-36; arrested, 36; secretary for exiles, 36-37; returns to Maryland, 38; Canadian mission, 43-53; at Rock Creek, 54-55; on Catholic guardians, 56; on clergy in 1782, 58; plans of organization, 59-60; petition to Rome of 1784, 61; on toleration, 61, 86-89, 92; on French ambitions, 65-66; on Franklin, 66, 68; named superior, 68-70; report to Antonelli, 73-75; visits Virginia, 75; visits Philadelphia in 1785, 76-77; Whelan-Nugent affair, 77-83; Wharton apostasy, 89-94; Smith attack, 94-97; La Poterie attack, 97-99; gifts to Arundells, 100-101; writes Beeston sketch, 101; interest in Miss Jefferson, 102-103; on foreign jurisdiction, 103; Nugent schism, 106-107; petition for a bishop, 107; services of Filicchis, 108; elected bishop, 108-109; and Catholics' Address to Washington, 111-112; receives official notice of appointment, 113; refuses Troy's invitation, 114; consecration at Lulworth, 116-118; promotes school at Georgetown, 118; on bishop-oath controversy, 118-119; confers with Nagot in London, 120-121; tells Antonelli of seminary plan, 121; sails for home, 122; arrives in Baltimore, 122; occupies pro-cathedral, 122-123; and Gallipolis colony, 125-127; and Oneida Indians, 127-128; plans for a synod, 128; work of synod, 129-130, 132-134; reply to

bishop, 190, 225, 253, 316, n. 48, 318, n. 28; Bishop Connolly arrives, 226; Connolly nominated and consecrated bishop for, 260, 280.

New Orleans, becomes part of United States, 175-176; Ursuline boarding school in, 176; Ursuline Nuns in, 177; voyage of the *New Orleans*, 232; Cathedral of St. Louis, 237; schism, 238; Dubourg arrives, 239; Jackson's victory, 278.

Newcastle, Delaware, 91.

Newtown, Maryland, 76.

Niles Register, 275.

Norfolk, Virginia, Carmelites land, 171; Fenwick arrives, 188; trusteeism, 212-213; priest of mentioned for New York, 220.

Northwest Territory, 234, 237.

Nugent, Rev. Andrew, in Whelan-Nugent affair, 79-83; charges against, 106; reported to Rome, 107, 121.

O'Brien, Rev. Matthew, and Mother Seton, 179; in New York, 219, 220-223; congratulates Carroll on winning lottery, 266; in Boston, 315, n. 30.

O'Brien, Rev. William, O.P., in Philadelphia, 76; and La Poterie, 98; replaces Nugent, 106; works in New York, 219-222.

Oellers, James, denies Carroll's authority, 207.

Ohio Company, 125.

Olivier, Rev. Donatian, 237.

Olivier, Rev. John, 239.

One Mile Tavern, 144.

Order of the Visitation, 173-175.

Otis, James, 84.

Paca, Governor William, invites Congress to Annapolis, 72; navigation of Susquehanna, 100.

Paca Street, Mother Seton's School, 182; Carroll's funeral, 283.

Paine, Thomas, 71, 84.

Pakenham, Lord, 277.

Pamphili, Archbishop Giuseppe Doria, and American peace commission, 62-68; on Carroll, 68-69; forwards Whelan's request, 78; gets Franklin's views on bishop for United States, 104; education of American Catholics, 137.

Parsons, Rev. Robert, S.J., 11.

Parter, James, 117.

Patterson, Mary Carroll, 282.

Patterson, William, 267.

Patuxent River, 2, 3.

Peggy Stewart affair, 40-41.

Pellentz, Rev. James, director of Georgetown, 138; sends views on academy, 141.

Pênet, Peter, 127.

Perrigny, Rev. Georges de, 159.

Philadelphia, Pennsylvania, Carroll there in 1776, 53; Carroll visitation in 1785, 76-77; Beeston there, 101; German troubles, 203-207; made see city, 225; Britt and Germans, 254-255; city of schism, 280.

Philadelphia, Diocese of, created, 225; question of successor to Egan, 259-261; Britt removed by Neale, 254-255.

Pilling, Rev. William, 93.

Pinaud, Jacques, 158.

Pinckney, Charles C., 270.

Pitt, William, 85.

Pittsburgh, steamboat from, 232.

Pius VI, confirms Carroll's election, 109; Carroll writes to, 119; death, 162-164; Leonard Neale's appointment, 215.

Pius VII, on St. Mary's Seminary, 150-151; elected, 163-164, 215; recognizes American Visitandines, 175; restoration of Jesuits, 193-194; divides Diocese of Baltimore, 225; and Louisiana, 239; refuses to annul Patterson-Bonaparte marriage, 268; persecuted by Napoleon, 271-272; freed, 276.

Plessis, Bishop Joseph A., acts as vicar-general in borderlands, 237; and

_____
_____
_____
_____
_____
_____
_____
_____
_____
_____
_____
_____
_____
_____
_____
_____
_____
_____
_____
_____
_____